HORSE RACING

The complete guide to the world of the Turf

Collins

Advisory Editor
Ivor Herbert

Contributors
Samir Abujamra, Julian Armfield, Richard Baerlein, Robert Carter,
Martin Eversfield, Tony Fairburn, Steve Haskin, Susan Helferty,
Wataru Ishikawa, Tony Kennedy, Frank E Kilroe, Sir Mordaunt
Milner Bart, Roger Mortimer, Richard Onslow, Leon Rasmussen,
Dick Ratcliff, Peter Rossdale, Michael Seely, Tony Sweeney,
Peter Towers-Clark, Peter Willett.

A QUILL BOOK

Published by William Collins Sons & Co Ltd,
London . Glasgow . Sydney . Auckland . Toronto .
Johannesburg

First published in Great Britain 1980
ISBN 000 411649-6

First published in Australia in 1980 by William Collins Pty
Ltd, Sydney

Front cover: Deauville (Bernard Gourier)
Back cover: Hurdling at Newbury (George Selwyn)

Editorial Director Jeremy Harwood
Art Director James Marks
Production Director Nigel Osborne
Designer Paul Cooper
Illustrators David Weeks, Antony Lodge
Picture Research Marion Eason, Francesca Serple
Editorial Thomas Rees, Michael Ross
Editorial Research Duffy White
Photographers Bernard Gourier, Laurie Morton, Jon
Wyand, George Selwyn
Cartography Ruecker (UK) Ltd.

Typeset in Great Britain by Parker Typesetting Service,
Leicester
Colour origination by Sakai Lithocolour Co Ltd,
Hong Kong
Printed in Hong Kong by Leefung-Asco Printers Ltd

The publishers gratefully acknowledge the advice and
assistance given in the preparation of this book by
Pacemaker International and its publisher, Nick Robinson.

Many individuals and organizations have helped in the preparation of this book. Among them are: American Horse Council, Australian Jockey Club, Ian Balding, Bloodstock Breeders Review, British Equine Veterinary Association, the British Racehorse, the Daily Telegraph, William Hill Organization, Horserace Betting Levy Board, International Racing Bureau, Japan Horse Racing Association, the Jockey Club, Mirror Group Newspapers, Mrs M Nakamura, the National Stud, National Trainers Federation, New York Racing Association, New Zealand House Information Service, David Nicholson, Gavin Pritchard-Gordon, Racecourse Security Services, Racing Information Bureau, South African Tourist Corporation, South Australian Jockey Club, Sporting Life, Western Australia Turf Club. Thanks are also due to the many other racing and turf clubs across the world, without whose help this book would have been impossible to compile.

HORSE RACING

Contents

Introduction

by Ivor Herbert

In one of the particularly green paddocks in the Golden Vale of County Tipperary, a stud manager points out a mare and foal.

'That's an Australian mare, covered out there by an exported American stallion. The foal's the produce of that mating. Now she's been flown here to be bred to one of our stallions. The stallion, like a lot nowadays, was bought in Kentucky as a yearling by a group of partners – Irish, American, English, French. The horse, though American-bred, did all his racing in England, Ireland and France.

'But then his pedigree's pretty international, fairly typically. On his sire's side two generations back it's 100 per cent English. But the dam's line came up into the States from South America.'

The Irishman shrugged, easily accepting the internationality of modern racing. 'The world of horse racing is nowadays no further away than our next door Irish county used to be.' He added a vivid Irishism. 'As thoroughbred racing has expanded, so its world has shrunk! Behind the band of grazing brood-mares and their bright, stilt-legged foals, rose a purple-topped mountain. Its name – and the story behind it – seem, like its setting, not inappropriate to this book, which deals with the development, administration and patterns – and with some of the greater personalities, equine and human – of racing around the world.

The name of the mountain is Slievenamon, which means, in English, Hill of the Woman. In the ancient Ireland of poets and princes, the local chieftain would sit upon its summit. He was waiting then, as the thoroughbred stallions wait now in the valley below, for female visitors who had proved their worth. The nearby women of the chieftain's time would, on a signal, race off and gallop gamely upwards to the chief. The one who won, who had best displayed the eternal pre-requisites of a race horse – speed, stamina, soundness, high courage and deep resolution – received her quick reward. She became his mate, his princess. She had proved that she probably possessed a better chance than the rest of producing the strong, fast, healthy and nimble offspring who could compete.

The Darwinian dogma of the survival of the fittest is excellently exemplified in the huge, rich world of horse racing. Breeding always will out. Now, of course, the business is managed by man. It requires not only expertise (which can be learned or hired) but, at the top, capital on the scale of a major industry. Its success also depends on a natural flair, on an instinct usually innate, which the great bloodstock breeders have always possessed.

The end results continually rearrange the pattern of the breed. There in droves struggle the thoroughbreds who have failed, the great majority whose deaths mark the ends of their lines. Rejected, down-graded, the classically-bred colts perform as geldings in petty races and in other fields of equestrianism where speed is not quintessential. Out of every 5,000 a mere handful survive, who have passed their racecourse tests at their summits and who will, if prepotent, stamp their assets on the breed. Marketed at the price of large factories, a few golden stallions each year are syndicated around the globe. Their services are sought by human millionaires of many races. They represent, standing in the USA, England, Japan, France and Australia, living capital equipment worth now, in some cases, more than $15 million a head. They earn for their fortunate shareholders incomes of $3 million annually. If their progeny emulate them and win in the highest class, their earnings will increase and keep several lengths ahead in the race against inflation.

The attractions to the very rich are very real. Almost every major racing country offers substantial tax advantages to those who invest in bloodstock. That is, of course, if their original investments prosper. The chances against this happening are so long that, for example, the Inland Revenue of Great Britain, which originally caught all bloodstock in its net of Capital Gains Tax, soon released them. The genuine and heavy losses of the many overwhelmed the rare great profits of the few.

But the stallions and brood-mares who make up the capital plant of the horse-racing industry provide a great deal more than the possibility of high profits and fiscal amelioration. The ordinary racegoer, the man in the street and his wife and children, would never pay a penny to stand and watch the clanking machinery which turns out trucks, shirts or shoes. They would derive little aesthetic pleasure from the spectacle. Nor would they have, from that sort of machine, any hope of gambling gain.

Horses are never machines. Racehorses, in their finely-developed, highly-tuned state, are extremely delicate creatures. The million dollar yearling can, through some trivial training accident, be a write-off for racing. The horse that probably would have won a Classic, but cannot run in it through sickness or lameness, can fall in value from £5 million to a few hundred thousand overnight. And the horse who is beaten by a neck in the Epsom Derby, for example, diminishes in value by those few feet, after one-and-a-half miles, by several million pounds.

The world of horse racing also offers two extraordinary attractions, setting it apart from other industries. It is connected with animals which are pleasures to look upon. It is connected with, and largely financed by, the dreams of poor punters.

The earth over, racegoers share a common interest. the man on Churchill Downs, at Epsom, at Sha Tin, Longchamp, Flemington and Baden-Baden is at one with his brothers round the racing world. They are passionately involved, not with the rattle of a ball round a roulette wheel nor with the flip of a card, but with the struggle of their choice, a man and horse combined, two animals on whom their hopes depend. Racing is a matter of the heart. The poorest punter is blood brother, for a few moments as the race climaxes, to the millionaire owner.
A third factor makes the racehorse special. A work of art – a Rembrandt, or a Turner, a genuine Chippendale sideboard, a Queen Anne silver cup can all afford comparable pleasure to the eye and to the investment portfolio. They can all be beautiful hedges against inflation. Their capital value may soar. But they cannot earn. They cannot, like the successful racehorse, breed.

Owners contribute the initial capital costs of racehorses and bear their running costs. Racing's work force contributes its labour. The cream is added by the losing punter in his millions. But much of this in every racing country is skimmed off by governments in betting duty and taxation.

In Britain, alone among the major racing countries of the world, betting on horses also enriches greatly another segment of the population – the bookmakers.

This loss of finance to racing has gradually reduced the standing of Great Britain from the 1930's. The pace of deterioration accelerated markedly after the Second World War. The country in which the modern thoroughbred evolved is no longer paramount. As Britain's general economic wealth declined, so more of the seed corn of its thoroughbred industry was exported by owners milked by taxes in life and death. Most of the best stock went to the USA.

The sales by the old Aga Khan of Blenheim and Mahmoud to America were followed by an avalanche of top-quality exports after the war. The American dollar was strong enough to buy what its bloodstock experts wanted. What Britain lost, the world gained. The blood of the British thoroughbred, which even the French still term *le pur sang anglais*, spread to the furthest corners of the earth. The racing world itself was expanding as new nations like Japan entered the top league of international racing. In the twelve years from Sir Ivor's Epsom victory in 1968, half the Derby winners went abroad as stallions.

Despite this the influence of British racing has remained in several sectors. Firstly, the admiration of other racing countries for the competence of its administration and for the overall honesty of its sport. Britain, in its turn, took over innovations from other countries, like the USA and Ireland. They were not all generally welcomed by the diehards. Starting stalls, for instance, were initially ridiculed as being fit only for greyhounds. Secondly, a preference among wealthy overseas owners towards running horses on the more attractive grass tracks of England, France and Ireland, and so sharing in the heritage and panoply of such days as the Epsom Derby and Royal Ascot. Thirdly, the generosity of a few foreign owners like Mr Paul Mellon of America, with Mill Reef, and Dr Carlo Vittadini of Italy, with Grundy, in allowing their British Classic winners to stand at Britain's National Stud.

A final major factor emerged in the early 1970s, emphasizing the internationality of racing and breeding as a sport and an industry. Into the breach left by the extinction in Britain of the old type of large owner-breeder like the Earls of Derby and Rosebery and the late Duke of Norfolk, moved a few businessmen with a cosmopolitan outlook. Spearheaded by Robert Sangster, they realized that racing's biggest earnings are not those of prize money. They derive from the stud potential of the great stallions. The era of the purchase-syndication of America's most expensive yearlings began. In the late 1970s, the tide gradually began to turn again. The flow of top-quality bloodstock was no longer only westwards into the USA. Many of the dearest descendents or original European bloodlines are now being plucked out of top American sales and brought to Europe to race, redressing in part the balance of the old world where thoroughbred racing first began.

The world of horse racing, as the Irishman remarked beneath the Hill of the Woman, is indeed shrinking. And this book, with which I am happy to be associated, aims to bring the more important corners of that world closer than the 'next door Irish county.'

Foreword

by R E Sangster

On 3rd September 1947 Arthur 'Bull' Hancock purchased the great stallion Nasrullah to stand at his Claiborne Farm in Paris, Kentucky. From that day on the boundaries of international thoroughbred racing and breeding started to shrink and they have been doing so ever since.

The most exciting and important stallion in the USA at the moment is Lyphard, raised in America and raced in France. Just a few stalls away stands Vaguely Noble, bred by the late L B Holliday in Yorkshire, raced in England and France before becoming one of the most sought-after stallions in the world today. In Australia, the most successful stallion is Without Fear, raised and raced in France by the American-bred stallion Baldric.

It is interesting to note that, although the majority of the world's leading stallions are American-bred, the most successful raced in Europe. Of these the names Sea Bird, Sir Ivor, Nijinsky and Mill Reef spring to mind, whilst Northern Dancer is probably the only American Classic winner to have been as successful at stud.

At the end of the Second World War there was a tremendous influx of the best European breeding stock to the USA, but this trend has been reversed to a great extent. For example, half sisters to recent Kentucky Derby winners Bold Forbes, Seattle Slew, Affirmed and Spectacular Bid were in training in either Ireland or England during 1980.

Ten years ago only a handful of Europeans were buying yearlings in America – now they dominate the market. Looking into the future, we can foresee the day of world championship classifications with perhaps a truly international classic to be staged in September over one and a quarter miles.

When Collins first approached me about the forthcoming publication of this book, I suggested that it was no longer possible to talk in the context of one country's racing – that it was time the real international concept of this exciting business was pulled together in one volume.

This, I believe, has now been achieved for the first time in *Horse Racing*. From the superb layout of Vincent O'Brien's gallops in Tipperary to the unexpected gradient of Santa Anita's six furlong turf track, from the exploits of Lester Piggott to Bill Shoemaker, we have at last a chance to take an overall look at the most fascinating sport in the world.

Robert Sangster.

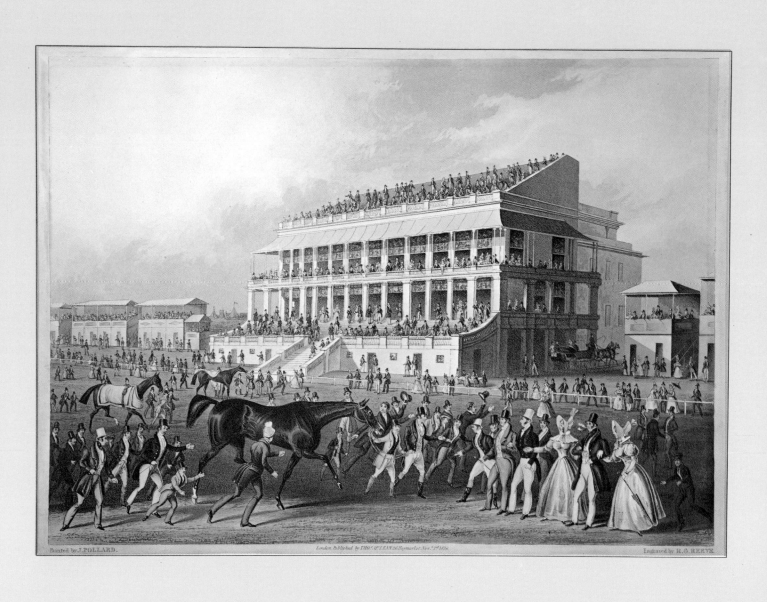

Painted by J.POLLARD.   London, Published by THO.S M.C LEAN 26 Haymarket Nov.r 7.th 1836.   Engraved by R.G.REEVE.

The Story of Racing

"A dark horse,
which had never been
thought of . . .
rushed passed the grandstand
to sweeping triumph."

Benjamin Disraeli
'The Young Duke'.

The Development of the Thoroughbred

'The English race-horse boasts of a pure descent from the Arabian, and under whatever denomination the original stock of our thoroughbred horses have been imported . . . they were regarded as the true sons and daughters of the desert.'

Thus wrote Admiral Rous in the preface to his book 'On the Laws and Practice of Horse Racing' published in 1850. Though the story of the modern thoroughbred begins in Britain, Rous – the virtual dictator of British racing in the third quarter of the nineteenth century – was mistaken in this opinion. The thoroughbred, in fact, had mixed origins, of which the Arabian was only one, while any comparison of the modern thoroughbred with the modern Arabian horse is bound to refute his assertion. The throughbred has superior size, scope and speed; it also differs in important physical characteristics, such as the high set and carriage of the Arabian's tail. Moreover, some thoroughbreds show a coarseness of limb and a convex profile which are wholly foreign to the Arabian.

The first thoroughbreds
The Arab's influence on the development of the thoroughbred began in midseventeenth century Britain. Before that time, the strains from which horses were drawn for racing were extremely diverse. Many of the racehorses were Galloways, ponies of thirteen to fourteen hands in height, which were used extensively for riding and racing in southern Scotland and northern England, especially Yorkshire. Other strains were of Eastern, Italian and Spanish origin. All of these strains tended to be deeply intermingled and, as a consequence, the racehorse breeding stock of early Stuart times was a veritable hotchpotch of breeds.

The vital formative period of the thoroughbred was the century that followed the Stuart restoration to the throne of England in 1660. The enthusiasm of Charles II for race meetings – particularly Newmarket – and racing in general was a powerful spur to the improvement of the racehorse; the king himself, though a breeder on only a small scale, gave direct support to its development by giving his Master of the Horse, James Darcy of Sedbury, a contract to supply him with twelve 'extraordinary good colts' annually for £800. In contrast to the recorded version in the General Stud Book, the bible of racing, which described the 'Royal Mares' as mares procured by Charles II abroad through the agency of the Master of the Horse, it is now thought that these were probably native-bred. In all likelihood, some of them were mares used by Darcy to

THE PENNY MAGAZINE

OF THE

Society for the Diffusion of Useful Knowledge.

102.]   PUBLISHED EVERY SATURDAY.   [NOVEMBER 2, 1833.

A ROMAN HORSE-RACE.

London : Published by C. Knight, Pall Mall East.—Printed by William Clowes, Duke-street, Lambeth :.

[Horses preparing to Start.]

Above *A nineteenth-century print of a Roman horse race. By this time, English racing had formulated most of its rules, but Roman racing was very different.* *Instead of being ridden by jockeys, the horses ran without riders.* **Right** *Charles II, Britain's royal patron of the turf in its early days.*

fulfil his contract, while others may have come from the royal studs which had been dispersed by Oliver Cromwell.

The breeders of late Stuart and early Georgian times turned to imports from the Middle East and North Africa in order to improve and impose greater uniformity on their stock. The Arabian was ideal for this purpose. It was not only the most elegant but also the most genetically pure breed of horse in the world. As good specimens of the Arabian breed were hard to buy, however, British breeders also imported horses

of related breeds, such as Turks and Barbs. James Darcy himself owned a White Turk and a Yellow Turk.

The precise details of these importations are impossible to discover in many cases. This is because of the contemporary habit of calling horses after their current owners and labelling them indiscriminately as Arabs, Turks or Barbs. Thus, it is believed that the same horse was described at different times as Honywood's Arabian, Sir J. Williams's Turk and Sir C. Turner's White Turk. With mares, the problem of identifi-

cation was further complicated by the practice of attaching to them the names of their sires; for example, the Layton Barb Mare and Burton Barb Mare, who were important thoroughbred foundation mares, were probably not imported, but were merely sired by Barb stallions.

The General Stud Book listed 103 imported stallions in the formative period of the thoroughbred after the Stuart restoration. As for the distaff side of the thoroughbred, the nineteenth-century authority Bruce Lowe traced all the British and Irish

thoroughbred mares of the 1890s back to about fifty original mares in pursuit of his aim to devise a sure system of breeding winners. Some modern researchers have narrowed the field even further, concluding that the present thoroughbred population may be derived from no more than a dozen foundation mares.

Three male lines

The mists of time which obscure some aspects of the origins of the thoroughbred will never be dispelled. On the other hand, it is certain that the present world thoroughbred population of perhaps 750,000 has an extremely narrow genetic base. One of the undisputed facts about the breed is that all modern thoroughbreds trace their ancestry in the direct male line to no more than three founding sires – the Byerley Turk (born about 1680), the Darley Arabian (1700) and the Godolphin Arabian (1724).

Direct genealogical lines are not necessarily equated to genetic contribution, however, and it was not until Professors G A T Mahon and E P Cunningham presented their findings on 'Genetic Studies in Horses' in March 1978 that a serious attempt to evaluate the real importance of the founding fathers was made. The research was based on a random sample of sixty mares drawn from volume thirty-five (1965) of the General Stud Book. From each great-grandparent, a line was drawn back to the foundation of the breed to produce a deep-sample pedigree. At each step in a line the sire or dam was chosen at random to be the representative of the next generation back and it was found that the lines were, on average, nineteen generations long.

The report stated that: 'The deep-sample pedigree enabled us to measure the relative genetic contribution of prominent foundation animals to the present-day population. Almost eighty-one per cent of genes in the modern thoroughbred derive from only thirty-one original ancestors'. This finding showed that the genetic base of the thoroughbred was even narrower than had been previously supposed. But at the same time it confirmed the importance of the

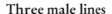

Above left *The last race to be run before Charles II, near Windsor Castle in 1684. The king's racing activities, however, were chiefly centred on Newmarket; the present-day Rowley Mile gets its name from his nickname, 'Old Rowley'.* **Left** *The Godolphin Arabian, one of the three founding*

sires of the English thoroughbred. The other two were the Byerley Turk and the Darley Arabian. As shown by modern research, the policy of Restoration breeders was to import such stallions to cross with native British strains. The ultimate result was the English thoroughbred.

founding fathers, who occupied three of the first four places among the contributing ancestors. The Godolphin Arabian was first with 14.6 per cent, the Darley Arabian second with 7.5 per cent and the Byerley Turk fourth with 4.8 per cent.

The interloper was the Curwen Bay Barb, in third place with a genetic contribution to the modern thoroughbred of 5.6 per cent. The role of this hero of the breed had gone unsung previously because he did not found an enduring male line, but his contribution was weighty. He was the maternal grandsire of Partner – champion sire four times between 1737 and 1743, the grandsire of Herod and the maternal grandsire of Matchem. Herod and Matchem were not only two of the greatest stallions of the second half of the eighteenth century; they were also essential links in the chain of inheritance of the Byerley Turk and the Godolphin Arabian lines respectively.

Although this analysis has confirmed the importance of the three founding fathers, it has destroyed at the same time the assumption that their genetic contributions were proportionate to the numbers of their descendants in direct male line. More than eighty per cent of modern thoroughbreds trace their descent from the Darley Arabian in the male line; however, the deep-sample pedigrees supply evidence to show that the genetic contribution of the Darley Arabian, at 7.5 per cent is little more than half that of the Godolphin Arabian, whose male line survives, for all practical purposes, only in the modern dynasties of Man O'War and Hurry On.

British ancestors

A further refinement of this method made it possible to determine, for the first time, the relative importance of the genetic contributions to the thoroughbred made by horses imported from the Middle East in the middle of the seventeenth century or later and by horses derived from strains already existing in Britain. The deep-sample pedigrees show that eleven of the thirty-one individual ancestors that contributed eighty-one per cent of the genetic make-up of the thoroughbred were British and were responsible for 15.8 per cent of that contribution. Therefore it is reasonable to suppose that about twenty per cent of the whole genetic make-up of the thoroughbred came from British sources. This is a much higher proportion than most earlier estimates.

The most important of these British ancestors was the mare by Mr Curwen's Shields Galloway, who was the great-granddam of Tartar, the sire of Herod. She contributed 2.5 per cent of the genetic

make-up, being closely followed in importance by the dam of Hautboy, who contributed 2.3 per cent.

All these eleven British ancestors were mares, whereas all but one of the most important imported ancestors of the thoroughbred were stallions. In this way, analysis of the deep-sample pedigrees provides strong corroboration for the idea that the policy of the post-Restoration breeders was to import stallions of Arabian and related breeds to cross with and improve existing British running strains; and that this policy, to which the evolution of the thoroughbred was due, was triumphantly successful.

General Stud Book

In tracing mares back to the foundations of the breed and to produce the deep-sample pedigrees, Mahon and Cunningham had to rely on the information contained in the General Stud Book. This is so-called because it embraces the breeding records of all thoroughbreds; in this respect, it contrasts to the private stud books kept by individual breeders.

The General Stud Book records are accepted as being generally accurate, but, since the first volume was not published until 1793, it had to rely on secondary sources that were not always complete or accurate. Many of the early breeders were unaware of their responsibility to posterity and did not keep consecutive breeding

Above Flying Childers, bred in 1715 at Doncaster, Yorkshire, and acknowledged to be the first truly great racehorse. As far as can be established, Flying Childers' record – particularly in trials and against the clock – broke new ground in racing history. He also had a lasting influence on the evolution of the breed, though his own ancestry is a matter of dispute.

The account given in the General Stud Book is disputed by some racing historians. Right Richard Tattersall, whose family became one of the great names of the horse world. The sales conducted by Tattersalls became world-famous.

records; this meant that some of the information reaching the compilers was little better than hearsay. Inevitably the authenticity of some of the details has been questioned in the light of later research.

One of the most striking examples is Flying Childers – the first truly great racehorse. Although few of his racing performances were recorded, he was acknowledged to be infinitely superior to all the other horses of his day, his feats in trials and against the clock becoming legendary. Flying Childers was bred by Mr Leonard Childers of Doncaster in 1715 and sold to the Duke of Devonshire as a young horse. The GSB version of his pedigree was that he was by the Darley Arabian out of Betty Leedes by Old Careless (by Spanker out of a Barb mare), out of Cream Cheeks by the Leedes Arabian, out of a mare by Spanker, out of the Old Morocco mare, who was

Spanker's own dam. The Old Morocco mare was also known as Old Peg, and was by Lord Fairfax's Morocco Barb out of Old Bald Peg, by an Arabian out of a Barb mare. Spanker was by the Darcy Yellow Turk.

If the accuracy of this account is accepted, then two very significant facts about the breeding of the first great racehorse emerge. The first is that it involved intense inbreeding to Spanker and the Old Morocco mare. The second is that he traced his origins back to ancestors of Middle Eastern origin without exception within six generations. On the other hand, doubt was cast on the validity of the GSB version by the historian C M Prior, who discovered a different version in the private stud book of the prominent contemporary breeders Cuthbert Routh. This stated that 'Childers was got by Darle's Arabian, his dam by Careless, his granddam by Leedes Arabian, out of a famous roan mare of Sir Marmaduke Wyvill's.'

Unfortunately, the pedigree of the roan mare was not given. But, even if the GSB pedigree of Flying Childers was partly fictional, it is certain that inbreeding was practised intensively by the early thoroughbred breeders. Mahon and Cunningham found that the average coefficient of inbreeding from the deep-sample pedigrees was 12.9 per cent, which is equivalent to the mating of half-brothers and sisters.

Influence of Eclipse

Flying Childers had a lasting influence on the evolution of the breed; his grandson Snap was an outstanding sire of broodmares. However, Flying Childers's brother Bartlet's or Bleeding Childers, who was unable to race because of his weak blood vessels, forged the essential link in the perpetuation of the Darley Arabian male line as the great-grandsire of Eclipse, the second truly great racehorse.

Eclipse lived until 1789 and, as a stallion, exerted a powerful influence on the progress of the breed. Although he was never the leading sire of winners, he was second eleven times, and was solely responsible for the survival of the Darley Arabian male line from which the large majority of modern thoroughbreds spring. But concentration on the male line would be misleading, because the influence of Eclipse was no greater than that of three other stallions whose careers overlapped his own. They were Matchem (1748–81), who was a grandson of the Godolphin Arabian, Herod (1758–80), who was a great-great-grandson of the Byerley Turk, and finally Herod's son Highflyer (1774–93). Matchem was leading sire of winners three

times, Herod eight times and Highflyer twelve times.

The importance of these horses cannot be measured in terms of breeding statistics alone, for their real value lies in the fact that their influence dominated the most critical phase in the evolution of the thoroughbred. They raced in the primeval era, when racehorses were allowed to mature slowly – Eclipse did not run until he was five – and the most prestige was attached to winning the 'King's Plates' – Eclipse won eleven of them. These were races dedicated to the promotion of strength and endurance, in which horses had to carry twelve stones in four-mile heats. But their progeny raced in a new and transitional age, in which speed and precocity were assuming growing importance. Two-year-old racing was then being introduced and the three-year-old classic races were beginning to develop as the supreme tests of the racehorse. The St Leger was founded in 1776, the Oaks in 1779 and the Derby a year later; the classic programme was completed by the addition of the 2,000 Guineas and the 1,000 Guineas early in the nineteenth century.

The most decisive influence on the new, speedier and quicker maturing type of thoroughbred was exerted not by any one of these four great stallions acting singly, but by Eclipse and Herod in concert. The Eclipse-Herod cross was at the heart of early classic breeding. Waxy, the winner of the Derby in 1793, was the finest of all examples of it. He was by Pot-8-0s (by Eclipse) out of Maria by Herod. Waxy sired the Derby winners Pope, Whalebone, Blucher and Whisker, and so permeated the breed with his own good looks and ability that he was once called 'the modern ace of trumps in the stud book.'

Development of the breed

This fundamental change in racing and the characteristics of the thoroughbred occurred under the aegis of the Jockey Club, whose control of the sport was gradually tightening, and the first so-called 'dictator of the turf', Sir Charles Bunbury. The process of improving speed and increasing precocity by selective breeding continued through the first half of the nineteenth century and the era of the second dictator Lord George Bentinck. In 1850 the third dictator, Admiral Rous, was able to write: 'It is generally believed by the most learned men of the Turf that a first class English racehorse would give 6 stone to the best Arabian which can be found.'

The thoroughbred had become a breed separate from, and far superior in speed to, its most important ingredient and incapable of further improvement by fresh infu-

sions of that ingredient. Rous also put his finger on a significant aspect of thoroughbred progress when he wrote, after regretting that the old system of not training horses until they were fully matured had been abandoned: 'The great expense of training induced horse-owners to bring forward all the important sweepstakes at two years old and three years old.'

The genetic plateau

Rous might have added that the great expense of breeding was an equally strong factor, but his message was clear. The costs of racing and breeding had soared and the whole thoroughbred system was assuming some of the aspects of an industry as well as a sport. Although great private breeders such as Sir Joseph Hawley, Lords Falmouth and Rosebery and the Dukes of Portland and Westminster produced most of the classic winners in the second half of the nineteenth century, the emergence of breeders for the yearling market like Blenkiron of Middle Park, Sykes of Sledmere and, curiously enough, Queen

Victoria herself at Hampton Court, indicated a more commercial approach.

The second half of the nineteenth century produced two unbeaten racehorses of surpassing brilliance – St Simon and the 1886 Triple Crown winner Ormonde – and three stallions of extraordinary importance – Stockwell, Hermit and the previously mentioned St Simon. This was the last period of measurable improvement in British thoroughbred performance. Evidence for this comes from the modern research of Cunningham, who, in 1975, examined the times for the Derby, the Oaks and the St Leger. He concluded that they showed steady improvement, at about two per cent per decade, up to 1900, with no evidence of further improvement since then. The thoroughbred had probably reached a genetic plateau.

Factors like the importation of speedy stock – for example Americus, Rhoda B and Sibola – from the USA at the turn of the century; the beneficial effect of inbreeding and line-breeding to St Simon, which was found in two of the most eminent classic stallions of the twentieth century, Hyperion and Nearco; the impact of other great stallions like Phalaris and Blandford; the responsibility undertaken by the National Stud to support quality breeding by standing top class stallions; the injection of money into racing through the betting levys: another more sophisticated American invasion in the last fifteen years providing top stallions such as Habitat and Mill Reef; and the introduction in 1969 of the Pattern race system, designed to aid selection by providing a comprehensive series of tests for high-class horses, have promised at various times to give fresh impetus to thoroughbred improvement. The inexorable logic of the times of classic races, however, is that the utmost efforts of breeders have been required not to secure improvement but to prevent retrogression. If progress is being made, or is to be made in future, it is more likely to be achieved in countries such as the USA, where much larger sums are available for investment and selection can be based on the best bloodstock drawn from all the principal breeding regions of the world.

Above left Ormonde and The Barb, two great horses of the nineteenth century, battle for supremacy in the 1886 running of the Epson Derby. **Left** Excursion buses on the way to Epsom for the Derby Day of 1913. By the mid-nineteenth century, the pattern of five three-year-old races had been established as the classic test of the racehorse in England; the Epsom Derby, in particular, was a national spectacle, as thousands of spectators made the trip to the downs where the race is still held. Even Parliament suspended business for the day.

Ireland

Ireland has always been associated in the public's mind with horse racing and the Irish horse itself has a history going back for at least 600 years. It is recorded that Richard II, on his arrival in Ireland, was met by the king of Leinster, Art Mc-Murrough Kavanagh, astride a magnificent white steed that 'without housing or saddle cost him four hundred cows.' But what races there were then – and for a long time subsequently – centred around private matches.

Perhaps the key document in the evolution of Irish racing was composed by Sir William Temple, when in 1673 he addressed to the then Lord-Lieutenant, the Earl of Essex, a work entitled 'An essay on the advancement of trade in Ireland.' A large portion of this centred around horses, who, Temple complained, were a drug on the market, but who, through a more selective use of a better type of stallion, could be improved to build up a valuable export trade. He made a particular point about the Irish environment, writing: 'The soil is of a sweet and plentiful grass which will raise a large breed and the hills especially near the sea coast are hard and rough and so fit to give them shape and breadth and sound feet.'

Trade and horses

To improve standards, Temple urged that 'there may be set up both a horse fair and races to be held at a certain time every year for the space of a week. At each races may be two Plates given by the King, one of £30, the other of £20 for horses proved to be Irish-bred.' Sir William had the foresight to see that money would not be the only motivating spirit in racing.

He also advocated that the Lord-Lieutenant attend the races and that the two winning owners be allowed to ride back with him to Dublin Castle to dine and receive the honour of the table. 'This to be done,' he added, 'what quality so ever the persons are of, for the lower that is, the more will be the honour, and perhaps the more the sport and the encouragement of breeding will by that means extend to all sorts of men.' Sir William may not have coined the phrase 'on the turf and under it all men are equal,' but he was certainly aware of the concept, as this account shows.

Charles II not only took up the scheme, but gave 100 guineas as a prize for a King's Plate. These Royal Plates still survive at Down Royal and Bellewstown, while a few years ago the prize money offered for them

at the Curragh was amalgamated with the Royal Whip. This is a trophy which the Curragh executive, with a delightful disregard for the passage of time, still describe as being presented by the late King William IV, the said king being now 'late' for over 150 years.

The Turf Club

The next landmark was the formation of the Turf Club some time in the mid-eighteenth century. As with the British Jockey Club, its origins are cloaked in mystery, but it probably grew out of a 'Society of Sportsmen' who are on record as putting up a £100 plate at the Curragh April meeting of 1750. Victory in the race went to one of the most discussed racers of the era, Sir Ralph Gore's Black and All Black. By 1790, when a certain Pat Sharkey published volume one of the Irish Racing Calendar (price 11s 4d), the whole apparatus of Irish racing authority as it is known today had come into being, with three stewards as its ruling body.

The pre-eminence of the Turf Club as the supreme body in Irish racing arose through the willingness of racecourses up and down the country to submit disputes to them for arbitration. The first Racing

Calendar named eighteen racecourses and gave the results of 154 races. By 1850, Robert J Hunter, the new Calendar publisher, was giving the results of 273 events contested by 521 individual competitors at various racecourses, the majority of which are now extinct.

Like much else in Ireland, racing suffered a severe setback as the result of the devastation caused by the great famine of the 1840s. But through the second half of the century it rose again and by 1869 there were more than 400 races being held annually. The total prize fund averaged between £30,000 and £40,000 – the level of £50,000 being attained for the first time in 1901. The £100,000 figure was finally reached in 1919, when post First World War inflation was at its height. The ensuing depression initiated a downward spiral and, by 1939, prize money in real terms was less than that which was on offer a century earlier.

The Racing Board

From out of this financial crisis emerged the Racing Board, the brainchild of Joe McGrath, who was not only a former government minister, but also founder of the Irish Hospitals Sweepstakes. McGrath was a man who, once he involved himself in racing and breeding, did so with his customary energy and success. He persuaded the government of Eamonn de Valera to pass a bill setting up an executive body with responsibility for improving Irish racing and the authority to charge a levy on all bets made on the course. Previously, these had not been taxed, though clients of Irish betting shops, legalised in the 1920s, had to pay a tax on their stakes to the exchequer. As a result of the bill, the Racing Board was founded; the levy, which started at five per cent, was reduced for a time to 2½ per cent, and is now six per cent, has proved the salvation of racing in Ireland.

In 1978, prize money totalled £2,756,675, of which £320,535 was contributed by sponsors. The notion of commercial sponsors is a long-established one in Irish racing, going back in origin to the beginnings of railway development there. With betting with on-course bookmakers totalling £40,208,250, and with the totalisator pulling in a turnover of £11,138,134 – both beating the rate of inflation – there were further increases in prize money in the pipeline.

The Racing Board was also able to claim a record attendance, with more than 1,100,000 paying customers spread over the 265 days of the racing calendar. The number of individual runners was 3,723; they competed almost 20,000 times, producing an eleven-runner average for the 1,712 flat and jumping events.

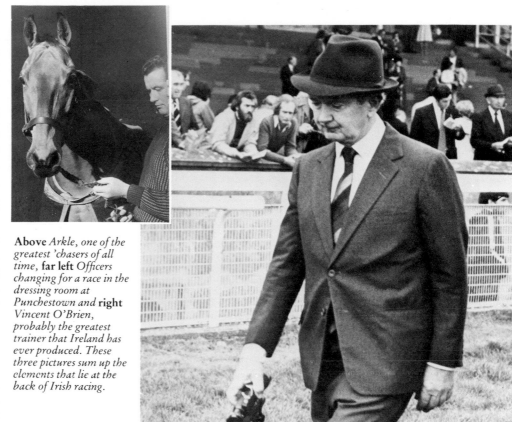

Above *Arkle, one of the greatest 'chasers of all time,* **far left** *Officers changing for a race in the dressing room at Punchestown and* **right** *Vincent O'Brien, probably the greatest trainer that Ireland has ever produced. These three pictures sum up the elements that lie at the back of Irish racing.*

Racing and breeding today

As a source of employment, racing today plays a prominent role in the Irish economy. Apart from the people employed in the betting industry, the Turf Club currently lists 307 licensed trainers, 333 permit holders, 424 jockeys and apprentices and over 2,000 stable lads, who have care of the 5,252 horses in training.

The post-war explosion in the size of the racing industry was sparked off by the Racing Board. It was then nurtured and sustained by a government which had the foresight to appreciate the value of a strong and prosperous horse breeding industry, able not merely to provide bloodstock for the home tracks but also to build up an immense export trade. For foreign manufacturers willing to set up in Ireland, a variety of tax concessions have been devised, but for bloodstock breeding these go even further, with complete exemption from income and capital gains tax for all bloodstock enterprises.

Top stallions

Whereas the general standard of sires available to Irish breeders before the war offered little chance of breaking into the lucrative top end of the market, tax-exempt stallions of the highest quality have been located at Irish stud farms throughout the country from the late 1940s onwards. In the post-war years, Irish breeders have had access to horses of the calibre of Nasrullah, Royal Charger, Sovereign Path, Habitat and Petingo and many others.

Another factor of major significance has been the skill of Irish trainers and the standards of Irish horse care. Talented men such as the trainers Vincent O'Brien and Paddy Prendergast have attracted a wealthy influx of foreign owners, with the money to purchase not just the best of Ireland's home-bred stock, but to buy choice colts and fillies at auctions all over the world.

In 1963, Paddy Prendergast became the first Irish trainer to top the list of leading trainers in England. He held the title for the next two seasons before handing it over in 1966 to Vincent O'Brien, who repeated the achievement in 1977 with a record prize money total. O'Brien is without a doubt one of the most successful trainers of the day.

Irish racing is thus as flourishing today as it ever has been in its long history. Wherever racing is held throughout the world, the name of Ireland – and the reputation of its horses, trainers, breeders and jockeys – is held in high renown.

France

Thoroughbred horseracing in France is a widespread activity. In addition to the seven courses – Longchamp, Chantilly, Saint-Cloud, Evry, Maisons-Laffitte, Deauville and Vichy – controlled by the three Paris-based 'Sociétés', there are some 200 provincial courses, of which no fewer than sixty held five or more meetings in the 1978 racing year.

Most of the races away from the metropolitan courses are confined to horses trained in the provinces, with relatively low prize money on offer. The large majority of provincial programmes are mixtures of flat racing, racing over hurdles and fences, and trotting. The larger provincial courses such as Lyon, Marseille, Bordeaux and Nantes, however, stage some valuable races open to horses from the stables of Chantilly and Maisons-Laffitte, which supply the metropolitan courses. Provincial prize money, too, generally was buoyant in the late 1970s, with a consequential improvement in the standard of racing. In 1978, the French provinces staged 2,807 flat races compared with 1,244 on the metropolitan courses.

Steeplechasing and hurdling play a subsidiary, but not unimportant, role in the French thoroughbred racing scene. Auteuil, situated in common with Longchamp in the Bois de Boulogne in Paris, is its headquarters; the 298 races run there in 1978 included nearly all the most important races over fences and hurdles.

French breeding, too, is on a large scale. In 1977, 5,644 thoroughbred foals were born in France, compared with 4,419 in England, Scotland and Wales and 3,784 in Ireland. Furthermore, the quality of the products of the French breeding industry ensures that they regularly attain the highest international standards.

A slow start

In view of the obvious importance of the present-day French racing industry, it seems strange that the introduction of horse racing and breeding into France was tardy and, in the early days, half-hearted. There are scattered references in French literature to horse races from the fourteenth century onwards, while it is known that a course was laid out in the Plaine des Sablons, near Paris, in 1776. But horse-racing failed to take root in the sporting tastes of the nobility of pre-revolutionary France and, in any case, all vestiges of the sport were swept away by the French Revolution of 1789.

Napoleon I tried to stimulate the sport into renewed activity when, by a decree of August 31, 1805, he created a series of races to be run in the six main horse-breeding

départements, with a final in Paris. But it was not until twenty-eight years later that an eccentric Englishman, Lord Henry Seymour, and his collaborator the Duc d'Orleans, the heir to the French throne, introduced the essential measures to ensure the foundation of a properly-organised French racing and breeding industry.

Their first step was to found the Jockey Club in Paris in 1833, but this remained an exclusive social club without taking on any of the tasks of control of turf affairs, as had its English prototype. Nothing daunted, Seymour and Orleans tried again. Together with a number of like-minded enthusiasts, they issued a manifesto in December 1833 which contained this analysis of the situation. 'The want of encouragement given to the breeding of thoroughbreds has for a long time past reduced this line of business to inactivity and sterility; yet nothing could be more important than to assist it and promote its development in every imaginable way, for it is the sole means ... of providing France with those lighter species ... in which she is so deficient,' they wrote.

In order to supply this missing factor, the two men founded the *Société d'Encouragement pour l'Amélioration des Races de Chevaux en France*. It was this body which assumed the same administrative and legislative functions as those exercised by the English Jockey Club; it also took responsibility for promoting and improving the breeding of horses in France. These aims and functions of the Société d'Encouragement, adopted nearly a century and a half ago, have remained unchanged down to the present day.

Imported stallions

Although English by birth, Seymour lived in Paris and identified himself completely with the interests of French racing. The founders of the Société d'Encouragement agreed that it was pointless to go back to the original stock and try to create a separate French breed of racehorse. They declared that they must build upon, and try eventually to improve, the long patient work of the English breeders; for this purpose, thoroughbred stallions and mares had to be imported from England as foundation stock. These ideas were incorporated in the French Stud Book,

Right *One of the great races of the nineteenth century, the inaugural running of the Grand Prix de Paris in 1863, and* **inset** *the beginnings of the sport in France. Founded at the instigation of Napoleon III, the Grand Prix was open to all and so became one of the chief battlegrounds between French horses and their foreign rivals. National passions ran high.*

which was compiled by government order, while the thoroughbred was designated the 'pur-Sang Anglais.'

Seymour himself took the lead by importing the 2,000 Guineas winner, Ibrahim, who was a failure as a stallion, and the non-classic Royal Oak, who, in complete contrast, was a great success. Royal Oak, who is commemorated in the name of the French equivalent of the British St Leger, was the sire of Poetess, who, in 1841, became the fourth and last of Seymour's four winners of the French Derby (Prix du Jockey Club), which had been founded five years earlier. Poetess became a great brood-mare, whose influence was of inestimable benefit to the developing French thoroughbred. Her son Monarque, the best horse bred in France up to that time, won the French Derby in 1855 and two years later was sent over to England, where he won the Goodwood Cup.

The battle for supremacy

Goodwood was the favourite target for the early French challengers to British supremacy. This was because its nearness to the south coast made it easy to reach, while it also offered generous weight allowances to the competing jockeys. Jouvence had been the first important French winner in England when she captured the Cup there in 1853. But, with growing evidence that French horses were not doomed to perpetual inferiority, French owners soon became more ambitious in the international field.

In 1865, the ability of France to produce thoroughbreds of the highest class obtained its final proof when Gladiateur, a son of Monarque, was sent over to win the coveted Triple Crown of the 2,000 Guineas, the Derby and the St Leger – a feat which led him to be described by his French fans as 'the avenger of Waterloo.' The victories of a horse who defied the handicap of chronic navicular disease by his sheer class and force of character were hailed with joy by the French public. Indeed, he lives on in French racing history today; his statue has the place of honour just inside the public entrance gates of Longchamp.

Gladiateur was owned by Count Fréderic de Lagrange, who poured a fortune into his attempts to improve the standard of the French thoroughbred. He had won the Oaks with Fille de l'Air the year before the triumph of Gladiateur. In the next fifteen years, he and his partner Joachim Lefevre won the 1,000 Guineas and Oaks with Reine, the 1,000 Guineas with Camelia, who also deadheated with

another French filly Enguerrande in the Oaks, the 2,000 Guineas with Chamant and the St Leger with Rayon d'Or.

However, the French classic races at that period were closed to foreign competition – a fact which caused considerable resentment among English breeders. With the introduction of the Grand Prix de Paris in 1863 and at the instigation of the Emp-eror Napoleon III opened to all, English owners were able to hit back at their continental rivals in what was intended to be the greatest French race of all. An English horse, The Ranger, won the inaugural Grand Prix; other English horses – Ceylon, The Earl, Cremorne, Trent, Thurio, Robert the Devil, Bruce, Paradox and Minting – had followed suit by 1886.

Honours even

For the last hundred years, there has been approximate parity between the thorough-bred in the British Isles and the thorough-bred in France, though sometimes one has held temporary supremacy over the other. British breeding survived the First World War in a better shape than the French industry; as a result, the British-bred horses Galloper Light, Comrade and Lemonora won the first three post-war runnings of the Grand Prix. Comrade also took the first Prix de l'Arc de Triomphe. This was introduced into the French racing calendar in 1920 and was destined to become one of the foremost of all international races.

Conversely, the thoroughbred in France emerged from the Second World War stronger than its British rival. This, however, was due less to the impact of the war itself than to the dominance of the studs owned by the French millionaire Marcel Boussac and their successful exploitation of the influence of the three great stallions

Pharis, Tourbillon and Asterus. French horses were kings of the international racing scene for a decade after 1945.

The traditional insistence by the French on the three virtues of soundness, toughness and stamina as far as the thoroughbred is concerned has been blurred in recent years by the downgrading of stamina tests such as the Grand Prix, the Prix Royal Oak and Prix du Cadran, together with a growing emphasis on sheer speed. But the Société d'Encouragement has remained faithful to its original pledge to work for the improvement of breeds of horses. French breeders, in recent times, have been subsidized by generous breeders' prizes, for example: these have been an integral part of overall prize money schemes, swelled by the proceeds of a tote monopoly. And it is clear that the excellence of the French thoroughbred is so broadly based to be proof against any adversity.

Right *Francois Dupre and his 'wonder horse' Tantieme, after winning the Prix de l'Arc de Triomphe, one of Europe's richest and most fashionable races.* **Far Left** *Fashion from a bygone era of elegance; Mme d'Erlanger, Princesse Guy de Faucigny-Lucinge and Princesse de La Tour d'Auvergne compare form and costumes at Deauville at the turn of the century. Fashion, wealth and racing have always gone hand-in-hand; it is not for nothing that racing is known as 'the sport of kings'.*

Below *Sea Bird II, the French favourite for the 1965 Epsom Derby, arrives at Gatwick airport. Sea Bird II's Derby victory was an exceptional French triumph; though many expected him to win, few predicted how easily he would triumph over his rivals in a phenomenal burst of speed in the race's closing stages.*

North America

The links between racing in the New and Old worlds go back to the times of the Stuarts. Charles II, who came to the English throne in 1660, was a passionate devotee of horse racing; naturally enough, where the king led, his courtiers followed. One of these was Colonel Richard Nicolls, the first governor of New York, who brought his own enthusiasm for the 'sport of kings' across the Atlantic to the Americas. Nicolls quickly built a course on Long Island and organized racing became a fact of North American life in 1665.

In this respect, however, New York was an island, surrounded by a sea of religious and political prejudice against the sport. Though in 1699 William Penn imported the stallion Tamerlane along with two mares, nothing of enduring significance took place on the American racing scene – at least, nothing which can be verified – until the English stallion Janus was imported as a ten-year-old in 1756. He was followed in 1764 by Fearnought.

Both these stallions were popular with breeders in Virginia and both proved extremely effective sires. Janus, indeed, was so popular that he was exposed to incredibly intense in-breeding. As a result, the names of both stallions can be found in the pedigrees of many successful US thoroughbreds to this day. This is particularly the case with horses who trace their female descent only as far as an American family mare – that is, a mare whose earliest-known distaff ancestress cannot be traced to a mare eligible for the English General Stud Book.

Family of Selima

In those pre-revolutionary, colonial days, a magnificent mare was also imported in the 1750s. A daughter of the Godolphin Arabian, one of the three founding sires of the thoroughbred, her name was Selima. She became the queen of the turf, winning several of the richest and most significant four-mile heat races in competition with horses owned by the most eminent patrons of the turf.

As breeding stock, however, Selima not only reflected her own talent, but magni-

Top Lexington, right Imported Messenger and far right Hambletonian. Messenger was one of the four imported sires who were to lead American racing into what is termed its 'heroic age'. His son, Hambletonian, became the cornerstone of the Standardbred breed. Messenger traced his ancestry back to both the Darley and Godolphin Arabians; other important influences were Flying Childers and Matchem. In its early years, American racing and breeding owed much to those of England; the links between the two countries survived both the War of Independence and the War of 1812.

LEXINGTON.
THE GREAT MONARCH OF THE TURF AND SIRE OF RACERS.
BY BOSTON OUT OF ALICE CARNEAL.
Winner of the great 4 mile heat race against Lecompte's time 7:26 for $20,000, over the Metairie Course, New Orleans, April 2nd 1855.
Time 7:19¾.

PUBLISHED BY CURRIER & IVES

IMPORTED MESSENGER.
THE GREAT FOUNTAIN HEAD – IN AMERICA – OF "THE MESSENGER BLOOD."
Foaled 1780 got by Mambrino, he by Engineer, he by Sampson, he by Blaze, he by Flying Childers, he by the famous Darley Arabian. Messenger's Dam was by Turf, he by Matchem, he by Cade, he by the great Godolphin Arabian, and the sire of the Dam of Messengers Dam was also by the Godolphin Arabian.

fied it. The name of this monumental matriarch is still to be found in the family trees of top-quality horses throughout America. Among her direct tail-female descendants, for instance, was the Belmont Stakes hero Hanover, four times champion sire in the USA.

The influence of Diomed

Political conflict was soon to cloud the American racing scene. As the tension and bitterness between the colonies and England escalated into open war, the importation of thoroughbred or blooded horses from England practically ceased. But, not long after the war was over, the newly-independent USA was, as in colonial days, buying horses from the former mother-country.

Before 1800, four stallions had been imported which were to have much to do in revitalizing American racing and breeding during what is termed its 'heroic age'. The stallions concerned were Medley, Shark, Messenger and Diomed, with Messenger's son, Hambletonian, becoming the corner-stone of the Standardbred breed.

It was the incredible Diomed, however, who had the most dramatic and dynamic effect on the breed in America prior to the Civil War and the end of the 'heroic age'. But this success story had uncertain origins.

Winner of ten consecutive races, including the inaugural Epsom Derby in 1780 and considered the best colt since Eclipse (1764), Diomed, by the time he was retired from racing, was appraised more for 'what you have done lately' than for what he had done at the age of three. His

stud fee was a paltry five guineas, which quickly dropped to two. He was poorly patronized and his foal crops were sur-prisingly small, with only sixty-eight foals over fourteen seasons.

Eventually, at the age of twenty-one, Diomed was sold to the USA, arriving there in 1798. There, the 'rejected stone,' who had cost his lucky buyer a mere $250, immediately became a fantastic success. His virility, which had been practically untapped in his prime years, found an outlet in his new home.

In the USA, in tail-male, Diomed's crowning glory was expressed through his son, Sir Archy, who had an even greater stud career than his sire. However, both were the victims of excessive in-breeding; as their superiority was so overwhelming, leading breeders did not hesitate to keep

HAMBLETONIAN.
THE PROPERTY OF WM. M. RYSDYK OF CHESTER, ORANGE COUNTY, NEW YORK.

'doubling up' their blood. It is one of the great mysteries of breeding that such an intemperate policy allowed the line to survive beyond one or two generations, but survive it did for nearly three-quarters of a century.

One of Diomed's English daughters, Young Giantess (1790), also ensured that his name lived on in the pedigree of every modern-day thoroughbred. Her son, Sorcerer, carried on the male line of Matchem, tail-male ancestor of the English Triple Crown winner, West Australian. The last-named horse was sire of Australian, founder of the 'native' American Fair Play line. Young Giantess is also one of the collateral lines of Orlando, the Derby winner of 1844 and sire of Eclipse (US), founder of the irrepressible male line of Domino. Her name is additionally prominent in the genetic make-up of Pocahontas, the daughter of Glencoe, who produced such sires as Rataplan, King Tom and the 'sire of sires' Stockwell.

Change of policy

Diomed, his daughters and his sons – especially Sir Archy – were thus significantly responsible for the American horse emerging as a type of its own. There were also other contributing factors. Firstly, the USA and England came into conflict again in the War of 1812 and, as a consequence, there was a further cessation of imports, which lasted on this occasion until around 1830. There was also the fact that Americans looked upon the shorter distances of the English classics as being effeminate, for 'degenerate sons of noble sires.'

Americans preferred the four-mile heat. This preference was to remain a fact of racing life until the USA reversed its policy in the post-Civil War era, patterning its racing more or less in England's image.

England and America

In retrospect, it also seems somewhat ironic that it was the first Epsom Derby winner, the discarded Diomed, who was startlingly responsible for giving the American horse much of his own personality. The irony comes from the fact that today the American-bred thoroughbred is the most successful in the world, if it is agreed, as some authorities claim, that the northern hemisphere thoroughbred is superior to all others. Such a statement is not necessarily parochial or nationalistic. It merely reflects the international nature of the thoroughbred today.

For many years, it was believed with some justification that Americans must constantly replenish their bloodstock by returning to England. For the most part,

Above *A hurdle race at Monmouth Park, New Jersey, in the heyday of nineteenth-century American racing.* **Left** *The first meeting at Jerome Park, New York. In common with Europe, racing expanded greatly in the USA during the nineteenth century. American horses started to race abroad, the first American-bred to capture an English classic being Iroquois, winner of both the Derby and St Leger in 1881. In the early 1900s, however, American racing suffered a body blow, when various states passed anti-racing legislation.*

Chief amongst these was New York, where racing actually came to an end in 1908. The target was not so much the sport itself, but rather the evils of uncontrolled gambling that were associated with it. Many race tracks believed that racing would be impossible without bookmakers; courses closed all over the country. But with the introduction of the pari-mutuel betting system, racing gradually became re-established.

this was true, because the English, with a few exceptions, refused to part with their proven sires and mares. Now, however, the situation has changed radically. The geographical centre of the world's finest breeding has shifted to North America. This proves that the best-bred horses will breed the best horses wherever the environment favours such activity.

First overseas successes

Although an American-bred horse was raced in England as early as 1843, while Richard Ten Broeck had moderate success with several horses, including Prioress, in 1856–57, the first American-bred to capture an English classic was Pierre Lorillard's Iroquois. This horse won both the Derby and St Leger of 1881, just over a century after Diomed. In the same year, James R Keene won the Grand Prix de Paris with Foxhall. Then, at the beginning of this century, the American-bred Rubio won the Aintree Grand National, the American-bred Norman the 2,000 Guineas, while Rhodora, a half-sister to the Derby winner Orby out of an American-bred mare, secured the 1,000 Guineas.

This was not the end of American influence. The Tesio-bred Nearco, unbeaten on the track and probably the most influential sire of this century, had 150 years of American dams in his tail-female line. His third dam, Sibola, was bred in the USA by Lorillard. She also won the 1,000 Guineas.

The Jersey Act

Just as US racing was increasing in popularity and prestige, it suffered several body blows from anti-racing legislation – not all, admittedly, undeserved. The worst of these occurred in 1908, when the state of New York banned racing – the Charles Evans Hughes ban.

As a result, prices of bloodstock became extremely depressed and owners who were wealthy enough to do so looked abroad for their racing opportunities. England countered with the Jersey Act in 1913, which effectively made a horse ineligible for registration in the General Stud Book unless it traced in all lines to animals previously registered in it. Thus, a horse sent to England before the Jersey Act was classed as a thoroughbred, while others of similar breeding who left the USA afterwards were not.

The Act was finally modified in 1949. However, the renaissance in US racing and breeding had begun to flower during the 'roaring twenties' up to the great stock-market crash of 1929.

First syndicated import

These years saw the importation of the French classic winner, Sir Galahad III, who was brought to the USA in 1925 by Claiborne Farm. This son of Teddy from Plucky Liege by Spearmint was to exert an influence unrivalled by any imported sire for many years. He was also one of the first stallions to be purchased by the syndicate, a method which is almost obligatory today because of the astronomical prices fetched by such horses.

Sir Galahad III was a landmark because he represented a new direction in US breeding. His purchase marked the beginning of a deliberate policy of buying the highest-quality European horses, instead of accepting what in most instances the English and French were ready to surrender. This policy reached a peak after the Second World War, when France and England both desperately needed dollars for post-war reconstruction.

Sir Galahad III became champion sire four times and champion brood-mare sire a record-setting twelve times. His brother, Bull Dog, followed him across the Atlantic in 1930, as did their sire, Teddy, in 1931. Bull Dog also topped the sire roster and was leading maternal grand-sire three times. His son, Bull Lea, headed the sire list four times and the brood-mare sire list three times.

Nor did the acquisitions stop there. In 1928, the fine English-bred Pharamond II came to the USA. Although he failed to top the sire list, he was an enduring success through his son, Menow, sire of the American Horse of the Year, Tom Fool. The latter was the sire of another Horse of the Year, Buckpasser.

The following year, Pharamond II's brother, Sickle, became a US resident. He was to head the sire roster twice. The male line he established, through his great-grandson, Native Dancer, has produced horses of such exceptional quality that it is today rivalling that of the great Nearco. The Horse of the Year, Affirmed, the world's first $2 million horse, is a great-grandson of Native Dancer.

Three Derby winners

As the USA emerged from the great depression of the 1930s, major breeders again turned to England for quality sires. In 1936, the Derby winner of 1930, Blenheim II, was purchased from the Aga Khan; in 1940, he was followed by his son, Mahmoud, winner of the 1936 Derby in record time. These two horses soon injected the influence of their classic pedigree into American breeding. This persists to the present day.

Above *Tod Sloan, one of the most celebrated American jockeys of his day. On his visit to Britain in 1897, Sloan completely revolutionized the then customary riding style, which was very much the same as that used in the hunting field. He introduced the idea of riding with short leathers, a long rein and in the characteristic crouch to a doubting audience. It took time for Sloan's innovations to become established and even today US jockeys crouch closer to their horses than their European counterparts.*

In the same year as Mahmoud, two more influential English exports reached the USA. These were the English Triple Crown winner Bahram and Hyperion's classic-placed son, Heliopolis. Bahram was soon to be re-exported to South America, but Heliopolis, though sparsely patronized at first at bargain fees, quickly attained star status. He was premier sire in 1950, as Blenheim II had been in 1941 and Mahmoud in 1946. His line has thrived through his brilliant son, Olympia.

Yet another great horse risked the perils of the U-boat-infested North Atlantic crossing to reach the USA in 1941. This was Princequillo, a scion of the revitalized St Simon male line by Prince Rose. He was to head the sire list twice and the brood-mare list a remarkable eight times. Through such marvellously successful sons as Horse of the Year Round Table and Prince John, Princequillo's influence – both in tail-male and through his producing daughters – seems inviolate.

Post-war policy

After the Second World War, American breeders and owners began a bloodless raid on European bloodstock, especially that of England. This came close to shattering the industry overnight and certainly changed it drastically. In the post-war years, ranging well into the 1950s and beyond, such distinguished names as Khaled, Alibhai, Tudor Minstrel, Court Martial and Tulyar found new homes in the USA. There, they did much to change the course of breeding history, creating what is now known as the Trans-Atlantic Thoroughbred.

Another remarkable change was to take place during this period, largely due to the power of the dollar. In the past, North America had found it almost impossible to persuade European breeders and owners to part with their prize broodmares belonging to classic distaff families. As events were to show, even these pearls now had their price in a changed world.

Influence of Nasrullah

The single most revolutionary acquisition, however, was undoubtedly Nasrullah. In common with Mahmoud, Jhaled and Alibhai, Nasrullah was bred by the Aga Khan. A son of Nearco and already a champion sire in England, he topped the American list for the first of five times in 1955. His son, Bold Ruler, headed the same list eight times, while Bold Ruler's son, What a Pleasure, topped it twice. An imported son of Nasrullah, Indian Hemp, sired TV Lark, the premier sire of 1974.

Still another son of Nasrullah, Never Bend, became the champion sire in England in 1971, when his superb son, Mill Reef, captured Horse of Europe honours. Mill Reef, in turn, was England's champion sire of 1978.

The USA also purchased Nasrullah's three-parts brother, Royal Charger. His grandson, Hail to Reason, headed the sire's roster in 1970, with his foals including the 1972 Derby winner, Roberto. Royal

Charger's son, Turn-to, was also imported. He proved to be a 'sire of sires', for, in addition to Hail of Reason, he fathered such exceptional sires of winners as Sir Gaylord, Best Turn and Cyane. Sir Gaylord's son, Sir Ivor, was a dual classic winner and the best horse of his age as a three-year-old in England. He is now one of the world's most successful sires, particularly of fillies.

Another imported son of Nearco, Nearctic, changed the history of breeding in Canada. A champion sire on several occasions, Nearctic sired seven different champions, including the Canadian-bred Northern Dancer, a champion at three both in Canada and the USA, where he set a new record time of two minutes for the Kentucky Derby. He went on to become a champion sire in both England and the USA, his progeny including the English Triple Crown winner Nijinsky II and the dual Derby winner The Minstrel. Like their sire, both these horses now stand at stud in the USA.

Ribot, the unbeaten dual Arc de Triomphe winner, also spent most of his stud life in the USA. Through such sons as Tom Rolfe and Graustark, Ribot's branch of the St Simon male line is also living gloriously on; Tom Rolfe's son, Hoist the Flag, for instance, is the sire of Alleged, another two-time Arc winner and European Horse of the Year. The male line of Son-in-Law has also probably been saved in the USA through the French Derby winner Herbager, whose several sons, including the French-bred Grey Dawn II, are displaying an ability to breed quality stock.

Left *Two views of the Kentucky Derby, probably the USA's most internationally-celebrated race. The inset shows the 1905 running, in which there were only three starters. Agile led all the way from start to finish. The race took time to reach its present stature; it was not until 1915, when Harry Payne Whitney's magnificent filly, Regret, similarly won by leading from the start, that the race captured the public* *imagination. Today, it is one of the most impressive spectacles of the racing world, with, on average, 100,000 spectators present on the course.* **Above** *The crowd at Belmont Park and* **Below** *the crowd at Cocaine. Founded by some of the richest men in American racing at the turn of the century, Belmont Park's relaxed, sophisticated atmosphere contrasts greatly with that of some of America's other leading tracks.*

Future prospects

The apparent strengths of these sire lines, coupled with many of the fine mares that have been brought to the USA, to blend with the 'native' blood of Fair Play and Domino augured well for the future. The breeding industry in North America, producing numerous yearlings capable of realizing over $1 million each at auction, seemed incapable of not moving from strength to strength.

However, economic factors have a merciless way of changing things. Today, as the value of the dollar declines, more and more of these impeccably-bred American horses are racing for foreign owners in Europe. Many of them will never be returned to the USA.

Yet, out of this dramatic change, the entire world of racing may benefit. Some of these horses may well serve as catalysts for improving the breed in other parts of the world.

Italy

Italy's bloodstock industry is small compared with that of the British Isles, France, and even that of Germany. However, its world-wide impact is out of all proportion to its size, largely due to the work of the great breeder Federico Tesio.

Tesio's impact on the entire world of the thoroughbred is well-nigh imperishable. The rider of 500 steeplechases, an artist in his own right and a lover of all the arts, he was an observant and practical man in everything to do with his horses. The scope and scale of his successful venture into breeding gave rise to a number of theories as to the reasons for his success, but it is impossible to discover the exact nature of his secret – the more so since, in his book 'Breeding the Racehorse', he did not lay down any hard and fast laws. All that can be said is that thoroughness was an essential part of his method, particularly in his studies of the characteristics of mares and their potential mates.

Origins and policy
Racing in Italy shows home-bred horses few favours; only the Derby Italiano and the Premio Parioli (the Italian 2,000 Guineas) are restricted to native stock. Convinced of the beneficial effect of regular infusions of foreign-bred bloodstock, and mindful and proud of what Italian horses bred on these lines have achieved abroad, the Italian racing authorities have ceased to bar foreign-breds from most of their pattern events. In 1978 alone, fourteen of the thirty-five principal two-year-old races, three Group 1 events and eight in Groups 2 and 3 were won by horses bred abroad. The 3,094 races were contested by 2,231 horses, of which 595 were two-year-olds and 701 were three-year-olds. There were 109 sires standing at Italian studs, but only forty-one had more than ten of the 869 foals to their name.

The story of Italian racing really starts in 1884, with the first running of the Derby Italiano, the Italian Derby. This was the real beginning of the country's interest in the thoroughbred horse, though there was racing before this. The sport was supported lavishly by the reigning King of Italy, Vittorio Emmanuele II, but the next step of importance happened in 1911 when Federico Tesio sent out Guido Reni to win him his first Derby Italiano. That ,year became both a milestone in Italy's turf history and a memorable date in the sport's development the world over, entirely because of Tesio's initial classic triumph.

Winning sixty-five classics
Guido Reni was followed by Tesio-bred winners of nineteen Italian Derbys, fifteen

Italian St Legers and nine Oaks d'Italia, in addition to many victories in the Premio Elena and Premio Parioli, the two remaining Italian classics. Dormello, the stud created by Tesio and still run today by the family of his partner, the Marchese Incisa, has increased the total to sixty-five classic victories by winning, since Tesio's death in 1954, another six Italian Derbys, ten Italian St Legers and five Oaks d'Italia. Marracci in the 1979 Derby Italiano is the latest classic winner to come from this illustrious nursery.

Tesio began his operations in 1898 by buying a mare in England, the country where he made his most successful pur-

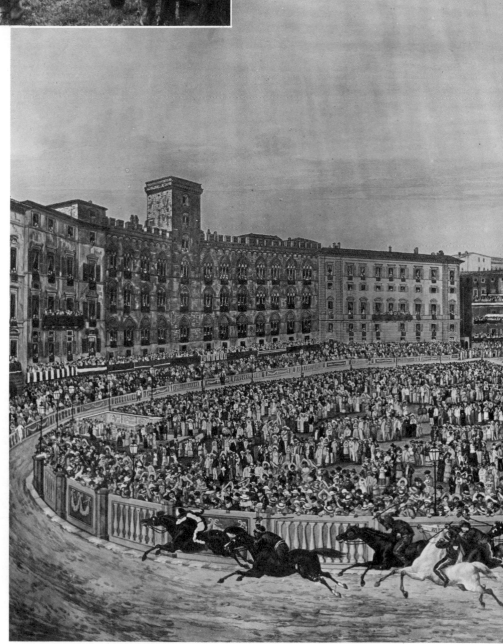

Left Gamici, *winner of the 1955 Milan Grand Prix,* **below** *the traditional horse race at Sienna and* **below right** *Ribot, one of the greatest horses ever to be bred. Though Italian interest in racing stretches back over the centuries, as the picture of Sienna shows, modern Italian racing owes much to the work of one genius – Federico Tesio. Ribot was the greatest horse that Tesio produced in a career going back to 1911, when he won his first Italian* classic. *This was the Derby Italiano, a race founded in 1884. Nicknamed 'Il piccolo' (the little one), Ribot was the outstanding horse of the St Simon line to race in Europe in the mid-twentieth century. In his first great international win – the 1955 Prix de l'Arc de Triomphe – he won by an easy three lengths from the top-class opposition. Repeating the feat the next year, he then retired to stud.*

chases throughout his career. He did not stand his own stallions, except during wartime, preferring to send his mares to stallions standing abroad or at other Italian studs. One reason for this was that he strongly believed this policy to be good for the mares, just as he liked to move them to and fro between his three studs. Briefly, Tesio possessed a strong belief in the advantages of changes of environment, always provided that the paddocks had the right type of soil.

Once Tesio was convinced of his horses' international calibre, he started sending them abroad to race. Scopas, certainly not one of his best, took the 1923 La Coupe in Paris before he easily triumphed in the 1924 Grosser Preis von Baden-Baden. His exceptional colt, Donatello, narrowly lost the 1937 Grand Prix de Paris, a race which the giant among sires, Nearco, took against formidable opposition in 1938. Both these sons of British-bred sires, Blenheim and Pharos, went to England and founded immensely important sire lines there. Tesio's filly, Tofanella, a daughter of the Tesio-bred 1928 Coronation Cup winner Apelle, who stood at stud in England, was not particularly outstanding in Italy but took Munich's 1934 Brown Ribbon, while her son, Tenerani, won both the Queen Elizabeth Stakes and Goodwood Cup in 1948. Marguerite Vernaut, whose dam was bought by Tesio's successors for 230 guineas, trounced Never Too Late (1,000 Guineas and Oaks) in Newmarket's 1960 Champion Stakes.

Federico Tesio did not live to see Ribot, probably the best of his legion of magnificent horses, win the Prix de l'Arc de Triomphe in 1955 and 1956, as well as Ascot's 1956 King George VI & Queen Elizabeth Stakes. Ribot, the unbeaten victor of sixteen great races, who was exported to the USA at the age of eight, became one of the most prepotent and influential progenitors of our times, siring in his first crop of foals the Razza Ticino colt Molvedo, victor of the 1961 Prix de l'Arc de Triomphe.

Other influential owners

Tesio was not the only Italian owner to venture abroad. There was Giuseppe de Montel's Ortello, the conqueror of the great Kantar and Oleander, the twin prides of German racing, in the 1929 'Arc'. Razza del Soldo's Crapom emulated Ortello's achievement in this event in 1933. Felice Scheibler and Edoardo Ginistrelli were pillars of Italy's racing establishment. The former was a shrewd and skilled judge of bloodstock; the latter, after he left his native Italy, went on to breed, train and own Signorinetta, who won the 1908 Epsom Derby and, forty-eight hours later, the Oaks. More recently, Ortis and Orange Bay, top-class performers in Italy, were sent to be trained in England and won Ascot's Hardwicke Stakes in 1971 and 1976 respectively. Thus, Italian racing continues the Tesio tradition today.

Germany

Organized thoroughbred racing started in Germany in 1822, when Doberan, a small spa on the Baltic, staged its first race meeting. The venture was a success and breeding began with imported British bloodstock. This produced, after two decades, horses good enough to carry off Goodwood's Stewards' Cup and Chesterfield Cup with Turnus in 1850, while the three-year-old Scherz took the Cambridgeshire in 1854. Turnus was paid the compliment of being bought by an English stud, where he sired the 1860 Oaks winner, Butterfly.

Such events were only a flash in the pan, however, since German horses were inferior, on the whole, to their foreign rivals. At times, quite modest foreign horses trounced the German runners at Baden-Baden, where the valuable prestige event, the Grosser Preis, fell more often than not to French and other foreign challengers. For its part, the Deutches Derby, run at Hamburg for the first time in 1869, went frequently to invaders from Austria. It seemed clear that there was something lacking in the breeding of the indigenous German thoroughbred, the answer probably lying in a combination of the climate and the soil.

The breeding associations

These limitations were a severe handicap, but successful efforts to overcome them were made by a number of breeders gifted with vision, expertise and initiative. In order to assist German breeders, who, on the whole, were poorer than their foreign rivals, breeders' associations were formed to undertake the importation of good-class bloodstock. This was then auctioned off to individual breeders to enable slow, but consistent, progress to be made in the right direction.

One such importation was Festa, a filly foaled in 1893 by the great St Simon out of the Oaks winner L'Abbesse de Jouarre. Festa was an immediate and enormous success at the Waldfried stud, near Frankfurt am Main. Her four sons and one daughter all won several classic or prestige events and the family which she created is still going strong.

Gestüt Schlenderhan, the oldest private stud in Germany, established near Cologne in 1869, became the lucky owner of Alvéole, whose descendants, together with those of the Hungarian-bred Kisasszony and Orsova, made the establishment the most important in Germany. Conditions in the Rhine valley seem particularly suited to the breeding of good horses.

The Ministry of Agriculture, concerned with the production of the ideal cavalry

horse, in the meantime entrusted the Prussian state stud, Graditz (today the National Stud of the GDR), with the importation of foreign-bred sires, whose progery were raced under the stud's silks. Count Georg Lehndorff acquired two grandsons of St Simon—Nuage, winner of the 1910 Grand Prix de Paris, and Ard Patrick, hero of the 1902 Epsom Derby. These two sires created one of the most successful 'nicks' ever known; this happy phenomenon was put on an even broader basis with the help of Dark Ronald.

Two world wars

German breeding and racing naturally was greatly influenced by the two world wars, though the results were different in each case. In spite of the damage caused by the First World War, the German-bred racehorse emerged from four years of hardship and fodder shortage a much better animal. Native-born horses now proved able to beat off foreign challengers for rich prizes at Baden-Baden, Berlin's high class course, Hoppegarten, and Munich. At the last-named, the unbeaten filly Nereide conquered France's legendary Corrida,

victress of two runnings of the Prix de l'Arc de Triomphe. In 1929, Oleander, produced by Gestüt Schlenderhan, finished a narrowly-beaten third in the Arc itself – an effort no German horse could have made before the First World War.

As a result of the Second World War, however, German bloodstock and racing were reduced to a tiny nucleus. German breeders still realized that judicious purchases abroad had brought about a remarkable improvement of the breed. Nevertheless, despite great efforts on the part of some breeders, the fact remained that, all too often, Germany's rich prizes were – and are – taken by foreign-bred and foreign-trained visitors.

For whatever reason, the present home-bred German horse does not measure up to the good horses that, between the wars, were able, for instance, to fight off many high-class challengers for the Grosser Preis von Baden. Since the Second World War, this has gone abroad fifteen times in twenty-eight years. Altogether, out of 273 pattern events open to foreign-bred horses, run between 1950 and 1978, fifty-four were lost to foreign-breds.

Left *Hurdling at the Hoppegarten racecourse in Berlin in 1963. Most German race meetings include steeplechase and hurdle races on the programme, although emphasis is on flat racing. Since the war German racing has largely been closed to foreign competition and great efforts have been made to improve the quality of the German thoroughbred. This race, won by Kastellan (No 6), was run in honour of the German National Stud at Graditz, in Prussia.*

Below *Herero, winner of the German Derby at Hamburg in 1962. Bred at the Gestut Römerhof, Herero is a representative of the Ticino male line in Germany. In the last ten years German stallions have played an increasingly important role in European racing, with Star Appeal, by Neckar, winning the Prix de l'Arc de Triomphe in 1975.*

The German answer

The Germans had two answers to this. The first was to reduce the competition and the second to improve the breed. The simple fact recognized by German breeders themselves is that German-bred horses are just not good enough to compete in truly international racing. Nor could the breeders – and the industry as a whole – survive the onslaught on prize money that would be the inevitable result of open racing.

German race-goers are optimistic that better horses will be bred in the not-too-distant future. There are about eighty-five sires standing in Germany, together with approximately 1,900 mares. These produced 2,837 contestants for 2,254 races run in 1978, 415 of whom were two-year-olds and 821 three-year-olds. The blood of Ticino has been of considerable influence.

The courses, too, do their best to encourage breeding. Prize money is high, together with breeders' premiums. These benefit from the tax on tote betting, which itself is growing yearly. On the other hand, National Hunt racing – once the pride of many flourishing courses – has suffered both recession and neglect.

Australia and New Zealand

Over the past century, Australia has made greater progress in the world of horse racing than almost any other nation in the world. This is the result of a combination of businesslike administration, which has led to the development of the country's superb race courses, spiralling prize money, the establishment of world-class studs, such as Lindsay Park, South Australia, and Stockwell at Diggers Rest, Victoria, and the production of a long line of class thoroughbred sprinters and stayers.

Yet, though horse racing in Australia has much to offer, few people outside the country realize how tremendously the industry there has grown. As a result, the status of Australian horse racing is extremely high and continues to attract massive investment in the thoroughbred horse. In this achievement, New Zealand, too, has played a major role. There, horse racing and betting turnover has never been more affluent, with the annual yearling sales at Trentham commanding a world market because of the proven quality of the stock. All Australia's leading trainers are prominent at these sales each year, while overseas buyers arrive with open cheques in search of the best available yearlings. Now, however, there is also strong competition from the Sydney Easter yearling sales, the Victoria sales, and the South Australian sales in Adelaide.

Foundation of Australian racing

It was the origin of the imported blood horse which started the process and Australians and New Zealanders are the first to recognize the fact. The story starts in 1799, when the first English thoroughbred stallion, Rockingham, arrived in Australia, though a cargo of well-bred mares had been landed in Sydney from the Cape of Good Hope four years earlier. Many of the early importations were Arabs and Persians, but, after 1820, the majority of imported horses were from England.

From the early days of the colony, individuals matched their horses against those owned by their neighbours, but the first organized race meeting in Australia was held at Hyde Park, Sydney, in 1810. This was a three-day meeting in the October of that year, staged by the officers of the British 73rd Regiment in conjunction with leading local politicians. Regular meetings took place at the Hyde Park course until 1814, when the regiment was transferred from garrison duty in Australia to Ceylon. This brought about a lapse in the sport until 1819.

Gradually, racing was re-established. It entered a new era with the formation of the Australian Jockey Club in Sydney in 1828. The AJC was to become the controlling body of racing in New South Wales and has retained that status ever since.

Spread of racing

Where New South Wales led, the other colonies followed. As the pioneers settled in all the Australian colonies, one of the first priorities was to establish a race course. Horse racing had been part of the English way of life for many years and lovers of the sport wasted no time in bringing Australia into line with the customs of the old country.

The island colony of Tasmania, first settled by white men in 1804, organized racing as early as 1814. Western Australia, settled in 1829, held its first race meeting at Fremantle in 1833. Victoria, settled in 1835, had its first course ready for racing in March 1838. Queensland had its first racing in 1842, shortly after the state was open for general settlement.

The settlers, too, framed their racing on the home pattern. By the 1850s, there were Australian equivalents of the Derby, Oaks and St Leger classics in all the various capital cities.

The revolution of 1860

The sport became increasingly popular and, by 1860, practically every race meeting was conducted with pure thoroughbreds. That year, however, saw a revolutionary change. Australian administrators came to believe that the pattern of feature races should be widened, with the biggest and richest events extending beyond just classic and weight-for-age races. This, they believed, would give the middle-class owner, with an average horse, the opportunity to share in the major prize money that was being offered.

This change was marked by the promotion of the first Melbourne Cup at Flemington in 1861. It set into practice a policy which has stood the test of time. It proved beyond a doubt that winning a high-class handicap with more than weight-for-age can carry more prestige than struggling home in a set weights race.

To the dismay of traditionalists, the 1861 Melbourne Cup over two miles (now 3,200 metres) was the richest prize of the carnival at £710. The 1979 Melbourne Cup was worth $A310,000 with a $A10,000 gold cup. In common with the principal cup handicaps in every state of Australia, it increases in value each year. The Australian Jockey Club and Sydney Turf Club also provide substantial prize money; the same story applies to the races staged by Queensland Turf Club, the Brisbane Amateur Turf Club, the South Australian Jockey Club in Adelaide, and the Western Australian Turf Club in Perth.

The reasons for the system

What purists fail to understand is that in Australia and New Zealand (to which the system spread), the top weight-for-age

Below *Flemington race track, Melbourne, at the turn of the century. Flemington staged the first Melbourne Cup in 1861, when the race became the richest race of the Melbourne carnival, despite being a handicap over two miles. Until that time classic and weight-for-age races dominated Australian racing. Now the Melbourne Cup merits a national holiday.*

horses frequently dominate the major handicaps. These, in turn, generate a huge proportion of the betting turnover distributed back to the race clubs.

Because capital city cups and other major handicaps are less predictable than the majority of classic – and particularly weight-for-age – races, the racing public enjoys a greater degree of speculation and bet more freely and widely in handicap events. Australia is unique in this respect, since cup handicap races attract more general interest and discussion than the majority of set-weight races.

The role of betting

The success story of Australian racing is thus closely linked to that of betting, which provides much of the revenue for the development of the sport. Betting in Australia has a long and fascinating history, but, on the money side, Australian racing entered a new dimension as recently as March 1961. On March 11 of that year,

the Victorian Totalizator Agency Board set up the Commonwealth's first legalized off-course tote betting system in Melbourne.

There were then thirteen agencies operating, a total which has now grown to 472. TAB turnover on that opening day was £43,226; for the 1977/78 season, it reached $A570,821,358, and the aggregate tote turnover for Victoria alone from March 1961 until the financial year ending July 28, 1978, was a staggering $A4,377,903,440. Other Australian states accepted the lead given by the Victorian government and the Victoria Racing Club. They, too, are now enjoying the rich benefits of the off-course tote betting system, which is the success story of modern Australian racing.

Three turf immortals

Breeding, too, is an essential part of the Australasian story. Much can be written of thoroughbred racehorses and their achievements, but, in the history of

Top *The finish of the 1979 Melbourne Cup with Hyperno beating Salamander and Red Nose. Australia is unique in international racing in that the top handicaps attract far greater interest than weight-for-age races from the racing public.*

Above *The gold trophy for the 1979 Melbourne Cup. Besides the cup, the race was worth $A310,000 to the winner, a prize that increases in value every year in common with the other principal cup handicaps.*

Australian racing, three immortals of the turf have inscribed indelible memories. In historical sequence, these were Carbine, Phar Lap and Tulloch – all foaled in New Zealand by imported sires. Only superlatives can describe their ability.

Many authorities claim that Carbine was the greatest Australian horse of all time. His story starts before the turn of the century as a race horse and then as a stallion. By Musket from the imported mare Mersey (by Knowsley), Carbine was in-bred – his pedigree showing as many as six strains of Camel, the sire of the great horse Touchstone. His record speaks for itself – he was unplaced only once in forty-three starts. After carrying a weight handicap of 10 st into second place behind Bravo in the two-mile Melbourne Cup in 1889, he shouldered an enormous 10½ st the following year. This time, he not only defeated his thirty-eight rivals, but set a weight-carrying record which has never been equalled.

After he retired from racing, Carbine had a powerful impact on the English thoroughbred. At stud in Australia, he sired 203 winners, the best-known of these being the outstanding racehorse and sire, Wallace, whose progeny won 949 races. Finally, Carbine was exported to England in 1895. There, he stood with the great St Simon at Welbeck Abbey, the stud of the Duke of Portland, where he sired the 1906 English Derby winner, Spearmint.

Carbine's blood has been carried to victory in almost every thoroughbred racing country in the world. This is particularly due to Spearmint, who, through his partnership with the mare, Plucky Liege, produced twelve great winners. These included Bois Roussel, Sir Galahad III and Bull Dog. All three of these became champion sires in either Britain or the USA.

The great Phar Lap

Phar Lap – the Ceylonese for 'lightning' – was by Night Raid from Entreaty. His alternative nickname – 'Red Terror' – came from his height and colour (he was a rich red chestnut, standing seventeen hands high) and some Australians believe that he was the greatest racehorse ever foaled anywhere in the world.

Bought at the 1927 New Zealand yearling sales for a mere 160 guineas, Phar Lap turned out a freak racehorse. He won a maiden race from five starts as a two-year-old; then, over the change of season, his development was colossal. As a three-year-old, he won thirteen races, including both the Australian Jockey Club and Victoria Derbys, and was third to Nightmare (also by Night Raid) in the two-mile Melbourne

Above *Runners at a meeting at Birdsville, a remote outpost of Australian racing 850 miles from Brisbane. Bush meetings in Australia are immensely popular; although facilities are far from sophisticated, there is no lack of enthusiasm and interest.*

Cup, after trying to lead over the final six furlongs. He reached his peak in the following year, when he won fourteen successive races. These included the Melbourne Cup that had eluded him the year before, even though he was handicapped with 9 st 12 lb – 15 lb over weight-for-age for a four-year-old gelding.

Phar Lap did not just win his races with a few lengths to spare; he won by anything from ten to thirty lengths, going half-pace, in both set weights and weight-for-age races. He more or less turned every race into a procession. For this reason, he became the only horse in racing history in any part of the world to alter the conditions of weight-for-age races. He continued to annihilate his opponents so mercilessly that penalties and allowances were introduced to weight-for-age races in Australia to try and even them up. This saw Phar Lap carrying 7 lb and sometimes more over the normal scale to try to bring him down to the level of the opposition. Only once, however, did this beat him. It was his first race after a rest and he was beaten by a neck in a mile weight-for-age event, in which he had to concede 21 lb to the winner, also a four-year-old.

Phar Lap's career was packed with drama and also a near-tragedy and a tragedy. Though he was idolized by the public, he was a thorn in the side of certain betting interests. A few days before his Melbourne Cup victory, an attempt was made to shoot him while he was being led back to his stable after track work. Lead slugs, fired from a car lodged in a nearby fence, just missed the horse. He was removed to a country hide-out and had armed police protection until he went to the barrier for the Cup start.

The tragedy occurred when he was taken to the USA to run in the Agua Caliente Handicap in Mexico in March 1931. He won easily, but just sixteen days later Phar Lap was dead. He was treated for colic, but the real cause of death remains a mystery.

Tulloch, in the eyes of many, is considered Phar Lap's successor (p. 234).

Racing in New Zealand

Racing in New Zealand began a year after the annexation of the two islands to the British crown, when a number of race meetings were held to celebrate the event. In New Zealand, as in every land they colonized, the British established a chain of race courses, as they extended their territory deeper into the country.

One man bemused by this addiction was Alexander Majoribanks, a dour Scot, whose book 'Travels in New Zealand' was published in 1846. 'It is curious,' he wrote, 'that the English cannot settle in a new

The racecourse stables at Awapuni, near Palmerston North, in New Zealand. Despite its small population, there are eighty eight registered racing clubs in New Zealand and the islands have been responsible for a high percentage of the best horses to race in Australia. Among them are numbered Carbine, Gloaming, Phar Lap, Dalray/and Rising Fast.

country without wasting time and money on that most absurd of all absurdities, horse races ... one would suppose that Aucklanders might have been better employed in sowing a little clover or turnip seed for their cattle than in setting a parcel of dumb animals to run against each other.' Despite his lack of interest, Majoribanks was present at the grandly-named Epsom race course in Auckland on January 5, 1841, when army officers and prominent citizens staged an anniversary meeting. The main event was the Town Plate, with an entry fee of three sovereigns, winner take all.

Wellington, at the other end of the north island, and Nelson followed suit, the latter holding its first meeting in 1843 on the anniversary of its foundation. It was here that New Zealand racing was first placed on a sound footing. A proper race course was established at Stoke, four miles out of the town; the first meeting was held there on February 3, 1845. Among other centres, Wanganui began racing in December 1848, while the first races in Dunedin were held in March 1849. Otago followed; as a result of the discovery of gold in the province, this was, for a time, the strongest racing centre in New Zealand.

Canterbury held its first meeting on December 16, 1851, with a programme of four events at Hagley Park. At about the same time, there was racing on the west coast and at Tranaki. However, Hawke's Bay, which was to play a prominent role in the development of New Zealand racing, did not have its first meeting until New Year's Day 1857.

Improving the breed

While the pioneer settlers firmly believed that poor racing was better than no racing at all, they were anxious to improve the quality of their horses as quickly as possible. In the formative years of the sport, they looked to accessible Australia rather than to England, the faraway home of the thoroughbred horse.

Not all the early importations had attested blood lines, but their worth was judged more on appearance than on pedigree. In 1845 and 1846, two mares from New South Wales of unknown pedigree produced filly foals in Wellington. Both of these foals were to have a significant role in the advance of the New Zealand thoroughbred to the world-class status it enjoys today. The first of these fillies produced in her turn the great tap-root mare, Sybil. The other filly was given the unflattering name of Sharkie. From her descended Advance, who so richly graced the New Zealand turf half a century later, while a crossing of the blood of both Sybil and Sharkie produced Equitas, a great racing mare of the early twentieth century. She passed on her quality to Oratress, winner of the New Zealand and Wellington Cups. In turn, a daughter of Oratress, Oratrix, won the Wellington and Auckland Cups, was second in the New Zealand Cup and third in Australia's most famous race – the Melbourne Cup.

The descendants of Flora McIvor

Important though the contribution was of those anonymous mares, it did not match the almost incredible story of the Australian-bred mare, Flora McIvor. Henry Redwood, whom many consider to be the father of New Zealand racing, imported Flora McIvor from New South Wales and her previous owner must have been delighted to get good New Zealand money in exchange for the horse. At the time of the sale, Flora McIvor was twenty-five years old, past the average lifespan of a thoroughbred, and far over the normal reproductive age. Yet, at the age of twenty-seven, she produced Io and two years later, Waimea.

From Waimea, there descended a host of good horses, including Nightmarch, Chide, Silver Scorn and Silver Ring. Io, too, produced innumerable winners, but none of these was greater than Trenton, whose record both in racing and at stud was truly remarkable.

Looking further afield

When the Australian importations convinced New Zealanders that their rich pastures could produce horses of the highest quality, they looked to England for fresh blood. Probably the best of the early stallions so imported was the immortal Traducer, a descendant of the Byerley Turk, one of the three stallions to whom every thoroughbred in the world traces its descent. Traducer's stock won nearly every race of importance in both New Zealand and Australia; his best son, Sir Mordred, was a top sire in the USA. Traducer also sired Lurline, who produced the Sydney Cup winner, Darebin, whose descendants included Commando, a brilliant racehorse in the USA in the early years of the twentieth century.

Great though the influence of Traducer was, it was surpassed by that of Musket, even though his stud career lasted a brief eight years. In 1885, his union with an English-bred mare produced Carbine, whose influence was to permeate racing wherever it was conducted.

Since those distant days of Musket and Carbine, New Zealand breeders have continued to look for the best of English, French, American and Australian blood. They have not bought the dearest, because they cannot compete in the sales ring with the tycoons of the northern hemisphere; but their skill, patience and the wonderful properties of the New Zealand soil make this tiny country a phenomenon in the world of thoroughbred breeding.

Control of racing

In the formative years of New Zealand racing, each club operated independently, fashioning its own rules more or less on the pattern of the English Jockey Club. The clubs did not recognize each others' jurisdiction and, in many cases, ignored disqualifications imposed by another club.

This chaotic system lasted until the 1890s, when the New Zealand Racing Conference was founded. This is not a racing club, but an administrative body, with complete control over all aspects of racing. Racing at the various courses is in the hands of the various clubs. The Auckland Racing Club has its home at Ellerslie, while Wellington has its headquarters at Trentham. The Canterbury Jockey Club, founded in 1854, is the senior club in the country.

The Far East

Racing in Japan began in the mid-nineteenth century, shortly after that country's centuries of self-imposed isolation from the rest of the world was brought to an end. With the development of Yokohama as a thriving international port and city, it was not long before the mainly English traders who had settled there laid out their first race course. This opened in May 1862; another course, Negishi, was opened in 1867, using part of the promenade around Yokohama Bay.

It was many years after this, however, before the Japanese were introduced to the thoroughbred horse. For a long time, the contestants were ponies, mainly imported from China, with most races being run from five furlongs to one mile. In 1895, fourteen thoroughbreds were imported from Australia for the first time, though in 1902 a regulation restricted such imports to fillies. One of the earliest arrivals was Mira, ancestress of Hikaruimai, who won the Tokyo Yuushun (Derby) in 1971.

Foundation of classics

The establishment of classic races on the English pattern had to wait until the 1930s, when the Japanese Racing Society was founded in 1936. The Ouka Shou (1,000 Guineas) and Satsuki Shou (2,000 Guineas) were first contested in 1939; the Yuushun Hinba (Oaks) and Kikuka Shou (St Leger) date from the previous year. Only the Tokyo Yuushun pre-dates the foundation of the club. This dates from 1932, while the ten furlong Satsuki Shou is not a direct equivalent of an English classic.

The Second World War hit Japanese racing severely. One of the first casualties was Negishi, which was bought by the Japanese navy. However, the old course has not been forgotten, as a 'Memorial Hall of Racing' was opened there in 1977.

All courses were finally closed to the public from December 1943 onwards, though a certain amount of test racing still took place behind closed doors in order to establish which were the best horses for breeding purposes. The sport resumed under the supervision of the Allied occupation authorities at Tokyo and Kyoto in 1946, but the number of horses involved was only about 250.

'National Racing'

The government eventually got control of Japanese racing back from the occupation authorities, its involvement lasting until 1954, when the Japanese Racing Association Law was passed. The JRA is now the ruling body for what is known in Japan as 'National Racing'. This takes place at ten tracks, staging about 290 days of racing a

year in total. Meetings are only allowed to be held on Saturdays, Sundays and public holidays. Large tracks in the national racing group hold five or six meetings per year, none of which may last more than eight days, while the smaller ones stage two or three.

Each programme is restricted to twelve races. This allocation is almost completely filled, the number of races run on 288 days in 1977 being 3,083. Of that total, 2,674 were flat races for thoroughbreds, 221 were restricted to Arabs and 188 were steeplechases. Only ninety-seven of the 2,227 events for three-year-olds or older thoroughbreds were contested at a distance greater than ten furlongs. A record total of 4,669 horses competed 30,658 times.

Prolific betting

The JRA is a non-profitmaking organization, whose capital is totally owned by the government. It is responsible for the complete operation of 'National Racing', including the pari-mutuel betting system Japan has adopted. Bookmakers are not allowed. Something over 4,000 horses are housed at two huge training centres – Miho (for Tokyo) and Ritto (for Kyoto) – but

many more are involved in the alternative to national racing. This is 'Regional Public Racing', a more everyday version of the sport which is conducted under the auspices of the local municipality or prefecture rather than the JRA.

Main events

The four most valuable races in 1978 each guaranteed a winner's prize of 55,000,000 yen (£119,500) – a figure that has subsequently increased. These were the Tokyo Yuushun and Tennou Shou, run at Tokyo in late May and late November respectively, the Tennou Shou at Kyoto at the end of April and the Arima Kinen at Nakayama in mid-December.

The Tennou Shou, or Emperor's Cup, was established in 1905 and has been contested twice a year since 1938.

Three other races were worth more than 40,000,000 yen (£86,950) in 1978 – Kyoto's Kikuka Shou, the Takarazuka Kinen, for four-year-olds and over run at Hanshin in June, and Tokyo's Yuushun Hinba. The most valuable races for two-year-olds are the Asahi Hai Sansai, at Nakayama, and the Hanshin Sansai, at Hanshin. Both are run over one mile in December.

Public support

Big race days are often sold out and attendances are vast; a crowd of 169,174 watched the 1973 Tokyo Yuushun, for instance. The Tokyo track is at Fuchu, seventeen miles west of the city, while Nakayama is nineteen miles to the east. Kyoto and Hanshin are near Osaka.

All Japanese tracks are right-handed – the exception being Tokyo – with a dirt track and a figure-of-eight steeplechase course inside the main turf oval. Huge stands run the length of the straight; this has a run-in of 600 yards at Tokyo, but under two furlongs at the other three.

Not only is public interest very high but Japan also takes its position as a racing power extremely seriously. The JRA was instrumental in setting up the Asian Racing Conference, which met for the first time at Tokyo in 1960. The ARC now has thirteen members, who confer on a regular basis.

Foreign-trained horses are not allowed to compete in Japan, while those Japanese horses which have raced abroad have not been conspicuously successful. However, the Japanese have imported a large number of high-class winners for stud purposes, including seven post-war winners of the Epsom Derby. They continue to import good stallions (the law of 1902 having been repealed), particularly stayers, and it is likely that they may well soon produce a horse of the highest class.

Above left *Horse racing – a Japanese view. The sport became established in Japan with the foundation of the first organized racecourse at Yokohama, opened by English traders in 1862; a second at Negishi was opened in 1867, using ponies imported from China.* **Left** *The Kikuku Shou, the Japanese equivalent of the St Leger, at Kyoto racecourse, worth nearly £120,000 in 1980. Run over 1 mile 7 furlongs at the end of the season, the race is open to home-bred three-year-old colts and fillies.* **Below** *The Tokyo Yuushun, the Japanese Derby.*

Malaya and Singapore

With only four race tracks – Singapore, Penang, Kuala Lumpur and Ipoh – Malaysia and Singapore nevertheless only have a fortnight in the year without any form of racing. Interest in the sport is extremely high; if, for instance, a course is closed, crowds still gather there to bet on races relayed by television from other courses.

The Singapore Turf Club, based at Bukit Timah, was established in 1842. Penang TC followed in 1864, the Selangor TC, with its racecourse in Kuala Lumpur, in 1869, and the Perak TC, with its course at Ipoh, in 1898. The last three each stage about twenty days' racing a year, all on the flat. Racing is controlled by the Malayan Racing Association, made up of members elected by the four clubs. Internationally, the association's chief claim to fame lies in its pioneering of pre-race dope testing. A system of saliva testing was introduced as early as 1951, while urine tests have been used since 1956.

Singapore and Penang

Singapore and Penang are the two most important tracks, though the former is by far the most developed. The stands there are palatial, while every box has the facilities of an executive suite. Average attendance is 33,000 – with the rebuilt stands, this will rise to 45,000 – with racing on thirty-four days of the year. In addition, the course is also opened for racing broadcasts from the other three tracks of the Malayan mainland.

The course belongs to 700 debenture holders and is a thriving business. Eight trainers, with approximately 400 horses, are stationed there; the horses, in Asian terms, are of a good standard, being much better than those racing at Hong Kong, as Singapore owners are allowed to import horses of their own choice principally from Australia and Europe.

Singapore also has one of the best equine hospitals in the world, with thirty stalls for sick horses, four of them air-conditioned. The hospital block additionally houses the superbly-equipped analytical laboratories of the Malayan Racing Association, while there is also an apprentice jockey training school.

Penang, too, has a notable apprentice school. This was opened in 1964 and is run by the course's official starter. It is responsible for seventy per cent of all local riders, who pass through the course in groups of ten. Successful applicants are between eighteen and twenty, of a limited weight, less than five feet tall, and of an accepted educational standard.

South America and South Africa

A continuously unfavourable balance of payments, together with chronic inflation, have combined to dramatically affect the once-thriving racing industries in several of the nations of South America. This is particularly the case in Argentina, Chile and Uruguay.

Few countries, for example, are more suitable than Argentina for the raising of quality stock, but that country's problems in the past three decades have had such sorry effects that racehorse owners and breeders fall easy prey to dollar-rich visitors from the northern hemisphere. Though the Argentine still produces good horses, poor prize money and uncertain political and economic conditions mean that even the best horses can be bought reasonably cheaply.

The decline of racing is also reflected in the number of race courses. Buenos Aires, for instance, used to have two magnificent tracks – Palermo (renamed Hipodromo Argentino in 1977) and San Isidro. The latter, however, has been closed since 1976. San Isidro had both turf and dirt courses, but Argentino has only a dirt track. So, too, does La Plata, the only other Argentinian track where top-class racing takes place. Of twenty-five Group One events in 1979, twenty-three took place at the Hipodromo Argentino and two at La Plata. There is also racing at the provincial centres of Cordoba, Mendoza and Rosario, but this is not of top-class standard.

This state of affairs is in complete contrast to the hey-day of Argentinian racing in the nineteenth century. Then, Argentinian cattle barons were rich enough to import such stallions as Ormonde – the Triple Crown winner of 1886 and one of the best horses ever to race in England – and another Triple Crown winner, Diamond Jubilee, as well as many top-quality mares.

Today, export, rather than import, is the name of the game. Forli, the most significant purchase among the thousands of South American horses exported to the USA in the last thirty years, was the sire of Forego, three times Horse of the Year in the USA, as well as of such successful European horses as Thatch, Home Guard and Lissadell.

Guests of honour of the Argentine Jockey Club at Palermo racecourse, renamed the Hipodromo Argentino in 1977. Of twenty-five Group 1 races in 1979, twenty three were run at Argentino, where the racing takes place on dirt.

Today Argentina exports a number of horses to the United States, significantly Forli, sire of Forego in the USA, and Thatch, Home Guard and Lissadell in Europe.

The same situation prevails in other South American countries. Cougar, the US turf champion of 1972, came from a female line which had thrived in Chile since the nineteenth century, while the 1976 Epsom Derby winner, Empery, is out of Pamplona II, the star of the 1959 classic generation in Peru. Indeed, in 1969, Peruvian breeders switched to northern hemisphere times for the official birthday of their horses – previously, in common with the rest of South America, this had been July 1. The idea was not only to discourage imports from Argentina, but also to make their own stock more attractive to North American buyers.

Progress in the north

However, the picture is not totally bleak. In recent years, economic strength on the continent has moved northwards to Brazil and Venezuela and so, too, has the strength of the racing industry. Even though the climate and the soil are less suitable for thoroughbreds, the prize money, particularly in Venezuela, is exceptional (the standard of racing, however, is still below that to the south).

El Chama and Prendase, both Venezuelan-trained, caused general amazement by taking the first two places in the 1955 Washington DC International, but this success has never looked likely to be repeated. Indeed, the Venezuelan record in the Classico Internacional del Caribe, a nine-furlong event for three-year-old confined to horses from countries in, or bordering on, the Caribbean, is also unimpressive. Venezuelan horses have won twice, compared to two from Panama, one from Puerto Rico and seven from Mexico.

A new track is being built near Valencia, partly so that Venezuela may once more stage the Classico. This is because new height regulations have ruled the old course out of court, with the discovery that altitude has as drastic an effect on horses as on athletes. This means that La Rinconada,

the Caracas track, could no longer play host to the race. Here, the subtraction of more than one-third on all totalisator bets, gives owners one of the best chances available anywhere of making a profit simply from prize money.

Imports from the USA

Although all South American countries still buy in Europe – Brazil is an especially good customer for French stock – they now mostly look to the USA as their chief source of supply, as well as their best customer. Telescopico, on whom the nineteen-year-old Marina Lezcano – the world's most successful girl rider to date – completed the Argentine Triple Crown in 1978, was by the American horse Table Play.

Many countries buy large numbers of cheap yearlings in the USA, often through their jockey clubs, which resell them on arrival. Canonero, winner of six races in Venezuela before returning home to take the 1971 Kentucky Derby and Preakness Stakes, was purchased in this way.

The problem of distance

The huge distances involved on the continent have traditionally meant that each studmaster relies on his own stallions for breeding purposes. This is often a severe limitation. Racing in most countries is just as restricted, being confined to the capital cities, as in Peru, Uruguay and Venezuela, or rigidly concentrated on the main centres, as in Brazil.

In Brazil, Cidade Jardim (São Paulo) is virtually independent of Gavea (Rio de Janeiro). The former opened in 1941. Racing is held there on Saturday and Sunday afternoons, when most of the events are on grass, and under floodlights on Monday evenings, when all the racing is on dirt. The two courses used to duplicate each other's racing pattern, but, since 1962, there has at least been a Brazilian Derby – the Grand Premio Cruzeiro do Sul – which alternates between them.

Separate statistics, even for breeding, are maintained, as they are for the principal supporting tracks at Cristal (Porto Alegre) and Taruma (Curitiba).

South America, nevertheless, has a great deal to offer world racing – from trainers such as Angel Penna, who has reached the top in four countries, to a legion of top-class jockeys and horses. Economic conditions have held the continent back, but the potential it possesses is vast.

Racing in South Africa

Racing in South Africa started at the beginning of the nineteenth century. As early as 1815, the governor of the Cape, Lord Charles Somerset (his name is commemorated in the Somerset Plate), was writing home about the importation of thoroughbreds to encourage the racing which had started at Green Point Common. There then followed the foundation of the South African Turf Club, the oldest racing club in the country. Its biggest race is the Metropolitan, run over 2,000 metres at the Kenilworth course at the end of January, but the race of which it is proudest is the Queen's Plate. This has a history going back for 120 years. The club's other big race is the Cape of Good Hope Derby, also run over 2,000 metres.

The other Cape track is at Milnerton, the home of the Cape Turf Club. This is a perfect course, two bends giving varying straights of three or four furlongs plus a seven furlong home straight. The major race there is the Cape Guineas.

Johannesburg's first race meeting took place in 1881, when the first running of the Johannesburg Turf Club Handicap was won, most inappropriately, by a horse called Second. Six months later, the race was held again; it then was known as the Johannesburg Summer Handicap. Now re-christened The Holiday Inns, it is the richest race in South Africa.

Run over 2,000 metres, the race is the stiffest test of South Africa's 'big three' races, the others being the Durban July Handicap – run at Greyville and one of South Africa's most popular races – and the Metropolitan. The climb to the far bend and the four furlong straight make it a searching test of stamina.

Below The course at Greyville, Durban, in South Africa. Surrounded by highrise buildings and houses, the course is bisected by a motorway running through two subways beneath the two sides of the track. The Durban July Handicap, sponsored by Rothmans, is to South Africa what the Melbourne Cup is to Australia.

Below *The paddock at the Hipodromo Argentino in Buenos Aires. A second track, at San Isidro, was closed in 1976, but there is also racing at La Plata, which stages two Group 1 races, Cordoba, Mendoza and Rosario.*

The World of Racing

The World of the Owner

"When I see a rival owner
or trainer
cheering home a winner
I have one reaction
— I say
good luck to him."

Robert Sangster.

The World of the Owner

Like marriage, people enter the world of racehorse ownership either for love or for money. Even the nuptial vows echo sentiments of the turf. Most owners will 'love and cherish' their horses until they become unfaithful and start losing races they should have won. Naturally the more successful the horse the more cherished it becomes. The Roman Emperor Caligula (AD 12–41) had his champion racehorse Incitatus fêted after each victory until, with all other honours exhausted, the colt was made a citizen of Rome and then a senator.

During the eighteenth century, the Prince de Condé built the magnificent Grandes Ecuries at Chantilly for his highly prized string of racehorses, though it must be said he had an ulterior motive. A firm believer in reincarnation, the Duke was convinced that in a later life he would return to earth as a thoroughbred and occupy his grandoise stables. At the other extreme Lord Glasgow, a prominent nineteenth century member of the British Jockey Club, took full advantage of one particular clause in the marital contract – 'till death do us part' – and shot all of his horses which failed to make the grade.

The modern day owner cannot afford to take such drastic culling measures and usually sticks with his horse 'for richer, for poorer; for better, for worse' for at least one season. Usually it is for poorer and for worse, but the rewards of owning a 'good un' are such that owners (collectively) never give up trying to find the perfect horse.

Record prices

Record prices do not count for much in a period of inflation. They merely serve to demonstrate with increasing regularity that sheer weight of money cannot guarantee success in racing. Even the technological genius of the Japanese cannot guarantee that the record-breaking $1.6m yearling they bought at the Keeneland Sales of 1979 will be some sort of super horse. For every million dollar yearling sold, there are several thousands that can be bought for less than average price, while it is a mathematical certainty that every season there will always be a few Davids around to floor most, if not all, of the Goliaths.

The yearling sales of 1976 provided an example. At the American Keeneland Sales that year, a colt by the Triple Crown winner

Below Paul Mellon holds the trophy after winning the 1971 Washington International at Laurel Park with Run the Gauntlet. With him are **(from left to right)** *Elliot Burch (trainer), Mrs Mellon, Robert Woodhouse (jockey) and John Schapiro, president of Laurel racecourse.*

Right *The Queen and her jockey Willie Carson in the paddock at Newmarket. The Queen takes every opportunity to discuss her racehorses with her trainers and jockeys.*

Saratoga (course)	Year	Lots sold	Aggregate	Average
(in dollars)	75	230	8,525,700	37,068
	76	237	10,510,700	44,349
	77	210	12,035,000	57,310
	78	210	16,821,500	80,102
	79	209	20,502,000	98,096
Newmarket Houghton (Tattersalls)				
(in guineas)	75	401	3,049,420	7,605
	76	416	4,103,880	9,865
	77	494	6,996,940	14,164
	78	477	9,849,800	20,649
	79	427	12,982,200	30,403
Goffs September				
(in guineas)	75	500	2,779,410	5,559
	76	451	3,402,920	7,545
	77	430	3,872,380	9,006
	78	527	6,282,570	11,921
	79	524	7,449,400	14,216
Keeneland July Select				
(in dollars)	75	342	18,344,000	53,637
	76	346	23,035,000	66,575
	77	324	27,651,000	85,343
	78	350	42,579,000	121,654
	79	305	47,448,000	155,567
Deauville				
(in francs)	75	755	26,861,900	35,579
	76	667	27,421,700	41,112
	77	604	32,293,600	53,466
	78	629	55,393,650	88,066
	79	609	64,340,600	105,650

Yearling sales *Prices at the major yearling sales show a significant overall increase during the last five years, despite a drop due to over-production in the early 1970s. Not surprisingly, since the top prices are paid by some of the world's richest men, trends in the prices of yearlings often pre-empt trends in the stock market. Today the highest-priced yearlings are bought with a view to their possible stud value after their racing careers.*

Below *Robert Sangster (left) in the process of spending $5,000,000 in two days at the 1979 Keeneland July Select Yearling sale. With him is Bart Cummings, the Australian trainer. Sangster, one of the world's most successful owners, employs the best trainers and jockeys and backs them with a huge investment in bloodstock.*

Secretariat was sold for $1.5m, while, a few weeks later at the Ballsbridge Sales in Dublin a small, unfashionably-bred yearling called St Terramar was bought for 220gns (£231). The Secretariat colt, Canadian Bound, was sent to race in France where, in three races spread over two years, the best he could do was to finish second once. St Terramar on the other hand, came to England, was syndicated among a dozen people and, up to the end of the 1979 season, had won eight races and had been placed fifteen times for earnings of more than £26,000. Similarly Thundersquall was sold at the 1964 Ballsbridge yearling sales for only 26gns (£27.30). As a three-year-old she won six races on the trot and was rated eleventh best filly of her age in Britain. At the other end of the scale in 1964, Keeneland again produced a world record price when One Bold Bid made $170,000 but he did not even reach the race course. History repeats itself in racing. The only difference between the high and the low prices of 1964 and 1976 was a ninefold increase.

But money, backed by expertise and experience, can improve an owner's chance of success. Robert Sangster, for one, has demonstrated this over the past few years with sale-toppers like The Minstrel and Alleged, who between them cost $375,000, won $1.1m and were syndicated for $22m.

Buying a yearling

If an owner does not breed his own horses, buying a yearling at auction is the normal way of acquiring a horse to race on the flat. In Britain and Ireland, thirty-three per cent of the thoroughbreds foaled each year are sold as yearlings, but, whatever price range the owner choses, he first has to get his animal to the track to stand any chance of winning. This is not as elementary as it sounds. The sobering fact is that due to premature death, accident, unsoundness, virus infection or simply because they are not fast enough, about half the annual crop of thoroughbreds never manage to achieve the purpose for which they were bred.

In 1976, some 8,700 foals were born in Britain and Ireland alone. Of these 2,902 ran as two-year-olds and at the most another 1,000 might be expected to appear as older horses – some as three-year-olds, the majority as jumpers who had been 'put away' to be given time to mature. But even when a horse reaches the course, the chances of it winning a race are little better than even money; of the 2,902 two-year-olds only twenty-five per cent won in their first season. The odds against a horse paying for its keep in one year are roughly 10-1, or almost 20-1 if it is a jumper.

The costs of ownership

From the 15,220 horses that ran on the flat and over jumps in Britain and Ireland in 1978, some 10,000 failed to win a race, while only 1,374 managed to top the £3,000 mark when represented the break-even point for that year. One hundred years ago it cost £300 a year to keep a horse in training, but in 1980, with the top trainers charging £80 a week and syndicate managers budgeting for an outlay of £120 a week to cover all expenses, between £5,000 and £6,000 is needed.

Overheads can be enormous. In 1980 owners in Britain were required to pay a tax of 15 per cent (VAT) on training bills and on every horse bought or imported. In Ireland this tax is zero rated for horses, while in France it is charged only on the animal's carcass value. Other principal expenses are accounted for by entry fees and forfeits, which although lower than in most countries still average out at £400 a year while transport costs, free or subsidized in many other countries, can vary from £30 for a thirty mile (Lambourn–Newbury) to £300 for an 870 mile (Lambourn–Perth) round trip by road.

Insurance premiums at rates of 2.7 per cent for flat horses, 5.5 per cent for hurdlers and 10 per cent for chasers, have to be considered together with jockeys fees which total £27.50 (flat) and £38.25 (jumps) when VAT and a percentage contribution to the jockeys compensation fund are added. In addition, registration fees for horse's name, owner's name and colours as well as items that are not covered by the basic training fee, such as veterinary and gallop fees, shoeing and clipping charges, all make up a long list of extras.

However, against these heavy and rising costs, there is the fact that in 1978 a record 12,432 owners had their colours registered in Britain. This represented an increase of twenty per cent in four years even though the production of horses during the same period had fallen by sixteen per cent from an all-time high of 9,767 in 1975 to 8,216 in 1978.

Syndicates and companies

The influx of new blood into British racing is due largely to the increase in the number of syndicated and company-owned horses over the past few years. Although it has always been common practice to own horses in partnership, it was not until 1963 that multiple ownership on a large scale was first pioneered by 200 enthusiastic townsfolk of Tunbridge Wells in Kent. They bought shares in a locally trained hurdler which was named after the town and won two races before the scheme had

Deauville sales *Between 1975 and 1979 the average price at these sales increased by almost 300 per cent. In 1979 the Irish sales company Goffs took over part of the sales at Deauville, following the success of their sales at Kill, Co Kildare, in Ireland.*

Far left *The Tattersalls Houghton sales at Newmarket 1979. Going through the ring is Ghadeer (Fr), the top-priced yearling at the sale. This Lyphard colt out of the Habitat mare Swanilda made 625,000 guineas despite the fact that the dam's only previous offspring, by Sandford Lad, had no more than moderate success. The record-breaking colt is now in training with H Thomson-Jones at Newmarket and is racing as a two-year-old in 1980.* **Above centre** *The pre-parade ring at the Ballsbridge sales at Dublin. Besides yearlings, a number of good three-year-old store horses for National Hunt racing are sold there.* **Below centre** *Harry Wragg, the Newmarket trainer, with his son David at the 1979 Houghton sales.* **Left** *The sale ring at Keeneland, in Lexington, Kentucky.*

to be abandoned in the face of Jockey Club opposition.

Four years later, however, the authorities partially relented and allowed up to twelve people to own shares in a horse, while under a leasing scheme it also became possible for companies and approved clubs to own horses. Now twenty per cent of the horses in training are either owned in direct partnership or by syndicates and companies. The latter form of ownership in particular is flourishing as, provided the Inland Revenue authorities are satisfied that the company is racing the horse solely for promotional purposes and that any profits will go straight to the company, expenses incurred in the venture are deductable against tax.

In 1979 history was made when One In A Million, running in the name of the textile firm Helena Springfield Ltd, became the first company-owned horse to win an English classic when she took the One Thousand Guineas at Newmarket. Her success is a portent of things to come and a far cry from the days when the aristocracy dominated the Turf and the leading owner could afford to donate his season's prize money of £73,858 to charity as the Duke of Portland did in 1889.

The first owners

When owners first registered their colours with the English Jockey Club in 1762 their number was made up of seven Dukes, four Earls, two baronets, one Marquis, Viscount and Lord and three commoners. They were men of immense wealth who established large studs and bred entirely for their own benefit. The only time quality horses came on the market was when their breeder died and his stud was sold at auction. Then towards the end of the nineteenth century a new type of owner entered racing.

These were the *nouveaux-riches*, many of whom used the sport to achieve their social ambitions. In order to mix with the aristocracy and win social acceptance, these men of commerce and industry were prepared to spend vast sums on well-bred yearlings. The nobility, for their part, were quite happy to release some of their better-bred stock and a few dinner invitations in return for the money.

One who did not take so kindly to the invasion of 'Jewburg owners and society parasites', as he called them, was Bob Sievier who owned and trained the brilliant filly Sceptre to win four of the five classics in 1902. Sievier, a great gambler and adventurer, particularly despised the owner J. B. (Jack) Joel whom he constantly attacked through the columns of his paper

Broad forehead, ears not too small.

Bold, kind eye.

Well balanced, well set on head.

Shoulders not too heavy, moderate slope.

Croup and withers at same level; back not hollow or too straight.

Generous chest with good heart room.

Flat knees and relatively short cannon bone.

Good feet and pasterns, not too straight or sloping.

Horse standing over plenty of ground.

The champion racehorse Mill Reef at the age of three. He serves as an example of what conformation of the thoroughbred should be and what an owner should look for when buying. Mill Reef was a neat bay, smaller than his great rival Brigadier Gerard, another horse with an almost perfect conformation.

The Winning Post. Among other things Sievier accused Joel of being 'an illicit diamond buyer, a thief's accomplice and a fugitive from justice'. Whether true or not, these virulent charges hardly impeded Joel's career on the turf and he became a leading owner-breeder in the years before the First World War, while his brother, Solly, won the Triple Crown with Pommern in 1915.

The owner-breeders

After the First World Ward, racing in England was dominated for thirty-four years by the stables and studs of the seventeenth Earl of Derby and the Aga Khan. Between 1919 and 1952, these two remarkable men more or less alternated as the season's leading owner and/or breeder. Together they headed the lists on thirty-

eight occasions. Lord Derby was leading owner seven times and leading breeder ten times; the Aga Khan was leading owner thirteen times and leading breeder eight times. Lord Derby won twenty classics and the Aga Khan seventeen including the 1932 St Leger in which his four runners finished first, second, fourth and fifth in a field of nineteen.

The Derby-Aga Khan domination was all the more astonishing, as they faced strong competition from the studs of the Lords Astor, Rosebery and Glanely, who only occasionally managed to break through to take an owners' or breeders' title. But since the war no peer of the realm has topped either list; taxation, which was only one shilling in the pound at the turn of the century, has hit the nobility hard, while death duties in particular have forced the

Croup sloping to tail.

Good strong flanks.

Straight line through hock from base of tail.

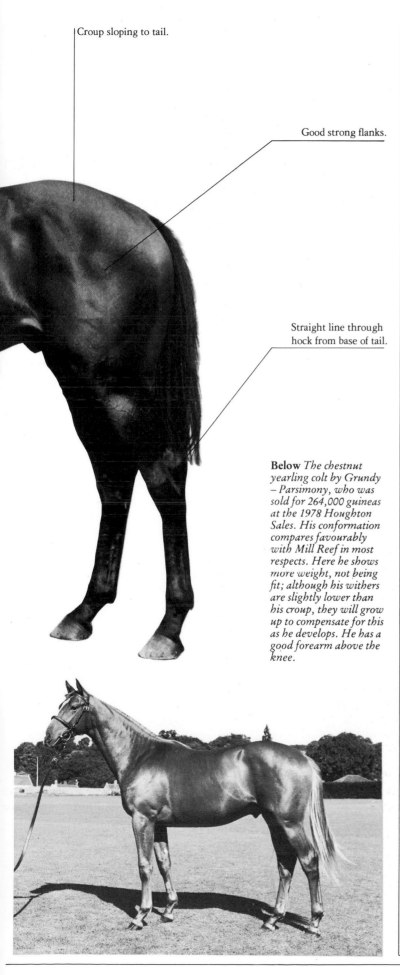

Below *The chestnut yearling colt by Grundy – Parsimony, who was sold for 264,000 guineas at the 1978 Houghton Sales. His conformation compares favourably with Mill Reef in most respects. Here he shows more weight, not being fit; although his withers are slightly lower than his croup, they will grow up to compensate for this as he develops. He has a good forearm above the knee.*

The chest, back and quarters of a horse provide significant clues to its likely performance on a race course, although there have been successful racehorses with any of the faults shown below. In general, the body should allow for flexibility and strength, with ample room for the lungs and heart. A good length between hip and hock is also a good sign; it is held that the greater this length, the more ground the horse will cover with each stride.

Below *A hollow back lacks strength and flexibility. It can be a sign of age.*

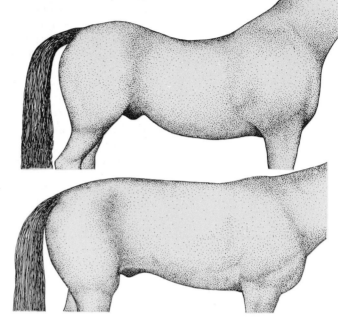

Above *A straight back restricts movement. The horse will lack power.*

Below *A shallow-bodied horse will lack lung capacity and, possibly, stamina.*

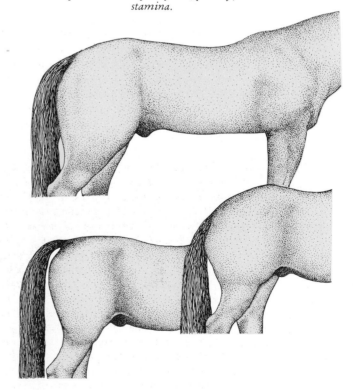

Above *A straight croup means less flexibility.*

Above *An acutely sloping croup means weak hind quarters.*

Right *Five examples of forelegs. The first shows good conformation. The hoof is centred between the shoulder and elbow points. In 2, the horse is under itself in front, making for less stability. In 3, the horse is camped in front, a conformational fault that causes tendon strain. A hollow-kneed stance (4) throws extra strain on the ligaments behind the knee. A knee-sprung stance (5) can make a horse stumble.* **Below right** *Five examples of* hind legs. *The first shows good conformation, with the hoof centred between stifle and buttock point, though some judges of racehorses prefer a straighter hock. In 2, the leg is camped behind; this can cause sway-back. The horse is under itself behind (3), a fault which can lead to forging. Back at the knee (4) is a fault that strains the tendons of the fetlock. Straight hocks (5) may give speed but also tend to limit movement.*

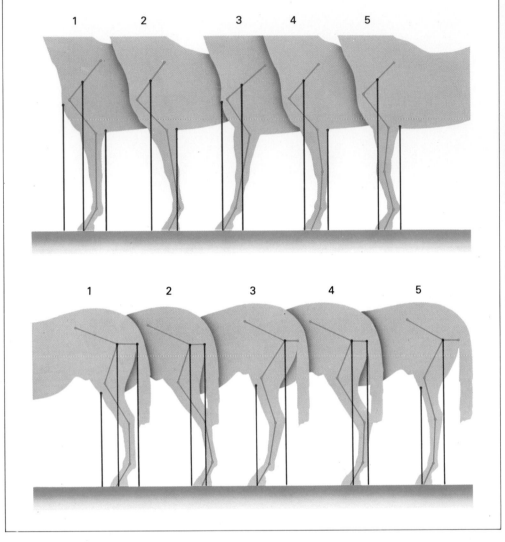

break up of many of the great studs. The Queen, however, remains one of Britain's largest owner-breeders.

It was in order to help pay off death duties that Brook Holliday was forced into selling his father's smart two-year-old Vaguely Noble at Newmarket in 1967. The colt went to an American buyer, Dr Robert Franklin, for a record 136,000 gns (£142,000). The following season, the horse proved himself to be the best in Europe through winning the Prix de l'Arc de Triomphe and three other races besides. He was syndicated for $5m and retired to stud in Kentucky where he proved himself to be one of the most influential European stallions ever to be imported.

Vaguely Noble has sired a string of champions, principally for Nelson Bunker Hunt who, as one of the world's largest owner-breeders, acquired a half share in the horse shortly after it was sold at Newmarket and eventually bought out Franklyn. Foremost among them was Dahlia, a remarkable filly who won Group I races in five different countries and a record $1.5m. Although trained in France, her wins in England in 1973 were responsible for Hunt beating David Robinson for leading owner honours that year, despite the latter having set a new British record for races won in a season with 115 victories.

America and Britain

The vast difference in the scale of operations between American and British owners can be gauged by comparing Robinson's record with the American equivalent which was set the following year by the thirty-two-year-old former hamburger salesman, Dan Lasater. Robinson won his 115 races worth £114,735 with a string of 130 horses (huge by British standards) divided among three trainers. Lasater, a self-made millionaire who

retired at twenty-eight, won a staggering total of 494 races worth over £1½m with a stable of 380 horses which were split up among thirteen different trainers.

Coincidentally, both owners cut back drastically on the number of horses they had in training after setting their records. But whereas Robinson, who had always claimed it was possible to make money as an owner, quit racing within three years of his triumph, Lasater held his position as leading owner for four years. He is still extremely active as an owner-breeder, benefitting from the various state-operated incentive schemes, which go a long way to improving an owner's chances of making a profit out of racing in the USA.

The premiums which the states hand out are funded from a fraction of the state's betting turnover and are principally aimed at breeders. But, as most American breeders race a good proportion of their own horses – only fifteen per cent of the country's foal crop are offered for sale as yearlings – the premiums are largely of equal benefit to owners.

Incentive schemes

Since the war, the American breeding industry has grown in spectacular fashion, from 5,819 foals in 1945 and 9,610 in 1955 to 18,850 in 1965 and 27,589 in 1975; but it is the increase in breeding in individual states which has been most dramatic. In 1973, only 115 foals were born in New York State. But a new incentive scheme, which paid breeders premiums of twenty-five per cent of any prize money won by a horse bred in New York racing in the state, with a further fifteen per cent awarded to owners of New York-based stallions whose progeny won prize money within the state, soon altered the climate of breeding in the state.

Leading owner-breeders began to move their bloodstock from established breeding centres such as Kentucky, Florida and California into New York in response. In five years, the number of state-registered foals increased by 600 per cent. In 1980 some 1,500 foals were expected to be born and a rich programme of races restricted to New York-breds is developing. Over the

Above *Some of 159 tints for owners' colours registered at Wetherby's secretaries to the Jockey Club in Britain. There are eighteen basic colours. About 750 new colours are registered each year, with a total of around 9,000. This figure is increasing due to the greater number of partnerships now being registered.* **Right** *Jockeys at Newbury racecourse,* *showing some of the different markings and colours, at the retirement presentation to Des Cullen in 1978, after he had been warned to give up riding by doctors.*

Washington Bridge in neighbouring New Jersey, owners in addition to breeders receive similar premiums and they are even paid a $100 'participant award' for running their horses in races confined to New Jersey-breds.

The American owner not only benefits from these premiums, which also operate in Europe – in France at a generous forty and even fifty per cent in certain races, while Britain and Ireland limit such payments to the owners of fillies – but, under what is known as a hobby law, he can offset any losses his stable makes against profits in other businesses. This is provided that his racing operations show a profit in two years out of seven. Elementary auditing and the timely sale of bloodstock can always ensure that this condition is met.

In addition the owner also has a higher average of prize money to aim at and more chances of winning a race. In 1977 there were 68,826 races for thge 61,938 horses in training compared to the 2,959 races that were on offer to the 6,440 horses in training on the flat in Britain in 1978. It is small wonder that the percentage of runners to win in America is as high as seventy per cent; but against this, however, US owners have to pay some of the highest training fees in the world. In 1979, top New York trainers were charging a basic of $55 a day for a horse, though the average fee was nearer $40.

Quantity and quality

The fact that so many American owners prefer to race in Europe is a further pointer to the fact that, although their races are rich in quantity, Americans do not necessarily have a monopoly on quality. True sportsmen in the mould of Paul Mellon, Raymond Guest and John Hay Whitney have had horses in training in England and Ireland for most of their lives; indeed, Whitney, in a speech he made to the Thoroughbred Club of America in 1963, warned of the dangers of commercialism engulfing the 'spirit of racing'. He made a plea then that a line should be drawn at the point where the horse begins to serve commercialism, rather than commercialism serving the needs of the horse. That point has long since been passed.

In an effort to increase the number of horses running at each track and so boost the betting turnover, the use of the drug butazolidin was legalized in all but one of the twenty-six racing states in America. The sole exception is New York. American horses are notoriously prone to leg trouble because of the strain imposed by tight, turning tracks and the unyielding dirt surfaces on which they race. But, by using the drug, a lame horse could be made sound just long enough for it to compete in a race. The problem was that because the horse could feel no pain in its legs due to the effects of the drug, there was an alarming increase in serious breakdowns and accidents.

After four jockeys had been killed and 1,500 others seriously injured in spills on the American tracks in 1977, Nick Jemas, managing director of the US Jockeys' Guild, spoke out against the use of bute. He blamed it for an 'increasing parade of lame, sore, worn-out and completely exhausted horses . . . these drugs appear to have been seriously abused for selfish gain. There has been complete inconsideration of the crippling danger to jockeys and horses.'

The 'spirit of racing'

In 1971 the 'spirit of racing' in America suffered another blow when jumping was

Plain — Seams — Epaulettes — Stripe — Braces — Stripes — Hoop — Hoops

Halved — Quartered — Sash — Cross belts — Chevron — Chevrons — Check/Squares — Diamonds

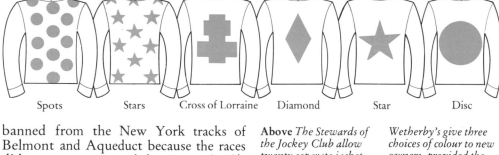

Spots — Stars — Cross of Lorraine — Diamond — Star — Disc

Above *The Stewards of the Jockey Club allow twenty separate jacket markings, plus the variation on a diamond of a star or disc.*

Wetherby's give three choices of colour to new owners, provided the combination is not used by any other owner.

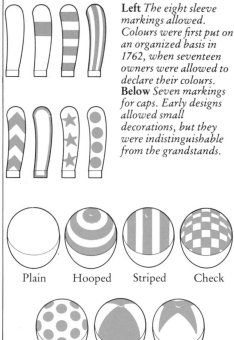

Left *The eight sleeve markings allowed. Colours were first put on an organized basis in 1762, when seventeen owners were allowed to declare their colours.* **Below** *Seven markings for caps. Early designs allowed small decorations, but they were indistinguishable from the grandstands.*

Plain — Hooped — Striped — Check

Spots — Quartered — Star

Below *Making racing silks at a factory in Nottinghamshire, Britain, before the start of the flat season. Of a jockey's equipment, only* *the silks are kept by the trainer for the owner.*

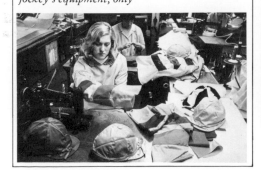

banned from the New York tracks of Belmont and Aqueduct because the races did not attract as much betting as the flat events. Although it has made a tentative comeback on some of the metropolitan courses in recent years, the sport still has a somewhat nomadic existence at once-a-week hunt meetings. At these betting is illegal; they owe their survival to an increasing amount of sponsorship and the support of some of America's wealthiest families. The outstanding example is provided by Marion duPont Scott, owner of the 1938 Grand National winner Battleship. She has financed the running of the international steeplechase, the Colonial Cup, at Camden, South Carolina, since 1970.

In contrast jump racing in Europe is flourishing. France has by far the best prize money to offer and it is even possible for an owner to make a profit there, but the vast majority of people go into this side of racing with no thought of gain. The fact that Red Rum won three Grand Nationals and £100,000 for his owner Noel Le Mare, who parted with 6,000 gns (£6,300) for the horse – now earning even more money as a limited company – was no more than a happy accident.

Many owners who go into jump racing do so in order to take part in the sport either as a trainer or rider. Some are quite content to confine their activities to the point-to-point field where the maximum prize money is £50 a race. They are just as much addicted to the sport through their love of the horse as Far Eastern owners are through their love of gambling.

In Hong Kong

The Royal Hong Kong Jockey Club has a five-year waiting list of potential owners. There are no pretensions to quality or improvement of the breed there, as races are restricted to geldings with an import value of no more than £5,000, the motivation apparently being to provide opportunities for betting. However, experiments are now taking place whereby a limited number of owners are being allowed to import horses of their own choice, mostly from Australia and in rare cases from Europe.

In Australia and South Africa owners are no less motivated by thoughts of profit through a well-worked coup. Although their racing is on a level comparable to Europe or America their prestige races continue to be the big handicaps and in particular the Melbourne Cup and the Durban July.

Owners' Biographies

Calumet Farm

In the early 1930s when Calumet Farm's fortunes were low, owner Warren Wright Sr wondered whether he had made the right decision in switching from breeding standardbreds to thoroughbreds. The stable won a stake race from time to time and the losses were not too hard to bear even in the depression years. But the future of the stable did not really impress Wright until Bull Lea won the 1939 Widener and later went to stud. That famous son of Bull Dog sired horses who were destined profoundly to influence the course of breeding and racing history.

The red and blue silks of Calumet dominated the sport from 1941 to 1949, and in the twenty years to 1961, the Kentucky-based farm near Versailles Pike topped the money standings no less than twelve times. This rise was sparked off by the advent of 'Plain Ben' Jones, a former Missouri mule-raiser who trained a string of champions that spread-eagled every division from coast to coast.

Wright left his racing and corporate empires to his widow, Mrs Lucille Wright Markey, who subsequently married the famed Admiral Gene Markey, the playwrite and author. She became the first lady of the turf in due course, remaining in the sport even when the stable was losing a fortune and nearly bankrupt. Her patience was rewarded in 1977 when her new trainer, John M Veitch, took over after the six years of spotty success that followed Jimmy Jones' departure to Monmouth Park. Today Calumet's trophy room is one of the wonders of the Kentucky racing world, with wall-to-wall memorabilia and memories that could fill several books.

Baroness von Oppenheim

Baroness Gabrielle von Oppenheim is not a familiar figure on British racecourses, but her Schlenderhan stud, midway between Cologne and Aachen, rates among the most successful breeding establishments in Europe. The winners of seventy-nine German classics, including sixteen Derbies, have been bred at the stud, founded by Baron Eduard von Oppenheim in 1869 and still owned by this Cologne banking family. The Baroness Gabrielle took it over on the death of her husband, Baron Waldemar, in 1952.

Schlenderhan has headed the list of German breeders thirty-three times and the Baroness, advised by her able manager, Meyer zu Düte, is constantly introducing new blood with mares, bought mainly at

Newmarket. There they struck a bargain by paying 3,700 guineas for Promised Lady in 1964. Her first six foals, all winners, included Lombard, winner of twenty races and £165,289 in Germany and France. Lombard's intended English programme was thwarted by a coughing epidemic, and he now stands at the Banstead Manor Stud near Newmarket.

Lombard had produced good winners in Germany and France before his daughter Sharifa scored at Newmarket in November, 1978, the first time that the Oppenheim colours had been successful in England since Weissdorm had won at Manchester fifty-three years ago.

The Baroness keeps about forty horses in training at Cologne, whilst in 1979 she sent for the first time some of Lombard's progeny to be trained at Newmarket.

Jacques Wertheimer

Jacques Wertheimer is the latest representative of a family of owners and breeders who have been winning high-class races in France and England for some sixty years. His father, Pierre, won the Stewards' Cup at Goodwood with Epinard in 1923. Thirty-three years later he won the Derby with Lavandin, his first runner in the race. Pierre Wertheimer died in 1965 and his widow carried on – she won the French Derby with Roi Lear in 1973 – until her son Jacques took over in 1975 and won that year's French Derby with Val de l'Orne. He won the following year's Arc de Triomphe with Ivanjica and was leading owner and breeder in 1978 when successful in the two French fillies' classics with Dancing Maid and Reine de Saba.

Jacques Wertheimer has therefore not only inherited his family Chanel cosmetics empire, but also one of the most powerful thoroughbred establishments in Europe. He has around eighty horses in training with Alec Head at Chantilly and more than fifty brood-mares at his stud in Normandy, as well as a few based in Kentucky to be mated in America.

Wertheimer is the perfect owner of whom his trainer, Alec Head, says: 'Jacques does not bet. He is very easy and leaves everything to me. The horses might be mine'. No owner could be paid a higher compliment by the man who has trained for the family since 1949.

Noel le Mare

It is likely that Red Rum has been seen by more people than any other horse in the history of racing. He ran for the first time, and won a selling race at Aintree in April,

1967, when he was two. He finished his career at nearby Haydock almost eleven years later. During this period he had run in a total of 110 races, won three of his five Grand Nationals and been second in the other two. Since his retirement he has been on show for charity all over the country.

Red Rum's veteran owner, Noel Le Mare, is not so well-known. Son of a missionary, he was born in India but he and his parents came to live in Lancashire when he was a child. Noel went to sea in trawlers as a boy. Later, he served in the merchant navy until 1918, having survived two days in an open boat after his ship had been sunk. After the war he founded a construction company, which spread to operate worldwide and was to make him an extremely rich man.

Noel Le Mare had been obsessed by racing – and the Grand National in particular – since his early days at sea. He was seventy when he bought his first racehorse and eighty-four when he paid 6,000 guineas for Red Rum. This resulted in a fairy story which can never be repeated. It was appropriate that the recipient should have been this Lancashire gentleman, who had always had the best out of life through hard work, native wit and shrewd business acumen – and whose love of racing and thoroughbred horses was inherent in his nature more than 60 years before Red Rum was foaled.

The Queen

Thirteen English classics have been won by the four reigning monarchs directly descended from Queen Victoria. King Edward VII won two, including the Derby with Minoru in 1909; his son George V one; his grandson George VI five, four of them during the war; while his great-granddaughter Queen Elizabeth II's current total is five, plus Highclere's Prix de Diane in 1977.

Though the three kings obviously enjoyed their racing, they were not experts on the subject. However, there can be few owner-breeders from any walk of life whose knowledge of racing and breeding can match that of the present monarch. 'It's amazing. She knows all about it. I just can't think how she has had the time to learn so much', said one of her former trainers, Sir Cecil Boyd-Rochfort, some years ago.

It is probable that the Queen's first personal contact with thoroughbreds was in 1942 when, as Princess Elizabeth, she went with her father and mother to Beckhampton to see Fred Darling putting Big Game and Sun Chariot through their paces before their classic successes for King

George VI. This side of racing has appealed to her ever since then. She will often break-fast with one or other of her trainers after early morning work or have tea with them before evening stables.

Since her Coronation, the Queen has won nearly 350 races and has been leading owner twice. The Royal Studs topped the list of English breeders in 1977. There is no doubt that her enthusiasm has done much to ensure that the public image of racing has not declined, as has been the case in some professional sports. There is a sense of personal satisfaction when her horses win, be they favourites or rank outsiders, which everyone in the world of racing shares.

Nelson Bunker Hunt

During his frequent trips to his father's oil wells in Pakistan and India, Nelson Bunker Hunt would stop over in France to attend the races at Longchamp, Chantilly and Saint-Cloud, He began buying broodmares from all over the world, and before long, had ten at Lee Eaton's farm in Lexington, Kentucky, five at Stephenson's farm in Virginia, and eight French mares at Egypt's Prince Tousson's farm outside Deauville. He also had six horses in training with John Cunnington in France, and two in America with Tommy Root Sr and Bob Wheeler.

After being the underbidder for Vaguely Noble in 1967, Hunt was offered a half-interest in the then two-year-old colt. Accepting the deal, he saw the son of Vienna capture the Arc de Triomphe as a three-year-old and eventually bought a controlling interest to become the majority owner of one of the world's leading sires. Over the years, Vaguely Noble sired for Hunt such top stars as Dahlia, Nobiliary, Exceller, Empery, Mississipian, Noble Decree and Ace of Aces. Hunt also bred and raced the international champion Youth, winner of the French Derby, Canadian International Championship and Washington DC International.

In July 1979, Hunt dispersed his entire crop of yearlings at the Kentucky Horse Center in Lexington. In all, sixty-nine yearlings were sold for $12,305,000.

C V and John Hay Whitney

Ever since John Whitney, the founder of the Whitney dynasty, arrived in Boston in June 1635, the Whitney family has been one of the most prominent in America. However, it was not until 1897 that William Collins Whitney became inter-ested in racing.

Through his oldest son Harry Payne, the Whitney stable dominated racing during the early to mid-1900s. Harry Payne's son Cornelius Vanderbilt inherited the power-ful stable, and has run it ever since. Among his most notable runners are Silver Spoon, Phalanx, Chompion and State Dinner. In 1940, he imported the English Derby winner Mahmoud to America, where he was leading sire in 1946 and sired more than seventy stakes winners.

William Collins Whitney's other son, Payne, was the principal heir of his uncle Oliver Payne's fortune. In 1902, he married Helen Hay, daughter of diplomat John Hay. In the mid-1920s Payne Whitney became an active partner in his wife's racing and breeding interests. When Mrs Whitney died in 1944, the stable was passed on to her two children, John Hay Whitney and Joan Whitney Payson.

In 1953, Greentree's greatest horse, Tom Fool, captured the Handicap Triple Crown and was named Horse of the Year. Over the years, the stables have raced such top stars as No Robbery, Late Bloomer, Shut Out (1942 Kentucky Derby), Capot, Devil Diver, Bowl Game and Stage Door Johnny (1968 Belmont Stakes).

H J Joel

Mr H J (Jim) Joel comes from a family which has bred and owned classic horses since 1900, when the late J B (Jack) Joel, a nephew of the South African millionaire Barny Barnato, registered the black with red cap colours which are still consistently successful under both sets of Rules of Racing. Jack Joel won eleven classics, including two Derbies, with Sunstar (1911) and Humourist (1921), and was leading owner three times. Jack's brother S B (Solly) Joel won the Triple Crown with Pommern (1915). Solly's son, Stanhope Joel, won the St Leger with Chamossaire in 1945.

On Jack Joel's death in 1940, his son, Jim, took over his stable, as well as the family stud, Childwick Bury. Four years later, Jim won the 1,000 Guineas with Picture Play, the great-grandam of Royal Palace. The latter was the winner of the 2,000 Guineas and the Derby in 1967, while his four-year-old successes included the King George VI and Queen Elizabeth Stakes in 1968. Joel, 86 on September 4th, 1980, is one of the best liked and most respected members of the Jockey Club.

Robert Sangster

Robert Sangster, born in 1937, has owned racehorses since he was twenty-three, but it was for sport only that he raced. In 1975,

however, he decided that his hobby must become a profession if it was to pay its way. With a natural business acumen developed as Chairman of Vernons Pools and following expert advice, he has invested a fortune into the sport; he now has interests in some 160 horses in training spread over England, Ireland, France, Australia and North America. He employs twenty trainers and holds a third share in the Irish studs, Coolmore and Castle Hyde, whose eighteen stallions sired winners of 354 races in 1978. His English-based mares are at his Swettenham Stud in Cheshire, while those in France are managed by Comte Roland de Chambure at the Etreham Stud in Normandy. The value of his bloodstock holdings probably exceeds £30 million.

Only the best in manpower is good enough for Sangster. His Irish horses are trained by Vincent O'Brien and ridden by Lester Piggott, whilst those trained by Barry Hills at Lambourn are ridden by the young American, Steve Cauthen, whom he brought to England in 1979. One of his Australian trainers is the world-famed Tommy Smith.

Sangster's equine investments have done well. He has won the Derby with The Minstrel and two successive Arc de Triomphes with Alleged as well as valuable races in Australia. His horses, in England alone, won £348,023 in 1977 and £160,542 in 1978.

J K Galbreath

Few other owner-breeders have done more to bring the equine worlds of Europe and America closer together than John Gal-breath. Galbreath has owned and bred winners of the Kentucky Derby, Preakness Stakes, Belmont Stakes, Coaching Club American Oaks and Epsom Derby.

Galbreath was born in Derby, Ohio, in 1897. After serving in the First World War, he went to work in Columbus, Ohio for a real estate broker before opening an office of his own. He eventually became a developer and builder, with major sites in New York, Pittsburgh, Louisville, Canada and Hong Kong. He was also instrumental in the reconstruction of Belmont Park.

The nucleus of Galbreath's breeding operation is the 620 acre farm in Lexing-ton, Kentucky, where he has stood such notable stallions as Swaps, Graustark, Ribot, Sea Bird II, Roberto, Summer Tan, Little Current and Chateaugay. In 1963, he won his first of two Kentucky Derbys with Chateaugay, who later won the Belmont Stakes after running second in the Preak-ness. Four years later, Proud Clarion gave

Top left *The Queen and Willie Carson with Prince Philip listening.* **Top right** *Nelson Bunker Hunt, whose filly Dahlia, by his own stallion Vaguely Noble, twice won the King George VI and Queen Elizabeth Diamond Stakes.* **Centre left** *Jack Joel with his trainer* Henry Cecil. The Joel colours of black with a red cap are among the most famous in Britain. **Centre right** *Mr and Mrs J K Galbreath. John Galbreath was responsible for taking Ribot and Sea Bird II to stud in America; he also owned the Epsom Derby winner* Roberto. **Above left** *Robert Sangster with Mrs Sangster and Lester Piggott. Sangster has some 160 horses in training in England, Ireland, France, Australia and the USA.* **Above right** *The American, Jock Whitney, a staunch supporter of racing in Britain.*

Galbreath his second Derby win, when he upset the favourite Damascus at odds of 30-1. In 1972, Galbreath became the first man to own and breed the winners of the Kentucky and Epsom Derbys, as Roberto captured the English classic by a nose. Later that year, Roberto handed Brigadier Gerard his only career defeat, winning in world record time.

The Aga Khan

The Aga Khan was not particularly interested in racing when he inherited an extremely valuable collection of horses following the tragic death of his father, Prince Aly Khan, in a car crash in Paris in 1960. This was surprising, for his grandfather, Aga Khan, who had won five Derbies, and Aly Khan, had been almost fanatical in their devotion to the sport.

In the year that his father died, the young Aga won the French Derby and the Grand Prix de Paris with Charlottesville and the Ascot Gold Cup with Sheshoon.

For three years, the Khan's horses were trained by Alec Head, but they were then transferred to François Mathet. Since then the Aga Khan – 'K' (for Karim) to his friends – has become increasingly enthusiastic and has had many successes. In 1977 he bought the entire stock of eighty-two horses which Mme Dupré had inherited from her husband, Francois Dupré. Two years later, Top Ville, one of the yearlings included in this deal, won the Prix du Jockey Club. He also paid nearly £5,000,000 for Marcel Boussac's stable and stud of almost 100 including the 1978 Prix du Jockey Club winner Acamas. He has sold his father's old racing stables at Green Lodge, Chantilly, but has built a fabulous new establishment at nearby Gouvieux while retaining the family studs.

Raymond Guest

Being born in New York City, the son of Captain Frederick E Guest, an Englishman, and American heiress Amy Phipps Guest, it was only fitting that Raymond Guest should own champion racehorses in England and the United States. In 1965, his Tom Rolfe captured the Preakness Stakes and was placed in the Kentucky Derby and Belmont Stakes to be voted champion three-year-old in America. Three years later Sir Ivor captured the 2,000 Guineas and Derby en route to championship honours in England. In 1975, Guest's great steeplechaser L'Escargot won the prestigious Grand National.

Guest's father was a Member of Parliament, who was a member of the government of David Lloyd George and served for a while as personal secretary to his first cousin, Winston Churchill. Raymond and his brother Winston graduated from Yale in the 1930s and became star polo players. Raymond began to breed and raise his own horses in Virginia and became Director of Bessemer Securities before serving as a commander in the US Navy during the Second World War. He was a Virginia state senator from 1947 to 1953 and in 1965 was named US Ambassador to Ireland.

Always interested in Irish racing, Guest purchased a yearling colt by Never Say Die out of Skylarking at the 1960 Ballsbridge Sales. Named Larkspur, he went on to capture the Epsom Derby before retiring to stud in Ireland.

Ken Cox

Kenneth Fabian Cox is one of Australia's leading industrialists, a committeeman of the Victoria Racing Club, Chairman of the Melbourne Cup Carnival Committee, which organizes and promotes Melbourne Cup Week, and above all owner-breeder and Governing Director of the Stockwell Stud at Diggers Rest in Victoria.

Cox, whose companies produce seventy per cent of the steel for Australia's building industry, first entered the thoroughbred breeding industry by buying Landau. Formerly owned by the Queen, the stallion was imported to Australia by E A Underwood and later leased to the Stockwell Stud. Landau was joined at Stockwell by Arctic Explorer.

In all Stockwell has had nineteen stallions, but none measured up to the colossal reputation of Showdown. In ten seasons to the end of 1978/9 Showdown's progeny earned $A 3,236,202. The total stakes earnings by all Stockwell stallions over twenty years has been $5,802,000.

Among many top class horses raced by Cox were four weight-for-age and classic winners, Tontonan, Toy Show, Show Ego and Kiss-Me-Cait. Cox is not a betting man, his maximum wager being $5. He is an untiring administrator, and breeds and races his horses with a view to projecting the industry to the best advantage. Besides his other posts, Cox is also President of the Equine Research Foundation.

Dr Carlo Vittadini

Dr Carlo Vittadini's blue and yellow colours were immortalized in 1975 when Grundy won the English and Irish Derbies, the Irish 2,000 Guineas and, following a memorable duel with Bustino, the King George VI and Queen Elizabeth Stakes from one of the highest-class fields ever to contest this great Ascot race.

It was in 1960 that Vittadini's four-year-old Exar, trained by Noel Murless, won four races in a row including the Goodwood and Doncaster Cups. This colt, bought for only 1,900 guineas, was to earn £25,840. Others to do well were Palatch, winner of the Musidora Stakes and the Yorkshire Oaks, and her son Patch who, after winning the Lingfield Derby Trial Stakes, was only just beaten by Val de l'Orne in the 1975 Prix du Jockey Club, thus robbing his owner of an English-French Derby double. Ortis, winner of the Italian Derby, the Hardwicke Stakes and some £100,000 in all, and Orange Bay, runner-up to The Minstrel in the King George VI and Queen Elizabeth Stakes in 1977, are two more good horses to carry Dr Vittadini's colours.

Dr Carlo Vittadini, not a medical man, is most people's idea of a wealthy Italian aristocrat, which he is. Always smiling and with a perfect command of English, this Milan-based millionaire has real charm. Regardless of his successes on the turf, he has the natural good manners inherent in the Italians as a whole.

Anne, Duchess of Westminster

It is said, with some justification, that great horses can make good trainers and jockeys. Unfortunately, they do not necessarily make good owners or even kind ones, which they certainly deserve.

So that great steeplechaser Arkle, three-times winner of the Cheltenham Gold Cup, twenty-four other races and £75,207 in prize money – and immortalized in literature, verse, sculpture and portraiture – was lucky when Anne, Duchess of Westminster, bought him for 1,150 guineas at the Dublin Sales in 1960 when he was a three-year-old. For the Duchess, Miss Nancy Sullivan of Co Cork, until her marriage in 1947, has been a horse lover all her life. It could only have been someone who loved horses who could say: 'I will never let my Arkle run in the Grand National, because I adore him, because he is one of the family, and because he is much too precious to me'.

Arkle was named after a mountain overlooking the Duchess's Scottish estate near Lairg, as was Ben Stack, one of his contemporaries. But winning races with these and her many other good chasers is not her only interest in bloodstock. She owns the Eaton Stud in Cheshire where her late husband's grandfather bred Bend Or, Ormonde, Flying Fox and other great

Top left *The Aga Khan, with jockey Henri Samani and his trainer F Mathet. Since taking over his father's horses the Aga Khan has developed a great interest in bloodstock and greatly increased his investment in racing.* **Top right** *Raymond Guest unveiling a plaque* to his own horse Larkspur, winner of the Derby, at the Ballsbridge sales ring in Dublin. He had a second winner of the Derby with Sir Ivor. **Centre right** Dr Carlo Vittadini holding the trophy after his Grundy had won the King George VI and Queen Elizabeth Stakes at Ascot. **Above left** Ken Cox, the governing director of the Stockwell Stud in Australia and a committeeman of the Victoria Racing Club. **Above right** Anne, Duchess of Westminster, with Lord Howard de Walden's Lanzarote.

horses. The stud still does well, selling its yearlings at the Houghton Sales.

Daniel Wildenstein

When Daniel Wildenstein's Lianga won the July Cup in 1975, it was the first time that one of the French-trained horses owned by this international art dealer had, after years of fruitless forays, been successful in Britain. The following season he became leading owner in Great Britain with the winners of ten races and £244,500, which included three classics and the King George VI and Queen Elizabeth Stakes at Ascot. He might have won this Ascot race also in the previous year but for his last minute and extremely unpopular decision not to run his subsequent Prix de l'Arc de Triomphe winner Allez France, successful in the 1973 French 1,000 Guineas and Oaks.

Wildenstein was subjected to adverse criticism again in 1978 when he alleged that Pat Eddery's riding tactics were responsible for the abject defeat of Buckskin in the Ascot Gold Cup. The horse's trainer, Peter Walwyn, was incensed by this slur on his jockey's judgement and the Wildenstein horses were despatched to Henry Cecil, for whom Buckskin that year won the Doncaster and Jockey Club Cups. Cecil made no attempt to hide his disappointment when in the 1979 Gold Cup, his last race, Buckskin was beaten by his stable companion, Le Moss.

Wildenstein's French trainers have been Maurice Zilber, Albert Klimscha and Angel Penna. The last-named is now in charge of his horses in America. Wildenstein, through his company Dayton Ltd, also has nearly sixty mares and shares in more than forty stallions.

Paul Mellon

Born in Pittsburgh, Pennsylvania, Paul Mellon attended Yale University where he became vice-chairman of the Yale Daily News. After graduating at Yale, he studied history at Cambridge, England. Art was his passion, however, and he has since built up one of the finest collections in the world.

In 1964 Mellon made his first impact on the racing world when Quadrangle upset Northern Dancer in the Belmont Stakes. Five years later, Arts and Letters became Mellon's first champion, winning the Belmont, Travers, Woodward and Jockey Club Gold Cup, and was nominated the Horse of the Year. The following year, he had his second consecutive Horse of the Year with Fort Marcy.

Mellon's string of champions continued the next year in England, when the great Mill Reef won the Epsom Derby, Eclipse Stakes, King George VI and Queen Elizabeth Stakes, and culminated the year with a success in the Prix de l'Arc de Triomphe. In 1972, Mellon's Key to the Mint developed late in the season to beat Riva Ridge as the leading three-year-old. Other good horses have been Summer Guest, Key to the Kingdom, Upper Nile, Glowing Tribute and Ivory Wand.

E P Taylor

Perhaps no other individual has done more for racing in his own country than Canada's Edward Plunkett Taylor. As Chairman of the Ontario Jockey Club, Taylor took an unprosperous industry and turned it into a first-class operation.

Born in Ottawa, Ontario, in 1901, Taylor attended McGill University in Montreal. In the Second World War, he became joint-director of munitions productions and supply, and later became president of War Supplies Ltd. He was appointed president of the British Supply Council in North America by Winston Churchill and Lord Beaverbrook. After the war, Taylor set up an investment company known as Argus Corp and eventually built an empire in oil, precious metals and various other commodities.

Taylor had attended the races as a youngster and set about using his business resources to revive the sport in Canada. He eliminated most of the minor tracks and concentrated on improving the better ones. He kept Fort Erie and Woodbine (renamed Greenwood) and built a new $13,000,000 extravaganza called the new Woodbine.

As an owner and breeder, Taylor has dominated racing in Canada, especially the historic Queen's Plate. Over the years, he has bred eighteen winners and owned ten of them, including the great Northern Dancer, winner of the Kentucky Derby and Preakness Stakes.

Baron Guy de Rothschild

Baron Guy de Rothschild is one of the few members of his international banking family who has yet to win an English classic. His colt Vieux Manoir was beaten by a length by Marcel Boussac's Scratch II in the 1950 St Leger. Nine years later his Shantung was desperately unlucky not to win the Derby, after being brought almost to a standstill when colliding with a stumbling horse. He was a long way last coming into the straight but still managed to finish third to Parthia and Fidalgo.

Apart from these reverses, Baron Guy has done well with his comparatively few runners in England. He won the Coronation Cup with Exbury and Tropique, the Eclipse Stakes with Tropique and Hardwicke Stakes with Guersant. These and other winners were trained at Chantilly by Geoff Watson, an extremely popular man, whose family had been employed by the Rothschilds for nearly a century. Sadly the partnership has now split up and Baron Guy's horses are now trained by François Mathet.

Rothschilds have raced in France and England for more than 120 years. Baron Guy's grandfather, Baron Meyer, won four English Classics in 1871, three of these, the 1,000 Guineas, Oaks and St Leger, with Hannah, whose full-brother Favonius took that year's Derby. Hannah was named after her owner's daughter who married the 5th Earl of Rosebery, father of the late and (from racing's point of view) famous 6th Earl.

The Queen Mother

The Queen Mother, like all owners of steeplechasers, has had to take the rough with the smooth. She lost Monaveen, her first and only horse at the time, when he broke a leg at Hurst Park in December, 1950, less than fourteen months after becoming her first runner and winner. Her Devon Loch had the 1956 Grand National at his mercy when he collapsed on the run in from the last fence. Many of her other horses have disappointed for various reasons, but there have been winners too – Manicou, The Rip, Double Star and Isle of Man among them.

Winning or losing the 'Queen Mum', as she is affectionately known throughout the racing community, never fails to congratulate or commiserate with her trainers and jockeys, as well as speaking to the stable lads who have looked after the horses. Though heartbroken by the Devon Loch tragedy, when sympathizing with her jockey Dick Francis, she rounded off the conversation by remarking, 'Well, that's racing I suppose'.

The Queen Mother delights in her racing, her horses and the men who ride and tend them. The majority of her horses, which are mostly steeplechasers, are trained by Fulke Walwyn at Lambourn, and she has one or two a year in training with George Fairburn in Scotland. Among the horses she races over hurdles and fences are those flat horses she leases from the Queen for the winter NH season. The successful novice hurdler, Rhyme Royal, was one such horse in 1979/80.

Top left *Daniel Wildenstein, whose Pawneese won the Oaks in 1976. Two other great Wildenstein fillies were Allez France and Flying Water; through his breeding company, Dayton, he was leading owner in France in 1976 and 1977.* **Top right** *Paul Mellon, who has* *owned champions on both sides of the Atlantic – Mill Reef, winner of the Derby and the Prix de l'Arc de Triomphe, and Key to the Mint in the USA.* **Centre** *Baron Guy de Rothschild. His family have raced in France and England for more than 120 years, and he is* *one of the few members of it not to have won an English classic.* **Centre left** *E P Taylor bred Nijinsky, winner of the Derby in 1970, and was largely responsible for the revival of racing in Canada.* **Above** *The Queen Mother with the Queen.*

The World of the Trainer

"I was a coaxing trainer
not like the genius
who taught me
– Fred Darling.
He would walk down the yard
at night with his little
stick under his arm
and all the horses would
stand to attention."

Sir Gordon Richards.

The World of the Trainer

The art of training a racehorse has changed little in 200 years, although advances in veterinary science have made the whole field more scientific as time has gone by. What has changed is the degree of responsibility of the trainer, concurrent with the increasing values of the horses he trains. It is now financially vital to preserve the successful reputation of horses, as their subsequent value at stud will depend largely on their racecourse performances. Thus a trainer now has to conduct a public relations exercise on behalf of a prospective stallion or mare while it is in training, while at the same time keeping his horses fit enough to win races through the racing season. The selection of the right races for a particular horse, so that it may have the greatest chance of winning in its particular class, is now more important than ever.

In England there are three main training areas – Newmarket, the downlands to the west and south of London, and Yorkshire. Newmarket is still the headquarters of British racing; every yard there is occupied and there are about 1,800 horses in residence. This represents a considerable proportion of the total racehorse population in the country. There are several hundred acres of gallops and to ensure their proper use, strict discipline is needed.

Training methods

The operations of Newmarket are under the control of Robert Fellowes, the agent of the Jockey Club, the owners of the gallops. With the exception of Warren Hill, which is only open in the spring, the majority of the ground is flat. Horses are therefore worked differently there than on the Berkshire or Sussex downs or the Yorkshire moors, where animals can be galloped uphill, or 'against the collar', and work is done at a slower tempo. The reasons for this are obvious, as anyone who has tried running up a steep incline knows to their cost. Those who have had experience of both methods prefer working on hills. Their contention is that, once a horse is fit, he is kept fresher for longer periods.

At Newmarket, horses have to gallop faster throughout and be made to quicken appreciably at the end of their work-outs. However, both methods are equally successful. Sir Noel Murless had equal success at Beckhampton, in Wiltshire, as he did at Newmarket. So, too, did Dick Hern when he moved from Newmarket to West Ilsley in Berkshire.

But, in addition to the main centres, there is hardly a county in the British Isles where racehorses are not trained, although larger operators, with teams of more than 100 horses, are normally based at training

Vincent O'Brien's training stables and gallops at Ballydoyle, Castel, Co Tipperary, showing the training complex with stables, covered ride and six barns where horses are exercised before working or in bad weather. **Top left** A view of the gallops showing the uphill five furlong straight and part of the 1¾-mile grass and peat gallops. There is also an all-weather gallop in the middle of the round gallops. **Upper centre** 'Tattenham Corner', a left-hand down hill bend, and the last four furlongs of the 1¾-mile gallops, which are up-hill. **Lower centre** The training complex with the 1¾-mile gallops in the background. In the foreground is part of the straight five furlong all-weather strip. The two-year-olds begin their training here. **Bottom** The whole of the 1¾-mile grass and peat gallops, running from right to left, and the all-weather gallop, all finishing up-hill.

centres. The facilities there are greater and more varied; there are also a more extensive variety of workgrounds available. The scientific and ancillary aids, too, are closer to hand. At Newmarket, for example, the Equine Research Centre is the most up-to-date in the country, while veterinary surgeons tend to be specialists. Both Newmarket and Lambourn have swimming pools, which are of enormous help for exercising horses with doubtful legs.

Permit holders

Apart from the more important trainers, who have anywhere between eighty and 120 horses in their yards, there are countless stables with twenty-five horses and upwards in their care. At the bottom of the scale are the permit holders, who can only train animals for their wives and immediate family. Some of these may only have as little as one or two animals to look after.

The top flat stables tend to be larger than their National Hunt counterparts of equivalent stature. Fred Winter, for example, the most consistently successful jumping trainer, seldom has more than fifty 'chasers and hurdlers in his Lambourn stables; a man like Henry Cecil, who trains only for the flat, always has 120 or more two-year-olds, three-year-olds and older horses at Warren Place, in Newmarket.

Like all forms of business, training race-horses tends to be something of a power game, with the same men always figuring at the head of the trainers' table. This has always been so to some extent. When the legendary John Scott of Whitewall used to farm the classic races with monotonous regularity in the nineteenth century, this extraordinary Yorkshireman had about ten per cent of the total population of horses in training in his Malton stables. Scott even had establishments near Doncaster and Epsom in order to put the final touches to the preparation of his runners for the St Leger meeting and the big southern fixtures, such as Epsom and Royal Ascot.

The entrepreneur

The modern trainer at the head of his profession has to be something of an entrepreneur. To train a classic winner is still the ultimate objective, and stallion promotion is an inherent part of the sport at the top level for the trainers as well as the owners. The only way a trainer can accumulate capital through racing is by being given a share in a potential stallion by its grateful owner. So the ambitious man in his profession has to be something of a salesman as well as a skilful trainer. In the old days, the successful breeders used to be loyal to the trainers of their choice. But nowadays,

with so much money at stake, even this formerly steadfast band is more fickle, and often switch to the trainer of the moment.

Every big stable tends to contain a mixture of home-bred animals and those bought at the sales. To give himself a good chance of winning a classic race a top trainer must command the resources to buy a collection of well-bred colts annually. Nowadays the tendency is to form syndicates to buy such yearlings. For obvious reasons, a syndicate owner would prefer to spread his risks by having a quarter share in four colts rather than one solitary yearling. And it is the trainer who must have the personality and expertise to attract this type of owner.

Training in Ireland

The pattern of training in Ireland is roughly the same as in Britain. Just as there is a group of leading trainers centred around Newmarket in England, so, too, are there a number of trainers based at The Curragh in County Kildare, near Eire's most important racecourse. Their problems are similar , too. One of the chief of these is the amount of travelling involved – far more than in France, for instance, where trainers tend to base themselves around one particular course or group of courses. A long journey can take as much out of a horse as a race. The consequent nervous tension, combined with physical activity, causes a far greater loss of weight if a horse has to be cooped up in a horse box for a 200-mile round journey than on shorter trips. An animal trained at Newmarket, who is running at his home meeting, might have lost only ten lbs after the race. On the other hand, if the same animal travels to one of the London meetings, he might shed from between twenty and fifty lbs or even more. This weight has to be regained before the horse can be

seriously worked again, let alone raced. Thus the disadvantages of the travelling that is entailed in the British Isles inevitably curtails the amount of racing that a horse can stand during a season.

In France

Racing in France is far more centralized. Chantilly, Lamorlaye and Maison-Lafitte are the main training centres and no horse has to travel more than about thirty miles to race in the Paris area. French trainers do send their horses to the provinces to race and also to the fashionable Deauville meeting in August. Here horses that are to race during the month-long meeting stay at the racetrack, similar to American arrangements, and are trained on the course. But, by and large, racing is confined to the Paris area with all the consequent advantages of centralization.

The main difference between the top French trainers and their English counterparts is that the Parisians operate on a much larger scale. Francois Boutin, for instance, has more than 200 horses in his yard. He would therefore be earning far more prize money than an English or Irish trainer, since not only does he have more horses, but the prize money in France is greater as well.

The United States

In the USA, the sport is organized on a different basis. There are few grass tracks; the main courses have a dirt surface, which permits almost continuous use. At a course like Santa Anita, for example, racing can go on for three months at a time.

All the training takes place on the racecourse itself, rather than on special gallops. As there is only limited stable accommodation available, trainers are allocated a set number of boxes for the period of the meeting. A leading trainer would be given about

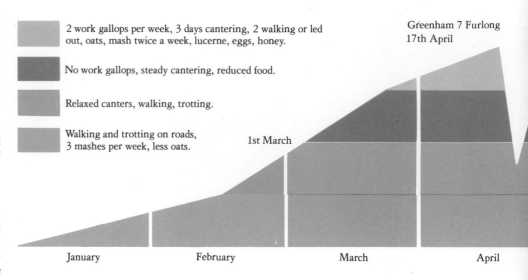

2 work gallops per week, 3 days cantering, 2 walking or led out, oats, mash twice a week, lucerne, eggs, honey.

No work gallops, steady cantering, reduced food.

Relaxed canters, walking, trotting.

Walking and trotting on roads, 3 mashes per week, less oats.

Greenham 7 Furlong 17th April

1st March

January   February   March   April

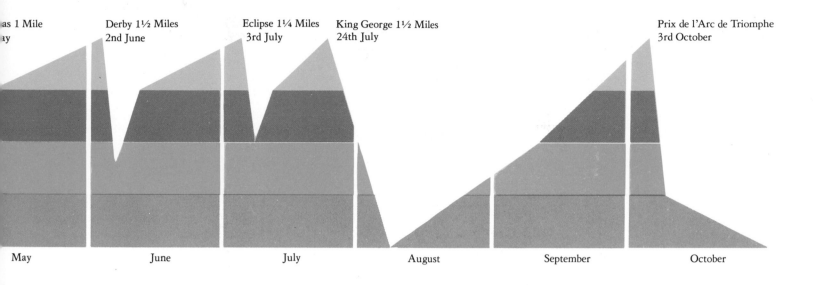

as 1 Mile
ay

Derby 1½ Miles
2nd June

Eclipse 1¼ Miles
3rd July

King George 1½ Miles
24th July

Prix de l'Arc de Triomphe
3rd October

May   June   July   August   September   October

Fitness and Feeding

The stages of fitness and feeding of a race-horse while it is being prepared for a series of top class races as a three-year-old is shown here in chart form. It is based on the races Mill Reef contested as a three-year-old and the programme of training used by his trainer, Ian Balding, at Kingsclere.

Preparation for the season begins in January, with six weeks of trotting and cantering on the roads in order to build up muscle and harden the legs. During this time the horse will be eating mostly bulk foods with three mashes a week. A mash is made up of bran, linseen oil, boiled barley and a handful of chaff.

There follows a period of five or six weeks of steady cantering, with increased protein food (oats) and less bulk food, before starting work gallops four weeks before the first race. Mill Reef had two work gallops a week, his last work being a short, sharp gallop three days before the race. Because the Greenham Stakes is a trial for the 2,000 Guineas, Mill Reef was perhaps not quite at peak fitness, the early season target being not the Greenham but his next race – the first classic.

After the Greenham Stakes, Mill Reef had an easy week, being led out on the days after the race and cantering towards the end of the week. A similar pattern was followed after each of his races, with a long rest after the Derby. Because of the long gap between the Derby and the Arc de Triomphe, Balding was able to rest his horse for six weeks. During this time, Mill Reef was walked and trotted around the lanes and footpaths near his stables, usually with another horse, away from the gallops and work grounds, so that he could relax and take his mind off racing.

The campaign of a racehorse in its three-year-old season depends greatly upon whether it will race as a four-year-old, as if it does so it will have greater opportunities to prove itself on the racecourse before its stud career than a horse that is to be retired at the end of its three-year-old season. Mill Reef was kept in training to race as a four-year-old, which he did before he broke a leg on the gallops.

In contrast, horses such as Nijinsky, who did not race as a four-year-old, are subjected to a far more demanding season as a three-year-old; Nijinsky ran in eight races and three different countries.

Another factor in selecting which races to run in is whether the horse is a good traveller or becomes nervous when flying. Mill Reef avoided flying to Ireland for the Irish Derby partly because of his dislike of travelling and partly because the date of the Eclipse Stakes at Sandown was more suitable to his training programme. The St Leger at Doncaster was not included in his programme because Mill Reef would have added little prestige to his career by winning it; he would also have further opportunities to prove himself the following season. Finally, despite his aversion, if slight, to travelling, he was taken to France to win the Arc de Triomphe because of the enormous prestige of the race.

Brigadier Gerard

Brigadier Gerard was unbeaten as a two-year-old. At the start of his three-year-old career, there were several options open to his owner, John Hislop, and his trainer, Dick Hern. Their early season target was the 2,000 Guineas – as it was of Mill Reef and the fastest two-year-old in 1970, My Swallow. Hislop did not want to take on Mill Reef in the Greenham Stakes, or My Swallow in his preparatory race for the first classic, as it was felt that such an encounter would represent a clash between the best horses of their generation in a trial rather than the classic itself.

Brigadier Gerard therefore went to Newmarket on May 1 for the 2,000 Guineas without a preparatory race. However, he worked over seven furlongs at Newbury racecourse on April 18 and had another trial on his home gallops on April 24, eight days before the Newmarket race.

After beating My Swallow and Mill Reef in the 2,000 Guineas, Hislop immediately decided not to run his horse in the Derby, as he was not bred to stay the distance of one-and-a-half miles. Instead, bearing in mind that he was to race as a four-year-old when he was likely to race develop more stamina, he was restricted to races over one mile, culminating the season with the Champion Stakes over one-and-a-quarter miles at Newmarket on October 16.

The programme mapped out for him was that of the St James's Palace Stakes at Ascot on June 15, the Sussex Stakes at Goodwood on July 28, the Goodwood Mile on August 28, the Queen Elizabeth II Stakes at Ascot on September 25 and the Champion Stakes. These races were selected in order to give Brigadier Gerard about a month between each of his races; although it was obvious that other prizes were more valuable, especially in France, it was realized that they did not provide an even pattern to the season's campaign.

Despite not competing for the most valuable mile prizes in Europe Brigadier Gerard met and beat all the best one-mile horses in 1971. He achieved this without becoming sour for his four-year-old campaign. In so doing, he established his reputation as the best one-mile horse in Europe seen for some years.

Above *Mist pervades the morning on the training ride at Belmont Park. All training in the United States is done at the racetrack, though preparatory work is done at the trainers' or owners' farms.* **Right** *A covered ride in England, used when frost or rain prevents the use of the training grounds. Covered rides are also used for preparatory work for two-year-olds.* **Below** *August by the sea at Deauville. Sea water is particularly good for horses' legs, and provides a welcome change of routine.* **Centre** *Arthur Pitt, the trainer, sorts out his work riders at the Epsom training grounds. The gallops rise steadily for seven furlongs, as does the all-weather gallop, and they are open to all the trainers in the Epsom area.* **Far right** *Working at Newmarket on an all-weather gallop.*

twenty boxes. Those horses which need resting are sent back to their owners' or trainers' farms and ranches to recuperate, with a fresh batch taking their places. Most of the major tracks have accommodation for about 2,000 horses at any one time.

There are two other great differences. The first is in the division of labour and the second lies in the way in which the horses are worked. In Europe one man – the stable lad – is in sole charge of his horses from day to day. The number of horses involved may range from two to three or four, depending on the availability of labour. The lad is entirely responsible for his charges; apart from looking after them in their boxes, he usually rides them out each morning for exercise. On workdays, they are often handed over to the jockeys who are likely to be riding them in their actual races, but this is only for the gallop itself. After work, the regular lad takes over again, and also rides them in all conditioning, cantering and half-speed work.

Timing and training

In the USA a groom generally looks after four horses and is entirely responsible for their well-being while in their boxes. He mucks them out, grooms them and often feeds them, a job which in Europe is usually done by the head lad. All the work in America takes place on the tracks, which are usually open from 6am to 10am.

On emerging from its stall, the horse is handed over by the groom to an assistant called a hot-walker. His job is to lead the

Stable staff at the Newmarket stables of Gavin Pritchard-Gordon, standing centre. Pritchard-Gordon has approximately seventy to eighty horses in his yard each season, with a staff of forty. Each lad will be expected to look after at least two horses, sometimes three. The head lad will supervise

these, as well as the feeding, while the one or two travelling head lads will be responsible for the horses when they travel to the courses for races. A secretary will deal with paperwork, while the assistant trainer will generally oversee activities on the instruction of the trainer.

animal around until he is warm and loosened up from his walk. The exercise rider then takes over and gives the horse whatever work has been specified – this can range from walking to jogging and galloping.

All work in the USA is done against the clock. The horses are timed from a central tower operated by two or three official clock watchers employed by the track. Such store is set by timing that a horse is not considered fit enough to do himself justice until his best time has been recorded.

The horses are usually fairly well conditioned – what racing circles term 'straight in condition' – when they arrive from their owners' or trainers' farms and about three weeks away from being able to race. All the muscling-up and conditioning has already been done; work on the track adds the final finishing touches.

However, there is much less preparatory work done over a horse's actual racing

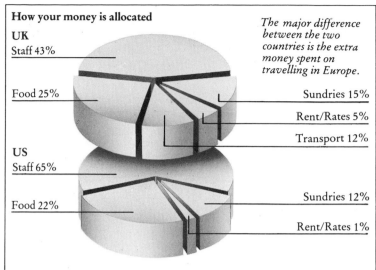

How your money is allocated

UK
Staff 43%

Food 25%

Sundries 15%

Rent/Rates 5%

Transport 12%

US
Staff 65%

Food 22%

Sundries 12%

Rent/Rates 1%

The major difference between the two countries is the extra money spent on travelling in Europe.

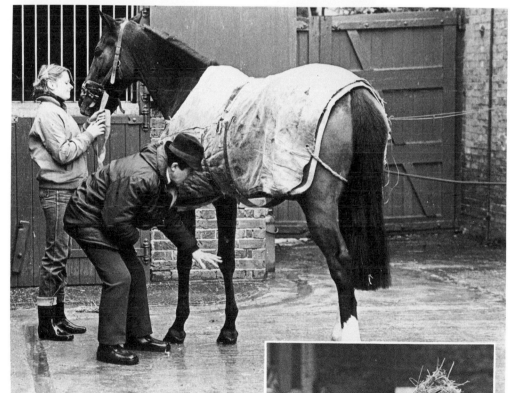

Top left *The head lad handing out feed. Each horse's diet will be adjusted to individual tastes and according to the amount of work the horse will do.*

Above *The watchful eye of the trainer checks a horse's legs for any heat or swelling. The strain on ligaments when racing is considerable, and with the career of the horse vulnerable to any injury, it is vital that the slightest infirmity be diagnosed at the earliest stage. The most common injuries are swelling due to overstrain of the ligaments and tendons, and splints, small bony growths below the knee on the inside of the leg.*

Right *The grim reality of racing life. A lad carries a muck sack after mucking out a box. Lads start work at about 6.30 or 7 am. After tacking up and riding out they return to muck out and groom. The process is then repeated. With afternoons free, they will be back at work at 4 pm for evening stables.*

distance in the USA than in Europe. Even a mile-and-a-quarter horse will be breezed along for only about four furlongs. It is common practice for the same horse to be given a run in a six-furlong race about ten days before his target.

The casualty rates among horses in training in the USA are higher than in Europe, due to the dead surface on which they race. They also race faster, going flat out from the starting gate to the finishing post. Both these factors place additional strain on the horses' limbs, causing a greater number of breakdowns. It is because of this that there is a demand for horses out of training from Europe to fill the ranks being depleted through injury.

Every racecourse in America is run under the auspices of the particular state in which it is situated, although in theory the New York Jockey Club has overall control of the sport. But regardless of the fact that a trainer holds a New York licence, he also has to have permission to train from the state controlling the track where he intends to run his horses.

Australian training

Training in Australia is organized on much the same lines as in the USA. A horse being prepared for the two-mile Melbourne Cup, for instance, might have several preliminary races over shorter distances. There is a slight similarity with England, too, as an Epsom Derby horse might be asked to gallop the full distance of the race of one-and-a-half miles only once before the race. This, however, is by no means the rule.

The trainer's year

In an English stable the flat trainer's year starts in the autumn with the intake of the crop of yearlings from the studs and the sales. In the USA, the process begins earlier. Since the huge American auctions at Saratoga and Keeneland take place in July, horses purchased at these sales will have already settled into life at the training stables and the process of their education will have begun.

The breaking-in of a yearling follows much the same pattern in most yards, though each trainer's methods vary slightly, and the length of time taken varies with the individual horse. Some young horses have been handled more than others at the studs where they were reared and are naturally amenable, while others may be nervous and so take more time to break-in.

A yearling will have been taught the rudiments of his trade by Christmas, although those trainers with yearlings of classic potential – such horses are unlikely to start racing before midsummer the following year – will not attempt too much before the turn of the year. The trainers concerned will be content if the horses have learnt to settle into their bridles and canter in Indian file.

The Newmarket Guineas meeting at the beginning of May is the earliest they will be thinking of running their yearlings, while those that might be Royal Ascot probables will appear even later. The potential classic horses will start racing at about the three-day July meeting at Newmarket or the Sussex festival at Goodwood.

The smaller stables, which have a preponderance of sharper and cheaper yearlings bred more on sprinting lines, will aim these at earlier races, in the hope that they can produce winners before the larger yards' better horses start running. Their animals will therefore have done more work and been more thoroughly educated before the turn of the year. They will have cantred upsides and perhaps even worked behind an older horse before he departs for his winter holidays, and these likely early winners will have been singled out and preparations for their work put in hand.

Breaking-in

A yearling's education begins with it being led about gently until it becomes accustomed to its new surroundings. Then it is lunged – that is to say, made to walk, trot and canter in a circle round its handler on a rein. This process must be done equally both right-handed and left-handed in order to prevent the horse developing a one-sided mouth. The next step is to accustom the yearling to having a roller put on, so that it does not feel constricted when the saddle is put on later. The roller is a strap fastened at the side of the horse so that it completely encircles the chest around its

girth. Sheets, rugs, saddles and bridles are fitted next – all new and alarming equipment that can frighten a highly-strung young thoroughbred. Some are long-reined, with the handler driving them on from behind, or driven through traces. Every trainer has his own method, but generally speaking the animals are not ridden until these procedures have been accomplished.

Almost as soon as a horse can be ridden it is taught to walk through the starting stalls. This is soon accepted by the horse as a natural part of its existence. This part of the tuition programme takes some time, and it is only a few weeks before the horses are first due to run that they are lined up and made to jump off together. The final part of this particular stage of their education is for them to stand and have the doors banged open and shut in their faces, so that they are accustomed to the whole procedure.

Stable staff

The head lad, who frequently has an assistant if there are two yards to be looked after,

Who rides what and where? The trainer pairs riders with horses and the work they have for the morning. Due to the different weights of the lads, they will be selected according to the type of work the horse must do and, in some cases, the temperament of the horse and the style of the rider. The trainer will use the different weights of the lads to provide a fair test between horses of different ability, not wanting to use additional weights if possible.

A canter on the all-weather gallop at Epsom. Made up of shavings, tan or peat, or a mixture of all three, the gallop does not freeze in cold weather or become hard during hot weather, thus providing a springy surface to work on throughout the year. In some rare cases horses do not stride out with confidence on the somewhat spongy surface and trainers will therefore want to work those horses on a grass gallop.

is the trainer's right-hand man in the stables. His day generally starts about 5.30am, when he gives the early morning feed and checks that the mangers have been cleaned up from the night before. Any horse not eating up may be sickening. About 7.30am the lads appear, start mucking out and preparing the first group of horses. The trainer's own routine varies. Some like to be the first man down in the yard, while others rise early to catch up with paperwork. Generally the trainer is in the yard about a quarter of an hour before the first group of horses is ready to leave. He and his assistant trainer – if he has one – will have organized the day's work the night before, and a list of the various work and horses to be ridden will have been posted up in the yard.

The gallops

Most yards have two work mornings a week, the days on which gallops take place. The other four mornings are spent walking and cantering, although it is not always a rigid timetable. During the middle of the

season a horse's gallop has to be timed to fit in with its next race. The gallop itself takes place four or five days before the race, with a sharp pipe-opener over a shorter distance being given two days beforehand in order to clear the animal's wind.

A flat race trainer with a large string of horses has a full and busy morning, as there are normally three groups to be exercised. Breakfast is eaten after the first have come in, at about 9 or 9.30am, according to the trainer's routine. After half an hour spent with his secretary discussing entries and declarations for races the second group will go out.

The third goes out about 11.30am. Before the start of the season the trainer will usually go out with them, but as the tempo of the season begins to quicken, so does the pace of the trainer's life, and he will invariably need to change and prepare to go to the racetrack. Horses in the third lot tend not to be in full work.

The season's plans

When the form of the horses has settled some trainers in England tend to cut down their racegoing, except for the major meetings or unless there is a horse that they particularly wish to see run. Long before midsummer, plans for the following season must be in preparation. The sales catalogues have to be scrutinized for possible purchases and prospective owners contacted, in addition to seeing that the stable is kept running smoothly. A travelling head lad – most leading stables employ two or three – is more than capable of attending to the racecourse side affairs, such as seeing to the well-being of the runners on the tracks, declaring them for their relevant races and giving instructions, if needed, to the jockey.

There is no doubt that the trainer's life is a high-pressure one. It starts early and ends late, and thus the hours between 2pm and 4.30pm are sacrosanct as a rest period in a training stable. It is the period between the drawn-out work of the morning and the comparative quiet of the evening stable, when the trainer will tour the stables to check on the condition of each horse. During the afternoon the lads are free to do as they wish, and the trainer often tries to rest.

Thus the trainer can be seen to be regarded as a horseman in the traditional sense, a businessman and employer of staff, an entrepreneur ready and able to take advantage of financial investment in bloodstock both for his owner and himself, and finally a student of the form book as capable of placing his winners as the most successful tipster.

Above *Indian file in a canter at Newmarket while the trainer and his hack look on. In England horses will start off at about half-speed, working up to about three-quarter speed towards the end of the gallop. Using one or two consistent handicappers as a yardstick, the trainer will determine the ability and fitness of his horse by the ease or otherwise* *with which his horse gallops with them or past them.*
Right *The office. Here the trainer will deal with entries, declarations for races, 'phoning through to Wetherby's, secretaries to the Jockey Club, before 11am on the day of the race.*
Below *Hacking back to the yard after morning's excercises.*

Right *Having sized up the foot, the farrier selects an already prepared shoe of the nearest approximate size and shape and forges it to fit exactly.* **Below** *While the farrier forges a shoe, his assistant hammers another into shape on the anvil.* **Centre** *A selection of training shoes and racing plates, with rasp, knife for cutting the hoof, buffer, pincers and shoeing hammer.* **Bottom left** *Here the farrier is taking down the* toe and side of the hoof so that when flat on the ground the foot will be at the correct angle. **Bottom centre** *Fitting the shoe after preparation. The farrier may need to forge the shoe or hammer it into an exact fit. The shoe is always made to fit the hoof, not the hoof to the shoe.* **Bottom right** *Nailing the shoe. The farrier will take great care to angle the nails correctly so as not to damage the foot.*

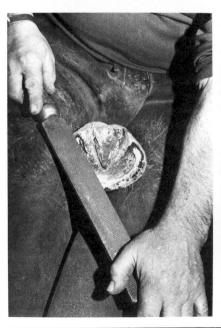

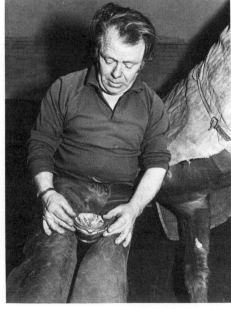

Trainers' Biographies

Francois Mathet

Francois Mathet, eighty-two in May 1980, controls more horses and has won more races than any European trainer since the war. He starts his campaign on the opening day of the Paris season at Saint-Cloud in February and produces winners on most racing days until the end of the French season at Maisons-Laffitte in December. In 1978, which was not his best by any means, he turned out 137 winners from around 250 horses spread over three widely separated yards at Chantilly and nearby Gouvieux where he lives. He has won all the major French races; his four English classics include the 1963 Derby with Relko, owned by hotelier Francois Dupré, his first big patron when he set up as a trainer in 1945.

After leaving the military academy at St Cyr, Mathet became a top-class amateur rider with 206 winners in his own country. He rode in steeplechases at Aintree, finishing second in the Foxhunters Chase, in the Pardubicc at Prague, in Milan and Merano. His patrons, as well as Dupré, have all been big names – Suzy Volterra, Arpad Plesch, Baron Guy de Rothschild and the Aga Khan are included amongst their number.

He has twice won the Prix de l'Arc de Triomphe, with Tantieme and Sassafras, the latter beating Nijinsky, the first time that horse was beaten. Among the many great horses he has trained are Tanerko, Bella Paola, Reliance, La Sega, Rheffic, Exceller and Top Ville.

Woody Stephens

It was fitting that Woody Stephens saddled Cannonade the winner of the centennial running of the Kentucky Derby in 1974. For the past forty years, a virtual assembly line of stakes winners has been turned out from his stables, more than any other East Coast trainer in the United States.

Born in 1913 in Woodford County, Kentucky, Woodford Cefis Stephens left his father's tobacco farm at the age of fourteen to try his hand at riding. Soon outgrowing the profession, he began to train for such stables as Woodvale, Woolford and Marlet, training his first stakes winner in 1945 with Marlet's Saguaro in the Excelsior Handicap at the Old Jamaica race track. By 1952 he had won the Preakness with Arthur Abbott's Blue Man. In 1956, he became private trainer to the Cain Hoy Stable of Captain Harry F Guggenheim, and in nine years he saddled sixty-eight stakes winners including Never Bend, Iron Peg, and Bald Eagle.

Stephens founded his own public stable in 1965, basing his operations in New York and taking on a roster of influential thoroughbred owners. Through the years he has chalked up important stakes wins with Mrs John A Morris' Missile Belle, John A Morris' Proudest Roman, Mrs Taylor Hardin's Kittiwake, Seth Hancock's Judger, and James Mills' Believe It among others.

Elected to the United States Hall of Fame in 1976, Stephens continues to excel with his charges and to accomplish the extraordinary. He recently developed three stakes winners in two years out of the same dam, when he trained Quadratic, Smarten and Smart Angle, all offspring of Smartaire, and now has more than 200 stakes winners to his credit.

Laz Barrera

Laz Barrera came from a poor family, spending his youth and early adult years in his native Cuba, where he was born on the site of the old Oriental Racetrack in Havana in 1924 and in Mexico. He first gained prominence in the United States in 1971 when he brought Tinajero from Puerto Rico and that youngster became a multiple stakes winner for the owner Rafael Escudero. Possibly no better yardstick of Barrera the man could have been provided than his enduring relationship with Escudero, a Cuban friend whom the emotional and loyal Barrera would not desert even when certain major success beckoned with a new owner. Fortunately for Barrera, he had earned the respect of Lou Wolfson, master of Harbor View Farm and the man whom he teamed with to earn national recognition.

Wolfson wanted an exclusive arrangement with Barrera in 1974, but Barrera told him he would not give up Escudero because his friend was seriously ill and had stuck with him when times were lean. Wolfson was so impressed with Barrera's character he hired Barrera on the spot and has never had an instant of regret. Under Barrera, Harbor View has fielded a brigade of champions, headed by the money-winning leader and Horse of the Year, Affirmed, who won the 1978 Triple Crown. Affirmed's success long after eclipsed Barrera's feat with Bold Forbes, who won both the 1976 Kentucky Derby and Belmont Stakes.

Mack Miller

Throughout his career, Mack Miller has trained for owners with strings on both sides of the Atlantic, and has gained a reputation as the finest developer of grass horses in the United States.

Born in Versailles, Kentucky in 1921, Miller's father bred and raced horses in a modest way. After attending the University of Kentucky, Miller went to work for Calumet Farm as a groom and handyman in the broodmare barn and later worked his way up to foreman of the Calumet string training in South Carolina. His break came when he started to work for trainer Kirkley Cleveland and in 1949 Miller became a public trainer. He immediately won success by saddling the good stakes winners Leallah and Lebkuchen.

In 1966, Miller teamed up with owner Charles Engelhard, for whom he trained Assagai, champion grass horse in 1967 and Hawaii, champion grass horse in 1969, plus major stakes winners Tentam, Red Reality, Larceny Kid, Mr Leader, Nijana and Javamine. Miller also saddled the former Epsom Derby winner Snow Knight to champion grass honours in 1975. Snow Knight was a temperamental horse, but under Miller's patient handling the son of Firestreak learned to relax and race off the pace. The following year, he scored wins in the Man o' War Stakes and Canadian International Championship to seal the grass title.

In 1977, Miller took over the training of Paul Mellon's Rokeby Stable and immediately won stakes with Glowing Tribute, Music of Time, and Ivory Wand.

Angel Penna

Angel Penna, born in Argentina in 1923, is undoubtedly the most successful international trainer of the century. He has been at the top of his profession in Argentina, Venezuela and France, as well as at the Saratoga and Miami circuits in the USA. When winning the King George VI and Queen Elizabeth Stakes with Pawneese in 1976, he was momentarily leading trainer in England, France and Italy simultaneously and, by the end of that year, he had become the first man since 1950 to have won three English classics with different horses all in the same ownership in one season. These were Daniel Wildenstein's Flying Water (1,000 Guineas), Pawneese (Oaks) and Crow (St Leger).

Penna's French career began in 1972, when he went to that country to train for Countess Margit Batthyany and later for Wildenstein. He left there in 1978 to train for Wildenstein in the USA, where he is still based. His European winnings were more than 25 million francs and around £270,000. In all, he has turned out some 1,400 winners since he started training at

Buenos Aires in 1946.

Penna is an exuberant, kindly man. His recipe for success is a love and understanding of horses. 'My best time of the day is not in the afternoon on the racetrack but the early morning with my horses at home. I try to get inside their heads and think as they do. If I can do this I have a chance of doing them justice.'

Fred Winter

When Midnight Court won the Cheltenham Gold Cup in April, 1978, there was scarcely a field left in National Hunt racing to be conquered by Fred Winter. Two of Winter's champion hurdlers, Bula and Lanzarote, had both been narrowly beaten in the Gold Cup, while Pendil, who was beaten by just a short head by The Dikler in the Gold Cup, was perhaps the best horse never to have won the race.

This success story followed Winter's success as a jockey. He started riding when he was thirteen, serving his apprenticeship with his father and one year with H Jelliss. He rode for a total of twenty-five years, during which he was four times leading National Hunt jockey. In this role, he won practically every big National Hunt race in Britain – two Grand Nationals, two Cheltenham Gold Cups, three Champion Hurdles and three King George VI Chases – while in France he won the French Champion Hurdle and the Grand Steeplechase de Paris, the equivalent of the Grand National. In that race, Winter's reins broke soon after the start, but he still managed to steer his horse, Mandarin, over three miles of fences to ride a finish to win.

Winter began training in 1964. In his first season, he won the Grand National with Jay Trump. The following season, he again won the race with Anglo. Since then, a succession of the best horses in National Hunt racing have been trained by Winter, including the ill-fated Killiney, a brilliant novice 'chaser killed in a fall at Ascot, Into View and Crisp, beaten by only three-quarters of a length by Red Rum in the Grand National when giving that horse almost two stone in weight. Winter has been leading National Hunt trainer seven times in the last eleven seasons.

W R Hern

Dick Hern, born the son of a Somerset hunting farmer and landowner in 1921, trains some 100 horses at West Ilsley, near Newbury in Berkshire, about fifteen of which are bred and owned by the Queen. Since training the royal horses, he has won three classics for Her Majesty, including the Prix de Diane in 1974. To date, this is the only French Classic to be won by a British reigning monarch.

Hern was a fine horseman before becoming a trainer. He was on the staff at the Porlock Equitation Centre, where the British show-jumping team received their final instruction before going on to win the Gold Medal at the 1952 Helsinki Olympic Games. He had also ridden as an amateur rider over fences and in point-to-points before taking out a licence to train in 1957 as private trainer to the late Major L B Holliday, the breeder of Vaguely Noble. Before that Hern had served four or five years as assistant trainer to Major M B Pope up to 1957.

Hern's first runner, Plaudit, won the Brocklesby Stakes at Lincoln for Major Holliday. Four years later he moved to the West Ilsley stables owned by the Astor family, for whom Hern trained. The stables are now owned by Sir Michael Sobell and Sir Arnold Weinstock and Hern also trains their horses.

Having won every other British classic, Hern achieved his greatest ambition in 1979, when Troy won the 200th running of the Derby by seven lengths, the longest winning margin for fifty-four years. Troy went on to win the Irish Derby and the King George VI and Queen Elizabeth Stakes and was syndicated for £7.2 million. He also trained Brigadier Gerard, who won seventeen of his eighteen races, including the 2,000 Guineas and the King George VI and Queen Elizabeth Stakes, and Lady Beaverbrook's Bustino, who won the St Leger and was just beaten by Grundy in their epic race at Ascot for the 'King George'. The first four horses home all beat the existing course record; so gruelling was the race that Bustino was retired afterwards, while Grundy ran in one more race, in which he was badly beaten.

Charlie Whittingham

For nearly two decades, Charlie Whittingham's hold on racing in the American west has been hard and unrelenting. Born in the Californian border town of San Diego in 1913, Whittingham began his career at the Mexican racetrack Agua Caliente. After working for the great Argentinian trainer, Horatio Luro, Whittingham set up on his own and his record since then has been full of success.

In 1971 he trained Ack Ack to be America's Horse of the Year. An inveterate sprinter, he was heralded for his speed but little else. In 1973, he won the coveted Santa Anita Handicap with Cougar II, bringing the brilliant South American stallion into the race off morning trials alone. In 1974 Whittingham runners finished first, second and third in the prestigious Hollywood Gold Cup, each horse owned by a different patron.

In 1978, Whittingham converted the international turf star Exceller into a peerless dirt track performer, ending the West Coast domination of Vigors in the Hollywood Gold Cup and defeating the reigning Horse of the Year, Seattle Slew, in the Jockey Club Gold Cup in New York four months later. Whittingham has won the Santa Anita Handicap five times, the Hollywood Gold Cup five times, the Californian Stakes six times and the Oak Tree Invitational eight times in only eleven runnings, and has been leading trainer five times. Whittingham was elected to the American Racing Hall of Fame in 1974.

Fred Rimell

Fred Rimell, born in 1913 and now training at Kinnersley, in Worcestershire, first achieved success in racing when he was twelve, riding a winner on the flat at Chepstow. He went on to ride another thirty-three winners before turning to National Hunt racing; before he retired in 1947, when he broke his neck (for the second time) when falling on Coloured Schoolboy in the Cheltenham Gold Cup, he had been champion National Hunt jockey three times.

Rimell then concentrated on training, having taken out a licence three years earlier. Since then he has trained four winners of the Grand National, the only man to achieve this feat, and is the only Englishman to have trained the winners of the Cheltenham Gold Cup and the Grand National in the same year, with Royal Frolic and Rag Trade in 1976. He also won the Cheltenham Gold Cup with Woodland Venture in 1967.

Comedy of Errors, who Rimell trained to win two Champion Hurdles and two Irish Sweeps Hurdles, is one of the few National Hunt horses to have been voted Racehorse of the Year. He also held the record for prize money won under National Hunt rules. In so doing, Comedy of Errors helped Rimell to become the first National Hunt trainer to win more than £1 million in prize money.

Rimell has been leading National Hunt trainer four times, with horses such as ESB, Coral Diver, Normandy, Gay Trip, Nicolaus Silver, Royal Gaye and Connaught Ranger. He works in partnership with his wife, Mercy, who is largely responsible for selecting the right races for

Top left *Angel Penna, who has been at the top of his profession in four countries, Argentina, Venezuela, France and the United States. In 1976 he was momentarily leading trainer in France, Italy and Britain at the same time, and that year won three* classics in Britain. **Top right** *Fred Winter, who twice rode the winner of the Grand National and twice trained the winner.* **Above left** *Dick Hern, son of a Somerset hunting farmer and now training for the Queen. In 1980 he trained Henbit and Bireme to* win the Epsom Derby and Oaks, both ridden by Willie Carson. **Above right** *Charlie Whittingham. Among the champions he has trained are Ack Ack, Cougar and Exceller.*

the stable's horses, as well as for the office work, while Rimell himself concentrates on the training and management of the stable.

Harry Wragg

Harry Wragg has been one of racing's true professionals for well over half a century. Born in 1902, Wragg was apprenticed to Bob Colling at Newmarket shortly after the First World War. He has been based in the town ever since. As a jockey, he won thirteen classic races, including three Derbies, the Eclipse Stakes five times and all the major handicaps. He was the first rider to explode the established theory that to win a Derby it was essential to lay up with the leaders most of the way. This he proved in 1928, when, coming with a late but perfectly-timed run on Felstead, he earned himself the title of 'The Head Waiter'.

Wragg first took out a licence to train in 1947. With the exception of the Oaks, he has won all the English classics, taking the 1961 Derby with Psidium. He has also won all the Irish classics bar their St Leger, including three Irish Derbies, and was one of the first trainers to realize that there were large prizes to be won outside Britain and France. In consequence he has won the Grosser Preis von Baden in Germany three times and the Gran Premio del Jockey Club in Italy twice, besides other major races on the Continent.

Among the best horses he has trained are Darius, Fidalgo, Espresso, Cynara, Miralgo, Salvo, Sovereign, Full Dress II, Intermezzo, Chicago and Moulton. The last is now beginning to establish himself as a stallion after winning the Benson & Hedges Gold Cup at York.

Francois Boutin

Francois Boutin had been a public trainer for only one full season when he won the 1968 Oaks with La Lagune, his first runner in England. Son of a farmer near Dieppe and apprenticed to a local trainer of trotters, Francois was lucky enough to be taken on as a pupil and later as assistant to Etienne Pollet at Chantilly in 1962 until that great trainer's retirement at the end of 1965. He was then one of Marcel Boussac's private trainers, before setting up on his own with two horses. The next step forward came with his introduction to the industrialist Henri Berlin, for whom he bought five yearlings which all won as two-year-olds.

These yearlings included La Lagune among their number. Since that filly's Epsom success, Boutin has never won less than 2½ million francs for his owners in any season. He now has about 150 horses in training; in 1978, when leading French trainer for the first time, his 111 winners netted 10,009,806 francs in prize money. He has won classics in France, Ireland (Derby and Oaks) and Italy. His English successes, apart from La Lagune, have included Nonoalco (2000 Guineas), Flossy (Champion Stakes) and Sagaro (three consecutive Ascot Gold Cups).

Tall, distinguished-looking and always impeccably dressed, this forty-two-year-old Norman is a perfectionist. 'In my job you must have one grand passion, the desire to win races. If you lose this passion for an instant, you will assuredly fail' is his dictum. Since he has already won nearly 900 races, it seems unlikely that his 'grand passion' will be lost for a long time.

H R Price

Like Vincent O'Brien, Ryan Price has reached the peak of his profession as a trainer both on the flat and over fences. Price first took out a licence in 1937, when he was twenty-five, and began by raiding the small West Country meetings for his wins in National Hunt races. As the horses in his yards improved, so, too, did the quality of the races his horses won. In due course, he won the Grand National with Kilmore in 1952. This was not the end of his achievements in National Hunt racing. He won most of the most important races over fences, including the Cheltenham Gold Cup, the Champion Hurdle (three times), the Whitbread Gold Cup and the Schweppes Gold Trophy – the richest handicap hurdle under National Hunt rules at the time – which Price won four times in the first five years of its existence.

Price gradually began to concentrate on flat horses. Although he still trains a few National Hunt horses, his attentions are now almost entirely devoted to flat racing. Ginevra won the Oaks for him in 1972, while Bruni won the St Leger in 1975. He has also won the Irish St Leger.

Giacometti and Sandford Lad, the champion sprinter of the year, are two other top-class horses Price has trained on the flat, as well as the very fast filly Truly Thankful. Other notable Price-trained horses include Star Ship, Whitstead, M-Lolshan and Obraztsovy. Besides racing, Price also farms at Findon in Sussex; a vigorously outspoken man, he never fails to maintain the closest possible connection with his horses. Three of his former jockeys, Fred Winter, Josh Gifford and Paul Kelleway, are now successful trainers.

Barry Hills

When Barry Hills, in his fourth season as a trainer, won fifty-five races and £52,628 in 1972, there were still those who considered his success a flash in the pan. A year later, these sceptics were silenced when this Worcestershire-born former stable lad's horses earned £92,060 for his ever-increasing band of satisfied patrons. By the end of 1978, he had turned out 569 winners with a total of £952,348; these figures do not include his many successes in France, notably with Rheingold, winner of the 1973 Prix de l'Arc de Triomphe and twice successful in the Grand Prix de Saint-Cloud, or Dibidale's 1974 Irish Oaks.

Apprenticed first to Fred Rimell and later to George Colling at Newmarket, Hills became travelling head lad to Colling's successor John Oxley. It was during his time with Oxley that he amassed sufficient capital to pay £15,000 for South Bank stables at Lambourn. This had been acquired principally by backing horses, a perk indulged in by most travelling head lads. The first instalment came when Frankincense, trained by Oxley, won the 1968 Lincoln Handicap at 100-8.

Hills rates Rheingold and Dibidale the best two horses he has trained, but also among good horses he has had in his stables are Our Mirage, Hickleton, Duboff, Proverb, Durtal, Hawaiian Sound, Sexton Blake, Enstone Spark, Dragonara Palace and Cracaval. All these were group race winners. Dibidale was perhaps his unluckiest horse, who was challenging for the lead in the 1974 Oaks – and likely to win – when her saddle slipped underneath her. Though she still managed to finish third, she was disqualified, as her weight cloth had been lost. If Dibidale was Hills' unluckiest horse, then the Oaks is certainly an unlucky race for him. A year later another Hills-trained horse, Durtal, was made favourite for the same race, only to shy after leaving the paddock. With her rider, Piggott, unable to control her, she galloped into the railings and staked herself.

Maurice Zilber

Maurice Zilber, born in Cairo in 1926 of a Hungarian father and a Turkish mother, arrived in Paris in 1962 with just sixty francs in his pocket. Twelve years later he became the first man to win the King George VI and Queen Elizabeth Stakes with the same horse two years running. This was the filly Dahlia (1973), the first of his three winners of the Washington International, the others being Nobiliary (1975)

Top left *Fred Rimell, who has trained four Grand National winners. His Comedy of Errors was the first National Hunt horse to win more than £100,000.* **Top right** *Harry Wragg, the 'Head Waiter', who won thirteen classics as a jockey and has been training since* 1947. **Above left** *Francois Boutin, whose Nureyev was disqualified after winning the 1980 2,000 Guineas.* **Above centre** *Ryan Price, whose career has often parallelled that of Vincent O'Brien. He has won the Grand National and the Cheltenham Gold Cup,* besides three classics. **Above right** *Barry Hills, former stable lad who set up as a trainer after successfully backing horses.*

and Youth (1976). All three horses were owned by Nelson Bunker Hunt. It was in 1976, too, that Zilber won the Epsom Derby with Empery and the French Derby with Youth, a double not completed by any trainer since 1950.

Zilber had trained more than 1,000 winners in the Middle East before he went to France. After eighteen months in Paris, he had amassed some 300,000 francs by shrewd investments on the race tracks. He was a shrewd judge of bloodstock, too, a fact recognized by Daniel Wildenstein, who took him on as his trainer in 1964. This profitable partnership was terminated in 1972 when he became trainer to Bunker Hunt.

An approachable man with a delightful sense of humour, he is now a successful public trainer at Chantilly, but often races in England.

Frank Whiteley.

Although Frank Whiteley has never led the trainer ratings in America, or set any earnings records, he has gained a reputation over the years for the impeccable conditioning of his horses, and his total dedication to the sport.

Born in Centerville, Maryland, in 1915, Whiteley came up through the so-called 'bush tracks' of Maryland and West Virginia. This was not a world of glamour, but of survival. At a small fair in Pennsylvania, he once ran a horse twice in one day, each race being worth $50. He would sleep in the back of his truck or in the nearest empty stall.

After a slow start in the late 1950s – his first winner in 1958 was not followed by another for four years – Whiteley came to national prominence with Raymond Guest's Chieftain and Tom Rolfe. The latter captured the 1965 Preakness Stakes, giving the 'Fox of Laurel', as he was now known, his first classic winner. In 1967, he saddled Edith W Bancroft's Damascus to Horse of the Year honours, including wins in the Preakness, Belmont Stakes, Woodward Stakes, Travers and Jockey Club Gold Cup.

In the early 1970s Whiteley had a number of top runners such as Icecapade, Loud, Cloudy Dawn and Forage, and in 1974 he trained the filly Ruffian to be undefeated in her first ten races, including a sweep of the fillies' Triple Crown. Then, in a fateful match race with the Kentucky Derby winner, Foolish Pleasure, Ruffian broke down badly, and the next morning had to be humanely destroyed. She was buried in the infield at Belmont Park, the first horse ever bestowed that honour in New York. The following year, Whiteley took over the training of Horse of the Year Forego, and saddled the great gelding to some of his most memorable victories. In 1978, he was given the honour of election into racing's Hall of Fame.

Alec Head

Alec Head's ancestors have been professional trainers and jockeys for nearly 150 years; one of them, Nat Flatman, rode ten English classic winners in the early part of the last century. His paternal grand-father rode and trained in France. His maternal grand-father, Harry Jennings, was a leading French trainer, and won the Triple Crown with Gladiateur in 1865. His brother Tom trained at Newmarket. Alec Head's father, Willie Head, was a top jockey and trainer. His son, Freddie, has been French champion jockey three times and is still at the top of his profession. His wife Ghislaine is sister of a leading Chantilly trainer and daughter of Louis van de Poele, three times leading amateur rider in France. His eldest daughter Christiane now trains with great success at Chantilly.

Following a career as a jockey, during which he won on both the flat and over jumps, Head took out a licence to train at the beginning of 1947. Since then he has won more than twenty French classics, as well as five in Ireland. In Britain he has won the Derby, the 2,000 Guineas and 1,000 Guineas, as well as the King George VI and Queen Elizabeth Stakes. Besides these, and the Prix de l'Arc de Triomphe, he has won nearly every major race in Europe. He now trains some 150 horses at Chantilly, north of Paris.

Besides training Head has a great interest in breeding, running a 500-acre stud in Normandy, where he is responsible for the mating of perhaps 100 mares besides his own. During the Deauville meeting in August he regularly plays host to up to 1,200 guests at his Le Quesnay stud, near the town.

Peter Walwyn

Peter Walwyn became a trainer in 1956, but for the next four years was so in name only. It was his job to assist and learn the job from his cousin, Helen Johnson Houghton, Fulke Walwyn's twin sister. Walwyn had previously been with G T Brooke for three years and had ridden in point-to-points and under National Hunt rules.

In 1961, Walwyn set up on his own at Windsor House, Lambourn, in Berkshire, but with only thirty boxes he felt he should find larger stables. In 1965 he bought the historic Seven Barrows establishment, with its extensive private gallops, a few miles outside Lambourn. He became the leading flat trainer for the first time in 1974 and again the following year, when he won the English and Irish Derbies and the King George VI and Queen Elizabeth Stakes with Grundy and turned out a record 121 winners. He has also trained the winners of the Oaks, the 1,000 Guineas, the Irish 2,000 Guineas and the Champion Stakes, as well as many valuable races in France.

In 1971 Walwyn trained Rock Roi to win the Ascot Gold Cup, only for the horse to be disqualified. The following year Rock Roi again won the race, but was disqualified yet again – the prize this time being awarded to Erimo Hawk, ridden by Pat Eddery. The following year Eddery became Walwyn's stable jockey, following Duncan Keith's retirement. The partnership has been consistently successful ever since, despite the outbreak of a virus in 1978 and 1979, which all but closed down Walwyn's yard.

Horatio Luro

Although he has been one of the top trainers in North America for almost four decades, Horatio Luro will always be remembered as the man who trained Princequillo. In one of the greatest bargain buys of all time, Luro, commonly known as 'The Senor' picked up the son of Prince Rose–Cosquilla for a mere $2,500 at Saratoga. He then turned the horse into one of the top handicap animals in America, winning the Jockey Club Gold Cup, Saratoga Cup and Saratoga Handicap among others. Retired in 1944, Princequillo became one of the most influential sires in the world.

Born in Buenos Aires in 1901, Luro went to France with his father at the age of ten and did not return for seven years. After serving for a time with the Argentine Legation in Paris, he again returned to Argentina where he went to work at the Haras el Morro while attending veterinary classes in Buenos Aires, and later became manager of the stud. In 1942, Luro went to Saratoga, training for the Boone Hall Stable, and on the advice of trainer David Englander, put in his famous bid for Princequillo.

Over the next few years, Luro saddled such top stars as Restless Wind, Nearctic, Rico Monte, How and Victoria Park. In 1964, training for E P Taylor, he saddled Northern Dancer to victories in the Kentucky Derby, Preakness and Queen's

Top left *Maurice Zilber, who arrived in Paris from Cairo with sixty francs. Since then he has trained Dahlia, Nobiliary, and Youth, and completed the French-English Derby double with that horse and Empery in 1976.* **Top right** *Peter Walwyn, a cousin of* Fulke Walwyn and leading British trainer in 1974 and 1975, when he trained Grundy, winner of the English and Irish Derbies, and the King George VI and Queen Elizabeth Stakes. **Centre left** *Frank Whiteley, trainer of Chieftain, Tom Rolfe, Damascus, Ruffian and* Forego. **Above left** *Alec Head with his son Freddie Head.* **Above right** *Horatio Luro, trainer of Nearctic and his son Northern Dancer, probably the most influential stallion in the world.*

Plate, as the little Nearctic colt went on to be voted champion three-year-old in America and Horse of the Year in Canada. Today, at the age of 79, 'The Senor' is still going strong, saddling George Pope's Jumping Hill to victories in the 1979 Widener and Donn Handicaps.

Henry Cecil

Henry Cecil broke all records for an English trainer when, in 1978, his 109 winners netted £382,812 (in Britain alone) for his patrons. This was the second time he had been the leading trainer of the season since 1969, when he took over his Newmarket yard from Sir Cecil Boyd-Rochfort, whom he had assisted for five years. In the same year, he won the Eclipse Stakes with Wolver Hollow.

Cecil's achievements were to some extent predictable. He is Boyd-Rochfort's stepson and Sir Noel Murless's son-in-law. But it is Cecil's own understanding of horses and men which has taken him to the top of his profession. He never over-estimates what his horses can achieve and is prepared to send them to any racecourse to find the right race, however unimportant, which he thinks suitable. He rarely comes home empty-handed. He has already won three classics and it seems only a question of time before he saddles his first Derby winner (a race won by his step-father with Parthia and by his father-in-law with Crepello, St Paddy and Royal Palace). By the end of 1978 he had won 572 races, worth a total of £1,313,972, and he was again champion trainer in 1979.

Cecil had more than 100 horses at his Warren Place yard at the start of 1978. A few months later, his stable became the largest in the country when he took on Daniel Wildenstein's English-based string following that controversial owner's split with Peter Walwyn. This partnership at once began to show results, and it was a source of great regret to Cecil when Buckskin, owned by Wildenstein, broke down in the 1979 Ascot Gold Cup, won by the stable's Le Moss.

Colin Hayes

The success story of Colin Sydney Hayes, born in 1923, began in 1951. His first venture was the purchase of an appropriately named jumper, Surefoot. This nondescript animal cost Hayes a mere nine pounds and went on to win £3,000 in stakes. This tidy sum from next to nothing set Hayes on the road to his horseracing and breeding empire.

Hayes first trained at Semaphore, a sea-side town a few miles from the city of Adelaide (South Australia) where his track was under lease from the South Australian Harbours Board. In 1965 he persuaded a syndicate including the jockey, Ron Hutchinson, to purchase a property at Angaston (SA) in the Barossa Valley, fifty miles from Adelaide, the famous Lindsay Park. Three years later Hayes was advised that his lease of the Semaphore property would expire in two years. He then built his own private training tracks at the Lindsay Park complex and transferred his horses there on August 1, 1970.

Lindsay Park stud has had tremendous success. The first stallion to stand there was the English horse Romantic. The first yearlings were sold in 1968 and to the end of last year the stud had bred 716 individual winners of 3,008 races, and over $A6,500,000 in stakes.

In the 1975–76 season Hayes set an Australian record of 186 winners. He has won the South Australian Trainers' premiership 17 times, and was top trainer in Victoria between 1977 and 1979.

Fulke Walwyn

Three young men, all destined to ride Grand National winners, were 'Gentlemen Cadets' at the Royal Military College, Sandhurst, in 1930. They were Frank Furlong and Fulke Walwyn (Reynoldstown, 1935 and 1936) and Bobbie Petre (Lovely Cottage, 1946). Furlong was killed in the Second World War, Petre retired from racing, while Fulke Walwyn went on to become one of the most successful National Hunt trainers since the war.

Walwyn rode his first winner while still at Sandhurst, his first ride in public. He was still an amateur when he won the National on Reynoldstown, but turned professional the following season. He rode with great success until the age of twenty-nine, when he set up as a trainer with a handful of horses at Lambourn in 1939.

In all Walwyn has been leading National Hunt trainer five times, winning the Grand National, the Cheltenham Gold Cup (four times), the Champion Hurdle (twice), the Hennessy Gold Cup (six times), the Whitbread Gold Cup (five times), the King George VI Chase (five times) and the Grand Steeplechase de Paris. Mandarin, the horse that won the Grand Steeplechase, is now in retirement at Walwyn's Saxon House stables, with his former jockey, Fred Winter, next door at Uplands.

Besides Mandarin, Walwyn also trained Mont Tremblant, Taxidermist and Mill House. The last was unfortunate to have raced at the same time as Arkle, but was still a winner of the Gold Cup. Team Spirit, who won the Grand National, The Dikler and Charlie Potheen were all trained by Walwyn, as well as the Queen Mother's horses. Walwyn also trained Tammuz, bred by the Queen, for the Queen Mother, when that horses won the Schweppes Gold Trophy at Newbury.

Vincent O'Brien

Born in Co Cork, Ireland in 1917, Vincent O'Brien trains at Ballydoyle, near Cashel, in Co Tipperary. O'Brien began training in 1944 after riding as an amateur jockey, his first winner coming in 1940. He quickly established himself among the best National Hunt trainers, winning the Grand National three times in successive years with Royal Tan, Quare Times and Early Mist. He also won the Cheltenham Gold Cup four times and the Champion Hurdle three times running with Hatton's Grace.

Concentrating his attention on the flat, O'Brien immediately produced Ballymoss, who ran second to Crepello in the Derby but who won the King George VI and Queen Elizabeth Stakes, the Irish Derby and the Arc de Triomphe. There followed from his stables a string of some of the best horses to have raced in Europe; these included Gladness, Barclay, Chamour, Larkspur, Long Look, Valoris, Glad Rags, Pieces of Eight, Sir Ivor, Gaia, Reindeer, Nijinsky, Roberto, Boucher, Home Guard, Abergwaun, Thatch, Apalachee, Alleged and The Minstrel.

In all O'Brien has won all the Irish classics at least once, all the English classics at least once (the Derby five times), the Prix de l'Arc de Triomphe three times, the King George VI and Queen Elizabeth Stakes three times, the Washington International (with Sir Ivor) and all other major races in England and Ireland. He is rightly regarded as the best trainer in Europe of the modern era.

As well as being a top trainer, O'Brien has always maintained a keen interest in breeding, and in recent years has developed this interest into a business, with shares in studs and stallions in Australia, the USA and Europe.

Bart Cummings

Bart Cummings was born in 1927 and after working for his father the late Jim Cummings, began training in 1954. He is unique among trainers, controlling training stables in Adelaide, Sydney and Melbourne simultaneously. He has had as many as 180 horses in work at once spread

over his three-state training establishments. Cummings' training empire is now based at Randwick, Sydney. It has become so huge that he has installed his own telex service, and spends much time each day conferring with his foremen in Melbourne and Adelaide. He has been openly criticised for this, on the grounds that it is impossible to train horses 500 miles away, but he continues to prove his critics wrong with winners in Melbourne, Sydney and Adelaide practically every race day. Cummings' training methods are superb, and expert staff adhere to his daily instructions to the letter. He has won the Victorian Trainers' Premiership five times and was the first Australian trainer in history to reach the million mark in stake money in one season. In the 1974–75 season he trained 165 winners and two deadheats for first for $A1,399,182 in stakes. The following season Cummings had 153 winners for $A1,324,852 and in the 1977–78 season, for the third time in succession he had 132 wins for $A1,337,632.

Cummings' most phenomenal feat has been in Australia's biggest race, the Melbourne Cup. He has won the famous handicap a record seven times with Light Fingers, Galilee, Red Handed, Think Big (twice), Gold and Black, and Hyperno. A feature of those seven cup wins has been to train the first and second on four occasions.

P J Prendergast

Paddy Prendergast is one of the most popular of the great Irish trainers who have been so successful in Britain since the early 1950s. It is difficult not to be charmed by

Top left Henry Cecil, with his brother David (right) of the Highcrest Bloodstock Agency. Cecil was champion trainer in Britain in 1978 and 1979. Top centre P. J. Prendergast, the Irish trainer. He has won all the British classics except the Derby, and all the Irish classics. Top right Fulke Walwyn, who trains next door to his great rival, Fred Winter, at Lambourn in Berkshire. Walwyn won the Grand National as an amateur on Reynoldstown in 1936.

this open-handed and extremely youthful septuagenarian extrovert.

Prendergast rode as a professional under National Hunt Rules, mostly at minor meetings, some fifty years ago, as well as in Australia. He began training in 1942. In his early days as a trainer at The Curragh, he concentrated mainly on two-year-olds and sprinters, The Pie King, Windy City, Whistling Wind, Young Emperor, Bold Lad (Ire) and Floribunda being among those to do well in England. He was always a force to contend with at Chester, York and later at Ascot. Prendergast graduated to the classics in the early 1960s, winning the 2,000 Guineas with Martial in 1960. He has won all the English classics, except for the Derby, and was leading trainer for three years in succession from 1963. His best year to date was that first championship, when he won the Oaks, with Noblesse, the Irish Derby, the King George VI and Queen Elizabeth Stakes at Ascot and the Doncaster St Leger with Ragusa. Two years later he took the Ascot race and the Irish Derby again with Meadow Court after running second to Sea Bird in the Derby.

Pourparler and Display are two of the classic fillies Prendergast has trained, while in 1978 his Icelandic, which he bred, won the Group III John Porter Stakes at Newbury. In 1980 Prendergast produced

yet another good horse in Nikoli, who won the Irish Two Thousand Guineas and was favourite for the 1980 Derby.

Prendergast has long been involved in breeding and keeps a dozen mares at his Meadow Court stud in Ireland.

Tommy Smith

The Randwick, New South Wales, trainer Tommy Smith boasts the extraordinary record of having won the New South Wales trainers' premiership twenty-eight times. Smith has also a record twenty-five Derbys to his credit, and like Bart Cummings there is not a major race in the Australian turf calendar he has not won, regularly winning more than a million dollars a season.

Smith was born at Griffith, a New South Wales Riviera town. Orphaned at the age of thirteen he was forced to leave school and headed for Sydney for work, becoming an apprentice with the trainer Mac Sawyer. Smith's father, Neil, had owned and trained a small team at Griffith. Smith hoped to be a jockey but suffered a serious thigh fracture in a fall which put him out of racing for two years.

Before Sawyer died he gave Smith an outlaw horse named Bragger. The animal was almost impossible to handle, but Smith, obviously with an innate ability to get the best out of a horse not only succeeded in taming Bragger but also won five races in succession with the gelding. He went on to win other races for Smith and launched the young trainer on what has been a fabulous success story. Smith has never looked back and has trained many immortals of the turf with the spotlight on his greatest horse, Tulloch.

The World of the Jockey

"If you are not prepared
for bad luck
you wouldn't last five minutes
in racing.
But in the end
it's the same whoever you are—
it's about getting on
with the horse."
Steve Cauthen.

The World of the Jockey

There is a great deal more to being a jockey than the standard dictionary definition – 'a professional rider of racehorses' – would lead the uninitiated to believe. In addition to being a first-class rider, the modern jockey must also be an expert assessor of a horse, a good judge of racing pace and a man possessed of a quick mind in order to seize any opportunity that may arise during a race. He needs to be physically strong and to keep himself 100 per cent fit throughout the racing season, despite existing very often on a meagre diet to keep his weight down. In Britain, for example, he must be prepared to travel many thousands of miles every year by road and air to meetings sometimes 500 miles apart. There it is quite common for a rider to attend two meetings and to ride in up to a dozen races in one day. In order to travel from an afternoon meeting at Folkestone on England's South Coast to Hamilton Park, near Glasgow, Scotland, for an evening fixture for example, many jockeys will join together with their colleagues and charter a private plane to cover the 500 miles involved. Some British jockeys work a sixteen hour day during the season and drive more than 25,000 miles in a year.

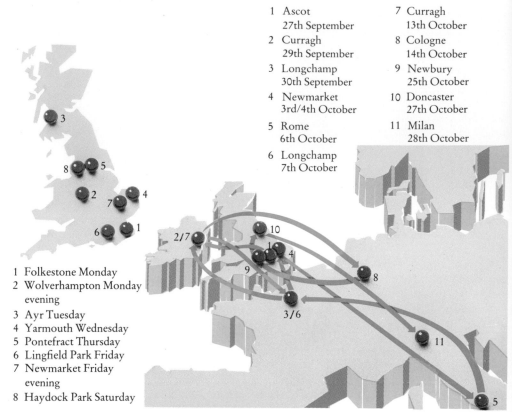

1 Ascot	7 Curragh
27th September	13th October
2 Curragh	8 Cologne
29th September	14th October
3 Longchamp	9 Newbury
30th September	25th October
4 Newmarket	10 Doncaster
3rd/4th October	27th October
5 Rome	11 Milan
6th October	28th October
6 Longchamp	
7th October	

1 Folkestone Monday
2 Wolverhampton Monday evening
3 Ayr Tuesday
4 Yarmouth Wednesday
5 Pontefract Thursday
6 Lingfield Park Friday
7 Newmarket Friday evening
8 Haydock Park Saturday

In America

So much travelling is uncommon in other countries. The existence of centralized racing in the USA means that jockeys there are based near the racing circuit tracks. Although many travel from coast to coast for the big races, most remain in one area only. The same is true of Australia, where there are two breeds of rider, the 'bush' jockey and the 'city' jockey. Although the 'bush' meetings are often only just outside the cities, the 'bush' jockey is not recognized as an equal by his counterpart in the city until he has ridden winners at a city track.

To become a jockey needs tremendous dedication and hard work. The competition is fierce and only the truly determined survive. The traditional way of learning the ropes has been to apply to a trainer for an apprenticeship. If the trainer is fully satisfied that the applicant has some potential and he is in a position to take on an apprentice, he will obtain a licence and the apprentice will move to the stables. By living in at the training stables, the embryo jockey will become fully versed in the day-to-day routine of the establishment. He will ride work each morning in addition to looking after probably two horses on a daily basis. When the trainer feels that the apprentice is ready, he will be given the chance to prove himself in a race with a weight allowance for inexperience.

Top *On the move. The map of Europe shows racecourses where important races are run in one month in September and October. A top European jockey could expect to ride in and travel to them all. The map of Britain shows one week's racing in August and the courses to which a jockey would have to travel. British jockeys expect to travel in the region of 1,000 miles a week in a car, the rest by plane.* **Above** *The American jockey Bill Shoemaker with his wife* *at Heathrow airport. Inter-continental travel is becoming more frequent for jockeys.*

Apprentice schools

There are now apprentice schools in most modern racing countries. These institutions are often run by ex-jockeys. Discipline is normally strict, but many stars of the future begin their racing careers at these establishments. Probably the best-known is the National Apprentice School of South Africa, situated near Durban. Here apprentices learn not only to become jockeys but also to achieve a good scholastic level. They are required to ride work for trainers every morning on the six tracks at the Academy, and they attend practical classes and lectures, in addition to completing a course of school work.

Similar academies exist in the USA and Australia. At Melbourne's Apprentice Academy, pupils who are attached to local trainers attend evening classes weekly, gaining invaluable knowledge of the veterinary science. At Britain's Apprentice School in Goodwood, Sussex, 50 boys and 10 girls a year are accepted. During the six week course, students are taught to ride, to look after a horse and the elements of stable management. Emphasis is placed on teaching the boys and girls to be useful members of a stable, as many youngsters who fail to make the grade as jockeys continue to work in racing stables. Many of the pupils at Goodwood have already had some experience of stable life but others have never even sat on a horse before.

Providing trainees reach the necessary standard of proficiency, the school will endeavour to obtain employment for them with a licensed trainer. Since the school opened in 1973 initially at Stoneleigh, Warwickshire, over 250 ex-pupils have gone into racing and more than 100 had ridden in races to 1979. All apprentice schools regrettably have to turn away many more applicants than they accept.

The first retainer

When the apprentice reaches the stage of riding in a race, he will normally start off by taking part in a race restricted to apprentices. As he rides more and more winners, so the amount of weight allowance he can claim diminishes until eventually he loses the right to claim any allowance at all. It is at this stage that he officially becomes a jockey and he must now compete on equal terms with the top riders. This is often the most crucial stage in a jockey's career, as he must prove to trainers and owners that he is just as effective a rider without the weight allowance.

At this juncture, if he is lucky, the jockey will be given a retainer by the trainer to whom he was apprenticed.

Alternatively, he may be retained by another trainer. Most trainers who retain jockeys ask their owners for a contribution towards the retainment fee; in return for this payment, the owners are guaranteed that the jockey will ride their horse, provided that the stable does not have more than one runner and that the jockey can ride at the weight. Some jockeys land second retainers with other trainers. This commits them to riding their second trainer's horse if their first trainer has no runner in the race.

In addition to his retainer fee a stable jockey receives a fee for each ride in a race – an insurance premium is deducted from this amount. He will also earn some income for riding work. Many jockeys ride freelance and have no ties. These individuals have usually been in the game for some years and have established their contacts. The jockeys' championship is dominated by those jockeys who are retained by the big stables as they are able to ride the best animals in training.

The agent

The American jockey's life is generally a good deal better organized than that of his counterpart in Britain. In the USA, most jockeys have an agent, who is paid a percentage of the jockey's earnings and in return offers extensive services to his client. The agent will spend many hours studying the form book selecting the best mounts for his jockey. The owners or trainers will then be contacted and asked if they will put his jockey up on their horses. Racing is the number one spectator sport in the USA so there is plenty of scope for the agent to negotiate business deals such as arranging for his jockey to appear in advertisements.

Few British jockeys have agents. Most have to do their own spadework with the form book and telephone, arranging spare rides. If a jockey is offered a ride on a horse he has not sat on before he will usually ring a colleague who has ridden the horse and who can advise how to get the best out of the animal. The interests of the profession as a whole are looked after by the Jockeys' Association of Great Britain Limited – a company limited by guarantee. The Association represents the jockeys on all official boards and negotiates riding fees and accident insurance. Similar associations also exist in other countries; the Jockeys' Guild

Above *Weighing in. Maurice Philliperon and Freddie Head in France; stewards check that the jockeys return with the correct weight.* **Right** *John Francome in the winners' enclosure with his 'guv'nor', Fred Winter, after winning the Cheltenham Gold Cup on Midnight Court.*

Left and far left *The rough and the smooth. The changing rooms in the luxurious jockey's quarters at Belmont contrast strikingly with the arrangements at Laytown in Ireland. The facilities at Belmont Park include a pool room, cafeteria, shower rooms and rest rooms with masseurs. The facilities at Laytown include wooden benches; there is also a bucket. The similarities do not end there, for at both courses the horses race on sand – at Laytown it happens to be the beach depending on the tide.*

Below *Dressed to kill as horse and rider leave the paddock for a race at Sha Tin in Hong Kong. Stable lads who prepare horses for their races are awarded prizes for the best turned-out horses.*

Right *One young man to another – Can I have your autograph please? Steve Cauthen signs the book for an admirer. Cauthen rode his first winner when he was sixteen, won 487 races and more than $6 million when he was seventeen and won the US Triple Crown when he was eighteen.*

Bottom right *You can't win them all. Jeff Fell reflects ruefully after a losing ride in Canada.*

in the USA covers the entire country, while most states in Australia have their own individual Jockeys' Associations.

Riding work

The majority of jockeys throughout the world ride work in the mornings, many riding out for more than one trainer. A senior jockey will often 'take the mount' on more than half a dozen different horses in one morning's session. In Britain a jockey will rise at around 6.30am and drive to the gallops, where all work is carried out. The work is likely to last for up to two hours; after this he will have his breakfast, sometimes with the trainer in order to formulate plans for future races.

In the USA, all work riding is done on the racecourse itself – often in front of hundreds of spectators. All workouts are advertised in the previous day's racing papers and each horse is given a number cloth so that spectators can follow the progress of each horse. They are even treated to commentaries, while professional racetrack watchers are employed by newspapers who report every gallop.

Work usually gets under way by 5.45am. Professional work riders — many on retainers — are employed who will ride over two dozen horses each morning. Jockeys also ride work daily. At the track, the jockey or work rider will be met by the trainer who gives instructions as to which horses the jockey should work alongside. He will also be met by a boy or girl on a lead pony – usually a quarter horse. A lead is attached and the pony then canters alongside the racehorse for about two furlongs; the lead is then whipped off and the pony goes off onto an outside track, leaving the jockey and racehorse ready for their workout. It is quite common for over a hundred horses to be working at the same time so the whole affair has to be highly organized. The lead ponies play a vital part in proceedings; there is usually one of these ponies positioned on each bend of the track to catch runaway horses.

Over the sticks

Britain and Ireland are the mainstay of steeplechasing, as in other countries the sport does not attract the public as much as flat racing. In these two countries, the sport is conducted during the winter months and racing therefore can take place in bitter conditions.

The riders have a tougher existence than those riding on the flat, due to the injuries they receive when horses fall. Besides the impact of being thrown to the ground at between twenty-five and thirty miles an hour, there is also the danger of being

Jump jockeys up and down. **Top left** *A fence being built at Liverpool for the Grand National, run over four-and-a-half miles and thirty fences.* **Centre left** *Jonjo O'Neill, champion National Hunt jockey, sits tight as his mount makes a mistake at Hexham.* **Bottom left** *Andy Turnell on Birds Nest flat out over hurdles. Turnell rides shorter than any other jump jockey in Europe.* **Above** *Matters go awry at Newbury during a novices' 'chase. Novice 'chasers of limited experience are usually the most dangerous rides.* **Left** *Pendil, with Richard Pitman up, shows how it should be done. Pendil took off before the wings for this jump but cleared it easily.*

kicked by other horses or being crushed beneath a falling horse. It is estimated that a jumping jockey will have a fall once in every twelve rides and riders regularly break bones during the season. The most common injuries are broken wrists and collarbones.

Many steeplechase jockeys begin their careers as flat race jockeys but grow too heavy for that sport; others start as amateur point-to-point riders or in show-jumping. If they survive the rigours of steeplechasing their careers are no shorter than flat race jockeys, although in many cases riders are forced to retire after serious injuries. In Britain the Injured Jockeys Fund was established to provide help for those unfortunate enough to have been disabled or prevented from working as a result of falls.

Steeplechase jockeys ride with longer stirrup leathers than flat jockeys, as they need the extra contact with the horse to maintain their security should a horse make a mistake at a fence. In rare cases there are jockeys who do not let their leathers down – notably Andy Turnell and Tommy Carberry – but they ride short not for any greater efficiency but rather because of personal style.

Apart from the length of their leathers, steeplechase jockeys must also be able to slip their reins when horses make mistakes. When hitting a fence, a horse naturally plunges forwards and, if a jockey does not slip his reins, he will be pulled over the horse's head.

Riders over fences are heavier than flat riders, due to the greater weights the horses are required to carry. While the highest weight a horse will carry on the flat is normally 9st 7lb, although in some cases this can go up to 10st and perhaps a few pounds due to penalties, the weights in National Hunt racing range between 10st and 12st 7lb. Most NH jockeys are therefore between 9st and 11st.

Except for the largest races, such as the Grand National and the Cheltenham Gold Cup, prize money in NH racing is well below that in flat racing, and jockeys do not accumulate the sort of wealth that is associated with the good flat jockeys.

Steeplechasing in America is now centred around Maryland and Virginia, with the Colonial Cup and Maryland Hunt Cup being the principal races there. The Colonial Cup is open to foreign horses, and British and Irish steeplechasers regularly compete. There are also a number of point-to-point meetings, with fences being constructed out of timber rails up to 5ft high rather than the soft birch of the British and French jumps. Although the fences take considerable jumping, the jockeys do not ride any slower over them. Steeplechasing has been phased out by most racecourses in the United States, due to the racetracks' policy of encouraging races which provide a heavy betting turnover. It was felt that steeplechases were too hazardous for racegoers to trust their money on the outcome. However, in Britain it has been shown that, despite the number of falls, more favourites win over fences than in flat races, and betting turnover does not decrease on jump races.

Steeplechasing in France does not have the attraction that it does here, although the prize money at the principal 'chasing course, Auteuil, is generally far greater than it is in Britain. The English jockey Martin Blackshaw regularly rides there, as his percentage of the winning prizemoney is higher that it is in Britain.

The highest prizemoney to be found anywhere for steeplechasing is in Japan, and there the riders earn at least as much as flat jockeys. However, to date, British riders have not ridden there.

Above 'Chasing at Leopardstown in Ireland. The leading jockey here sits back, taking the impact of landing through his legs, and has slipped his reins to allow the horse greater freedom as he lands. He will pick up the reins as the horse starts running again. **Right** Over the water jump at Newton Abbot, a small National Hunt course in the west of England, popular with holidaymakers. Its main meetings are held at the beginning and end of the NH season, in the summer.

The styles of racing

Riding styles vary considerably from country to country. Up to the turn of this century, jockeys in Britain traditionally rode with long leathers and great length of rein; there was in fact little difference between the racing style and the traditional hunting seat. In 1897, however, an American jockey named James Todhunter Sloan came to Britain, where he revolutionized riding fashions. He rode with short leathers and rein, crouched over his mount.

The style used by jockeys all over the world today is based on that created by Sloan, although it took a long time for his style to be accepted by European jockeys at the turn of this century. Riding on a lightweight saddle, the modern jockey uses even shorter leathers than his illustrious counterpart. He crouches down behind his mount's head to reduce wind resistance, enabling his horse to run faster, and is poised over the horse's centre of gravity. Nevertheless, he is able to exercise full control over the animal, despite the instability this posture might suggest.

The American jockey crouches even closer to his horse than his British or Australian counterparts. He also sits further forward in the saddle and often makes use of so-called 'Acey-Deucy' technique. This involves riding with one leather shorter than the other to improve balance. He can lean his weight over to the left as he speeds round the ever-turning course. Australian jockeys, in particular, are renowned for their superb balance; many look as if they are part of the horse they are riding.

Clothing and amenities

The jockey is responsible for purchasing much of the equipment he needs during a race. The exception are the racing silks, which are bought by the owner of the horse but kept by the trainer. The most expensive item of equipment is the saddle; many jockeys have up to four of various weights and sizes. He also needs stirrup leathers, stirrup irons, a girth, weight cloth, whip, crash helmet, goggles, breeches and boots. Master valets provide jockeys with a service which relieves them of the reponsibility of maintaining their equipment between race meetings, delivering boots, saddles, breeches, lead cloths, tights and more to the changing rooms before a race. Valets provide ninety-five per cent of all the equipment a jockey needs, although some jockeys provide their own special saddles and most prefer to keep their own whips.

A British valet travels some 25,000 miles during the seven month flat racing season,

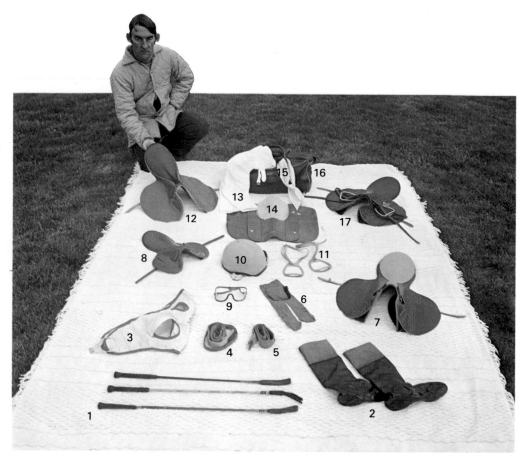

Above Greville Starkey with his kit. 1, whips for different horses; 2, boots; 3, blinkers; 4, circingle; 5, girth; 6, thin nylon socks; 7, 3 lb saddle; 8, 1 lb saddle; 9, goggles; 10, skull cap (helmet); 11, irons; 12, 2 lb saddle; 13, breeches; 14, lead cloth; 15, silk scarf; 16 grip; 17, 4 lb saddle. Jockeys normally keep three sets, one held by the valet in the south of England, one by the valet in the north of England, and one spare. *Right* Racing silks are kept by the trainer for the owner, and are delivered to the jockey at the course.

arriving at the course with between thirty and forty saddles, twenty pairs of boots and breeches, and equivalent amounts of sundry equipment. During a day's racing, he will tend to the needs of eight to twelve jockeys – because of the weight range of the jockeys and the handicap weights of the horses they will ride, the valet will need that number of 1½lb, 3lb and 5lb saddles. After racing, the valet will sponge down equipment and wash any laundry, while in the evening he will need to mend and maintain equipment that needs attention.

Valets are licensed by the racing authorities after serving a three year apprenticeship. Due to their close contact with riders, they are not allowed to bet; if they are discovered doing so, they are liable to have their license revoked. They are paid a

standard fee for providing the necessary equipment for each ride, and an additinal fee if the jockey they are attending to rides a winner.

Racecourse amenities for jockeys vary country to country. In Australia and the USA, jockeys are particularly well catered for, with excellent saunas and Turkish baths in the jockeys' rooms. First rate medical facilities are usually provided and life at the racecourse is generally more comfortable than in Britain. Racecourse security, however, is tight in the United States and jockeys are not permitted to mingle with the public. They cannot leave the jockeys' room unless they are taking part in a race, though they are able to watch the other races on a closed-circuit television unit

Above *Valet and jockey. The valet is responsible for looking after all the jockey's equipment and delivering it to the changing room at the* *racecourse.* **Right** *Steve Cauthen, with trainer Jeremy Tree, carries his saddle and weight cloth back to the scales for weighing in.*

The day of the race

Having arrived at the racecourse, the jockey will change into the colours of the owner of his first ride. His valet will hand him his saddle and weight cloth, the jockey will then gather all his equipment and report to the officials – in Britain the Clerk of the Scales – to be weighed out. Once this has been done, he will pass his tack, number cloth and weight cloth to the trainer so that the horse can be saddled up.

The paddock is the next port of call. Here the jockey meets his trainer and probably the owner of the horse he is to ride in that race. Together they will discuss race tactics, although a detailed plan may already have been formulated. The 'jockeys please mount' signal will be given by the racecourse announcer and the jockey will walk his horse on to the track and then canter down to the start.

At the start the starter or his assistant will take a roll call and tell each jockey his draw. Girths will be checked and then the horses loaded into the starting stalls. The next few minutes will be laced with excitement and will hopefully be climaxed by a visit to the winner's enclosure.

The life of a jockey is always exciting but it is glamorous for only a few. Every jockey knows that, should he falter, there are plenty of others waiting in the wings to take his place. Despite all the pressures, however, few jockeys would consider exchanging their chosen lifestyle.

Women in the saddle

Women were slow to enter the world of racing. At the beginning of the century, women were virtually unknown even as owners – and then generally under male pseudonyms. With the First World War came women trainers, albeit unofficially, and then in the late 1960s and 1970s the professional woman jockey arrived on the scene.

Now nearly every racing nation, with the exception of Moslem and Far Eastern countries, has a score or so of professional women jockeys, backed up by far greater numbers of amateur lady riders. Conditions still vary widely from country to country, with girls sometimes confined to gymkhana-type events, as in India, or to country tracks or non-betting races, as in Australasia until very recently. Some, like North America and most of Europe, give women jockeys parity with the men.

Only a handful of women have as yet broken through to success as professional jockeys. If they have not yet reached stardom, however, women riders have become widely accepted as responsible and hard-working. They have sensitive hands, and are particularly good at introducing two-year-old fillies to racing and at riding sour or nervous horses. Because of their lighter weight more girls are able to make flat race weights, giving them a theoretical advan-

Above *Two amateur women jockeys. Miss Lucy King on the inside of Mrs Jenny Hembrow.* **Top right** *Joanna Morgan, the first professional woman jockey to ride at Royal Ascot. While riding in Australia in 1979 she suffered severe concussion in a fall.* **Above right** *Lorna Vincent, the most successful woman rider in Britain over fences.*

tage over men. On the other hand, women are not as strong as men pound for pound, and are at a disadvantage when riding a strong finish.

Fences and flat

The record of women against men is better over fences than on the flat. Eva Palyzova has even won the dreaded Czechoslovakian Pardubice, a steeplechase far tougher than the English Grand National. Up to 1979, no woman had completed the Grand National course, although several have successfully jumped all the Aintree fences in lesser races. France early permitted women to ride over fences against men, the first woman to win a mixed steeplechase being Janet Slade.

In England, where girls have been allowed to ride under National Hunt rules since January 1976, well over 200 jumping races have been won by girls. About a score of girls are professionals or apprentices; Lorna Vincent, attached to Somerset trainer Les Kennard, won fifteen hurdle

races in her first season – 1978/79 – and more than doubled the score in the following season.

But the biggest impact by a woman rider over hurdles was the win by Ann Ferris, the widowed daughter of a famous Irish rider and trainer Willie Rooney, of the Sweeps Handicap Hurdle at Leopardstown in Ireland on December 27, 1979, when she held on riding the 25-1 outsider Irian, to win by a short head from a top-class field of twenty-nine.

Women in the Americas

Women first began to make their mark as professional flat race riders in North America around the end of the 1960s, headed by Kathy Kusner, a former show jumper. The first stakes race was won by the former film star, Robyn Smith, who first rode in races in 1970 and who has a big score of successes to her name. As American jockeys are confined to their quarters throughout the whole of the racing day, this mean solitary confinement for Robyn on many tracks, as she was not allowed to use the restaurant or the pool room. However, she said the racing made up for it; her annual earnings were in excess of $30,000. Nor did she eschew publicity gimmicks, sometimes riding on a mink-covered saddle. Among leading Canadian women riders is Joan Phipps, who had won over 300 races before she added the sixteen-nation-strong international ladies championship at São Paulo, Brazil, in 1977.

Women jockeys have done well in South America, the star being Marina Lescana in the Argentine. She won a classic race as early as 1976, when she took first place in the Gran Premio Nacìonal (the Argentine Derby) on Serxens in a field of nineteen runners. She followed this in 1978 by winning the Gran Premio Pellegrini (equivalent of the Arc de Triumphe) on Telescopico by an extraordinary eighteen lengths.

Australia, New Zealand, Europe

Although there have been women race-riders in the Antipodes for some time, it is only recently in most places that they have been given parity with men. In New Zealand women riders were only allowed to ride in totalizator races in 1978; before that they could only take part in non-betting races. In one week after permission had been given, Sue Day became the first woman to win a New Zealand race covered by tote betting.

Australia's tracks followed suit in March 1979. The first woman to win a race there was a New Zealander, Linda Jones, at Doomber, near Brisbane. The first winner of a race on a metropolitan track was Pam O'Neill, at Brisbane in June 1979.

In most European tracks, professionals ride without sex discrimination. The first woman professional in Italy was the stylish Tizziana Sozzi, who has ridden over 300 winners. Another top Italian woman jockey, Maria Sacco was, in 1979, kidnapped, and spent some months tied up, with her eyes covered with sticking plaster, before her father was able to ransom her. Pluckily, she is continuing to ride.

In Ireland Joanna Morgan, a Welsh girl who tried in vain to become apprenticed to an English trainer, has had an outstandingly successful career thanks to Seamus McGrath, the Curragh trainer to whom she was apprenticed. Among many firsts she was the first woman to ride in the Irish Derby and the French Arc de Triomphe; she also once beat Lester Piggott in a photo-finish.

Britain has the largest number of women riders under the rules of racing. Around 700 different girls have ridden under rules there from the introduction of the first flat races for amateur riders in 1972 to the end of 1979. Girls were allowed to be apprenticed in 1974 and to ride as professionals on the flat in 1975, jumps following in 1976. Only twenty to thirty of them are at present riding as professionals, and no English-based girl has really broken through as a professional on the flat.

Above *Robyn Smith, the former film star, now riding with success professionally in the United States, with earnings of more than $30,000 a year.* **Right** *Franca Vittadini with Tebaldi. The daughter of Grundy's owner, Dr Carlo Vittadini, she has twice ridden the winner of the Diamond Stakes at Ascot.*

Jockeys' Biographies

Lafit Pincay Jnr

When he came to America from his native Panama in 1966 at the age of nineteen, Lafit Pincay Jnr was joining a parade of fine riders from the Canal country that included Braulio Baeza, Jorge Velasquez, and Jacinto Vasquez. Since then Pincay has ridden more winners and earned more money than any of them, being leading jockey at Belmont Park, Aqueduct, Arling-ton Park, Santa Anita, Hollywood Park and Del Mar. He has won nearly 4,000 races and almost $50 million in prize money on horses such as Desert Vixen, Susan's Girl and Sham.

But it was not until 1979 that his name became linked with a horse of the very highest class, Affirmed. Up to 1979 Pincay considered Sham the best horse he had ridden. In 1973 it was Sham that pushed Secretariat to new heights in the Kentucky Derby and the Preakness Stakes before injuring himself in a final pursuit of that horse in the Belmont Stakes.

Pincay and Affirmed became a team during the early part of the 1979 season and in succession won the Charles H Strub Stakes and Santa Anita Handicap at Santa Anita, the Californian and Hollywood Gold Cup at Hollywood Park and the Woodward Stakes and Jockey Club Gold Cup at Belmont Park. Pincay became the first man to ride the winners of more than $7 million that year.

Pincay has always had a weight problem, but controls it with a spartan diet. Without it he would easily turn the scales at 130 lb.

Freddie Head

The Frenchman Freddie Head has never been popular with British racegoers, principally because of his unfortunate record in the Derby – he has been well beaten on heavily-backed colts three times in the last nine years. Some people allege that no jockey riding with such short stirrups can maintain proper control of his mounts, especially on the turns and gradients of Epsom. But no one who has ridden more than 1,400 winners and been French champion jockey three times can be anything but a first-class horseman.

Head's successes include all the French classics at least twice, the Prix de l'Arc de Triomphe four times, one Irish classic and wins at Royal Ascot, Newmarket and Doncaster. 'I am a small man with very short legs but, in comparison to our heights, I ride no shorter than Lester Piggott. That would be impossible', he claims.

Head is amusing and quick-witted. An excellent host, he lives in considerable style at Gouvieux, near Chantilly, with his wife, a daughter of banker Louis Dreyfuss. At thirty-two, he can look forward to more years in the top rank of French jockeys.

Bill Shoemaker

Bill Shoemaker, at the age of forty-eight, had won almost 7,800 races and $75 million in prize money by 1979. In his thirty-first year of riding he still rode more than 160 winners, among them Spectacular Bid, the country's leading three-year-old colt.

A premature baby, Shoemaker was incubated in a shoe box by his grandmother and grew to 4 ft 11 in, weighing just under 100 lb. Shoemaker and his lifelong agent, Harry Silbert, began by dominating the California circuit in the late 1940s and the early 1950s. They moved on to New York, Chicago and Florida, riding against Eddie Arcaro, Johnny Longden, Steve Brooks, Ralph Neves, Bill Hartack and Ted Atkinson.

Shoemaker led the United States in money won a record seven consecutive years in the late 1950s and early 1960s. Until Sandy Hawley came along in 1973 to ride 515 winners in a season, Shoemaker's record of 485 winners stood for seventeen years. Shoemaker has won the Kentucky Derby three times, the Belmont Stakes four times and the Preakness Stakes twice, riding such horses as Swaps, Round Table, Forego, Gallant Man, Northern Dancer, Gun Bow, Damascus, Cougar II, Ack Ack and Exceller.

Among his successes Shoemaker particularly remembers winning his first major stakes race, the 1951 Santa Anita Maturity on Great Circle, winning the 1962 San Juan Capistrano over fourteen furlongs on the short runner Olden Times, and returning from more than a year off after a broken leg to win his first three races.

Joe Mercer

Serving his apprenticeship with Major Sneyd for fifty pence a week, Joe Mercer was eighteen when he won the Oaks on Lord Astor's Ambiguity in 1954. The filly's trainer, Jack Colling, immediately asked Mercer to join him, and he stayed with him until Colling retired in 1962, when the Astor horses, the West Ilsley stables and Mercer were taken over by Dick Hern. When he left Hern to join Henry Cecil at Newmarket in 1977, Mercer had served the same stable for twenty-four years.

By the end of 1978, Mercer had ridden 2,272 winners in England and had won classic races in France, Ireland, India and Sweden as well as in his own country. In 1979, in his second season as stable jockey to Henry Cecil, he became champion jockey for the first time at forty-five with 164 winners.

Mercer rates Brigadier Gerard as the best horse he has ridden, followed by Hornbeam, Song and Bustino, but claims that the highlight of his career was winning the Prix de Diane for the Queen in 1974. He had won the 1,000 Guineas on the same horse earlier in the year. Among the other races he has won are the Oaks, 2,000 Guineas, St Leger, Irish Derby, Irish St Leger, Ascot Gold Cup, King George VI and Queen Elizabeth Stakes, Champion Stakes and the Prix Vermeille.

Harry White

Harry White, born in 1939, first rode twenty years later and has since won the Victorian Jockeys' Championship on three occasions, in addition to most of the major Australian races. His greatest triumph was to win successive Melbourne Cups on the Sobig horse, Think Big. Since the inception of the race in 1868 Think Big in 1974/5 is only the third horse to win the race twice in succession. Archer won in 1861/2 and Rain Lover in 1968/9. White's third winner of the Melbourne Cup was Arwon in 1978, while he won again in 1979.

White's forté is his quiet style of riding, and he is referred to as the coolest but strongest rider in Australia. Though the epitome of patience through a race, White is a tremendously powerful finisher. Whether using the whip or merely riding out with hands and heels, White is acknowledged to be a perfectionist.

In 1978 White flew to England and while there did much to establish the reputation of the fast two-year-old filly Greenland Park, trained by one of the Queen's trainers, William Hastings-Bass. In her six races that season Greenland Park won four times, each time ridden by White, while on the two occasions she was beaten she was ridden by Lester Piggott and Joe Mercer.

Jorge Velasquez

Although Jorge Velasquez had to settle for second place on so many occasions aboard Alydar in his duels with the great Affirmed, he has made a career out of being number one at the finish line more often than not. After a successful stint as a jockey in Panama where he was born in 1946, Velasquez was persuaded by Fred Hooper in 1965 to try riding in America. Two years later, he led the nation with 438 winners and in 1969 earned $2,542,315 to top all riders in prize money earned.

Velasquez has captured the New York riding title an unprecedented five times and is the only jockey to ride two filly Triple Crown champions – Chris Evert in 1974 and Davona Dale in 1979. The confidence that inspired trainers to choose him for their mounts is borne out by the horses he has ridden, among them the champions Snow Knight, Desert Vixen, Proud Delta, Fort Marcy, Our Mims, Late Bloomer and Tempest Queen.

Velasquez has consistently excelled each year. He has ridden four winners of the Man o' War Stakes – Czar Alexander, Fort Marcy, Hawaii and Snow Knight; has won the Jockey Club Gold Cup three times with Shuvee, Prove Out and Group Plan; and was victorious in four runnings of the Display Handicap with Fast Count, Copte and Paraje twice.

Lester Piggott

Though Lester Piggott does not dominate the day-to-day racing scene as he did year in and year out until 1971, the year of his ninth British championship, he is still the most sought after rider for a big race almost anywhere in the world. His nerve, judgement of pace and finishing powers are still unimpaired, as is his knack of obtaining the best possible mount in a classic race.

Born in 1935, Piggott rode his first winner when he was thirteen, and his first classic winner, Never Say Die, when he was eighteen, in the 1954 Derby. He has since won the Derby another seven times, the Oaks four times, the St Leger seven times, the 2,000 Guineas three times and the 1,000 Guineas once.

Of all the Derby winners he has ridden, Piggott rates Nijinsky as his best ride. It was on this horse that he won the British Triple Crown as well as winning the King George VI and Queen Elizabeth Stakes. Only two defeats marred this pattern, notably his defeat by Sassafras in the Prix de l'Arc de Triomphe when Nijinsky had probably gone past his peak for the season. Piggott was criticized for leaving Nijinsky with too much to do in the race, but the subsequent camera patrol showed that he had given the horse every chance.

Although defeated in that running of the Arc de Triomphe, Piggott has won the race three times, notably when winning in two successive years with the Vincent O'Brien-trained horse, Alleged. He has won the King George VI and Queen Elizabeth Stakes a total of six times, the Irish Derby four times, the German Derby three times and the Washington International twice,

the second time on another great O'Brien horse, Sir Ivor.

Christy Roche

Few Irish trainer/jockey partnerships have been more stable that that between Paddy Prendergast and Christy Roche. The Roches hail from Bansha in Co Tipperary and four of them served their apprenticeship at Rossmore Lodge, Prendergast's stables. Although it was Paddy who initiated the post-war Australian jockey invasion when, in 1950, he signed up the stylish and strong Jack Thompson, he always nurtured a dream that one day he would groom a local champion. The dream was realized in 1975 when a total of seventy-three winners made Roche champion jockey.

Roche was an outstanding apprentice and was made stable jockey to Prendergast when he finished his time. In 1972 he was on the unraced Ballymore in the Irish 2,000 Guineas. With the English 2,000 Guineas winner High Top in the field, few backers gave this 33-1 chance a second thought but Roche, riding a patient, educational race, brought Ballymore through to lead in the final half furlong and win going away by three lengths.

He has always rated Ballymore one of the best horses he has ever ridden. As a four-year-old partnership they won a thrilling Nijinsky Stakes at Leopardstown beating the Epsom Derby winner, Roberto, the classic winners Weavers Hall and Pidget and the Champion Stakes winner Hurry Harriet in the highest quality clash of two generations ever witnessed in Ireland.

Roy Higgins

Roy Higgins, who has won the Victorian Jockeys' Championship no less than eleven times, which equals the record of Bill Duncan, is one of the greatest jockeys Australia has produced. His best individual record was in the 1971/2 season when he rode a record seventy-five winners, riding at only one or two meetings each week.

Higgins has won the majority of major races in the Australian turf calendar, including two Melbourne Cups on Light Fingers and Red Handed, both trained by Bart Cummings. After Light Fingers's 1965 victory, Higgins was heard to say to the trainer, Cummings, 'I'm sorry, Bart'. The Cummings stable had backed the stablemate Ziema for a fortune, but Light Fingers, who had been a doubtful runner because of a shoulder injury, got up in the

last stride to beat the stable choice. Higgins was naturally pleased to have won, but was sorry for the connections of Ziema. This typifies the man.

Higgins has now ridden close on 2,000 winners, and is still keen to win more jockeys' championships. Known as 'The Professor' because of his eloquence, Higgins is untiring in his work for charity, and also gives up much of his time to help young apprentices over the early years of their careers.

Pat Eddery

Pat Eddery was born into racing. His father, Jimmy Eddery, a top Irish jockey, had won the Irish Derby and Oaks; his uncle, Con Eddery, was assistant trainer to Seamus McGrath, who signed on Pat as an apprentice in 1965 when he was thirteen; and his maternal grand-father, Jack Moylan, was a leading steeplechase rider.

Eddery was transferred to 'Frenchie' Nicholson's Cheltenham stable in 1967, but he had to wait until April, 1969, for his first winner. This was Avaro, on whom he scored four more times over the next five weeks, and has not looked back since then. His first major success was Erimo Hawk's Ascot Gold Cup in 1972. Two months later, following Duncan Keith's retirement, he was retained by the trainer Peter Walwyn for 1973. He rode 119 winners that year and has topped the hundred mark every season since. He won the Oaks on Polygamy and was champion for the first time in 1974; the following year, he took the English and Irish Derbies on Grundy as well as the King George VI and Queen Elizabeth Stakes.

Eddery's early recklessness – he was suspended four times when an apprentice – has been replaced by an ice-cool temperament. The trainer Peter Walwyn says of him: 'After horses he has ridden appear to have hard races, they come back to me as if they had never had a race at all'.

Tommy Carberry

Jockeys who are equally effective on the flat and over jumps are a central and attractive ingredient of the Irish racing scene. Joe Canty and Martin Molony were two of the most celebrated all-rounders of the century and Tommy Carberry, champion National Hunt jockey in 1974 and 1976, belongs in the same league.

Born in Co Dublin of farming stock, Carberry served his apprenticeship firstly with Dan Moore at Fairyhouse and later with Jimmy Lenehan at the Curragh. He rode forty-two winners on the flat before

Top left *Joe Mercer in Daniel Wildenstein's colours. After being moved aside to make way for a younger man at Dick Hern's stables, Mercer joined Henry Cecil and promptly became champion jockey.* **Top right** *Bill Shoemaker, who has ridden more winners* than any other man alive, among them Swaps, Round Table, Forego, Gallant Man, Northern Dancer, Gun Bow, Damascus, Cougar II, Ack Ack and Exceller. **Centre left** *Christy Roche lobbing down to the start. In 1972 he won the Irish 2,000 Guineas on the unraced* Ballymore. **Above left** *Jorge Velasquez, the only man to have ridden two winners of the American fillies' Triple Crown, Chris Evert and Davona Dale.* **Above right** *Roy Higgins in winning mood at Moonee Valley.*

increasing weight sent him back to Dan Moore and his first love, jumping.

In 1978 Carberry won the Group 2 Beresford Stakes on the flat, on the 50-1 outsider Just A Game while, the following autumn, he outmanoeuvred Steve Cauthen to win the Group 1 Joe McGrath Memorial Stakes on another outsider, Fordham. However, it is as a National Hunt rider that he has enjoyed his finest hours. He was twenty-five years old when he was champion jump jockey in Ireland, while four years earlier he had a winning introduction to Cheltenham, taking the Gloucestershire Hurdle on Tripacer.

The winning streak that Carberry will never forget came in the spring of 1975 when he became the first and only rider ever to complete a historic treble, winning the Cheltenham Gold Cup on Ten Up, the Aintree Grand National on L'Escargot and the Irish Distillers Grand National on Brown Lad. It was an achievement that may not be equalled for a long time to come. He was again first past the post in the Cheltenham Gold Cup on Tied Cottage in 1980.

Willie Carson

Not since Sir Gordon Richards retired has there been a jockey with such an obvious desire to win every race he rides in as Willie Carson, who halted Lester Piggott's lengthy monopoly of the jockey's championship by becoming champion himself for the first time in 1972. This was the same year that he won his first classic – the 2,000 Guineas – on High Top. Carson's strength and energy are amazing for such a small man – he can still ride at seven stone nine pounds. He will not accept defeat until he has passed the post.

Carson is a real horseman. He rode bareback over the last two furlongs of the 1974 Epsom Oaks, after Dibidale's saddle had slipped round. Most jockeys would have fallen off, but Carson's determination meant that he still finished third although he was disqualified because he had lost his weight cloth. He is one of the few flat race jockeys to spend his winters hunting.

Born in 1942, Carson rode his first winner in 1962, his only success that season, three years after being apprenticed to Gerald Armstrong at Middleham. But to 1980 he had ridden more than 100 winners in the previous eight seasons. In 1977 he won the Oaks and the St Leger for the Queen on Dunfermline. In the latter race, he defeated Alleged. The following season, he was champion jockey for the third time with 182 winners.

In 1979 Carson, who has retainers for the trainer, Dick Hern, and the Queen and Lord Derby, rode Troy to win the Derby, the Irish Derby and the King George VI and Queen Elizabeth Stakes.

Philippe Paquet

Philippe Paquet, son of the proprietor of a car driving school near Chantilly, came into racing via his local labour exchange in 1966 when he was fourteen. He had applied to be an apprentice jockey and was taken on by Francois Boutin, then on the threshold of his great training career. Pacquet showed such promise and did so well that Boutin promoted him as first jockey to his 120-horse stable in 1974 and the young rider celebrated his appointment by winning that year's French Derby on Caracolero, his first mount in the race. He was French champion jockey in 1976 when he completed the Irish Derby–Oaks double on Malacate and Lagunette. Earlier that year he 'won' the Prince of Wales Stakes and the Eclipse Stakes on Trepan, only for the horse to be later disqualified from both races on 'technical grounds'.

Paquet is one of the most popular French jockeys to have ridden in England for many years. He is modest, co-operative and speaks good English, thanks to his wife Michelle, daughter of the great Australian rider George Moore, now top trainer in Hong Kong.

John Francome

John Francome is the most stylish National Hunt jockey seen for some years. The son of a Swindon builder, John, a member of his local Pony Club, represented Britain in the Junior International Show Jumping at Dinard in 1969, when he was seventeen, and again when the team was successful at St Moritz. He is still connected with this branch of riding, his sister Jill being married to the top show-jumper Derek Ricketts.

The champion NH trainer Fred Winter took Francome on a two month trial at the end of 1969, when he won his first race at Worcester. He took over the job as first jockey to the Winter stable when Richard Pitman retired and was champion NH jockey in the 1976/7 season. In 1978 he won the Cheltenham Gold Cup on Midnight Court, and he now considers that horse to be the best that he has ridden.

Francome is distinguished on the racecourse for his quiet style, with a good length of leather, not always fashionable in modern race-riding. Nevertheless, he is a perfect horseman, and his horses always jump well for him without ever over-exerting themselves. His calm approach to the Grand National circuit, on which he takes the more dangerous inner course, is an example for all young steeplechase riders.

With typical foresight Francome has already built himself a set of stables at his house in Lambourn, and it is his intention when retiring from the saddle to start breeding and training.

Greville Starkey

Greville Starkey was champion apprentice in 1957, a year after he had ridden his first winner. Since then and up to the end of 1977 he had been a consistent if not spectacular jockey. His first big chances came when, having completed his apprenticeship with Harry Thompson Jones, he was retained by John Oxley. He was second on Merchant Venturer in the 1963 Derby and won the following year's Oaks on Homeward Bound. In 1975 he won the Eclipse Stakes and Prix de l'Arc de Triomphe on the German Star Appeal.

Until then, Starkey's personal best for a season was eighty winners in 1971. The breakthrough came in 1978 when he boosted his score to 107 winners, nine of which were Group 1 races with a total value of £383,613. Among them were the English and Irish Derbies (Shirley Heights), the English and Irish Oaks (Fair Salinia), the Ascot Gold Cup (Shangamuzo) and the Champion Stakes (Swiss Maid), an unprecedented achievement.

Born in 1939 in Ireland, where he first started to ride in the hunting field, Starkey is presently retained by the trainers Guy Harwood, Michael Stoute and Frank Durr. Although Durr and Stoute train at Newmarket, near Starkey's home, Harwood trains at Pulborough, in Sussex, and in order to maintain a close touch with the horses there Starkey spends much of his time driving the several hundred miles between Sussex and Suffolk.

Yves Saint-Martin

The son of a civil servant, Yves Saint-Martin was born at Agen, midway between Bordeaux and Toulouse, in September, 1941. With no racing background he was fortunate to be apprenticed to François Mathet, a great horseman, a strict disciplinarian and a stickler for good manners. These characteristics did much to mould Saint-Martin as a rider and a man.

Saint-Martin was seventeen when he rode his first winner, at Le Tremblay in Northern France, and only twenty when he won his first British classic, the Oaks,

Top left *Tommy Carberry, who rode Tied Cottage first past the post in the 1980 Cheltenham Gold Cup.* **Top right** *Harry White, the Australian jockey unbeaten on Greenland Park in England.* **Centre far left** *Pat Eddery, the former champion jockey whose*

early recklessness has been replaced by an ice-cool judgement. **Centre left** *Phillipe Pacquet, disqualified after winning the 2,000 Guineas on Nureyev.* **Centre** *The irrepressible Willie Carson, in the Queen's colours.* **Centre right** *John Francome, former*

champion National Hunt jockey. **Above left** *Lester Piggott, with Gordon Richards, the greatest jockey seen in Britain this century.* **Above right** *Greville Starkey, winner of the English and Irish Derby and Oaks in 1978 on Shirley Heights and Fair Salinia.*

on Monade. The following year he won the Derby on Relko. In 1970 he won his first Prix de l'Arc de Triomphe on Sassafras, beating Lester Piggott on Nijinsky, and four years later won it for the second time on Allez France.

It was in 1974 that Saint-Martin left Mathet to accept an offer to ride for the owner Daniel Wildenstein, who owned Allez France, and Saint-Martin rates that horse the best he has ever ridden. In all, he has won the French Derby five times, the Prix de Diane (French Oaks) five times, the Grand Prix de Paris three times, all the British classics, the King George VI and Queen Elizabeth Stakes twice and the Washington International.

Edward Hide

Edward Hide is a countryman, a lover of animals, a successful breeder of racehorses and has been a consistently good jockey for many years. His father, Bill Hide, was a Shropshire farmer who combined agriculture with training. Edward was apprenticed to him and rode his first winner in September 1951, when he was fourteen. He has never been champion jockey, for he was generally too involved in North country racing for that to be possible, although he did spend a period as first jockey to Sir Gordon Richards and also to Clive Brittain's Newmarket Stable.

Hide has won all the English classics except the 2,000 Guineas. His Epsom Derby success on Morston (1973) was remarkable in that he had never been on that horse's back before being legged up in the paddock at Epsom. He regularly rides abroad on Sundays and has won the Danish and Norwegian Derbies and the German 2,000 Guineas. His best English season was 137 winners in 1974 but he has topped the 100 mark on four other occasions.

He rode for many years with great success for the Elsey family at Malton and it is at Huttons Ambo, near that Yorkshire market town, that Hide and his wife Susan set up a small stud in 1965. His hundredth winner in 1972 was on his home-bred horse Rhine King at Warwick.

Among the many good horses he has ridden he lists Cantelo (St Leger), Pia (Oaks), Tudor Melody, Alcide, Waterloo (1,000 Guineas), Mrs McArdy (1,000 Guineas), Morston (Derby), Julio Mariner (St Leger) and Lochnager (Sprint champion, 1976) as the best.

Wally Swinburn

For generations a hundred flat race winners in one season represented the equestrian equivalent of the four minute mile for Irish jockeys. An apprentice Martin Quirke scored 86 winners in 1923 and that was a record that stood for half a century.

However, the century was in sight for Liverpool-born Wally Swinburn when on November 9, 1977, with ninety-nine winners on the board, he was his way down to the start at the Curragh on a wet and windy afternoon riding Lady Nugent's Blue Doc in the Chains Stakes. Initiating his run at the two furlong pole and urged on by a wildly partisan crowd, only a portion of whom can have backed him, Blue Doc and Swinburn drew clear to score by 1½ lengths.

The first championship which had come Swinburn's way was in the boxing ring while he was still serving his apprenticeship with Fred Armstrong at Newmarket and in 1954 he made racing headlines with a runaway Ebor Handicap success on the gambled-on By Thunder! Two years later, he started a regular winter practice of going to India and his association with R M Puttsanna was destined to yield twenty-seven Indian classic wins, including the Indian Derby on Prince Khartoum. At the end of his apprenticeship Swinburn rode two seasons in Ireland for Paddy Prendergast and after an interval returned to Ireland in 1974 as a professional to ride for Richard Annesley and subsequently Dermot Weld.

Champion jockey in Ireland in 1976 and 1977, Swinburn won the Irish 1,000 Guineas on Pidget in 1973, although he rates Romulus, the champion miler, as the best horse he has ridden

Angel Cordero

After failing to succeed in America on two separate occasions, Angel Cordero returned a third time from his native Puerto Rico, in 1965, and has since earned over $45 million in prize money. He has won the Kentucky Derby twice, and in 1976 was the leading jockey in America with record earnings of $4,709,500.

Cordero has been connected with horse racing throughout his life. His father was one of the first jockeys to come to America from the Caribbean, where he later became a trainer. Cordero himself was raised in the stable area at the old Quintana Racetrack. After his two unsuccessful attempts at riding in America, he was finally given mounts by trainer Sam Cardile and in 1966 he teamed up with the agent Vince DeGregory. By the following year Cordero was the leading rider in New York with a record 277 wins. In 1968 he led the nation with 345 winners.

In 1974 Cordero had the distinction of winning the hundredth running of the Kentucky Derby on John M. Olin's Cannonade. Two years later, he teamed up with trainer Laz Barrera to capture his second Derby on Esteban Rodriguez Tizol's Bold Forbes and the following month guided Bold Forbes to a neck win in the Belmont Stakes after leading from the start. In 1978, Cordero replaced Jean Cruguet as the rider of the Triple Crown winner Seattle Slew, and piloted the son of Bold Reasoning to brilliant wins in the Marlboro Cup, defeating Affirmed, and the Woodward Stakes, beating Exceller.

Known for his vigorous riding style and powerful finish, Cordero has been quoted as asking only one thing of his mounts: 'Get me to the eighth-pole, and I'll take it from there'.

Steve Cauthen

By the age of eighteen, Steve Cauthen had made the front cover of *Time* magazine, was voted 'Athlete of the Year' by *Sports Illustrated*, had swept the US Triple Crown, won three Eclipse Awards in one year, and set a new mark for prize-money earned in a single season. Born in 1960 in Covington, Kentucky, to a blacksmith father and trainer mother, Cauthen began riding under his parents' tuteage at an early age and he analyzed film footage of races at Latonia Racetrack and River Downs as part of his training.

His first big year was 1977, in which Cauthen scored six winners in a day three times, five winners in a day four times and fourteen four-win days.

On October 5, Cauthen surpassed Cordero's single season's earning mark set in 1976 of $4,709,500. Nineteen days later he went over the $5 million mark and on December 10 he passed $6 million. When the year ended, his 487 wins and $6,151,750 in purses topped all jockeys in the USA and he was voted best rider and apprentice jockey.

In 1978, Cauthen's spectacular series of wins continued on Affirmed, culminating in their sweep of the Triple Crown. But after he was replaced by Laffit Pincay on Affirmed and suffered 110 consecutive losses, he signed with Robert Sangster to ride in Europe in 1979.

Cauthen had his first ride in England at Salisbury on April 7, riding a winner, and followed up by taking the 2,000 Guineas at Newmarket on Tap On Wood. His contract was to ride horses trained by Barry Hills, but the stable became badly infected with a virus in mid-season, severely reducing his winning rides.

Top left *Wally Swinburn, the champion jockey in Ireland 1976 and 1977, and the champion apprentice in the boxing ring.* **Top right** *Yves Saint-Martin, the French champion jockey, is to France what Piggott is to Britain.* **Centre right** *Angel Cordero with his agent, Tony Matos. Cordero has twice won the Kentucky Derby, with Connonade and Bold Forbes.* **Above left** *The Kid, Steve Cauthen.* **Above right** *Edward Hide, who rode Morston to win the Derby in 1973. He had never ridden the horse before he got up in the paddock before the race. He has won all the English classics except the 2,000 Guineas.*

The World of the Breeder

"The thoroughbred exists
because
its selection has depended
not on experts, technicians
or zoologists
but on a piece of wood:
the winning post of
the Epsom Derby.
If you base your criteria
on anything else
you will get something else,
not the thoroughbred."

Frederico Tesio.

The World of the Breeder

The role of the thoroughbred breeder has undergone a fundamental change during the twentieth century. In an earlier chapter, the development of the thoroughbred in the studs of the great owner-breeders, who still held sway up to the Second World War, has been portrayed. The best mares and access to the most influential stallions lay in the hands of immensely rich and influential men whose aim was exclusively the production of classic horses.

The traditional owner-breeders – men such as Lord Derby, Lord Rosebery, Lord Woolavington, the Joels, Lord Dewar and his son, J A Dewar, Lionel Holliday and Giles Loder – were joined by new men and women of wealth and power such as the 'old' Aga Khan, Sir Victor Sassoon, the self-made millionaire Lord Glanely and the eccentric Dorothy Paget, whose interest lay both in the flat and in jumping. In the twenty-six years from 1920 until the end of the Second World War in 1945, eighteen winners of the British Derby were home-bred; not an American-bred horse was among them, with Bois Roussel, only the third French-bred horse to capture the race, being the only winner bred in France.

The Derby winners

The changing pattern of breeding in Europe is epitomized by the contrast in the breeding of Derby winners since the war. In the thirty-four years from 1946 to 1979, only twelve were owner-bred in British or Irish studs; of these, only the half-brothers Blakeney and Morston from Arthur Budgett's small Oxfordshire stud – Blakeney was in fact submitted to the sales but did not realize his reserve – Shirley Heights and Troy have won during the last twelve years. Seven (all before 1965) were bred in France and another seven came from across the Atlantic, predominantly since 1968.

The reasons for the decline of the traditional owner-breeder in Britain are not hard to establish. They are namely low prize money, increased overheads and increased taxation. The large studs of previous days have now largely been replaced by commercial establishments, which sell their horses at auction and a proliferating number of small breeders. The continual process of the breeding and racing of home-bred fillies to build up equine families, so vital to success in earlier years, now plays a less prominent role. Many of the best mares are concentrated with the large commercial breeders, who are located mainly in Ireland where a benevolent government offers substantial tax advantages. Foremost among them are the two leading breeding complexes of

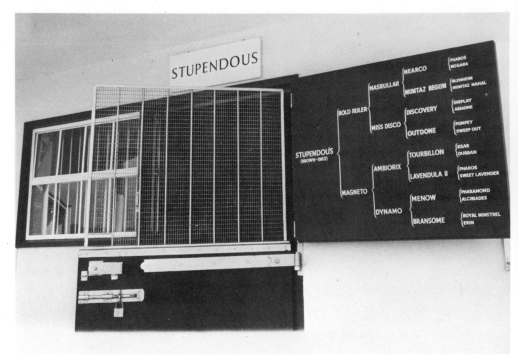

The stud tree board over Stupendous's box at the National Stud in 1967. His pedigree shows a 4×4 cross to Pharos. Mill Reef, sire of the English, Irish and French Derby winners, stands at the stud.

Coolmore-Castle Hyde in County Tipperary and County Cork, under the management of Vincent O'Brien's son-in-law, John Magnier, and the Airlie Stud organisation controlled by Captain 'Tim' Rogers in County Dublin.

The advent of commercialism

Though it is generally accepted that the quality of British bloodstock has deteriorated in the past forty years, there has been no reduction in the numbers. Indeed, the reverse is the case. In 1920, the General Stud Book recorded the birth of 3,102 live foals; by 1939, the figure had risen to 4,084; and at the height of the first post-war upsurge in 1951 it increased to just over 5,000. In 1964, it topped 6,000 live foals for the first time and then steadily went up until, at the height of the boom in 1974 and 1975, more than 10,000 foals were being produced. Such over-production could not last and the catastrophic fall in bloodstock prices in 1974 resulted in a drop in numbers to 8,045 in 1978.

The break-up of the big studs is emphasised by the fact that, in 1979, there were 8,784 owners in Great Britain and Ireland who kept one or two mares, whilst only twenty-four owners had twenty-one or more mares.

The increase in commercialism brought a change in the pattern of breeding. With the dramatic rise in costs of keeping a horse in training, owners increasingly came to look for a quick return on their money. That meant buying yearlings that looked likely to develop early and win as two-year-olds. The greatest demand was still for the classic-type horse, where the expectations were tilted highest, but little enthusiasm was shown for the produce of middle-distance stallions just below the top class, or of stayers. Breeders had to adapt to the requirements of their customers. Coinciding with this came the altered pattern of stallion ownership.

Stallion syndication

Whereas the great stallions of the past had been privately-owned, taxation now produced the introduction of stallion syndication. Through this, as long as the horse was sold before he left training, his capital value could be transferred tax-free to his owner by selling shares in the horse.

Stallion syndicates normally comprise forty shares in Europe and thirty-two in the USA. Each share entitles its owner to send one nominated mare to the horse each year. Those breeders not wishing to send a mare, or having none suitable, can sell off the nomination; a flourishing trade has developed in the sale of shares and nominations as a result. When Doncaster Bloodstock Sales began to hold public auctions, the other sales companies followed suit. People who had never owned a mare in their lives began dealing as in shares on the Stock Exchange. It proved a lucrative pursuit for some years and it can still be one if the right horse is selected. But it did a good deal of harm to the traditional pattern of the breeding industry.

Almost all the best colts are now syndicated for stud at three or four years of age, being restricted to about thirty-six to fifty-five mares in their first season. Additionally, one or two shares are given free to the stud standing the horse, while some are sold to defray expenses. Most syndicated stallions, therefore, receive up to seventy mares each season until, as they grow old, the number has to be reduced. Privately-owned stallions may take up to seventy or more mares, whilst in the lower price ranges, for horses standing mainly to produce jumpers, the number is higher still. In contrast to the top class horses, stallions in the latter category may stand as low as £100.

In every category there has been a trend towards what is generally, but not strictly correctly, called 'no foal, no fee'. Under these terms, the fee is not payable if the mare is certified barren on 1st October in the year of covering. Such a procedure, or a 'split fee' under which part of the fee is payable immediately and the remainder if the mare foals safely, is almost universal in the USA and is now generally employed in such establishments as the English National Stud at Newmarket and its Irish equivalent.

Stallion selection
The selection of stallions for stud depends on the three criteria of performance, appearance and genetic make-up, usually described as pedigree. The combined appeal of these three attributes will decide the popularity of the horse and therefore the price of the shares and nominations. On the whole, it is true to say that American breeders place greater emphasis on track performance than do their European counterparts – and the same applies to fillies.

With a stallion covering forty-five or more mares a year, it necessarily follows that the selection of mares for stud is far less rigorous. Figures in *The Statistical Record* show that in 1978 just over 1,200 stallions covered more than 14,000 mares in Great Britain and Ireland, resulting in more than 8,000 foals born in 1979. In France, some 500 stallions covered 7,700 mares, with 4,500 foals resulting; in the other two main European breeding countries, the numbers are smaller still. Germany has about 100 thoroughbred stallions and 1,600 mares and a foal crop of about 900, whilst the Italian figures are roughly the same. Many of the best mares from the leading studs in these two countries are sent to stallions in England, Ireland and France.

United States, Australia, New Zealand
The USA presents a contrast. Spread over the vast continent at the latest count were 5,997 stallions and 55,700 mares, resulting in an annual thoroughbred production of 32,192 foals. But then everything is on a colossal scale, for 70,000 races are run annually to accommodate all these horses, compared with under 4,000 on the flat in Britain and Ireland, and approximately the same number in France, of which only about 1,250 are run in the Paris area.

As the large owner-breeder studs largely disappeared in Europe, so in North America the great breeding complexes grew up. The area of Lexington, Kentucky, became the commercial hub of the industry, with examples such as Claiborne, Spendthrift Farms and the empire of the great Canadian breeder, E P Taylor, which spreads over farms in both Canada and the USA.

There are just over 10,000 breeders in Australia, with about 1,600 active studs and a stallion population of 2,500. There are more than 28,000 registered brood mares, with 13,420 foals being produced annually.

The pattern of breeding
Whatever the continent or country, the pattern of breeding is basically the same. The mare will spend about eight months of her year at her owner's stud (termed a private stud) or boarded out at one of the many studs who cater for those who have no establishment of their own. Then, some three weeks before she is due to foal, she will normally move to the stud at which stands the stallion she is going to visit, unless her owner foals her at home.

At the public stud – there are about a hundred of these in Britain and Ireland that cater for the more important stallions – all has been peaceful since the last of the visiting mares left in the previous June, with only the stud's own mares in residence. Then, from soon after the New Year, the visiting mares begin to arrive, the season running from February 14 to July 30 in the Northern Hemisphere and from September to January in the Southern Hemisphere.

With a gestation period of about 340 days – approximately 11 months – covering

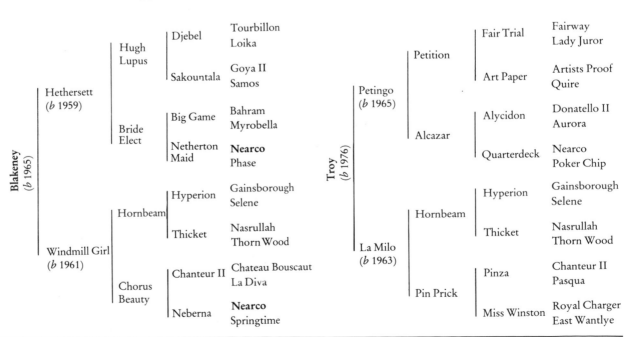

The pedigrees of two of the only four home-bred Derby winners between 1967 and 1979, Blakeney and Troy. Troy's pedigree is an example of outcrossing, with no duplication in any of his first four generations. Blakeney, whose maternal grandsire is also Hornbeam, has a 4×4 cross to Nearco. Blakeney's half-brother, Morston, who also won the Derby, was by Ragusa, by Ribot, while Troy's half-brother Admetus, who won the Washington International, was by Reform, by Pall Mall-Country House, by Vieux Manoir.

Blakeney (b 1965)	Hethersett (b 1959)	Hugh Lupus	Djebel — Tourbillon / Loika
			Sakountala — Goya II / Samos
		Bride Elect	Big Game — Bahram / Myrobella
			Netherton Maid — **Nearco** / Phase
	Windmill Girl (b 1961)	Hornbeam	Hyperion — Gainsborough / Selene
			Thicket — Nasrullah / Thorn Wood
		Chorus Beauty	Chanteur II — Chateau Bouscaut / La Diva
			Neberna — **Nearco** / Springtime

Troy (b 1976)	Petingo (b 1965)	Petition	Fair Trial — Fairway / Lady Juror
			Art Paper — Artists Proof / Quire
		Alcazar	Alycidon — Donatello II / Aurora
			Quarterdeck — Nearco / Poker Chip
	La Milo (b 1963)	Hornbeam	Hyperion — Gainsborough / Selene
			Thicket — Nasrullah / Thorn Wood
		Pin Prick	Pinza — Chanteur II / Pasqua
			Miss Winston — Royal Charger / East Wantlye

The Foaling Unit of the National Stud at Newmarket, with twenty foaling boxes. **Inset** *are* **right** *The Irish National Stud at Barrets Town Castle,* **centre** *the Westerly Stud Clinic building in California, recently bought by a group including Vincent O'Brien and Robert Sangster.* **Far right top** *The Bunbury yard at the National Stud, which accommodates mares prior to foaling and older mares with foals at foot and* **far right bottom** *the interior of the Bunbury yard.*

in the Northern Hemisphere cannot start until mid-February to ensure that no foal is born before the following January 1st; all thoroughbreds 'North of the Line' take their birth dates from that day and any foal born in December would become a yearling a few days later, with obvious impossible racing disadvantages. There are, however, many knowledgeable horsemen who are convinced that overall fertility would be improved if the season were put back to conform closer to nature.

Coming into season about eight to ten days after foaling and at three weekly intervals until she conceives, the mare will be veterinarily examined to ensure that she is 'on' and then normally cross-covered two days later. At forty-two days, a pregnancy examination will reveal whether she is in foal; if so, she will return to her private stud until she is due to go away again in the following spring. Despite the advances in veterinary science since the war, however, the sad fact remains that one mare in three overall fails to produce a foal every year.

Bloodstock sales

Whereas in Britain and Ireland it is customary for the majority of mares to remain at the public stud until they are in foal or until the end of the season, the American practice in the main breeding areas is for the mare to be 'vanned in' for covering. Thus, in contrast to Europe, it is not uncommon to find some of the major stallion farms comprising only a few acres, with a number of small railed paddocks each allotted to one stallion, and a covering barn, with no mares resident there at all. In contrast, few European studs stand more than four or five stallions, an exception being the Irish National Stud with twelve. Until the advent of Contagious Equine Metritis, a disease affecting mares, in 1977, 'walking in' to public studs was much practiced but it is now officially frowned on due to possible spread of infection.

For the commercial breeder, the years of anxiety, expenditure and expectation since he first decided on the mating of his mare come to fruition when his yearlings go to the sales in the autumn. Perhaps he has

decided to limit his liability by selling the horse as a foal (weanling) before the close of the year, when it will pass to another breeder, probably to reappear in the sales ring nine months later. The purchase of foals for resale has grown immeasurably since the war; in Europe the Irish breeders are the acknowledged experts. It is something to which the sales companies, who charge a five per cent commission to the vendor, have every reason to encourage, for they draw a commission twice on the same horse.

From July onwards in the Northern Hemisphere, the great sales circus begins for trainer and international bloodstock agents, who between them make the most of the purchases. The world's richest bloodstock sale by the Keeneland Sales Company in Kentucky is followed by Fasig-Tipton's Saratoga Sales outside New York in August. Then it is over to Deauville in France, Goffs' Kill Sales in Ireland and Europe's major dispersal, Tattersalls' Houghton Sales. In between, minor sales are staged by Doncaster Bloodstock Sales, Ballsbridge Sales and Tattersalls.

Profit and loss
In 1979, 305 yearlings at Keeneland averaged $155,567; at Saratoga the average price was $98,096; while the mean price of the 427 yearlings sold at the Houghton Sales worked out at 30,403gns ($60,000). Against these figures must be counted the fact that, with the cost of nomination, keep, depreciation of the mare and allowance for years in which she is barren, it is estimated that it now costs over $70,000 to get a yearling into a selected American sale and £15,000 to produce a Houghton yearling. Then, in November and December, the big breeding stock sales are held.

South of the Equator, with sales held in the first half of the year, prices have risen markedly but do not compare with the levels reached at the top American or European sales.

Sales techniques vary in different parts of the world. The animated routine of the American sales rings, based on the old tobacco auctions, contrasts with the less flamboyant but equally effective style at Tattersalls. But the aim of those cluttered around the ring remains the same – to buy the best horse available within their cash limits. For the breeder the objective is to breed the best that his financial resources allow, whether he intends to race himself or sell.If he is to sell, he must aim to pre-emp fashion at the sales when planning his mating, so that his yearling is a popular one.

Breeding a champion
In contrast to the breeders of other livestock, whose aim is to raise the overall quality of the herd or the flock and to increase, say, milk yield or carcass weight, the bloodstock breeder's target is to produce a champion horse that can outstrip his rivals – a Derby winner at best. Clearly, the higher the general quality of the bloodstock, the greater is the possibility of obtaining such an animal and the better the breeder's chance of a profit.

As he passes the winning post at the head of the field, the Epsom Derby winner becomes worth something over a million pounds, while the Kentucky Derby victor is valued in millions of dollars. Pressure is enormous to buy the top colts, most of all from the USA, where bloodstock prices are far in excess of those in Europe. After he had won the Derby and King George VI & Queen Elizabeth Stakes in 1977, Sangster's colt, The Minstrel, was sold to the USA at a valuation of $9 million. Lord Halifax and his son, Lord Irwin, preferred to keep his successor of the following season, Shirley Heights, in England. This horse was syndicated to stand at the English National Stud at £40,000 a share, to give a capital value of £1.6 million. The capital value of Troy, winner of the 1979 English and Irish Derbies and the King George VI & Queen Elizabeth Diamond Stakes, was £7.2 million.

The importance of conformation
The sales returns provide an almost endless list of expensive yearlings who were abject failures on the racecourse. Beauty in horses, as in women, is in the eye of the beholder, and this truism applies just as much to pedigree as to confirmation. One expert may spot in the animal before him, or in the tabulated pedigree that records its ancestry, something which another equally knowledgeable judge does not appreciate. Or it may be that the attributes that make the horse great – perhaps an outsize heart or lungs and the vital factors that give it courage – are hidden away

As far as conformation is concerned, perhaps the most successful horse in post-war Britain that came nearest to perfection was Brigadier Gerard. He serves as an illustration of the closest thing to a perfect thoroughbred that anybody is likely to see.

Breeding theories
It is never difficult to find examples of good horses to substantiate any breeding system; what matters is whether the particular system provides a higher proportion of such winners in relation to the number bred in that way.

Close inbreeding, on the lines demonstrated in the early days of the development of the thoroughbred, is now seldom practised. Every thoroughbred is of necessity inbred, but, in practical terms today, inbreeding means the recurrence of the same name within the first five generations. The 1969 Derby winner, Blakeney, was deliberately bred *inter alia* to carry a 4×4 cross to Nearco, with another cross in the next generation. With the duplication of genes, whether dominant or recessive, in inbreeding, it should normally be aimed at only with the best horses.

The most celebrated case of inbreeding in the past half century was that of the filly Coronation V, bred in 1946 by Marcel Boussac, who was by a son of Tourbillon out of a daughter of Tourbillon – yet Tourbillon had a reputation for producing horses with bent hocks. Coronation V proved a brilliant filly, winning the Prix de l'Arc de Triomphe, but was impossibly temperamental and failed to breed a single foal at stud. A similar mating, by a son of Firdaussi out of a daughter of Firdaussi, produced Flagette, dam of the fine French racehorse Herbager, who went to stand in the USA. An equally close inbreeding, this time to a mare, was practiced by the incomparable Italian breeder Federico Tesio, when he sent the dual classic winner Tokamura to Ribot's sire Tenerani. They were half-brother and sister, each out of Tofanella. The resultant filly, Tanaka, won eight races of no particular account.

In general terms, the nearest that most breeders would dare to inbreed today would be 2×3, but more normally 3×3 or 3×4. Examples of successful 2×3 inbreeding include Hugh Lupus and the St Leger winner Aurelius. But it is obviously impossible to know the number or names of horses so bred that never won a race.

Outcrossing
Outcrossing is the opposite of inbreeding and by definition means that the parents do not carry the names of common ancestors close up in their pedigrees. A system that has certainly provided a good share of high-class horses is the crossing of a stallion and a mare who are both closely inbred, but are unrelated to each other, it being suggested that a superior racing performance may thus be produced as a result of hybrid vigour. In 1970, the Queen sent her mare Highlight, who was inbred 3×2 to Hyperion, to the stallion Queen's Hussar, who was inbred 3×3 to Fair Trial. They carried no close-up common ancestors. The resultant product, Highclere, was winner of the 1,000 Guineas and the Prix de Diane.

The role of the veterinary surgeon

Breeding horses is part of the same biological pattern by which all mammals reproduce. The male (spermatozoon) and female (ovum) cells (gametes) are combined to form a new individual. This develops within the female until it is delivered as a newly born male or female individual to be further nourished by its dam until it is weaned. From this age it develops towards sexual maturity when it, too, can take part in a further generation of the reproductive process.

The gametes are produced by the sex organs – the testes (testicles) of the stallion and the ovaries of the mare. In each case, they are delivered into the genital tract, a tube which extends to the outside of the body. The essential difference between the two genital tracts of the sexes is that the mare has to nourish the developing foal during pregnancy and to deliver it at birth, whereas the stallion has only to deliver the spermatozoon in a fluid known as semen.

The breeding organs of the mare and stallion are controlled by hormones. These are produced in special brain cells in the pituitary gland and known as releasing and gonadotrophic hormones. They stimulate the gonads and control the production of the sex cells. The gonads produce hormones (in the mare oestrogens and progesterone: in the stallion testosterone) responsible for sexuality.

The breeding cycle

In the natural state, mares have a breeding season restricted to late spring and summer months. In practice, many mares have oestrous cycles in winter or early spring. This is because they are kept under special conditions and, further, they are selected not for their natural breeding capacity and function but, rather for special purposes, such as racing and jumping. It is therefore possible to breed mares at any time of the year, although not all mares perform to this 'unnatural' pattern.

During this period, the mare undergoes a series of sexual or oestrous cycles, making up a complex biological rhythm. These typically consist of a phase of heat, or oestrus, when the mare will accept the stallion, lasting for about five days, and a period of dioestrus, when the mare will not accept the male, lasting for about fifteen days. The complete cycle is therefore about twenty days; it is repeated if the mare does not conceive. If the mare becomes pregnant, the oestrous cycles come to an end until she has foaled. After this, she comes into heat again on about the ninth day – this is known as foal heat.

The stallion is not as influenced by the

Sexual Organs of the Mare

Kidneys
Vagina
Ureters
Vulva
Cervix
Ovary
Fallopian tube
Right horn of uterus
Bladder
Body of uterus
Urethra
Floor of pelvis
Teat

Sexual Organs of the Stallion

Kidneys
Bulbourethral gland
Prostate gland
Ureters
Seminal vesicle
Bladder
Sperm duct
Floor of pelvis
Spermatic cord
Urethra
Penis
Epididymis
Testis
Sheath
Scrotum

seasons as the mare, although the quality of his semen and his sexual vigour are usually better in late spring and summer than in the winter months.

Sexual behaviour

The hormonal patterns in the mare are responsible for corresponding changes in behaviour. During oestrus the mare repeatedly adopts a straddling stance with tail raised, vulva elongated and its lower part everted, exposing the clitoris and showing what is termed the Flehmen's posture. These visual signs are signals to the male horse that the mare is in a receptive state, encouraging him to investigate by smell and taste before mating. Dioestrus is marked by an absence of these encouraging signals and a show of hostility – the ears laid back and kicking – if approached. These signals of rejection will, under normal circumstances, keep the male horse at some distance. Mares that are pregnant or those which are sexually inactive (anoestrus) show similar behaviour.

The teasing of mares

In the wild, the stallion interprets the sexual signs on his own. However, in most systems of horse breeding, the stallion is kept separate from his mares and it is the breeder who has to interpret the sexual state at any given time. It has to be decided if an individual is in oestrus ('in season', 'in heat', 'on') or in dioestrus ('not in heat'. 'out of season', 'off'). If a mare 'not in heat'

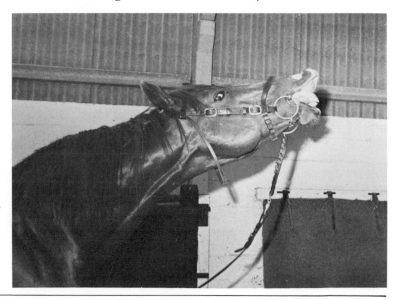

Right *The Flehman's posture, one of the visual signs a mare will show a stallion when she is receptive to him, encourgaing him to investigate by smell and taste before mating.*

Above *The stallion man bandages the tail of the mare before covering.* **Far right** *The stallion is also washed down. Special care has to be taken over cleanliness and hygiene as infection spreads quickly, mares being covered twice a year and stallions covering forty mares in a season. Mares are also moved from country to country for covering, particularly within Europe, and to and from the United States.* **Right** *The mare is fitted with protective shoes before the covering. Leg hobbles are also fitted when necessary, but must be removed at the point of mounting. Some mares kick out prior to or* *after mating, and without protective measures can easily damage the stallion.* **Bottom left** *The mare is held still while the stallion approaches. The groom at her head has a twitch on the mare, a stick with a loop of rope at the end which is twisted to contract around the fleshy upper lip of the mare. A second groom holds up the near fore foot of the mare, so that she cannot move any of her other feet without becoming unbalanced. The stallion man has the stallion on a lead for extra safety.* **Bottom right** *The covering procedure. The groom has released the near fore of the mare so that she* *can support the weight of the stallion, although the groom at her head still maintains the twitch for control. The stallion man aids the stallion to ensure penetration of the mare. Mating normally takes one or two minutes, during which the mare must be kept still as possible, especially during ejaculation.*

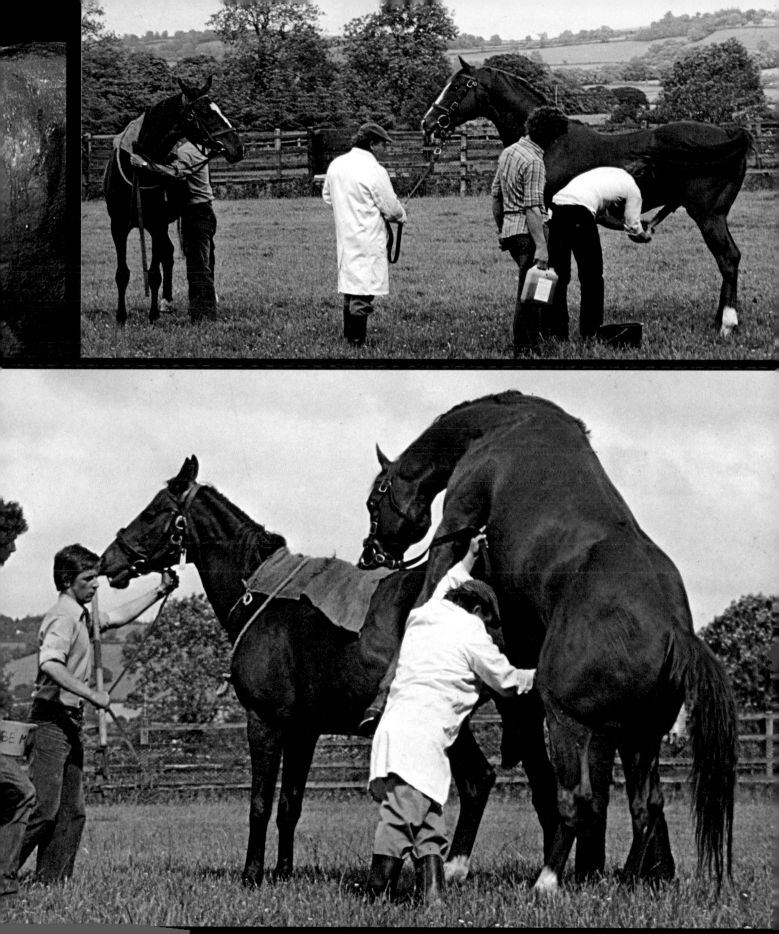

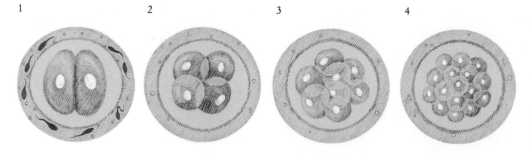

1   2   3   4

The cellular division of the ovum.
1, Once the fertile ovum has split into two cells no further sperms can penetrate its outer envelope. 2, Four cells. 3, Eight cells. 4, The embryo in its primitive stage consists of a cluster of globular cells presenting a surface like a mulberry or blackberry.

Below *Stages of birth. The foetus is connected to the dam by the umbilical vein. Normal presentation is followed by the breaking of the waters. Finally the forefeet begin to emerge.*

is inadvertently presented to the stallion in the mating yard, she may kick and injure the stallion in his attempts to mount. It is therefore essential that the mare is in a state of receptivity (oestrus) and it is for this reason that the ritual of trying or teasing mares has been devised. This entails subjecting mares to the attention of a male horse – either the stallion or one kept specifically for this purpose (the teaser) – to evoke sexual signs.

Veterinary surgeons also help in this. They can palpate the ovaries and uterus through the rectum and observe the cervix through a vaginal speculum to confirm the sexual state and to diagnose problems of infertility. Thus it is possible to determine whether or not a mare is in oestrus or in dioestrus and, after twenty to thirty days, to diagnose pregnancy. These examinations may be performed with the mare restrained in stocks or at the entrance to a stall or loose box.

Mating, pregnancy and birth
At the selected time of oestrus, when it is anticipated by veterinary rectal examinations that a 'ripe' follicle is present in one or other of the ovaries, the mare is presented to the stallion. The covering shed or yard should have a firm and dust-free floor. Many stud farms prefer sand or sawdust for the purpose. Mating takes place with mare restrained and the stallion led in hand.

The egg is fertilised in the fallopian tube and rapidly divides as it descends, by the sixth day, into the uterus. In the uterus it develops for a minimum of 320–360 days, and a maximum of 340 days being the average. The developing foal (foetus, embryo) depends on its placental membranes for nourishment. It starts as a single cell formed from the fertilization of the egg (the size of a very small grain of sand) and the sperm (about a thousandth of the size of the egg); in thoroughbreds, it grows to about fifty kg and 120 cm in length.

It is thought that the mare probably has the capacity to decide the hour of birth. Generally, she will prefer to foal during the hours of darkness. However it is accepted,

in scientific circles, that the foetus determines the day or week of foaling through its hormonal system acting on the mare's uterus. The event can be divided into three phases – the first, second and third stages of labour. During the first stage, the foal turns into an upright position with its forelegs and head extended. The uterine muscles contract causing the mare to show signs of pain. As the placenta ruptures and the fluid it contains escapes, the mare goes into second stage labour with powerful expulsive efforts that expel the foal within a maximum of an hour, given normal conditions. The foetal membranes are then delivered as the after birth which completes third stage labour.

The newborn foal
The foal stands for the first time within an hour of being born and sucks from the mare within about two hours. Thereafter it develops a close bond with its dam, following her and feeding from her. However, as it grows older, it indulges in bouts of play with other foals in the herd and becomes increasingly independent of its mother, grazing and wandering further from her immediate vicinity and returning only for bouts of suckling. In this way the foal develops the social bonds of the herd.

Weaning
In natural circumstances the mare weans her foal just before she is due to give birth to her next foal. Under most modern systems of management, however, the foal is weaned artificially at about the age of five months. Some studs prefer to separate a group of foals from their dams at a given moment, confining them to loose boxes while removing the mares out of earshot. A different and normally successful method is to wean from a paddock, in which a group of mares and their foals have been running together. One or two mares are then removed from the paddock at intervals of two or three days, leaving their foals running with the 'herd'. The weaned foals settle reasonably quickly without their mothers; the process is continued until all the mares have been removed.

Foetal Position

The Embryo

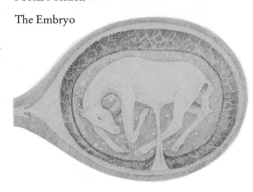

1st Stage of labour

2nd Stage of labour

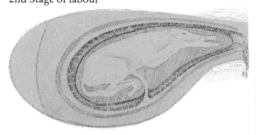

3rd Stage of labour

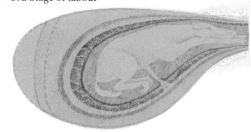

A foal after birth. Almost immediately after birth the foal will begin to feel the need for food. The mare will push the foal to encourage it to stand, and soon after it will seek the udder. It may need to be guided to the udder. The colostral (first) milk clears the bowels of the new-born foal and empties them of the pitch-like substance with which the intestines of all new-born mammals are filled.

Diseases of breeding horses and foals

Red worm parasites

Perhaps the most dangerous threat to young horses is that of the red worm, *Strongylus vulgaris*. This parasite lives in the large gut, its females laying eggs which pass on to the pasture in the horse's droppings. From here, the eggs hatch into larvae, which are then eaten by grazing horses. It is the larvae that do the most serious harm because they get into the blood system.

Young horses under the age of three years are most susceptible to the wandering red worm larvae. They should therefore be grazed only on paddocks which are comparatively free from the parasites.

The control of red worm, however, rests largely on feeding drugs at regular intervals to destroy the parasites in the gut and to prevent the females from laying eggs. Treatment on a monthly or six weekly basis is the pattern favoured by many stud managers and veterinarians.

Microbes

Microbes are another common cause of disease in horses of all ages. The most serious consequence come with the infection of pregnant mares with the 'rhino-pneumonitis' virus. This can cause abortion and, in a small number of instances, paralysis and even the mare's death. Fortunately these outbreaks are relatively uncommon. The abortions usually occur in the last third of pregnancy, although the virus may cause stillbirth or illness and death in the newborn foal.

Venereal diseases caused by bacteria may be a cause of infertility and can be spread extensively by a stallion, should he be allowed to cover an infected mare. Other causes of infertility include non-infectious diseases of the uterus, tumours of the ovary, poor conformation of the vulva and perineum and old age. The mare's productive life decreases markedly after the age of twelve years.

Diseases of foals

There is still quite a high incidence of foal deaths in the first month of life from infectious and non-infectious causes. Prematurity, deformities and brain damage contribute the largest proportion of loss. Disorders of bone growth may affect the foal and yearling. Strangles and respiratory infections from virus and bacteria may cause a 'snotty nose' condition, enlarged glands and fever in epidemic proportions if not strictly controlled.

A mare and foal at the National Stud at Newmarket. At the start of their lives, foals are almost completely dependent on their mothers, but show increasing confidence and independence until they are weaned away from the mares at about five months old. Two basic methods are to separate mare and foal completely, out of earshot, at a given moment or to move the mares gradually to another paddock while the foals are left to run together.

The Leg and Foot

The way in which horses gallop when racing accentuates the risks to which half a ton of body subjects such slender limbs, however well adapted they are for the task of carrying such a weight. The sprain or injury to any of the tissues in the structures of the limb may be the result of one misstep or the cumulative effect of the work the horse is asked to do; but the background to these problems lies in evolution, genetic structure (inheritance) development during foetal, neonatal and formative development in the paddocks and stables where the individual horse has been reared.

The diagnosis

Development depends on feeding, exercise and other factors which are in the hands of management. Thus injuries of the forelimb in horses should not be approached in isolation to the moment at which they occur, as a substantial number are pre-determined by prior events. Of course, there are many injuries that are specifically the result of trauma, inadventently sustained by stumbling or knocks incurred during sports such as polo or showjumping.

The question which has to be solved is which injuries fall into one or other of these groups and, following this diagnosis what can be done to prevent similar occurrences in the future. This is a matter for research based on some defined endpoint regarding gait and stride and recent studies using cinematograph techniques to measure stride and gait may provide this definition in the future.

During the evolution of the horse, the muscles in the lower part of the limbs have become superfluous because the limb is not adapted for grasping or for rotating on itself. There is thus no need for the muscles below the knee. The horse's muscles end above the carpus (knee) in the forelimb and the tarsus (hock) of the hindlimb. The powerful muscles of the hind quarters and of the back are those which are most commonly affected by injury (sprains) because these represent the driving power of the horse.

The forelimb

In the forelimb the muscles above the knee are attached by tendons to the pastern and pedal bone below. The extensor group is bunched in front of the forearm bone (radius) and the flexor group behind. The suspensory system is formed by the check ligament and the deep flexor tendon. The stay apparatus is completed by the suspensory ligament, consisting of entirely ligamentous structures that prevent over-extension of the foreleg should the muscles fail to keep sufficient tension on the deep and superficial flexor tendons. A similar arrangement is found in the hind limb.

Common injuries include sprains of the superficial flexor tendon, particularly in the middle region behind the cannon and fractures and inflammation of the splint bones. These two bones represent the second and fourth digits, similar to those of the human hand, that have become superfluous during evolutionary development. They may fracture, become inflamed on their surface and/or in their ligamentous attachment to the third metacarpal (cannon) bone. In these circumstances a callus of fibrous or bony tissue develops following a period of pain and, possibly, lameness. The callus can be seen and felt as a hard enlargement, commonly referred to as a splint.

Other points of damage, where the surface of the bone may become damaged and inflamed resulting in a fibrous or bony growth (exostoses), are to the fine outer lining of the cannon bone (periosteum) often due to small fissure fractures resulting from concussion. This condition is known as sore or bucked shins.

Inflammation at the front of the fetlock joint (osselets) can result from tearing of the insertion of the joint capsule extending across the fetlock joint.

Ring-bones

Sesamoiditis commonly occurs due to excessive strain on the suspensory ligament where it inserts into the seasmoid bones behind the fetlock joint. These bones may fracture causing added complications to this particular condition. Ring bones are another common ailment, and usually arise from tearing of ligaments or joint capsule as they insert into the periosteum lining the bones of the first, second or third phalanx.

Above *A mare and foal running together in the paddock. It is at this early stage that particular care has to be taken over the development of the limbs, as injuries or deformities, however slight, will have a significant effect on a foal's later performance on the racecourse. The foal will also tend to copy the action of its mother in her paces.* **Right** *Landing over the water. The two front legs take the strain of perhaps half or threequarters of a ton landing at around thirty miles per hour.*

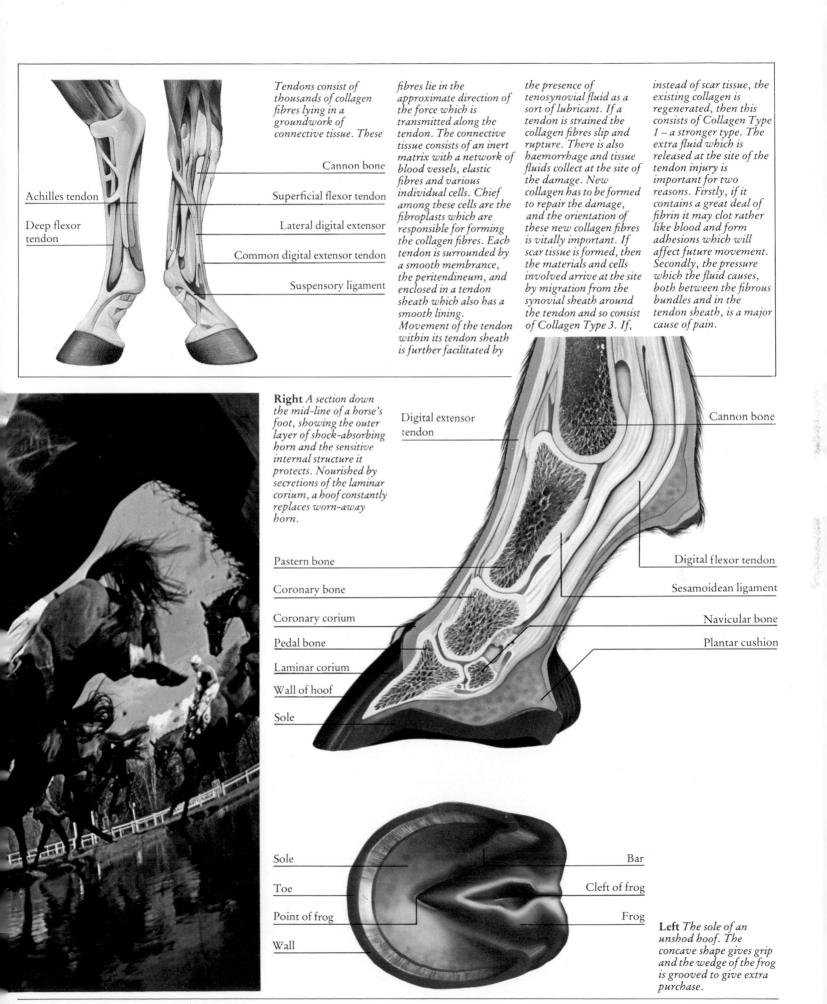

Tendons consist of thousands of collagen fibres lying in a groundwork of connective tissue. These fibres lie in the approximate direction of the force which is transmitted along the tendon. The connective tissue consists of an inert matrix with a network of blood vessels, elastic fibres and various individual cells. Chief among these cells are the fibroplasts which are responsible for forming the collagen fibres. Each tendon is surrounded by a smooth membrane, the peritendineum, and enclosed in a tendon sheath which also has a smooth lining. Movement of the tendon within its tendon sheath is further facilitated by the presence of tenosynovial fluid as a sort of lubricant. If a tendon is strained the collagen fibres slip and rupture. There is also haemorrhage and tissue fluids collect at the site of the damage. New collagen has to be formed to repair the damage, and the orientation of these new collagen fibres is vitally important. If scar tissue is formed, then the materials and cells involved arrive at the site by migration from the synovial sheath around the tendon and so consist of Collagen Type 3. If, instead of scar tissue, the existing collagen is regenerated, then this consists of Collagen Type 1 – a stronger type. The extra fluid which is released at the site of the tendon injury is important for two reasons. Firstly, if it contains a great deal of fibrin it may clot rather like blood and form adhesions which will affect future movement. Secondly, the pressure which the fluid causes, both between the fibrous bundles and in the tendon sheath, is a major cause of pain.

Achilles tendon

Deep flexor tendon

Cannon bone

Superficial flexor tendon

Lateral digital extensor

Common digital extensor tendon

Suspensory ligament

Right *A section down the mid-line of a horse's foot, showing the outer layer of shock-absorbing horn and the sensitive internal structure it protects. Nourished by secretions of the laminar corium, a hoof constantly replaces worn-away horn.*

Digital extensor tendon

Cannon bone

Pastern bone

Coronary bone

Coronary corium

Pedal bone

Laminar corium

Wall of hoof

Sole

Digital flexor tendon

Sesamoidean ligament

Navicular bone

Plantar cushion

Sole

Toe

Point of frog

Wall

Bar

Cleft of frog

Frog

Left *The sole of an unshod hoof. The concave shape gives grip and the wedge of the frog is grooved to give extra purchase.*

Virus infection

In recent years, there is probably no topic that has caused greater comment in the world of racing than what is commonly termed 'the virus'. Every season, horses seem suddenly to lose their form, necessitating in some cases a whole yard closing down for several weeks without having a runner. Even then, when the horses return to races, some of them run far below what is expected of them, and perhaps never recover their true form. Even for trainers, the first indication that his yard has been hit by 'the virus' may come only when his horses start running badly.

The virus of popular belief covers in fact six or seven different types of respiratory infection. These not only produce different symptoms and effects, but in some cases respond to vaccination while in others they do not. It takes several weeks to obtain results from the laboratory to confirm which form of infection is concerned, so that by the time the results are to hand the horse may have recovered. In acute cases, signs of the virus may be clinically apparent, but it is also possible for the horse to be incubating an infection without it being visible. So long as it is not subjected to all-out strain, it therefore shows no signs of ill health during training. It is only when put under extreme pressure at the end of a race that it drops out suddenly.

The complexity of the problem the virus sets to scientists and vets is clear when facts show that in England alone new forms of respiratory infection were isolated at Lambourn in 1972, at Epsom in 1974 and at Newmarket and Malton in 1975, in addition to numerous isolations of both equine influenza and rhinopneumonitis. The horse can be suffering from influenza, pneumonitis, adenovirus, rhinovirus or from any number of other problems that cause loss of form.

Clinical experience in veterinary practice suggests that the affected horse will show one or more of the following signs: poor performance; blowing after cantering or fast work; lack of appetite; raised temperature; 'staring' coat; discharge from the nose or lungs; coughing; small evil-smelling faeces; and signs of stiffness or setfast.

There are two main groups of respiratory infection, equine influenza, and other virus infections, of which rhinopneumonitis is the most prevalent. Equine influenza responds to vaccination and a programme is now routine practice. Young horses sent to the sales are required to be vaccinated and, fortunately, a requirement for vaccination is now becoming a required pre-requisite for many horse activities outside racing.

The virulent outbreak in the Newmarket area in England in 1979 made it evident that, after the initial two vaccinations, the booster given annually did not provide adequate protection and six-monthly booster vaccinations are now recommended. But it is essential to realise that influenza vaccination gives no protection against other forms of virus infection.

The respiratory form of pneumonitis, a virus which can also cause abortion in mares, is endemic and most young horses suffer from it. It is highly infectious, especially where a large number of horses are closely congregated, such as the yearling sales. Unfortunately, primary injections give immunity for only a few months; the horse then becomes susceptible to re-infection. This short duration of immunity, together with the many different strains of the virus, make it very difficult to produce a successful vaccine.

A form of vaccination used in the USA, mainly against abortion rather than respiratory infection, will probably be licenced for field trials at the Equine Research Station in England and elsewhere during 1980. In the same year a new Equine Viral Diagnostic Unit is being established at the Animal Health Trust laboratories outside Newmarket.

Contagious Equine Metritis

Contagious Equine Metritis, or CEM, was first diagnosed in 1977 when the disease reached epidemic proportions in Europe. It is a venereally transmitted disease caused by the bacterium *Haemophilus equi genitalis* and is capable of being spread either from an infected mare to a stallion or vice versa at the time of service. The most apparent symptom of CEM is a copious vaginal discharge and whilst never fatal to the horse, it makes it virtually impossible for an infected mare to give birth.

However, a mare can be a carrier, infecting a stallion at first covering after foaling, and with a stallion covering forty to forty-two mares in a season, an outbreak of CEM can have disastrous consequences for the

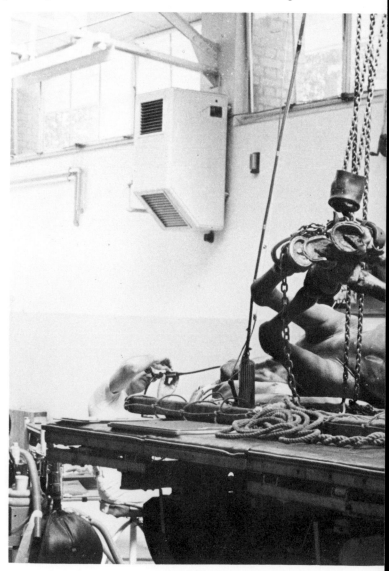

An endoscopic examination of the upper respiratory tract of a horse under general anaesthesia at the Animal Health Trust at Newmarket. Adenoviruses are associated with respiratory diseases in horses, along with five or six other types of virus that cause infection. Signs of infection are poor performance, blowing after cantering or fast work, lack of appetite, raised temperature, staring coat and a discharge from the nose or lungs.

breeder. Treatment for the disease usually means a course of antibiotics, such as penicillin or streptomycin.

Unlike Equine Infectious Anaemia or Equine Influenza, CEM is not a notifiable disease but most racing countries have taken stringent measures to ensure against another epidemic. The USA, in particular, is extremely stringent; in August 1977 the importation of all horses from outside the USA was banned. Three months later, however, the rules were relaxed and young stock and mares under 731 days old were allowed entry, but still not stallions.

In Britain, the Horserace Betting Levy Board, in conjunction with the Thoroughbred Breeders Association, drew up a code of practice for the 1978 covering season. Similar codes of practice were introduced in Europe. By 1979 the incidence of the disease had greatly diminished. Horses for export between countries have to be accompanied by certificates of clearance, as do horses travelling between stud farms within their own country.

Right An ultramicrotome for cutting very thin sections of tissues for investigation under the electron microscope.
Bottom right An electron microscope, a powerful weapon in the investigation of virus diseases in the horse. This instrument is capable of magnifying up to 100,000 times.

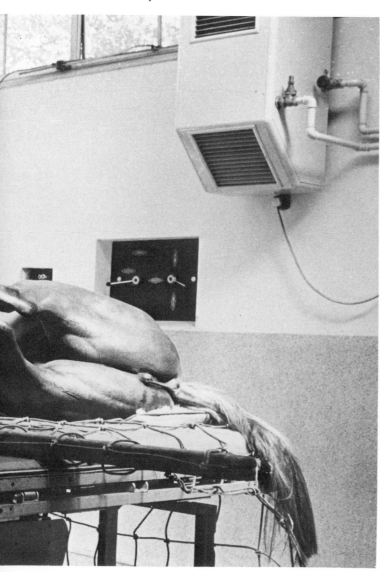

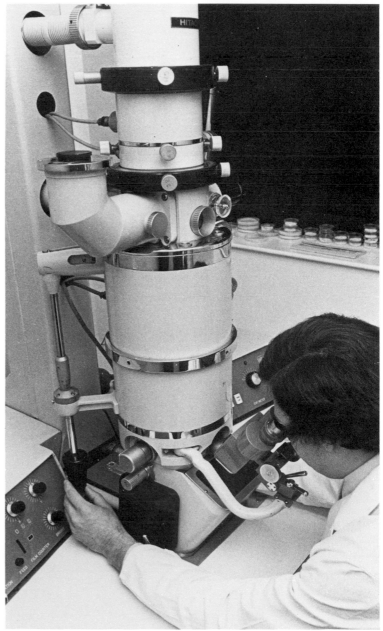

The World of Administration

"Ideally the umpire should combine
the integrity of a
Supreme Court justice,
the physical ability of an acrobat,
the endurance of Job
and the imperturbability
of Buddha."

Time Magazine.

The World of Administration

The administration and control of racing is as complex as might be expected in a sport which, in little more than a decade, has turned into an industry in which the computer has replaced the quill pen very rapidly, if not overnight. But one factor has remained constant; countries throughout the world have looked to Britain to provide a lead in almost every aspect of the control of racing. Rules are not markedly different in the various racing countries. There are Jockey Clubs in five European countries and it is to England that racing authorities still turn for advice on administration and control.

The sport as it is known today has its roots in the mid-eighteenth century. It was at that time that 'control' began. In Britain, the home of racing, corruption was rife, rules were virtually non-existent and fortunes were being won and lost on the turf with scant regard to justice. This led to the formation of the Jockey Club as a means of regulating at least some of the more disreputable practices in the ever-growing racing world.

Formation of the Jockey Club
The Jockey Club was formed, however, not so much to control and administer racing, but as a means by which prominent owners could meet, arrange matches between their horses and make and settle bets. Yet soon it began to influence racing, bringing a degree of honesty and order to the sport, which, up to that time, had been sadly lacking. It published its rules, settled disputes and generally established a reputation which spread throughout the country. As a consequence of this, other race courses began to refer their own disputes to the Jockey Club, which, in turn, agreed to adjudicate only in those cases where it was agreed that its own rules would apply.

Quite rapidly, the Jockey Club had power thrust upon it. Over the next century, it was fortunate enough to number among its members men such as Sir Charles Bunbury, Lord George Bentinck and Admiral Rous. These three great reformers of the turf laid the foundations for the multi-million pound and dollar industry which exists today.

The secretaries
Such a development demanded a formal organization. From 1770 through to the present day, the Jockey Club has been well served by the Weatherby family firm, who have provided the club with its own highly-efficient secretariat. Over the years, the firm of Weatherbys gradually extended their areas of responsibility from looking after the club's business and stakeholding to operating accounts on behalf of owners, collecting entry fees and paying out prize money. The firm maintains the *Stud Book*, produces the *Racing Calendar* and handles entries, forfeits and overnight declarations. Generally, it provides British racing with its own civil service, without which it would be totally unable to function.

Court of final appeal
Making the rules, imposing discipline, licensing participants and controlling the fixture list have been the primary responsibility of the Jockey Club throughout the last century. For most of the time, it has been a self-electing, self-perpetuating oligarchy – autocratic, élitist and dictatorial. Nevertheless the justice it imposed was usually impartial, if often rough; it commanded enormous respect and, in general, served racing well. A similar authority was established by the National Hunt Committee, which governed racing over hurdles and fences; the club and committee eventually amalgamated in 1968.

Modern developments
Developments of the past twenty years, however, have probably been more dramatic than any of those in the club's previous history. The first of these was a consequence of the legalization of off-course betting in Britain.

Until 1961, anyone could bet on a British race course, but, once outside it, it became a crime to do so, unless the punter had a credit account with a bookmaker. For the working man, however, wagering a small sum on a horse involved using a bookie's runner and the risk of prosecution. Legalization was the only answer. It was followed very quickly by the foundation of the Horserace Betting Levy Board, which was responsible for assessing and collecting monetary contributions – or levy – from the betting proceeds. It was laid down that these contributions were to be used for 'the improvement of breeds of horse, the advancement or encouragement of veterinary science or veterinary education, and the improvement of horseracing.'

The last-named was the most important as far as the British racing industry was concerned. With betting shops on almost every corner, the traditional source of revenue – the turnstile – was cut dramatically. Since it was no longer necessary to go to the course to bet, attendances were decimated.

The newly-formed Levy Board came to the rescue, but, as a statutory body, it needed to exercise control not only over raising the levy, but also how it was spent. In order to achieve this, the Joint Racing Board was formed under the joint chairmanship of the Senior Steward of the Jockey Club and the chairman of the Levy Board. Although this is a non-executive body, it provides a valuable forum for the two organizations to meet and formulate policy.

Uses of the levy
The Horserace Betting Levy Board now provides British racing with its lifeblood. Since its formation in 1961, it has produced a total of £97 million for the industry; in the year from March 1978 to March 1979 alone, it raised £13 million.

Prize money accounts for a major part of the Board's expenditure; of the estimated income for 1980/81, a total of £10.1 million will be allocated to it. Courses receive a prize money allocation for each day's racing, the sum varying with the grading of the course. In addition, more than £1 million is made available to boost the value of pattern races.

Over the years, the board has spent more than £21 million on course improvements. Either through grants or loans, it has

helped to finance practically all major rebuilding work on the great majority of courses; there is hardly a new stand in the country which could have been built without Levy Board aid. Starting stalls, photofinish cameras and camera patrol films – technical aids that are all comparatively recent innovations – are all financed by the levy. Similarly, Racecourse Security Services, financed by the Levy Board, has developed dope detection techniques in its fine laboratories which are among the most efficient in the world.

The grants system

Prize money, race course improvement, technical aids and security all come under the heading of 'improvement of horseracing'. The Levy Board also has the statutory obligation to spend its income on the improvement of horse breeds and veterinary education. To date, £4.2 million has been spent in pursuit of these aims. Not only are grants made to horse and pony societies; the board is also responsible for the National Stud, at which stand a number of top-class stallions. These include the Derby winners Mill Reef, Grundy and Blakeney, who, but for the board's intervention, might well have been exported.

Veterinary science and education are matters upon which the board is advised by its own committee of experts. Each year, the board makes a major grant to the Equine Research station and, in addition, it finances research scholarships and special projects.

Pressure groups

While the Jockey Club and the Levy Board are the dominant elements of British racing's administration, various associations representing special interests within the industry have a growing influence. The oldest and most influential of these is the Racecourse Association, which represents the sixty racecourses in Britain. Licensed by the Jockey Club and, in many cases, dependent to a great extent on the Levy Board for their financial viability, the courses are nonetheless major sources of finance for the industry. Turnstile revenue of some £12 million a year, television

income of £2 million, sponsorship worth almost £2.5 million and the £1.2 million earned from the relay of race commentaries to betting shops puts the association in a powerful negotiating position, though, curiously enough, few individual courses produce profits commensurate with their capital investment.

The Racehorse Owners Association, representing a substantial number of the owners of the 11,500 horses in training, has, like the Racecourse Association, an efficient administration of its own to negotiate on behalf of its members. So, too, do trainers, jockeys, breeders, bookmakers and stable staff.

The Advisory Council

The growing role and importance of these associations led the Jockey Club to establish the Racing Industry Liaison Com-

Left *The Stewards' Room at the Jockey Club in Newmarket, where offenders appear on the carpet in front of the horseshoe table.* **Top** *Ken Allday, the Jockey Club's controller of programmes, with the* chart of the 1980 Pattern Races. **Above** *The dining room at the Jockey Club rooms.*

mittee in 1976. This has now been replaced by the Horseracing Advisory Council, an entirely independent body, although it is financed by the Levy Board. With its own chairman, who has taken over one of the Jockey Club's seats on the Levy Board, it provides an independent forum for all sides of the industry to come to and express their views.

Such is the structure of British racing today. In essentials, its aims – the efficient and fair running of the industry – are shared by all racing authorities across the world. But, though the rules of racing differ little from country to country, the mechanism by which they are administered and interpreted does to a greater or lesser extent, as the following examples show.

US administration

As in Australia, the administration of US racing is the responsibility of the individual states that conduct the sport. Not all states allow racing; it is banned in twenty-two states, including Texas. In the remaining states, there are 138 tracks, ranging from Longacres in the north to Del Mar in the south. The task is a formidable one; racing is the largest spectator sport in the USA, with almost double the attendance of baseball.

Until 1930, the American Jockey Club, which was founded in 1939, had overall responsibility for the sport. In that year, however, a New York court decision stripped the club of its authority to license and control racing. It is still the controlling power in New York and Delaware, with authority over the New York Racing Association. On the whole, its rules form the outline for rules in other states, but it has no power to enforce these regulations. Today, its main purpose is the registration of thoroughbreds in the USA; each state requires a registration from the club before it will allow a horse to run on its tracks. The club also maintains the American Stud Book.

Each state has a Racing Commission, responsible to the state governor and controlled by state legislation and the state courts. The National Association of State Racing Commissioners, formed in 1934, provides a standard procedure for disciplinary action at its annual convention, but, again, it has no power to instigate action in individual states.

Bookmakers in the USA ceased to operate in the 1930s; today each track runs its own pari-mutuel pool system. Because of the compulsive nature of racing enthusiasts, the revenue from the tracks payable to the state is considerable. Thus, great efforts are made to ensure the con-

tinuing popularity of racing, both by the race courses' large and highly efficient publicity machines and the states themselves.

Racing in New York

Racing in the USA has no central authority, unlike the major European racing countries. Administration of the sport is the responsibility of the individual tracks, or the state in which the racing takes place. The three major tracks in New York – Aqueduct, Belmont Park and Saratoga – for instance, are run by the New York Racing Association. This was formed in 1955 as a non-profit-making organization to protect the interests of racing in the state.

Before 1955, the race tracks in New York were independent. The tracks themselves were in bad repair and their managements found it difficult to meet operating costs. In 1955, the newly-formed NYRA bought all three tracks referred to above, plus the one at Jamaica, New York, which they promptly closed. Aqueduct had been rebuilt by 1959 and the new Belmont Park was completed in 1968, though Saratoga, almost a national landmark in the United States, has never been rebuilt, but merely maintained so that it might retain its character. Between them, the three tracks now provide racing throughout the year. Aqueduct operates from mid-October until the last week in May, Belmont for the remainder of the year with the exception of August, and Saratoga racing in August.

The three tracks between them account for some 10,000 employees in New York State, from the Off Track Betting Corporation workers to the private stable-owners, as well as those who actually work at the tracks. The three tracks themselves employ 3,000 of these, a figure made up of approximately 1,000 people employed directly by the NYRA and 2,000 independent contractors such as concessionaires, Pinkerton security guards and maintenance crews.

Of those employed by the NYRA, only the accounting staff and the administration stay in Aqueduct throughout the year. The remainder move from track to track, although certain maintenance personnel stay at each track throughout the year.

The administration of the NYRA is headed by the President, who is responsible to a board of trustees. A secretary and council deal with legal matters, while there are five vice-presidents in charge of properties, marketing, customer service, public relations, and administration and finance. The vice-presidents are served by the director of racing operations, who is in charge of all three tracks and decides what

races will be staged where and how the horses are cared for at the tracks. 500 horses are stabled at Aqueduct throughout the year, and 2,500 at Belmont Park. There are training facilities at all three tracks.

While the NYRA is non-profit making, racing certainly is. The average daily handle – so-called because it is the amount of money handled at the track every day – was $2.9 million for the first three months of 1980, a figure significantly up on the previous year. The record daily take was $6,972,209 taken for the 1971 Belmont Stakes. That race was also responsible for the record daily attendance of 82,694 people, who had come to see if the Argentine horse Canonero II could complete the third leg of the US Triple Crown. In the race itself he finished fourth to Pass Catcher, Jim French and Bold Reason, the second and third horses being two he had beaten in the Kentucky Derby.

All profits made by the NYRA are passed to the state government. In this New York is atypical of the US racing scene. For example, the Maryland state government gives a franchise to operate to the owners of Pimlico, and sanctions the number of days racing allowed. Pimlico pays the state five per cent of the daily handle, plus an admissions tax and a property tax. The rest of the money not taken up by operating expenses is profit for the owners. They pay tax on this money to the federal government as income tax.

The NYRA, however, pays the state a smaller percentage of the handle – the figure is two per cent – plus all profit after

Above *At the starting stalls at Aqueduct in New York. Aqueduct is run by the New York Racing Association, along with Belmont and Saratoga. Aqueduct was rebuilt in 1961.* **Top right** *One of the four patrol cameras at Aqueduct. The views of all four feed into the Steward's Room and are also seen simultaneously by the racing press.* **Right** *One of the car parks at Aqueduct which has facilities for 5,000 cars. The track also has its own subway station.* **Below** *Santa Anita racecourse in California, run as an independent company with its own rules of racing.*

operating expenses in the form of 'direct tax revenue'. The federal government receives almost no money from this operation.

The NYRA also pays property taxes to the local governments in whose jurisdiction the tracks are located. The property tax on Aqueduct, for example, makes the NYRA the largest tax payer to the New York City government. Since the NYRA began operations in 1955, it has paid $1.5 billion in total to the state. This accounts for 99.4 per cent of all NYRA revenue after operating costs are deducted. The remaining 0.6 per cent was re-invested as capital improvement of grounds and equipment.

All bets in New York are placed on the pari-mutuel, the United States pool system. NYRA pari-mutuel odds are calculated on betting at the track in combination with betting at OTB offices.

French administration

Racing in France is controlled by the Societé d'Encouragement pour l'Amelioration des Races de Chevaux en France. Although formed at the start of the nineteenth century, this did not take complete control of French racing until 1833, its most conspicuous achievement being the establishment of Longchamp as one of the most successful courses in the world.

The Societé conducts racing in France along the same lines as the English Jockey Club, except for its fruitful dependence on the return from gambling. The Tiercé, a bet which requires punters to select the first three in correct order in a specified race, not only provides huge dividends for anyone lucky enough to win. It is also largely responsible for the healthy economy of racing in France today. As an example of this, during the Second World War some 700 thoroughbreds were taken to Germany and Hungary by the occupying forces, depriving France of her best stock. Nevertheless, due to the profits produced by the pari-mutuel and the high percentage returned to racing from the government taxes on betting, racing in France soon regained its high standard.

Administration in Australia

Australian racing has no less than six individual equivalents of the British Jockey Club. Five of Australia's six state capitals have a principal race club and it is this which acts as the controlling body of racing for the state.

Each club has its role to play and they are not answerable to each other or to any supreme governing body. They are run on a committee system of twelve men or more, elected from the club members by ballot. They all give their time voluntarily and their duty and responsibility is to organize and administer. From the full committee, sub-committees are formed to deal with all business activities associated with courses and meetings.

The exception is Tasmania. For many years there, a deadlock existed between the Tasmanian Turf Club in Launceston and the Tasmanian Racing Club in Hobart. Neither would recognize the other as the senior body, so the simple way to settle the duel for authority was for the state government to set up a Racing Commission. Though the generally-held Australian view is that, in general, commissions of control are generally set up with men of questionable ability and experience serving on them, the Tasmanian Racing Commission has proved a success.

Professional stewards

Another major difference is the Australian use of the steward system to control horse racing. While the British Jockey Club favours amateur stewards, with paid secretaries, only professional stewards officiate in both Australia and New Zealand. Which is the better system is one of the most controversial areas in all racing.

Colour film

Australians regard their professional stewards as having no superiors in the world of horse racing control. For instance, they use colour film for their race patrol filming, a major advantage over the black-and-white film used in Britain. Colour film gives a much more positive picture of any race incident. On this point alone, Australia is well ahead of Britain in its system of race control.

Above *The betting ring at Flemington, Australia, on Melbourne Cup day. Flemington is now to stage a £750,000 race, the richest in the world.* **Below** *The parade ring at* Longchamp in the Bois de Boulogne.

Doping: Drugs and detection

Sophisticated techniques of doping detection now mean that the main areas of doping legislation are concerned with which drugs are allowed and which are not. Although there is a high degree of consistency among the international racing authorities there are some drugs which are permitted in the United States, for example, that are not permitted in Europe.

Some 5,000 racehorses are tested for dope at British tracks each year. This figure represents approximately nine per cent of all horses competing in races. 'Non-normal nutrients', as specified by the British Jockey Club, can find their way into a horse's system no matter how diligent a trainer may be over feeding. Regular feeding with proprietary complete horse foods can lead to a build-up in the tissues of a prohibited substance. In Britain in 1979, of eighteen enquiries following a dope-positive sampling, more than half occurred as a result of branded foods, and in some cases trainers have been successful in recouping losses from manufacturers of such foodstuffs.

In all racing countries, the condition of the horse is the ultimate responsibility of the trainer even if substances have been administered without his knowledge.

In the United Kingdon, breaches of discipline regarding doping are dealt with by the Jockey Club. They are advised on all aspects of doping by the Horserace Anti-Doping Committee. This committee is made up of the chairman of Racecourse Security Services,who monitors the testing and analysis of samples, representatives of the Jockey Club, eminent pharmacologists, analytical chemists, veterinary surgeons and veterinary scientists. In turn, the HADC also advise Racecourse Security Services on anti-doping procedures and policies.

There is no international anti-doping committee, but the HADC attends conferences and meetings with the racing authorities of other countries to keep abreast of developments.

For serious infringement of the Rules, the Stewards may fine the trainer not less that £300 and his licence or permit may be withdrawn at their discretion. However, the Stewards may waive the fine if they are satisfied that the substance or substances were administered unknowingly and that the trainer had taken all reasonable precautions to avoid a breach of the rules.

No matter what the outcome of the preliminary investigation or the subsequent inquiry, a horse tested for dope and found positive is automatically disqualified, no prize money is paid out, and it is listed in the Racing Calendar as an 'also ran'.

Drugs acting on the central nervous system
Drugs acting on the autonomic system
Drugs acting on the cardiovascular system
Drugs affecting the gastro-intestinal function
Antibiotics, synthetic anti-bacterial and anti-viral drugs
Antihistamines
Anti-malarials
Anti-pyretics, analgesics and anti-inflammatory drugs
Diuretics
Local anaesthetics
Muscle relaxants
Respiratory stimulants
Sex hormones, anabolic steroids and corticosteroids
Endocrine secretions and their synthetic counterparts
Substances affecting blood coagulation
Cytotoxic substances

The Jockey Club list of prohibited substances, introduced after an international symposium on doping in Rome in 1977.

Outside the UK

Racing in Australia is organized by individual clubs such as the South Australian Jockey Club, the Queensland Turf Club or the Western Australian Turf Club. They liaise closely with one another and Conferences of Principal Clubs are held to determine their fixture lists and racing rules, including anti-doping procedures.

As a result of these discussions, a standard procedure is followed on all Australian tracks. As horses arrive at the track on race days, they are led to a testing station and every horse has a blood sample taken. Within ten to fifteen minutes the on-course analyst can announce 'all-clear' or recommend to the stewards that the horse be withdrawn because of the presence of a prohibited substance. The clear horses are then taken to the stables where they are kept under close surveillance up to the time of the race. This system effectively prevents drugs being administered to horses without the trainer's knowledge.

The Japanese Racing Association lists over forty prohibited drugs, mostly stimulants and depressants. Horses which have received medication with other drugs are not allowed to race within ten days of their administration.

On race days horses are kept under close watch for 130 minutes prior to the start of the race. After the race, the first three placed horses and any other horse selected by the stewards are led off to a specimen collection area for urine or saliva samples to be taken. The samples are hermetically sealed and JRA personnel transport them to the Laboratory of Racing Chemistry in Tokyo, often by air.

The samples are tested with thorough

---

efficiency as the penalties under Article 31 of the Horse Racing Law for administering substances are heavy – a fine of up to 300,000 yen or even three years hard labour.

Anti-doping legislation in America varies from state to state as there is no national body governing horse racing. The National Association of State Racing Commissioners advise the twenty-six states which hold race meetings and there is now parity on some aspects of dope testing.

Testing is usually post-race by urine sample, and because race meetings last between six to eight weeks at any one track, there are facilities for analysis at most tracks. All winners of the eight or nine races a day are automatically sampled together with a random choice in each race and any others 'on suspicion'. A positive result can mean that the trainer is fined heavily, the horse automatically disqualified and placed last and any purse money returned.

The list of prohibited drugs and their use differ widely. For example, in Arkansas and New York no medication at all is allowed, many other states allow medication up to seventy-two hours before racing, while New Jersey allows medication except on race day. Stimulants and barbiturates are, however, banned by all states. American horses are notoriously prone to leg trouble because of the unyielding dirt surfaces and tight turns of the tracks on which they race, and in an effort to increase the number of horses racing, the use of Butazolidin was legalized in all states save New York. 'Bute' as it is commonly known, is a non-steroidal anti-inflammatory drug which reduces swelling and fever and is also a pain reliever. Whilst this meant that its use enabled a lame horse to race, the problem was that many horses literally ran until they dropped. By 1977 as many as seventy-five per cent of horses at some tracks were racing on 'bute' and following an alarming increase in serious accidents and the death of four jockeys, many states have now banned its use.

France carries out its anti-doping measures in the same way as other European countries and the procedures are comparable to those of the United Kingdom. The stewards of the Société d'Encouragement, under whose rules racing is conducted in France, select horses for urine sampling after each race and use the same list of prohibited drugs. The penalties for administering non-normal nutrients and drugs to horses are similar – heavy fines and the possibility that a trainer may have his licence suspended. In France, however, every winning horse is tested.

Racing in Japan

Japanese Racing Structure

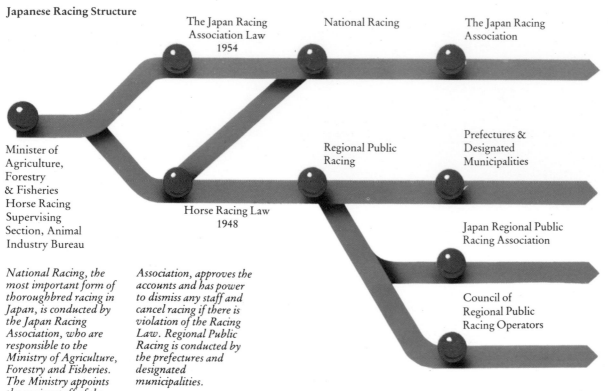

The Japan Racing Association Law 1954

National Racing

The Japan Racing Association

Operation of national racing at 12 racecourses (2 not in operation)
Sale of pari-mutuels
Registration of owners, horses & racing colors
Licensing of trainers & jockeys
Training jockeys & rearing of horses

Minister of Agriculture, Forestry & Fisheries Horse Racing Supervising Section, Animal Industry Bureau

Regional Public Racing

Prefectures & Designated Municipalities

Operation of regional public racing at 31 racecourses
Sale of pari-mutuels
Paying of about 1.2% of pari-mutuels to Japan Regional Public Racing Association

Horse Racing Law 1948

Japan Regional Public Racing Association

Registration of owners & horses
Licensing of jockeys
Subsidy for livestock industry promotion

Council of Regional Public Racing Operators

Liaison and coordination of regional public racing operators (34 operators)

National Racing, the most important form of thoroughbred racing in Japan, is conducted by the Japan Racing Association, who are responsible to the Ministry of Agriculture, Forestry and Fisheries. The Ministry appoints the senior staff of the

Association, approves the accounts and has power to dismiss any staff and cancel racing if there is violation of the Racing Law. Regional Public Racing is conducted by the prefectures and designated municipalities.

The enormous wealth of the Japanese racing industry is derived from the fanatical dedication to gambling shown by Japanese racegoers. Twenty-five per cent is deducted from the betting pool in Japan, with ten per cent going to the national treasury and fifteen per cent being reinvested in racing. With something around one billion US dollars invested on horses each year, the financial viability of racing in Japan is in no doubt.

The Japan Racing Association, responsible to the Minister of Agriculture, Forestry and Fisheries, was formed to run racing after the Horse Racing Law of 1954. Organized racing has been in existence since 1861, but it was after the association had been formed that Japanese racing showed startling growth. A non-profit-making organisation, the association relies on the Japanese government for its working capital of more than £800,000,000. It employs about 1,800 full-time officials and clerks and, in addition, some 2 million casual staff are employed throughout the season, which has around 280 days' racing.

An advisory council of twenty members, who are non-professional, has been established within the association to promote and ensure the impartial conduct of racing. The members include representatives of owners, breeders, trainers and jockeys; they have to be consulted before the association can make any major decisions that will affect any of the groups within the council.

At a lesser level, Regional Public Racing is organized by the various prefectures and designated municipalities. Although they have many more racing days – more than 2,000 – attendances at these meetings is lower than at the twelve racecourses supervized by the Japan Racing Association.

The twelve courses of National Racing provide 288 days of racing a year, with an attendance of approximately 12 million. They generate a turnover almost double that of Regional Public Racing, which has more than 2,000 days racing each year. The higher standard of National Racing shows how much more popular it is with racegoers.

Betting turnover is also considerably lower than at the JRA meetings. Regional Public Racing came into being after the 1948 Horse Racing Law. In order to upgrade the standard of racing in Japan, a series of international races open to foreign competition are being studied.

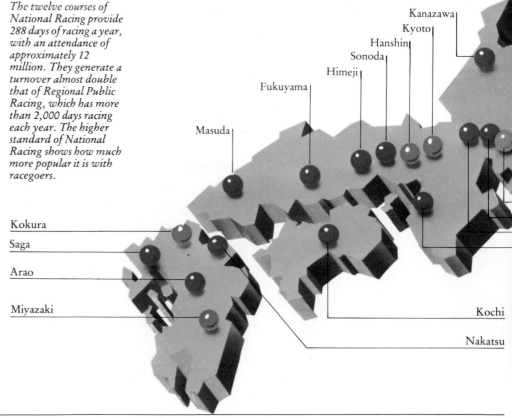

Kanazawa
Kyoto
Hanshin
Sonoda
Himeji
Fukuyama
Masuda
Kokura
Saga
Arao
Miyazaki
Kochi
Nakatsu

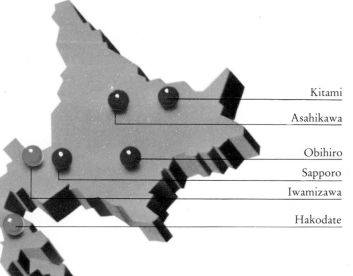

Kitami

Asahikawa

Obihiro

Sapporo

Iwamizawa

Hakodate

Morioka

Mizusawa

Kaminoyama

Fukushima
Miigata
Sanjo

Ashikaga
Nakayama
Funabashi
Ohi
Tokyo
Urawa
Yokohama
Kawasaki
Takasaki

Chukyo
Nagoya
Kasamatsu
Kimiideba

● National racing

● Regional public racing

● National and regional public racing

Principal Races in Japan

Race	Age	Grade	Furlongs	Track
Asahi Hai Sansai S	2	I	8	Nakayama
Hanshin Sansai S	2	I	8	Hanshin
Kikuka Shou	3 F C	I	15	Hanshin
Satsuki Shou	3 F C	I	10	Nakayama
Tokyo Yuushun	3 F C	I	12	Tokyo
Ouka Shou	3 F	I	8	Hanshin
Queen Elizabeth II Commemorative Cup	3 F	I	12	Hanshin
Yuushun Hinba	3 F	I	12	Tokyo
Arima Kinen	3+	I	12.5	Nakayama
Takarazuka Kinen	4+	I	11	Hanshin
Tennou Shou (Spring)	4+ C F	I	16	Kyoto
Tennou Shou (Autumn)	4+ C F	I	16	Tokyo

Nakayama racecourse, twenty miles from the centre of Tokyo. The home of the Japanese 2,000 Guineas and the Arima Kinen, the course has a circumference of eight furlongs with a straight course of one-and-a-half furlongs.

Betting around the World

Betting and bookmakers are as old as racing itself. It has been suggested, for instance, that bookmakers operated on the chariot races in ancient Rome; other sources indicate that bookmaking began in England during the reign of George IV in the early nineteenth century. But, whereas bookmakers have remained the traditional way of betting in Britain, virtually all other racing countries have either banned them or restricted them to racecourses, preferring to rely on the pari-mutuel, or pool, system of betting.

The more betting systems around the world are examined, the more surprising it is that the racing authorities in Britain, which gave racing to the world, was so slow to realize the opportunities to be gained from organized gambling. In France, for instance, the pari-mutuel system of betting had been adopted before the end of the US Civil War; in the USA, though Americans had been slow at first to adopt the French system, all bookmakers had been banned by 1913. Australia allows bookmakers only on the course, while in all other big racing countries, they are not allowed to operate. Yet Britain did not have a tote system until 1929 and the bookmakers' lobby has always been several lengths ahead of the tote monopolists.

British individuality

One reason the British never adopted the pari-mutuel system was the fact that racing in Britain was entirely in the hands of the Jockey Club and there was no interference whatsoever from outside. It was not until after the Second World War that the press gradually became effective with constructive criticism.

Some of the most influential Jockey Club members, such as the late Earl of Roseberry, indeed regarded some of the bookmakers as their friends. He and others like him respected them and, in return, the bookmakers gave them a point or two over the odds, knowing full well that this would be worth their while in the long run. In the circumstances, it is easy to see why the idea of a tote monopoly did not appeal to Jockey Club members.

In due course, the bookmakers went one stage further than Moses in establishing an eleventh commandment – 'Thou shalt not win'. As they gradually became public companies, the commandment changed to 'Thou cannot win'.

Curiously enough, the British betting tax – especially its increase to nine per cent off-course and four per cent on-course, as charged by the bookmakers – helped them considerably in the elimination of the shrewd punter. For instance, Alex Bird,

A £100 book. In the first example the bookmaker will make a profit of £18 He is said to be betting eighteen per cent overround. In a strong market as at Royal Ascot, he may bet less overround than this due to the volume of his turnover. At a small provincial racecourse with a weaker market, he will bet considerably more overround. In the lower example, after taking an extra £50 on horse A the bookmaker has increased the odds on horse B from 3-1 to 4-1 to attract more money to cover the bet on horse A.

Horse	Odds	Max stake	Wins	Payout incl stake
A	6/4	£40	£60	£100
B	3/1	£25	£75	£100
C	5/1	£16	£80	£96
D	6/1	£14	£84	£98
E	6/1	£14	£84	£98
F	10/1	£9	£90	£99
Total staked £118			Max payout £100	

Horse	Odds	Max stake	Wins	Payout incl stake
A	6/4	£90	£135	£225
B	4/1	£45	£180	£225
C	5/1	£37	£185	£222
D	6/1	£32	£192	£224
E	6/1	£32	£192	£224
F	10/1	£21	£210	£220
Total staked £257			Max payout £225	

one of the biggest British backers, had a turnover of about £3 million a year, on which he made one-and-three-quarters per cent. The five per cent turnover tax, as originally imposed, meant a loss of three-and-a-quarter per cent on balance.

This was a great deterrent to heavy backers, especially as, at the same time, the bookmakers reduced their place odds from a quarter to a fifth. While Alex Bird continues to operate on a greatly reduced scale, other professionals found that the tax and the increased general expenses involved in racing made the task of showing a profit not worth the effort.

The pari-mutuel

Pari-mutuel wagering was actually introduced by Pierre Oller, the owner of a perfume shop in Paris in the nineteenth century. Oller consistently lost to bookmakers and disliked the odds they were offering him. He therefore hit on a scheme by which the public could produce its own odds.

Oller sold tickets in his perfume at a standard price on the different horses in each race. From the money thus collected, he deducted five per cent commission and then distributed the remainder among holders of winning tickets in proportion to the numbers sold.

Oller's scheme was such a success that the owners of the Parisian tracks soon took it up themselves. It rapidly replaced bookmaking entirely, becoming the only legal form of wagering at French tracks.

The pari-mutuel is still the basis of the prosperity of French racing today. However, it is the tierce which is responsible for the high prize money. Here the punter has to name the first three in the selected race of the day. On Sunday mornings in practically every cafe in France, backers can be seen filling up their tierce forms in the

hopes of winning a dividend of enormous proportions.

Betting in the USA

The history of American racing suggests that the most important development in that sphere between the end of the US Civil War and the start of the First World War was the introduction of pari-mutuel betting. Copied from France, this gradually became one of the most powerful and richest betting systems in the world.

The first bookmakers in America were the Philadelphia firm of Sanford, Sykes and Eaves, who operated around 1866 with business based primarily on cricket, sailing regattas and trotting races; the American racing manual lists James E Kelley of New York, who opened a book on the 1871 Belmont Stakes, as the pioneer specialist in horse betting.

The industry quickly developed. In an article on the subject published in 1894, the *New York Herald* estimated that the bookmakers at Brighton Beach handled an average of $3,000 each per race. As there were about sixty bookmakers in action and six races per day, the gross handle was in excess of $1 million on a typical afternoon.

The bookmaker usually paid $100 a day to metropolitan tracks for his franchise. Assuming that there were sixty bookmakers, say, in action, the track's revenue was only $6,000. The situation today, however, is dramatically different. Some recent figures show that a New York City track would receive $50,000 and the state $100,000 from a $1 million take.

This was not the only revolutionary change to affect the American racing scene. In the 1870s and 1880s, pari-mutuel betting was tried out in New York, New Jersey, Kentucky, Maryland, Washington DC and Chicago. It received great publicity in October 1872, when a four-year-old gelding called Nickajack won a race at Gerome Park and paid $1,178. The book-makers had been offering the horse at odds of between 5-1 and 20-1, but the mutuel paid an astounding 234-1.

Nevertheless, public prejudice was against the new system. The new fangled machines were even satirized by the comedian Joe Frisco in a cabaret routine. Had a large group of American tracks given pari-mutuel an extended trial, the system would probably have gained acceptance, but, in the event pari-mutuel had to be forced upon the track operators as well as the betters.

The Hart-Agnew bill

In 1908 the Kentucky State Racing Commission ordered that mutuel betting only be adopted in the middle of the Datonia spring meeting. Louis A Cella, the owner of the track, complained that he could not afford to continue operations without books. It was then shown in the *Cincinatti Post* just how much the track benefitted from mutuel betting, compared to the benefits it received from the bookmaking system.

As Cella controlled the books as well as the track, his response was swift. He announced that the track would be closed if bookmaking ceased. Closed it was ten days before the end of the meeting.

The next step came in 1908. On June 11, Governor Charles Evans Hughes, after a long fight to get it through the state legislature, signed the Hart-Agnew Bill into law. As a result, betting became illegal in New York, though, in fact, the bill contained a number of legal loop holes. These meant that wagering could be conducted on an oral man to man basis. Accordingly in 1910 a new law prohibiting oral betting was passed under the Director's Liability Act. Race tracks were made responsible for its enforcement and, as a result, racing was suspended in New York for the next two years.

A more positive step came as a result of events in Kentucky. In 1908, the Mayor of Louisville, home of the Kentucky Derby at Churchill Downs, decided to enforce the law against bookmakers just as the meeting was about to open. On appeal, however, the courts decided that, though book-making was illegal, pool betting was not.

This ruling paved the way for the introduction of the pari-mutuel system, as other tracks followed suit. It was given a further boost when Stonestreet's Derby victory produced a dividend of $123.60 for a $5 ticket. Pari-mutuel thus gradually became the medium through which racing was restored in most states and eventually became the only form of betting in all of them. New York, the first state to try the system, was the last to adopt it.

Betting in Australia

Though betting in the USA is very big business indeed, in the field of betting the Australians have no equal in the world today. The rules vary from state to state and there is great jealously as to which state has the most efficient system.

When, for instance, it was mentioned to some of the officials at Ascot races, Perth, Western Australia, how impressive was the off-course betting system in Melbourne, they replied 'Ours is much better. We invented it, Melbourne and Hong Kong are copying us!'

In Perth, the off-course totalisator pays out after every race and they cannot understand how, in Victoria, that punters accept only one pay-out at the end of the day. When the Perth authorities were told that their Melbourne equivalents were adamant that they did not lose any turnover by this method, they simply could not accept it.

Betting in Victoria is highly developed, largely due to the work of Milton Nicholas, chairman of the Totalisator Agency Board and vice-chairman of the Victoria Racing Association. It was out of his visit to England that Victoria adopted its proposals to deal with off-course betting. The great aim was to avoid the introduction of the English betting shop system, in which punters can hang around the shops all day.

The most impressive feature of the Victorian system is the speed at which the totalisator dividends can be announced. Including all forecasts, this takes place before the horses have had time to pull up after the race. This is largely due to the use of the largest and most sophisticated computer in the world, first introduced in 1963.

Off-course betting has to be completed twenty minutes before each race. The payments are not made until the end of the day to keep punters out of the betting shops. In practice, eighty per cent of all off-course betting is completed by 10am.

A deposit system has also be instituted. The 60,000 accounts with the tote must be accompanied with a deposit. When a client has no credit left, the computer reports this fact and he cannot bet again until another deposit has been made. All betting is cash or credit in hand, so there are no bad debts.

Two sides of the coin in Australia. **Far left** *The computer of the Totalizator Agency Board, run by the government of Victoria, in Melbourne. The main control panel, with two television screens, shows instantly what functions the computer is performing at any time.* **Left** *Seconds after the result of these deliberations has been concluded at Flemington the computer will have adjusted the odds accordingly.*

The deposited money helps the totalisator authorities to defray running costs.

Bookmakers in every state in Australia are allowed to operate only on the course. The system works well and the bookmakers have no complaints. The Waterhouse brothers are two of the biggest operators; one of them, for instance, layed £18,000 to £4,000 on a horse, without even shortening the price. This would be impossible in Britain.

Another bookmaker, Mark Read, who is also a director of the Toolers Vale Park Stud, reports that his turnover by the end of the year amounts to $A10 million. This is based on racing on no more than two days a week.

There is one further fact about the betting industry in Australia which Australians believe has lessons for the rest of the racing world. They argue that the history of betting in Australia clearly indicates that the presence of off-course betting shops — the system so dominant in Britain — serves to hold back the horse racing industry and not to encourage its

development.

Australia can, it is claimed, produce irrefutable evidence during different periods of racing history that horse racing in Perth (Western Australia), Adelaide (South Australia) and Tasmania sunk to a deplorable financial state because of the existence of off-course bookmakers' shops. In each case, when off-course bookmakers were replaced by off-course tote betting, the benefits were almost immediate. Stake money, for instance, rocketed, while the thoroughbred breeding industry also boomed.

Hong Kong and the east
The biggest gamblers on horses in the world can be found in Hong Kong. The turnover per race on the tote at Sha Tin exceeds £1 million. From a day's racing alone, betting supplies the government with £1 million and the track with three-quarters of that sum. Yet the total take-out from the pool is only about 16.5 per cent, nearly ten per cent less than in England and France.

Sha Tin could never have been contemplated, let alone built, without an effective tote monopoly. A tote monopoly also enables racing to thrive in Malaysia and Singapore. There, bookmakers are totally banned and boards all round the rings continually remind you that to bet with bookmakers is strictly illegal.

When there is racing at one of the other three tracks in the area, the gates at Singapore are still opened. The average crowd drawn to bet on away meetings is about 11,000, who get commentaries on each race, together with all betting details. The racegoers appear to become just as excited as when they are watching live racing on the track, which gets ten per cent of all money betted on non-racing days.

The world's biggest bookmaker
No man did more to improve the image of the bookmaker in England — and indeed throughout the world — than the late William Hill, who built up Hill House from scratch and was able to advertise himself as the world's biggest bookmaker.

Far right *The heady atmosphere of the pari-mutuel windows at Arlington Park in the United States.* **Top** *The totalizator board at Gulfstream Park, in Florida. It shows, from left to right, the odds on the third race, how long to the start, the time, the time of the race, a dividend, times at the furlong poles in the last race, the result, and dividends paid.* **Right** *Café betting in France.*

William Hill never bet on a racecourse proper until the Second World War in 1940. He amassed some capital betting on pony races at Northolt, Middlesex, before the war, where he found the jockeys particularly co-operative. This was especially true of the leading rider, the late Tommy Carey, and the two men's friendship continued long after they had both graduated to racing under Jockey Club rules.

Hill's big chance came in 1942. In that year, Big Game, owned by King George VI, had won the 2,000 Guineas and was a short-price favourite for the Derby, for which the leading trainer, Fred Darling, thought him a certainty. Hill, however, decided that Big Game on his breeding would not stay the Derby distance. He therefore laid against him to the tune of £20,000 and, after his defeat, never really looked back. Throughout his career, he was never anxious to discuss the race; nor was he prepared to indicate whether he could have settled up if Big Game had won. There was no doubt, though, that this was

the foundation of his fortunes.

Five years later, Hill took another chance in the Derby. Again it was another 2,000 Guineas winner, Tudor Minstrel, trained by Fred Darling and ridden by Gordon Richards. Tudor Minstrel had won the Guineas in a canter, but was not originally the stable's Derby favourite, a fact unknown to the public. In fact, this was Blue Train, as Hill discovered. He then set about laying Tudor Minstrel, confident that the horse would not stay and knowing that it had not been the original stable hope.

Hill's total liabilities, as admitted by his accountant, Lionel Barber, were £175,000. He also admitted that Hill could not have paid this immediately if the horse had won. Even Hill's closest colleagues at Hill House were nervous, but he knew that he was so firmly established that he would be given time to pay if necessary.

From then on, Hill became a fearless better. In 1959, he said that he had already accumulated bad debts of £750,000, which he considered a total write-off. He also

became a great judge of a classic horse, setting up studs, buying stallions and putting back a great deal of his winnings from punters into the racing industry.

The great coups

George Cooper and Percy Thompson were the two most friendly and popular British bookmakers of the post-war era. Yet they both ended up bankrupt. So did the biggest backer, Hughie Rowan. On one occasion at Windsor, he bet a staggering £48,000 in cash on Montignac, owned by Percy Thompson and trained by John Goldsmith. On this particular race, Rowan was successful, but there was only one end for a man who bet in such figures and who only operated on hot favourites. Before he finished, he was glad to get £25 for his race glasses from another backer.

Other great coups are equally few and far between. In 1925 the American owner A K MacKember landed the autumn double with Fersetti (Cesarewich) and Masked Marvel (Cambridgeshire). The £50,000 cheque paid to him still hangs on

Above *Night racing at Sha Tin, with the race shown simultaneously on* *a giant screen and* **inset** *Sha Tin racegoers.*

the wall at the head office of Ladbrokes. Six years later, H F Clayton went out to win £100,000 when Six Wheeler finished second to Noble Star in the Cesarewich and Disarmament, who won the Cambridgeshire. But what would have been the biggest single win on any one horse by any one backer in the history of racing went down by a neck when Royal Tan beat Tudor Lane in the 1954 Grand National.

The man who lost was Alex Bird. He did not add up the final sum, but calculated that he stood to win £250,000 some time before he finished his betting. Bird's biggest single day's winnings of over £100,000 came in 1952; after having won £70,000 on Teal, he won the following event with his own horse, Signification, backed for a fortune from 100-6 to 7-2.

Bird was the only backer to play the game almost entirely alone. He did not want to know what the trainer or jockey had to say; if the horse came out on top on his figures, he backed it regardless of all other opinion.

Tom Westhead, another professional gambler, landed a tremendous coup when his own horse, Punch, won the Cesarewich in 1937. He also organized the first coup after the war, when Langton Abbot, trained by Teddy Langton and ridden by Tommy Weston, was backed from 33-1 down to 7-1 to win the 1947 Lincoln Handicap in a canter, netting the successful backers over £100,000. Westhead scored again in the same race in 1950.

On an entirely different scale, the eccentric owner Dorothy Paget bet furiously, but almost entirely on her own horses. She was lucky enough to win the Champion Hurdle two years running with Insurance and the Cheltenham Gold Cup five years in succession with Golden Miller, the winner of the 1934 Grand National. To a large extent she relied on the

Right *A bookmaker's pitch on the course in the Tattersall's enclosure. These bookmakers will relay bets to the rails bookmakers via the tic-tac man. Rails bookmakers lean over the rails of the Members' enclosure as they are not allowed in. They will create a market, which will be relayed to the betting shops. Betting shops with heavy liabilities will relay their bets back to the course to force the price down.*
Top *Betting on the tote at Newmarket.*

Horse	Total stakes £	Take-out stakes included £	Longest price laid	Biggest single Bet £	Hill win (+) or Lose (−) £
Accomplice	355	16,551	66	6,600×100	+ 71,546
Chetinkaya	5	2,505	500	2,500×5	+ 85,592
Cracaval	2,728	83,135	66	40,000×1,000	+ 4,962
Dickens Hill	2,111	59,402	25	10,000×500	+ 28,695
Ela-Mana-Mou	7,629	64,677	33	11,000×1,100	+ 23,120
Halyudoh	72	6,622	100	2,500×25	+ 81,475
Hardgreen	4,852	125,596	66	50,000×2,000	− 37,499
Lake City	1,518	52,278	40	33,000×1,000	+ 35,819
Laska Floko	440	20,836	50	5,000×100	+ 67,261
Leodegrance	25	12,525	500	12,500×25	+ 75,572
Lyphard's Wish	7,566	131,234	50	20,000×1,200	− 43,137
Man of Vision	1,918	97,295	66	20,000×300	− 9,198
Milford	7,950	84,320	50	16,000×1,000	+ 3,777
Morvetta	9	3,909	500	2,500×5	+ 84,188
New Berry	1,890	63,077	100	10,000×200	+ 25,020
Niniski	34	2,076	66	250×5	+ 86,021
Noelino	9,313	176,549	66	32,000×2,000	− 88,452
Northern Baby	105	4,315	66	1,000×30	+ 83,782
Saracen Prince	—	—	—	—	+ 88,097
Son of Love	5	335	100	132×2	+ 87,762
Tap on Wood	5,671	84,203	16	14,000×1,000	+ 3,894
Troy	17,122	192,079	25	50,000×2,000	−103,982
Two of Diamonds	1,676	32,643	100	16,000×1,000	+ 55,454
Non-Runners	15,102				
Total Field	88,097				

Above *William Hill's ante-post 1979 Derby book, showing liabilities on each horse. These show only the credit clients' bets and not the huge volume of betting the firm will accommodate on the course and in their betting shops.* **Left** *Luxury beckons punters in William Hill's betting shop in Park Lane. No other country in the world allows off-course betting shops controlled by bookmakers.*

advice of Gordon Richards for her big bets and he rode for her whenever he could. During the Second World War, she failed to arrive in time for her race because of a car breakdown and promptly took steps to ensure that this should never happen again. In spite of petrol rationing, she ordered a spare car to follow her whenever she went racing.

Not all coups have been honest ones. In May 1935, a gang headed by the Welsh bookmaker Gomer Charles attempted a coup on Francasal in a two-year-old selling race at Bath. The plan was to bring in a horse from France to take the place of the English-trained entry and then cut all the telephone lines to the course so that the money bet could not be laid off with the big hedging bookmakers. The horse duly won at 10-1, but, as news of the coup leaked out, hardly anyone was paid. The ring leaders went to court and received jail sentences.

When released from prison, Gomer Charles was murdered on his own doorstep by robbers who knew that he kept large sums of money in his house. They shot him and made off with any money they found, although how much was never established.

The World's Great Racecourses

"Racecourses mean people –
betting, shouting,
chewing, spitting, drinking,
forgetting, counting their money,
cursing their wives.
They come
from every walk of life."
David Hedges.

Epsom

As the home of the English Derby, Epsom, fifteen miles from the centre of London, is the most famous of English racecourses. Visitors from the USA, accustomed as they are to the flat, uniform tracks of their own country, can hardly credit that Britain's most important race takes place on a course that is noted for its gradients. The mile-and-a-half Derby course runs uphill to begin with, this phase being followed by the steep descent to Tattenham Corner. Rising ground is only encountered again in the final furlong of the straight. Horses with indifferent conformation rarely win the Derby as they cannot act on the bends and gradients. The five furlongs course at Epsom starts sharply downhill and is one of the fastest in the country.

There has been racing at Epsom for well over 300 years. In the latter part of the eighteenth century, the twelfth Earl of Derby used to entertain friends for the races at his country house there, The Oaks. At that time there was a growing tendency to replace the long-distance races, usually run in heats, for mature horses with events for younger animals with more emphasis on speed. With that object in view the Oaks, a mile-and-a-half race for three-year-old fillies, was instituted in 1779, and the Derby, a one mile race for both colts and fillies, in 1780. Its distance was extended to a mile-and-a-half four years later. The first Derby winner was Sir Charles Bunbury's Diomed who, at the advanced age of twenty, was exported to America. He retained his virility until he was thirty, and founded a dynasty of great thoroughbreds. From Diomed are descended some of the most famous horses, among them Lexington, in US racing history.

It took the Derby some forty years to achieve recognition as the most prestigious race of the year. It was helped in this process by the greatly increased amount of space given to racing in newspapers and by the rapid growth of the railway system. This did away with long journeys on foot for horses and enabled followers of the sport to travel in reasonable speed and comfort from meeting to meeting. Racing was becoming the business and pleasure of many rather than the recreation of the privileged few.

By the middle of the nineteenth century it had become the custom for Parliament not to sit on Derby day; the prominent politician Lord Palmerston, for example, referred to the Derby as 'our Olympian Games'. During Queen Victoria's reign there was a cheerful air of carnival about Derby day. People went to Epsom less to see the race than to have a generally enjoy-

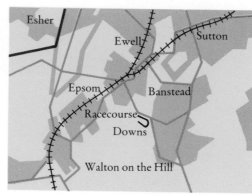

Epsom racecourse is on Epsom Downs, two miles outside Epsom and fifteen miles south-west of London.

The course is horseshoe-shaped, one-and-a-half miles long. The turf lies on chalk, draining well, and there is a watering system. The course rises to the long turn, dropping as it turns into the straight. There is a slight rise in the last furlong. The Great Metropolitan Handicap over two-and-a-quarter miles starts in front of the stands, cuts across the downs and rejoins the course on the far side.

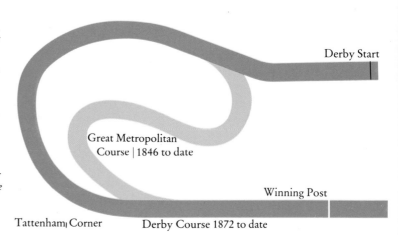

Epsom Downs, Surrey

Turf, LH, 1½m horseshoe and Great Metropolitan H'cap (2¼m) course. 3½f straight. 5f straight course. 6f, 7f starts on chutes.

Major races: The Derby, Oaks, Coronation Cup (all Gp I).

able outing. The downs were transformed into a gigantic fairground, with Sanger's Circus year after year occupying a large area between Tattenham Corner and the winning post. Dancing and other forms of merriment continued far into the night. In this century, however, the fairground atmosphere diminished and the actual race assumed an ever-increasing importance.

The first success of the royal colours in the Derby came in 1788 when Sir Thomas won for the Prince of Wales, later George IV. The previous year Sir Peter Teazle won for Lord Derby. Despite lavish patronage of the turf, no member of the Stanley family was successful again until, on a pouring wet day, Sansovino scored for the seventeenth Earl in 1924.

At least until the middle of the last century, racing was conducted on hap-hazard lines and villainy frequently passed undetected. At least two of Lord Egremont's five Derby winners were four-

Empery, trained in France, winning the 1976 Derby from Bustino who later won the St Leger. The course slopes toward the inside rails, with a rise towards the post. Horses tiring here can hang towards the rails as they meet the rising ground. Winning the Derby puts a stud value on the horse at least ten times as much as the prize money, and often considerably more.

year-olds without their owner being aware of the fact. Lord Egremont usually had over 300 horses in training at Petworth, where the management was notoriously lax. In the 1844 Derby the favourite's chance was ruined by foul riding and the second favourite was stopped by its jockey. First past the post was Running Rein, in reality a four-year-old named Maccabaeus. Largely due to the energy and determination of Lord George Bentinck, one of the leading lights of the Jockey Club, the swindle was exposed. But for him, English racing might have sunk into disrepute.

The first French Derby winner came in 1865. This was Gladiateur, nicknamed 'The Avenger of Waterloo'. Intermittently lame, Gladiateur carried off the Triple Crown, the Grand Prix de Paris and the Ascot Gold Cup. Iroquois (1881) was the first American-bred winner and news of his success caused the temporary suspension of business on Wall Street. The fifth Earl of Rosebery held office as Prime Minister when he won in 1894 with Ladas. There were memorable scenes at Epsom in 1896 when the Prince of Wales won with Persimmon. Four years later he won the race again with Persimmon's evil-tempered

brother Diamond Jubilee. The last royal victory in the Derby was in 1909 when Edward VII won with Minoru, named after Colonel W Hall-Walker's Japanese gardener.

The first Irish-trained winner was Orby in 1906. It was Italy's turn the following year, when Chevalier Ginistrelli's filly Signorinetta won the Derby at odds of 100-1 and followed that up by winning the Oaks. In 1911 Sunstar broke down a week before the race but was skilfully patched up to triumph on three legs and a 'swinger'. Controversy still surrounds the 1913 race when the stewards disqualified the favourite Craganour on their own initiative and awarded the race to the 100-1 outsider Aboyeur. Humorist won in 1921 when suffering from a tubercular lung condition and was dead a fortnight later. The Aga Khan's grey, Mahmoud, set up a record time of 2 minutes 33⁴/s seconds in 1936, while Mid-day Sun (1937) was the first Epsom Derby winner to carry a woman owner's colours. In 1978 The Minstrel was Lester Piggott's eighth winner of the race.

At the summer meeting, besides the Derby and the Oaks, there is the valuable Coronation Cup for older horses run over the Derby course. The most important races at the spring meeting are two events for three-year-olds – the Blue Riband Trial Stakes and the Princess Elizabeth Stakes.

Left *Looking across the course to the stands. The course is owned by United Racecourses Ltd, who also own Sandown Park and Kempton Park racecourses.* **Below right** *The small Princes Stand on Derby Day.* **Bottom right** *Runners parade before the stands. Horses often become unsettled during the parade or during the walk across to the start.*

Newmarket

Newmarket, sixty-two miles from London, is the headquarters of English flat racing and the home of the Jockey Club. It is also the biggest training centre in England, the site of many studs, including the National Stud, and the scene of the principal bloodstock sales. The last jumping meeting there, at which Lester Piggott's grandfather rode a winner, took place in 1900.

It was the Stuarts who developed Newmarket. That uncouth, ramshackle monarch James I enjoyed the hawking and hunting and built a royal palace there. Charles I maintained the royal connection but it was Charles II who made Newmarket a centre for racing. He genuinely loved the sport, rode in races himself and founded the Royal Plates. The Rowley Mile, one of the features of the Newmarket course, is named after him as his nickname was 'Old Rowley', derived from a favourite hack who bore that name.

The Jockey Club was founded around 1750 – the precise date is unknown – and acquired premises at Newmarket. At first the club's authority covered only Newmarket but was gradually extended to include racing all over the country.

There are two courses at Newmarket – the Rowley Mile course and the July course. The former, where racing takes place in the spring and the autumn, is straight for the final mile-and-a-quarter. From the Bushes, a point two furlongs from home, it runs downhill for a furlong into the Dip while the final furlong is uphill. Races of a mile-and-a-half or more start beyond the Devil's Dyke and turn right-handed into the straight at the ten furlongs start. In long-distance races, little can be seen of the early running; hence the description of Cesarewich (two-and-a-quarter miles) spectators as 'hanging about in Suffolk to see a race that is run in Cambridgeshire.' Many horses dislike the long, staring Newmarket straight and even the lion-hearted Brown Jack is alleged to have drawn the line at the Cesarewich.

At one time the Jockey Club adopted a take-it-or-leave-it attitude to Newmarket racegoers that seemed to imply that on the whole they would prefer them to leave it. However urgent financial considerations compelled a change of tune and today care is taken to ensure that visitors feel welcome. The Rowley Mile course used to be distinctly on the bleak side but a modernization scheme, devised by the late Duke of Norfolk and carried through at comparatively low cost, proved completely successful. In 1971 the Rowley Mile course was voted 'Racecourse of the Year' by the Racegoers Club.

Newmarket is partly in Suffolk and partly in Cambridgeshire, seventy miles north-east of London.

Newmarket, Suffolk

Turf, LH (for races above 1m on July Course, 1¼m Rowley Mile Course).

Major races: Rowley Mile – Champion Stakes, 1,000 Guineas Stakes, 2,000 Guineas Stakes, William Hill Cheveley Park Stakes, William Hill Dewhurst Stakes, William Hill Middle Park Stakes (all Gp I), Sun Chariot Stakes (Gp II), Cambridgeshire H'cap, Cesarewich H'cap. July Course – William Hill July Cup, (Gp I), Princess of Wales Stakes (Gp II).

There are two courses at Newmarket, the Rowley Mile Course, which extends around the bend to the Cesarewich Course, and the July Course, used during the summer meeting. The Rowley Mile, over which the Two Thousand and One Thousand Guineas are run, is straight with a dip about one furlong home.

16 furlong Summer Course
14 furlong Summer Course
18 furl... Cesare... Course
16 furlong Cesarewich Co...
12 furlong Suffolk Stakes Co...
14 furlong Cesarewich Course
10 furlong Suffolk Stakes Course
12 furlong Cesarewich Course

Post — July Course

5 furlong Chesterfield Course
6 furlong Bunbury Mile Course
7 furlong Bunbury Mile Course
8 furlong Bunbury Mile Course

Rowley Mile Course
Post

5 furlong Rous Course
6 furlong Bretby Course
7 furlong Dewhurst Course
8 furlong Rowley Mile
9 furlong Cambs Course
10 furlong Across the Flat

The two main races over the Rowley Mile course, both run at the spring meeting, are the 2,000 Guineas, instituted in 1809, and the 1,000 Guineas for fillies only, first run five years later. These two events form part of the five classic races and both are run over a mile. The most notable race for the 2,000 Guineas in recent years was in 1971 when Brigadier Gerard trounced Mill Reef and My Swallow. The Queen won the 2,000 in 1958 with Pall Mall and the 1,000 in 1974 with Highclere.

Two handicaps, the nine furlongs Cambridgeshire and the Cesarewich, form the once highly popular 'Autumn Double'. These races used to inspire heavy betting and some famous coups were achieved. In recent years, though, there are signs that both these events are losing their attraction for the public.

The mile-and-a-quarter Champion Stakes is run in October. It was in this race that the great Nijinsky's career ended with

defeat at the hands of Lorenzaccio. The seven furlongs Tote Free Handicap, frequently a useful guide to the classics, is run at the Craven Meeting in April. In the autumn there are three two-year-old races of primary importance – the Cheveley Park, Middle Park and Dewhurst Stakes – all now sponsored by the bookmaking firm of William Hill Ltd.

The July course, on the other side of the Devil's Dyke, is used in June, July and August and is ideal for mid-summer racing. The paddock is shady and the atmosphere agreeably informal. There is a straight mile; beyond that distance races start on the Cesarewich course and turn right-handed into the straight at the one mile start. The course runs downhill from six furlongs out to the final furlong which is uphill.

The best racing on this course is at the three-day July meeting when the main events are the mile-and-a-half Princess of Wales's Stakes; the one mile Child Stakes; and the Cherry Hinton Stakes, July Stakes and July Cup, all run over six furlongs. The July Stakes, first run in 1786, is the oldest two-year-old race in this country.

It was Newmarket in 1791 that one of the most celebrated of racing rows took place. On October 20, Escape, owned by the Prince of Wales, later George IV, and ridden by Sam Chifney, finished last behind three moderate opponents. The next day Escape ran again and won comfortably. The stewards, headed by Sir Charles Bunbury, held an enquiry and informed the Prince that 'if Chifney were suffered to ride the Prince's horses, no gentleman would start against him'. The Prince stood by Chifney and despite the pressures put on him, refused to take any action that implied condemnation of his jockey. Instead, he disposed of his stud, shook the dust of Newmarket off his heels and gave up the sport that had afforded him great pleasure.

Left *The stands on the Rowley Mile course.* **Right** *Going down to the start on the Rowley Mile. The long, staring expanse of the course has often been known to unsettle a horse, and few successfully lead from start to finish.* **Below** *Crowds during the summer July meeting, when the atmosphere is less formal than at the Rowley course.*

Below *The paddock behind the Rowley Mile stands. The course is named after King Charles II, who was nicknamed 'Old Rowley' because of his favourite hack.*

Doncaster

Records show that racing took place at Doncaster in 1595. The first English classic race, run over one mile six furlongs and 132 yards, named after Lieutenant-Colonel Anthony St Leger of Park Hill, was run at Doncaster in 1776, the course then being at Cantley Common. Two years later, racing itself was transferred to the Town Moor where it has remained ever since. The course is considered a fair one; it is pear-shaped, left-handed and with a straight run-in of four furlongs. There is also a straight course of a mile. Since the Second World War, steeplechasing has been revived at Doncaster. It took place there intermittently in the nineteenth century but the sport was then not of great importance. The present jumping course is reckoned a good one.

As soon as racing was established on the Town Moor, a grandstand was built for under £3,000. It had become positively Dickensian when eventually replaced in 1968. Until 1958 Tattersalls held their main yearling sale in the Glasgow Paddocks at Doncaster, but the sale was then transferred to Newmarket, Tattersalls being unable to accept the new terms offered by the Doncaster corporation, which also runs the racing. The loss was unquestionably Doncaster's, as that grim Yorkshire town can hardly be compared to Deauville in the matter of social amenities, and the sales did much to augment the pleasure and interest of St Leger week as well as attracting a host of visitors from Ireland.

There have been many remarkable races for the St Leger. In 1857 Mr W l'Anson's Blink Bonny, winner of the Derby and the Oaks, was a hot favourite but her jockey, Charlton, had been bribed to pull her by John Jackson, one of the leading bookmakers of his day. The Yorkshire crowd was justifiably furious and gave the filly a hostile reception on her return. The unfortunate l'Anson, who in fact had no part in the plot at all but had foolishly, despite warnings, trusted his jockey, was nearly lynched, his life being saved by the intervention of Tom Sayers, the prize-fighter.

Other controversial St Legers were run in 1924 and 1951. In 1924 certain bookmakers, one in particular, believed that

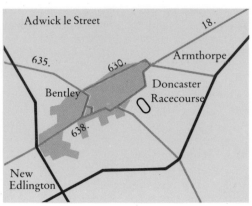

Doncaster is in Yorkshire, 156 miles north of London, and the course, on the outskirts of the town, is easily accessible by train and by car.

Salmon Trout, belonging to the Aga Khan and much fancied by his trainer Dick Dawson, could not possibly win and betted accordingly. At one point the race looked at the mercy of Polyphontes but close to home he suddenly faltered. Then, Salmon Trout, ridden by Bernard Carslake, appeared from nowhere and finished so fast that he won by two lengths. There were some long and disgruntled faces after the race among those who had laid the winner as if his victory was out of the question and the word 'betrayal' was commonly used.

In 1951, Marcel Boussac's Talma II behaved quite abominably in the paddock. He sweated profusely and his conduct indicated clearly that his mind was not on racing. Nevertheless money continued to pour on to him. In the race he went right away from his opponents and won by what the judge estimated as ten lengths but in fact was nearer twenty. No routine dope test was taken afterwards, even though Talma II had never showed comparable form either prior to the St Leger or subsequently.

A less successful St Leger favourite was Cameronian in 1931. Winner of the 2,000 Guineas and the Derby, Cameronian was usually the calmest and most amenable of colts but on this occasion he was in a savage temper. Before the start, he kicked Orpen severely and during the race he pulled impetuously for his head, ran himself out

---

Doncaster, Yorkshire

Turf, LH, flat and jumping. 1m 7¾f circumference, 4½f straight. Straight and round mile courses; all races beneath 1m on straight course. Inside jumping course 12 fences, run-in 247y.

Major races: St Leger, William Hill Futurity Stakes (both Gp I), Laurent Perrier Champagne Stakes, Park Hill Stakes (both Gp II), Doncaster Cup (Gp III).

The grandstands at Doncaster, with the paddock in front of the stands. There is both steeplechasing and flat racing at Doncaster. The St Leger, the final classic, is run over one mile, six furlongs and 132 yards.

2¼ mile start (Doncaster Cup)

Flat Course Winning Post

2 mile 150 yds start

National Hunt Winning Post

1 mile 6 furlong 132 yds start (St Leger)

1½ mile start

1 mile start

7 furlong start

6 furlong start

5 furlong 152yds start

5 furlong start

2½ mile start

Post (6 furlongs)

1 mile start

Post (mile)

3 mile 122 yds start

Post (1 mile 1 furlong)

1¼ mile start

1 mile 3 furlong start

Doncaster is a flat galloping track, with a straight mile. The steeplechase course is inside the flat course. There is also a round mile, starting from a chute.

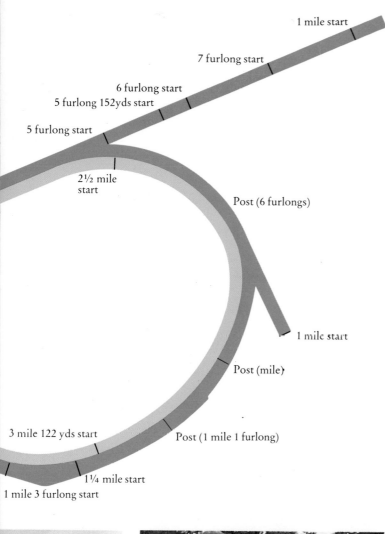

Left *Lester Piggott on J O Tobin at Doncaster. J O Tobin went on to become a champion in America.* **Below** *Owners, trainers and jockeys before the start of the 1977 St Leger. Standing centre is W Carson in the Queen's colours before winning on Dunfermline.*

and finished at the tail-end of the field. The stewards made no enquiry and ordered no tests. For nearly a year afterwards Cameronian ran a slight but persistent temperature.

Four great fillies have won the St Leger this century. They were Sceptre, Pretty Polly, Sun Chariot and Meld who carried off thirteen classics between them. Robert Sievier, who owned Sceptre, was always short of cash and he insisted on running her in the Park Hill Stakes, 'the fillies' St Leger', as well. It was a case of taking the bucket to the well too often and she was beaten. William Hill's Cantelo won the 1959 St Leger after being beaten two days previously in the Park Hill Stakes and her triumph in the classic met with a distinctly mixed reception in consequence. There was a memorable race for the St Leger in 1977 when the Queen's Dunfermline wore down and beat the supposed certainty from Ireland, Alleged, a really good horse that won the Prix de l'Arc de Triomphe that autumn and the following year as well.

The St Leger was run at Newmarket as the September Stakes from 1915 to 1918; at Thirsk as the Yorkshire St Leger in 1940, at Manchester as the New St Leger in 1941, at Newmarket as the New St Leger from 1942 to 1944 and at York in 1945. There was an enormous crowd on the Town Moor when the St Leger returned to Doncaster in 1946, the estimated attendance being 140,000. Recently, however, there have been signs that the St Leger is beginning to lose something of its former prestige and attraction and there have been moves, so far resisted, to make the race open to older horses as well.

Other important races besides the St Leger at the September meeting are the Park Hill Stakes; the seven furlongs Laurent Perrier Champagne Stakes and the five furlongs Flying Childers Stakes, both for two-year-olds; and the two-and-a-quarter miles Doncaster Cup. When the Lincoln racecourse closed in 1964, the one mile Lincolnshire Handicap, run as the Irish Sweeps Lincoln, was transferred to Doncaster and was run as the William Hill Lincoln in 1979. Unfortunately the draw is apt to play a significant part and low numbers are thought to have little chance. It was run on the round course in 1978 but went back to the straight course in 1979. The big race at the October meeting is the one mile William Hill Futurity Stakes, the season's richest prize for two-year-olds. Instituted in 1961, it was originally the *Timeform* Gold Cup and from 1965 to 1975 the *Observer* Gold Cup. The most distinguished winners so far have been Noblesse and Vaguely Noble.

Ascot

Ascot is the only English racecourse that belongs to the Crown. The meeting was founded at the request of Queen Anne who, while driving out one day from Windsor, decided that Ascot Common was the ideal site for racing. The Queen Anne Stakes is traditionally the opening race at the Royal Meeting in June.

The Ascot course is right-handed, triangular in shape and just over fourteen furlongs round. It runs downhill into Swinley Bottom a mile from home and rises for the rest of the way, finishing with a severe hill and a run-in of three furlongs. The Royal Hunt Cup course is a straight mile, uphill all the way. All races over shorter distances that that of the Hunt Cup are run over part of this course. The Old Mile is on the round course and is less severe than the former.

In modern times Ascot has been modernized. In 1961 a new cantilever stand in Tattersalls – the Queen Elizabeth II Stand – was completed at the cost of £1,000,000; three years later the new Royal Enclosure Stand was added.

During this century, up to the Second World War, this magnificent racecourse was used only for the four days of the Royal Meeting at which there were seven races each day, the first race being run at 1.30pm followed by an interval of an hour for lunch. Since 1945, however, there has been a large increase in the number of meetings that take place there – not without some resistance from traditionalists. The late Duke of Norfolk, for instance, declared early in his term of office as the Queen's Ascot Representative that jumping would take place at Ascot only over his dead body. However, the day came when it looked as if there might be need for another jumping course in the metropolitan area, since Hurst Park had fallen into the hands of property developers and the future of Sandown Park appeared to be insecure. Accordingly a course was constructed and jumping began at Ascot in 1965, but it has been no more than a moderate success. The big stands can be lonely places on a winter afternoon, while the racing itself appears distant and remote, strongly reminiscent, it has been said, of Blackpool with the tide out.

The Royal Meeting now consists of six races each day, starting at 2.30pm. There is thus no luncheon interval, as there was in the leisurely days before the war. The long row of tents and marquees on the far side of the course has ceased to exist, though little else has changed. The meeting is a significant social occasion combined with racing of the highest class and a touch of royal pageantry. The Royal Procession, intro-

Ascot is in Berkshire, thirty miles west of London.

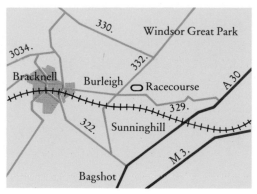

Ascot, Berkshire

Turf, RH, flat and jumping. Flat, 1m 6f 34y circumference, 2½f straight. Straight and round (old) mile courses; all races beneath 1m on straight course. Inside jumping course 10 fences, run-in 210y.

Major races: King George VI and Queen Elizabeth Diamond Stakes (Gp 1), Gold Cup (Gp 1), King's Stand Stakes (Gp 1), Coronation Stakes, Coventry Stakes, Hardwicke Stakes, King Edward VII Stakes, Prince of Wales' Stakes, Queen Elizabeth II Stakes, Queen Mary Stakes, Ribblesdale Stakes, Royal Lodge Stakes, St James's Palace Stakes (all Gp II), plus 11 Gp III races.

Ascot is a right-handed course with a straight mile and a round mile starting from a chute at Swinley Bottom. There is a relatively short straight, and horses must be well in touch with the leaders at the home turn to win. The steeplechase course is inside the flat course.

Old Mile Racecourse

Old Mile

Swinley Course

Ascot Heath

Holloway Gate

Golf Course

Winning Post

duced by George IV in 1820, still trundles down the course before the first race and experienced observers claim to be able to detect the state of the going by the amount the carriage horses are blowing when they pull up.

The most prestigious event at the meeting is still the two-and-a-half miles Gold Cup instituted in 1807, though now most of the best of the older horses are trained for the major european middle-distance events. The last Derby winner to win the Gold Cup was Lord Rosebery's Ocean Swell in 1945. From 1845 to 1853, however, the race was called the Emperor's Plate. This stemmed from an event in 1844, when the Czar of Russia accompanied Queen Victoria to Ascot and saw Lord Albemarle's Defence win the Cup. To honour the Czar, Lord Albemarle changed Defence's name to The Emperor; the Czar in return offered a piece of plate worth £500 to be awarded each year to the winner of the Cup, the title of which would be changed to the Emperor's Plate. However in 1854 the Crimean War broke out and the race became the Gold Cup once again.

There was a sensational race for the Cup in 1907 when the French competitor Eider was disqualified because of George Stern's indisputably foul riding, the prize being awarded to The White Knight. While all the excitement was going on, some enterprising individual whipped the cup off its little table in front of the stand and it was never recovered. Another long distance event at the Royal Meeting is the Queen Alexandra Stakes of two-and-threequarter miles. This is the race the famous stayer Brown Jack won six years running.

The two-year-old events at Royal Ascot form the basis for top-class two-year-old form at least until the autumn. The biggest betting races at the meeting used to be handicaps, such as the Royal Hunt Cup, the Ascot Stakes and the Wokingham Stakes, but betting habits have changed and today more money is wagered on the condition and weight-for-age races. Sprinters also now get a fairer share of the prize money than used to be the case. Less than twenty years ago the winner of the five furlongs King's Stand Stakes received just over £2,000. That race now carrys £35,000 in added money.

In 1951 the Duke of Norfolk and Major (later Sir) John Croker Bulteel, the Clerk of the Course, devised the King George VI and Queen Elizabeth Festival of Britain Stakes, to be run over a mile-and-a-half at the July meeting. It proved such a success that it was decided to make the race an annual event. Today, sponsored by De Beers, it is named the King George VI and Queen Elizabeth Diamond Stakes and in 1973 became the first £100,000 race staged in Britain. Notable winners include Tulyar, Pinza, Aureole, Ribot, Ballymoss, Ragusa, Royal Palace, Nijinsky, Mill Reef, Brigadier Gerard, Dahlia, Grundy and The Minstrel. The 1975 duel between Grundy and Bustino was reckoned the most memorable race at Ascot since 1936 when the 1935 Oaks winner Quashed just beat the American challenger Omaha in the Gold Cup.

There is an important three-day meeting at Ascot in September. Feature races are the one mile Queen Elizabeth II Stakes, the six furlongs Diadem Stakes, and the one mile Royal Lodge Stakes for two-year-olds. Royal Ascot, however, remains a favourite target for radicals who would like to see drastic changes made. There are perhaps certain aspects that seem outdated and a trifle ridiculous but the late Duke of Norfolk always took the view that Royal Ascot was unique and that its popularity in its current form was proved by the very big attendances.

New Mile Lodges

Straight Mile

New Racecourse

Right The winners' enclosure at Ascot with the Royal procession about to enter before the start of the Royal Ascot meeting. Below Looking down the straight mile from the stands. Below left Ascot fashions are as noteworthy as the racing, with an astonishing array of hats on Ladies Day, Gold Cup Day. Far left The parade ring during the Royal Ascot meeting.

Cheltenham

Cheltenham is the home of English steeple-chasing. Some of the most distinguished and colourful characters in steeplechasing history were Cheltenham men; George Stevens, the only man to ride five Grand National winners; 'Black' Tom Olliver who rode in nineteen Grand Nationals and won three; Tom Pickernell who, as 'Mr Thomas,' won three Grand Nationals; Fred Archer's father, William, who won the National on Little Charley; and Adam Lindsay Gordon, the poet of steeple-chasing.

Originally, Cheltenham races took place high up in the Cotswold hills but in 1830 it was decided to move down to the more temperate valley below. There have been four or five different courses in the valley including the present one at Prestbury Park. For many years local opposition to racing, headed by the formidable Dean Close, was strenuous and it was not until 1902 that sport at Prestbury Park was firmly established.

In recent years there have been many changes at Prestbury Park and there are now two courses there – the Old and the New. Neither offers quite the test and the excitement of the original course, when there were four fences from the final bend, starting with an open ditch at the top of the hill, then two downhill fences and the final jump just short of the stands. However, it is undoubtedly an advantage to have an alternative course when the going is heavy, as this means that the Gold Cup, run on the final day, need not be contested on badly churned-up ground. Both courses are left-handed and undulating with an uphill run-in of 237 yards. In general, Cheltenham can be said to represent a fairly tough test for horse and rider.

For many years now Cheltenham has been the permanent home of the important three day National Hunt Meeting in March. For a long time the big race at the National Hunt Meeting was the four miles National Hunt Chase for maidens at entry ridden by amateurs. On the old National Hunt Chase course not a single fence was jumped twice. The National Hunt Chase, though, began to diminish in importance after the foundation of the three-and-a-quarter miles Gold Cup in 1924 and the Champion Hurdle in 1927. Originally

Cheltenham racecourse is at Prestbury Park, on the outskirts of Cheltenham, in Gloucestershire.

There are two courses at Cheltenham, the old and the new. They use the same route, but alternate to provide good going during wet weather. The course is undulating with a hill on the far side, and a severe uphill finish. Jumping ability is at a premium, and a number of horses who have established their reputations with wins at easier courses fail at Cheltenham.

Bottom left *Runners gallop up the hill to start a second circuit during a long distance hurdle race.* **Top right** *Jumping away from the stands to start the final circuit.* **Right** *Hurdlers going down the back stretch.* **Centre** *The second last, with Prestbury hills in the background.*

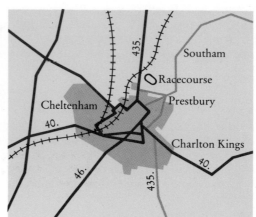

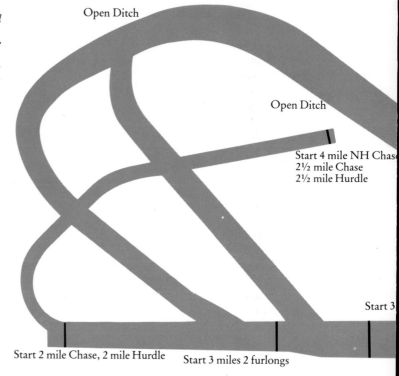

Open Ditch

Open Ditch

Start 4 mile NH Chase
2½ mile Chase
2½ mile Hurdle

Start 3

Start 2 mile Chase, 2 mile Hurdle

Start 3 miles 2 furlongs

Prestbury, Cheltenham, Gloucestershire.

Turf, LH, jumping only. Old course 14 fences, 1½m circumference, run-in 237y. New course, 1½m circumference, run-in 237y.

Major races: Gold Cup, Champion Hurdle. Queen Elizabeth the Queen Mother Champion 'Chase, Sun Alliance 'Chase, *Daily Express* Triumph Hurdle, Arkle Trophy 'Chase, Mackeson Gold Cup H'cap 'Chase, Massey Ferguson Gold Cup H'cap 'Chase.

both these races were run on the opening day and both were worth less than £700 to the winner. In 1979 the winner of the Cup earned £30,293 and that of the Champion Hurdle £22,730. In 1930 only the National Hunt Chase was worth over £1,000 to the winner; now there are nine races worth over £10,000.

The most famous Gold Cup winner to date is Golden Miller, who won the race five years in succession. In 1934 he landed the Gold Cup–Grand National double. Other distinguished Gold Cup winners are Easter Hero, both of whose victories were achieved by twenty lengths; and the Irish horses Cottage Rake and Arkle who both won three years running. The great stayer Brown Jack won the Champion Hurdle as a four-year-old, while Hattons Grace and Sir Ken both recorded three victories each.

Other important Cheltenham races are the *Daily Express* Triumph Hurdle in March; the Mackeson Gold Cup in November; and the Massey-Ferguson Gold Cup held the following month.

Water Jump

Start 3 mile hurdle

Winning Post

Liverpool

Liverpool's racecourse is situated at Aintree, a suburb of that great city. The course owes its existence to the Molyneux family; without them there would probably have been no Aintree racecourse. When the head of that family, the seventh Earl of Sefton, died heirless in 1972, the Molyneux had been associated with Aintree and the surrounding country for 850 years. It was the second Earl and his eldest son, the third Earl, who supported William Lynn, a sporting hotel-keeper, in laying out a course at Aintree in the 1820s. Steeplechasing began there in 1836 and the first Grand National was run in 1837. At that race Lord Molyneux acted as 'umpire' and he continued in that capacity after his father's death in 1838.

The Topham family – immortally associated with the Grand National – became involved with Aintree from 1843, when Edward Topham became Clerk of the Course and handicapper. In 1949 Lord Sefton, acting on financial advice, sold the Aintree course to the Tophams and full control passed into the hands of Mrs Mirabel Topham, a former musical-comedy actress.

There were manifold changes both in the course and in the nature of the fences in the early years of the Grand National but in due course the race came to possess immense appeal to the sporting public. The distance, four-and-a-half miles, and the formidable aspect of the big thorn fences faced with gorse rendered the Grand National a searching test of stamina, jumping power and courage for the horses that competed, and of skill and pluck for the riders. Even now that the fences have been rendered considerably easier by a friendly slope on the take-off side, they still need plenty of jumping. There has always been something heroic about winning the National, and a degree of prestige attaches even to horses and riders that succeed in completing the course. In 1921 only four horses finished, and all, bar the winner Shaun Spadah, had fallen and been remounted. Mr Harry Brown finished second on The Bore with a broken collar-bone. In 1928 the only runner to finish without a fall was the 100-1 outsider Tipperary Tim ridden by a young solicitor.

It can be said that the Grand National reached its heyday between the wars, when on one occasion the attendance is alleged to have totalled 300,000. After the war, however, though the National established itself as a popular television spectacular, the attendance began to dwindle ominously and there was much talk of developing at least part of the the course for building. Indeed, there have been times in recent

Aintree is a suburb of Liverpool, in Lancashire, 250 miles north-west of London.

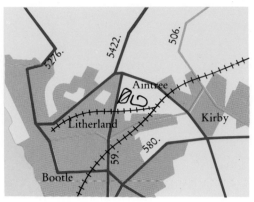

Aintree is a flat, left-handed course, with the smaller Mildmay course inside the Grand National course. The Grand National is run over two circuits, a distance of four-and-a-half miles.

2 miles 7 furlongs 110 yds start

2 miles 6 furlongs start

Plain Fences

Fence followed by Ditch

Elbow

The Chair

Water

Winning Post

4 miles 856 yds start

Plain Fence

Open Ditch

years when it looked as if Aintree was unlikely to survive.

Mrs Topham eventually sold Aintree to a property developer, who, however, soon found himself in difficulties. Luckily the situation has been saved, at least for the time being, by the massive support of Ladbrokes, the bookmakers, while the Grand National has found successive sponsors in a popular newspaper and a Japanese car company. The National, though, has forfeited some of its former dignity and status. The best horses today tend to give the race a miss and concentrate on the Gold Cup, with the result that the bulk of the Grand National field tends to be composed of mediocre performers. Unquestionably the race received a much-needed shot in the arm from the superb achievements of Red Rum.

Two of the greatest Grand National winners were Manifesto and Golden Miller. Manifesto won in 1897 with 11st 3lb and with 12st 7lb two years later. He was third with 12st 13lb, 12st 8lb, and, at the age of fifteen, with 12st 3lb. Golden Miller is the only horse to have won the

Gold Cup and the Grand National in the same year, a feat he accomplished in 1934. In the National he carried 12st 2lb and won in what was then a record time. The following year he was a hot favourite but unseated his rider. The wildest sort of rumours were in circulation after the race and, after he failed in the Champion Chase the following day, his owner, Miss Dorothy Paget, removed him from Basil Briscoe's stable.

The two most gallant losers must surely have been Easter Hero and Crisp. In 1929 Easter Hero carried 12st 7lb in a field of sixty-six. Despite heavy ground and spreading a plate he finished second to Gregalach, a high-class horse to whom he was giving 17lb. The Australian-bred Crisp, carrying 12st, gave a memorable display of jumping in 1973 and was only caught close to home by Red Rum to whom he was giving no less than 23lb. The time was nearly nineteen seconds faster than that of Golden Miller.

There has been a wide variety of successful riders. An American, Tommy Smith, won on Jay Trump and in 1980 another

Aintree, Liverpool, Lancashire

Turf, LH, jumping only. National, 4 ditches (incl The Chair), 2 rail, fence and brook (Becher's, Valentine's), water, 9 plain thorn and spruce fences, 2¼m circumference, 494y run-in. Mildmay course, 8 fences, 1½m circumference.

Major races: Grand National, Topham Trophy, Foxhunters' 'Chase, Mildmay 'Chase.

Top *The former dual champion hurdler Night Nurse leads the field over a hurdle.* **Centre left** *The water jump in front of the stands.* **Centre right** *Red Rum training on the course.* **Bottom** *The ditch at the Chair fence.*

Open Ditch

Plain Fence

Valentine's Brook

Canal Turn

Plain Fence

Becher's Brook

ain Fence

American, Charles Fenwick, won on his own Ben Nevis; an Austrian diplomat Count Kinsky, on Zoedone; and the Frenchman George Parfrement on the five-year-old Lutteur II. Captain Coventry and Lord Manners were officers in the Grenadier Guards, while David Campbell was a future general. Major J P Wilson, partner of Double Chance, destroyed a Zeppelin and played cricket for Yorkshire. Bob Everett, whose heart was always in flying, was awarded the DSO and was killed in the Second World War. Percy Woodland won the Grand National twice, the Grand Steeplechase de Paris twice and the French Derby twice. George Stevens, winner of five Grand Nationals, was killed while on a quiet ride near his home.

The famous fence Becher's Brook got its name from Captain Becher, a somewhat enigmatic character whose military career was of a slightly dubious nature. In 1839 Becher riding Conrad, fell heavily at the brook, was completely submerged and came out declaring that water without brandy was even nastier than he had imagined.

Sandown/Newbury

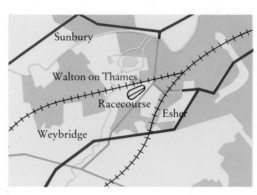

Sandown Park only fourteen miles from the centre of London, is modern as major English racecourses go, the first meeting there having been held in 1875. It was the first enclosed course; until then, charges had been made for entry into the various stands and enclosures, but the bulk of the course was open and free to all.

The man chiefly responsible for Sandown was Hwfa Williams. His brother General Owen Williams was a friend of the Prince of Wales who gave Sandown his support from the start, while Hwfa Williams was chairman and Clerk of the Course at Sandown for fifty years.

The site of Sandown was well chosen, as it is adjacent to a main railway line, while the stands are set on a hill, which, from the point of view of spectators, is ideal. Because of the excellent view of the fences, particularly on the far side of the course, steeplechasing at Sandown has always been particularly popular.

The course is oval, right-handed, and a mile and five furlongs round. From the final bend, there is a steady climb of four-and-a-half furlongs to the winning post. The separate five furlongs course rises steadily throughout. Because of the course's conformation, there are no races over six furlongs or over a mile-and-a-half. A new £3,000,000 grandstand was opened in 1973 and the course now has only two enclosures, the Silver Ring having been abolished, while the Royal Pavilion has ceased to exist.

The main flat race at Sandown is the mile-and-a-quarter Eclipse Stakes run in July. Instituted in 1886, it was the first £10,000 race to be held in this country. King Edward VII won it with the brothers Persimmon and Diamond Jubilee, and the present Queen has done so with Canisbay. The most famous race for the Eclipse came in 1903, when the 1902 Derby winner Ard Patrick just beat the famous mare Sceptre, winner of four classic races, with the 1903 Triple Crown winner Rock Sand a well beaten third. Another great race was in 1968 when the 1967 Derby winner Royal Palace beat the French colt Taj Dewan, with the 1968 Derby winner Sir Ivor close up third.

The five furlongs National Breeders Produce Stakes used to be the most

Sandown Park is at Esher, twelve miles south-west of London.

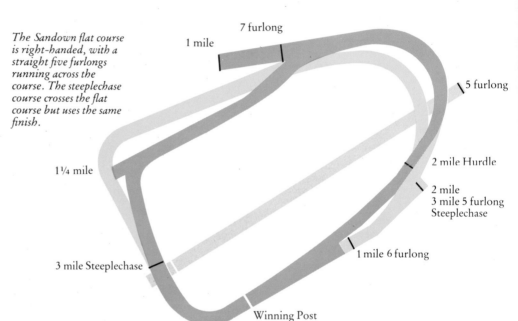

The Sandown flat course is right-handed, with a straight five furlongs running across the course. The steeplechase course crosses the flat course but uses the same finish.

Fighting out the finish on the straight five furlong course, uphill all the way. Horses who win over this course are usually capable of winning over six furlongs at easier tracks. There are no six-furlong races at Sandown.

valuable two-year-old prize of the season and was won this century by such famous horses as Pretty Polly, Cicero, Bayardo, The Tetrarch, Tetratema, Mumtaz Mahal, Tiffin, Orwell, Myrobella, Colombo, Bahram, Tudor Minstrel, Abernant and Palestine. However, since becoming the National Stakes in 1960, it has forfeited nearly all its old glamour and prestige.

For many years Sandown has staged the two-day Grand Military Meeting, once a notable jumping fixture both from the social and the racing point of view, but today the race is not in the least grand and barely military. The Imperial Cup was the most prestigious hurdle race of the season prior to the institution of the Champion Hurdle but it is now no more than an ordinary handicap. The big race over fences at Sandown is the three miles five furlongs Whitbread Gold Cup in April, a race that set the trend in sponsored events under National Hunt Rules. In 1965 it was won by the mighty Arkle under 12st 7lb.

Esher, Surrey

Turf, RH, flat and jumping. 1m 5f circumference, 4f straight. Separate 5f straight course. Jumping course 11 fences, run-in 300y.

Major races: Coral Eclipse Stakes (Gp I), six Gp III races, Whitbread Gold Cup H'cap 'Chase.

Newbury

Quite frequently John Porter, who trained seven Derby winners at Kingsclere, used to travel to London by train from Newbury. In the course of these journeys he came to the conclusion that some land adjacent to the Great Western Railway line and belonging to Mr L H Baxendale would make an excellent racecourse. He obtained an option on the land, but the stewards of the Jockey Club poured cold water on his scheme, saying that in their opinion there were enough racecourses already in existence. Shortly afterwards, however, Porter expressed his disappointment to King Edward VII, for whom he had at one time trained, and the King proved sympathetic. The stewards granted Porter a second interview at which he was given permission to go ahead. The first Newbury meeting was held in September, 1905, with 15,000 people present to christen the course.

Thanks to the railway and to the M4 motorway, Newbury is readily accessible. It is by general consent one of the fairest courses in the country, both for the flat and for racing over jumps. The track is left-handed, oval, nearly a mile and five furlongs round with a run-in of almost five furlongs. There is also a straight mile. Throughout the year the sport is of a consistently high standard. The membership is a large one and, vital for the future of the course, many young people attend the Saturday fixtures.

During the First World War, Newbury was in succession a prisoner-of-war camp, a hay dispersal centre and a tank testing and repair park. A worse fate was in store in the Second World War. In 1942 the course was taken over by the United States armed forces and, in due course, it became one of the main American supply centres. Layers of concrete and hard standing covered the turf and there were thirty-five miles of railway lines. It looked as if racing might never take place there again. It was not until 1947 that the course was released and the task of re-conversion to racing was formidable indeed. Thanks largely to the energy and wisdom of Geoffrey Freer, work was completed and racing was resumed in 1949.

Two significant trials for the 2,000 and 1,000 Guineas – the Clerical, Medical Greenham Stakes and the Fred Darling Stakes – are run at the spring meeting at which another important event is the Group 2 John Porter Stakes of a mile-and-a-half. In May there is the one mile Lockinge Stakes, which in 1979 was worth over £21,000 to the winner. Two-year-old events that can be relied on to attract high-class fields are the Mill Reef Stakes and the Horris Hill Stakes.

Newbury is in Berkshire, fifty miles west of London. There is a station at the course.

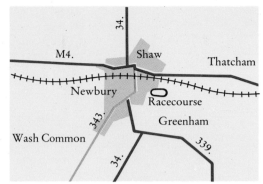

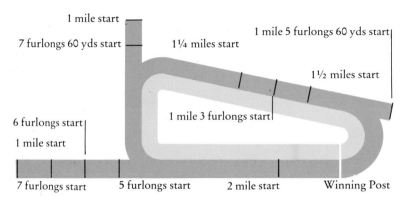

Newbury is a flat, galloping, left-handed course with a good four furlong straight which provides a fair test of horses. The steeplechase course is inside the flat course.

Newbury, Berkshire

Turf, LH, flat and jumping. 1m 7f circumference, 4¾f straight. Straight mile course. 7f 60y, round mile starts on chutes. Inside jumping course 11 fences, run-in 255y.

Major races: Geoffrey Freer Stakes, John Porter Stakes, Lockinge Stakes, Mill Reef Stakes (all Gp II), Hennessy Cognac Gold Cup H'cap 'Chase, Schweppes Gold Trophy H'cap Hurdle.

Jumping at Newbury is particularly popular because such a good view of the running is obtainable. The main steeplechase is the Hennessy Cognac Gold Cup run over three and a quarter miles at the end of November. Arkle won this in 1964 and 1965, carrying 12st 7lb on each occasion, but in 1963 he met with one of his few defeats in this country when he finished third to Mill House. Arkle's second defeat in the Hennessy was in 1966 when he failed by less than a length to give 35lb to the very useful Stalbridge Colonist.

The Schweppes Gold Trophy, a handicap hurdle, was originally run at Liverpool but has now been transferred to Newbury where it has proved an outstanding success, invariably inspiring some very lively betting. Some of the races for the Schweppes have been nothing short of sensational but at least the sponsors have not been in a position to complain over lack of publicity. The Queen Mother won the Schweppes with Tammuz in 1975.

Above *Hurdlers in the straight in front of the stands.* **Below** *Carroll Street leads Jimmy Miff over the water in front of the stands. The Hennessy Gold Cup is a long established sponsored 'chase at Newbury, as is the Schweppes Gold Trophy, run over hurdles.*

Goodwood/York

Goodwood, sixty-five miles from London, stands high on the Sussex downs and forms part of the Duke of Richmond's estates. It is not, and never has been, easily accessible by rail but the reward for the journey is to see racing on what is generally acknowledge to be the most beautiful racecourse in England. The track is right-handed, undulating to a marked degree and not reckoned severe. It was laid out by the third Duke of Richmond and the first meeting took place in 1801. Early on, Goodwood's survival seemed far from certain but both the nature of the course and the quality of the sport were greatly improved in the 1820s.

In due course the four day Goodwood meeting at the end of July was taken to mark the close of the now defunct London 'season,' the fixture combining top-class racing with a social side which, though significant, was far more informal than of Royal Ascot. It was by far the most important meeting of what used to be known as 'the Sussex Fortnight', which also included racing at Lewes and Brighton. Today the quality of the sport at Goodwood's main fixture has tended to suffer due to competition from the Ascot July meeting and from the big prizes that are offered at Deauville. The social side is largely a memory of the past.

Goodwood has, however, retained its popularity with the general public, though the inadequacies of the stands have caused a costly re-building scheme to be undertaken. Until quite recently Goodwood was absurdly under-used, there being only four days racing per year, but happily the season's programme has been considerably extended. The Predominate Stakes, a mile-and-a-half classic trial, is run in May, the valuable Waterford Crystal Mile at the end of August. The Predominate Stakes is named after H J Joel's popular old gelding, who won the Goodwood Stakes in 1958, 1959 and 1960 and the Goodwood Cup, at the age of nine, in 1961.

The Goodwood Cup, instituted in 1812, is run over two miles and five furlongs and is started by flag in front of the stands. A memorable race for the Cup was in 1910 when the great Bayardo, starting at 20-1 on, was defeated by the three-year-old Magic, largely due to the over-confidence of Bayardo's jockey, Danny Maher, who permitted Magic to get a furlong in front. Notable winners of the Cup this century include The White Knight, Son-in-Law, Brown Jack and Alycidon.

The most valuable race at Goodwood in July is the Group I Sussex Stakes run over a mile. In 1978 it was worth over £34,000 to the winner. In recent years it has been won

Goodwood is in Sussex, sixty miles south-west of London, on the Duke of Richmond's estate.

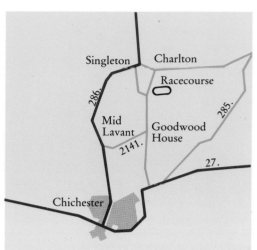

Goodwood is an undulating course on chalk, and provides a test of a horse's conformation and ability to act round turns and on dips and rises. The straight six furlongs starts with a rise, descends for three furlongs and flattens out with a rise at the finish.

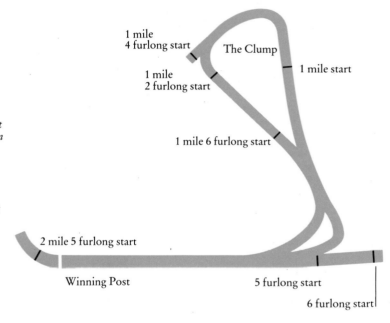

Goodwood, nr Chichester, Sussex

Turf, RH. Straight 6f. 1¼m and up races, 5f straight. 1m races, 4f straight.

Major races: Sussex Stakes (Gp I), Goodwood Cup, Nassau Stakes, Richmond Stakes, Waterford Crystal Mile (all Gp II), Spillers Stewards Cup H'cap.

In the straight, going for the line. Laid out in 1801, the course provides the setting for the 'Glorious Goodwood' meeting at the end of July.

by such fine horses as Brigadier Gerard, Sallust, Thatch, Bolkonski and Wollow. The big betting race of the meeting is invariably the six furlongs Spillers Stewards Cup, a handicap that always attracts a smart field of sprinters. One of the best horses to win that race was the French colt Epinard who landed a huge gamble as a three-year-old in 1923. The main events for three-year-olds are the Gordon Stakes and the Nassau Stakes, the latter for fillies, while the biggest prize for two-year-olds is the six furlongs Richmond Stakes.

One of the most distinguished of Goodwood winners was the gallant Hungarian mare Kincsem, who carried off the Cup and retired to stud the unbeaten winner of over fifty races in five different countries.

York, sometimes referred to as 'the Ascot of the North', is one of the best and fairest racecourses in the country, although in wet weather the going becomes very heavy. Racing first took place on the area of ground known as Knavesmire in 1731. The biggest crowd ever to assemble there was to see the execution of Eugene Aram; the next biggest was in the spring of 1851, when 100,000 spectators came to watch the famous match between Lord Zetland's Voltigeur and the Earl of Eglinton's The Flying Dutchman. Both horses were Derby winners. In 1850, two days after dead-heating for the St Leger and winning the run-off, Voltigeur beat The Flying Dutchman in a sensational race for the Doncaster Cup. The Flying Dutchman, though, had his revenge in the match, which he won by a length.

The course at York, where the profits made are ploughed back for the good of the sport, is a flat, left-handed one of two miles with a straight run-in of five furlongs. The five furlongs and six furlongs courses are dead straight but there is a slight left-hand elbow to the seven furlongs course. A new five-storey grandstand was built in 1965.

The most important meeting at York is the three day one in August, which provides racing of the highest class. The most valuable event is the ten-and-a-half furlongs Benson and Hedges Gold Cup, which, in 1979, was worth £49,200 to the winner. In 1972, the year of its inception, the cup was won by the Derby winner Roberto, who inflicted on the great Brigadier Gerard the solitary defeat of his career. The famous American-bred, French-trained mare Dahlia won in 1974 and again in 1975.

Other important races at York in August are the mile-and-a-half Yorkshire Oaks, which attracts top quality fillies; the mile-and-a-half Great Voltigeur Stakes, often a highly informative St Leger trial; the mile-and-three-quarters Tote-Ebor Handicap, invariably a big betting race; the six furlongs Lowther Stakes for two-year-old fillies; the six furlongs Gimcrack Stakes for two-year-olds; and the five furlongs William Hill Sprint Championship, a race that for many years was named the Nunthorpe Stakes and is still usually referred by its former title.

The Gimcrack Stakes, named after the little grey horse Gimcrack, was first run in 1846. By tradition the owner of the winner makes the principal speech at the annual York dinner of the Gimcrack Club in December. It was at the 1887 Gimcrack dinner that Lord Durham sparked off a notorious racing quarrel by directing highly-critical remarks at the stable in

York racecourse is on the Knavesmire, on the edge of York city, 200 miles north of London.

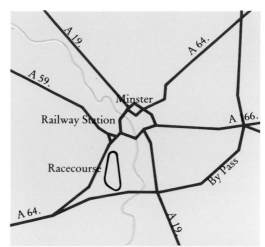

The track is a flat, left-handed horseshoe, which provides a good galloping test. The Mecca-Dante Stakes here is a popular Derby trial, despite the difference in the courses at York and Epsom.

Below *A close finish in a sprint at York. The August meeting at York attracts top class horses, and the Benson and Hedges Gold Cup, run over one mile two-and-a-half furlongs, is often a natural target for winners of the King George VI and Queen Elizabeth Stakes at Ascot.*

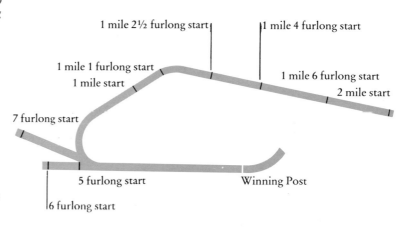

1 mile 2½ furlong start | 1 mile 4 furlong start
1 mile 1 furlong start
1 mile start | 1 mile 6 furlong start | 2 mile start
7 furlong start
5 furlong start | Winning Post
6 furlong start

York, Yorkshire

Turf, LH, 2m horseshoe, 4¾f straight. 6f straight course. 7f start on chute.

Major races: Benson and Hedges Gold Cup, Yorkshire Oaks (both Gp I), Gimcrack Stakes, Great Voltigeur Stakes, Mecca-Dante Stakes, William Hill Sprint Championship, Yorkshire Cup (all Gp II).

which Sir George Chetwynd, a former Senior Steward of the Jockey Club, had a leading interest.

The best horse ever to win the Ebor was Isonomy who carried 9st 8lb to victory in 1879. The course was under water in places and he conceded between 31lb and 56lb to his opponents. He had been the best three-year-old of 1878 but his owner refused to run him in the Derby, preferring to land a gigantic gamble in the Cambridgeshire. Before winning the Ebor, Isonomy had won in succession the Gold Vase, the Gold Cup, the Goodwood Cup and the Brighton Cup. In 1958 the Irish-trained mare Gladness, winner of the Gold Cup, won the Ebor with the utmost ease under 9st 7lb from twenty-four opponents, being backed as if defeat was the remotest of contingencies.

Another important York meeting comes in mid-May. There are two significant classic trials, the Mecca-Dante Stakes and the Musidora Stakes, both run over ten-and-a-half furlongs. Another good race is the Yorkshire Cup, originally run over two miles but since 1966 over a mile-and-three-quarters.

The Curragh

The Curragh holds a unique position amongst the great racecourses of Western Europe. It is the home of all Ireland's five classic races. Long before Lord Derby and Sir Charles Bunbury had tossed a coin to decide whose name would christen a new race at Epsom and still longer before the concept of an Irish Derby was dreamed of, The Curragh was the scene of historic horse races.

To go no further back than the seventeenth century, the first Kings Plates endowed by Charles II were held there. When the inveterate diarist and gossip John Dunton embarked on his Irish travels in 1698, The Curragh was on his itinerary. He described it in the following terms: 'It is a very large plain covered in most places with heath; it is said to be five and twenty miles around; this is the New-Market of Ireland where the horse races are run and

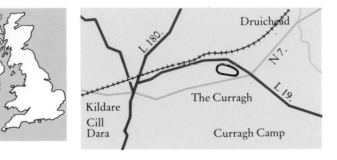

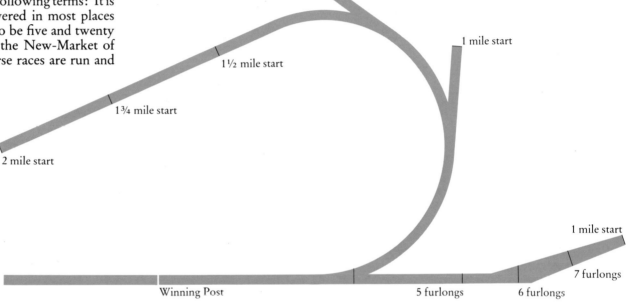

The Curragh racecourse, on which the Irish Derby is run, is a right-handed horseshoe. A wide, galloping course, it is often regarded as a more severe test of stamina than the one and a half miles at Epsom. There are not as many gradients, but there is a gradual rise throughout the last half of the race.

also hunting matches made, there being great store of hares and more game for hawking, all of which are carefully preserved'.

Dunton arrived on the afternoon of Thursday, September 13, to witness the King's Plate. 'There was', he wrote, 'a vast concourse of people to see it from all parts of the Kingdom. My Lord Galway (one of the Lord Justices) was present and other persons of great quality'. While he did not deem it worthy of notice to report the outcome of the race, he did at least record the conditions. 'The horses that run are to carry 12 stone each and the course is four measured miles.'

In view of The Curragh's subsequent development, Dunton revealed an interesting sidelight when he disclosed that, as early as this, 'there are several fine horses kept hereabouts for the Race in stables built on purpose.' By the early nineteenth century, the subscriber lists to the Irish Racing Calendar reveal that not merely were there private trainers engaged by the

big land owners but that public trainers had come into being.

For a long time Irish newspapers shared Dunton's disinterest in carrying racing results; it was not until John Cheng, publisher of the earliest English Racing Calendar, widened his field to take in Ireland in 1741 that the beginnings of a regular set of racing results on even a limited scale were published.

The Curragh of Kildare was described by him as 'Nigh Dublin' and in the light of the many disastrous upsets in form endured by punters in the intervening centuries, it was a nice touch that the first meeting was held on April Fools Day.

The first attempt to initiate Irish equivalents of the Derby and Oaks in 1817 did not succeed, as both the Irish O'Darby (sic) and the Irish Oaks Stakes were shortlived. A more orthodox nomenclature was utilized when the Irish Derby was restarted in 1866 and the Irish Oaks in 1895. Even so, the Irish Derby only barely struggled along in its beginnings. Mr J

Cockin's Selim had two opponents in its first running, while two years later, there was still less money at stake as Mr Holland's Madeira earned £115 for upsetting the odds on Bee Quick in a match race. There were also other unconventional aspects. Selim, for instance, contested four races in the week he won the Derby.

To increase interest in the race, a complex series of penalties and allowances were adopted for the Irish Derby as the other Irish classics came into being, the same procedure was followed for them. It was not until 1946 that five Irish Classic races without penalties and no allowance, other than one for sex, took place.

Of all the riders who have won Irish Derbys few could have matched the versatility of Tommy Beasley. He won the race three times in the space of five years on Pet Fox, Tragedy and Narraghmore and into the bargain rode the winners of three Aintree Grand Nationals and one Grand Steeplechase de Paris.

In 1907 'Boss' Croker's Orby became

the first Epsom victor to contest the Irish Derby and the odds of 10-1 betted on were landed with consummate ease. Subsequently several Epsom seconds like Zionist and Dastur found Irish Derby compensation, but it was not until the intervention of the Irish Hospitals Sweepstakes and the change in name from Irish Derby to Irish Sweeps Derby in 1962 that the event became the new automatic objective for English Derby winners. For a spell,

Right *A rousing finish at the Curragh, the headquarters of the British Army up to 1922.* **Below** *Runners for the Derby. In 1962 the Irish Sweeps organisation boosted the prize money for the Irish Derby from £7,000 to £50,000.*

the Irish race was the richest Derby but those who had imagined that the Derby double would be easy to complete had reckoned without the enormous difference in lay-out between the sharp gradients of Epsom and the splendid wide galloping track of The Curragh.

Larkspur was the first Epsom scorer to put his reputation to the test, but, after an interrupted preparation, he could only finish fourth to Tambourine II. A year later Relko went lame on the way to the post to become the most sensational classic withdrawal of the century. The Derby double, however, was completed by Santa Claus, Nijinsky, Grundy, The Minstrel, Shirley Heights and Troy, although it was destined to elude Charlottown, Sir Ivor, Blakeney, Roberto and Empery.

The Irish Oaks was run at a mile between 1895 and 1914 – a fact which explains why a mare like Americus Girl, one of the supreme influences for speed in the modern thoroughbred, came so near to victory in 1908. A mile was her limit and carrying 10st 4lb she failed by one-and-a-half lengths to give twenty-six pounds to Steve Donoghue's mount Queen of Peace.

Since the Second World War, there has been a regular French presence in the Oaks, an interest that intensified when in 1963 the Guinness brewery took up the sponsorship of the race. Though Marcel Boussac failed with his Prix de L'Arc winner Coronation in 1949, he was back a year later with the winning Corejada. These were fine fillies, but the greatest filly classic ever staged in Ireland was the 1973 Guinness Oaks in which Nelson Bunker Hunt's Dahlia beat the English 1,000 Guineas and Oaks winner Mysterious and the Champion Stakes winner Hurry Harriet as a prelude to a historic victory seven days later in the King George VI and Queen Elizabeth II Stakes.

Yet another filly, La Paloma, won the first Irish St Leger in 1915 while inaugural runnings of the Irish 2,000 Guineas (1921) and Irish 1,000 Guineas (1922) went to Soldennis and Lady Violette.

The Curragh received a new grandstand for the first Sweeps Derby but a more fundamental change came about in a different sphere. Since time immemorial, The Curragh has been common land and those who lived around its perimeter had sheep-grazing rights on it. It was a major revolution in land tenure when all land owners voluntarily surrendered these rights. This permitted The Curragh to fence in the race-track area and add a complex watering system to promote a lush vegetation that would have astonished the racegoer of an earlier day.

The Curragh, nr Newbridge, Co Kildare.

Turf, RH, 2m horseshoe, 3f straight. 6f 63y straight course. 7f (5f straight), new mile (4½f straight), old mile starts on chutes.

Major races: Irish 2,000 Guineas Stakes, Irish 1,000 Guineas Stakes, Derby, Oaks, St Leger (all Gp I), Beresford Stakes, Blandford Stakes, Gallinule Stakes, Moyglare Stakes, National Stakes, Pretty Polly Stakes, Sean Graham Ballymoss Stakes (all Gp II).

Phoenix Park/Leopardstown

Phoenix Park, one of the most impressive and, at 1,752 acres, certainly one of the largest parks in any European capital city, has in its day witnessed a variety of sporting, political and religious events. These included providing, in 1979, the venue for a Papal mass which attracted more than 1¼ million people to the congregation.

As a venue for racing it made its first appearance in 1842 when the Dublin garrison staged a three day meeting there. Initially the venture was so successful that it expanded into a fourth day, but it only survived for a decade and then collapsed. Yet situated as it was less than a mile from the centre of Dublin, it was inevitable that the park would one day rise again; and by the turn of the century, a blueprint for a new course was in existence. This was devised by J H Peard and drew largely on the design of Hurst Park.

Two families – the Arnotts and the Loders – put up most of the money and in 1902 Phoenix Park opened its gates. It made a spectacular impact as the feature race, a five furlong two-year-old event, was worth £1,500, outstripping in value even the Irish Derby. The first running was won by Bushey Belle, trained by J J Parkinson and ridden by John Thompson.

The Phoenix Plate – though few called it anything but 'The 1500' – was subsequently tied-in with the Dublin Horse Show. To this day it provides an electrifying sub-sixty second dash to counterpoint the activities of the more slow-moving show jumpers. Trigo, who won the following year's Epsom Derby, and Astrid Sun, destined to breed another Epsom winner Arctic Prince, were headline winners. Speed is an essential characteristic of the track; in 1979 Miami Springs set a new world record for six furlongs on grass when scoring there.

In atmosphere, racing at Phoenix Park much resembles a garden party, an image fostered by a profusion of roses and bushes and an orchestra situated on top of the tote building playing a repertoire of popular operetta music. Phoenix Park took over the St Patricks Day fixture when Baldoyle closed and now has eighteen days racing during the season.

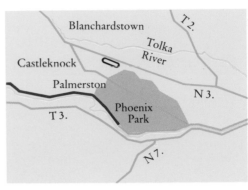

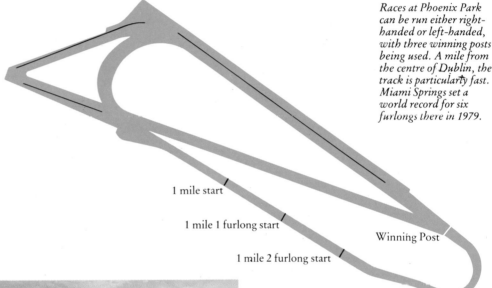

Races at Phoenix Park can be run either right-handed or left-handed, with three winning posts being used. A mile from the centre of Dublin, the track is particularly fast. Miami Springs set a world record for six furlongs there in 1979.

1 mile start

1 mile 1 furlong start

1 mile 2 furlong start

Winning Post

Above *The straight at Phoenix Park. The course has eighteen days racing a year.*
Left *The paddock. With a profusion of roses and an orchestra, the atmosphere resembles that of a garden party.*

Pheonix Park, Dublin

Turf, 1½m circumference. LH, 5f straight for 8f, 9f, 10f races. RH, 4½f straight for other distances 1m and up. 7f start on chute. 5f, 6f straight courses.

Major races: Gallaghouse Pheonix Stakes (Gp I), McCairns Trial Stakes, Mulcahy Stakes, Whitehall Stakes (all Gp III).

Leopardstown

In 1888, amid a welter of newspaper publicity, an enormous crowd made its way out to the fashionable Dublin suburb of Foxrock for the opening of Leopardstown racecourse. With the erection of the first 'Park' course, a new chapter in Irish racing history had begun.

During a slump in land prices a few years earlier, Captain Gerard Quinn had bought more than 200 acres cheaply and he proceeded to lay out an Irish equivalent to Sandown Park, already a proven success in Britain. Not even the discovery that the original five-furlong course was half a furlong short of its correct length detracted from its reputation as the best all-year-round track in Ireland, catering for a mixture of top-class racing on the flat, over hurdles and over fences.

For the greater part of its existence, Leopardstown was managed by Harold and Fred Clarke, but, as land values escalated, the racecourse came under ever-increasing pressure from would-be property developers. Recognizing that it would be a tragedy were the course not to survive, the shareholders decided in the late 1960s to offer Leopardstown to the Irish Racing Board for a fraction of its value.

The Racing Board had not previously involved itself in racetrack operation but this was one offer that it felt bound to accept. Two years later, the new owners embarked on a £1,000,000 re-building scheme, the end product being the most modern and best equipped stands in Ireland offering full under-cover facilities for betting, watching the horses in the parade ring and following the races themselves. Four restaurants and ten bars are among the assets of a giant complex that changes character every night when it houses one of the city's top discotheques.

Leopardstown, which has taken over many of the dates formerly held by Baldoyle, is the most often used course in Ireland with twenty-four days of racing a year. These start in early January and continue through to Christmas. It is quite a change for a place that in mediaeval times served as a leper colony.

Leopardstown is in the suburb of Foxrock in Dublin, some three miles from the centre of the city.

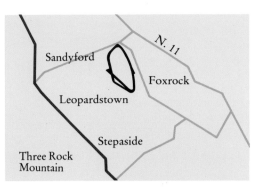

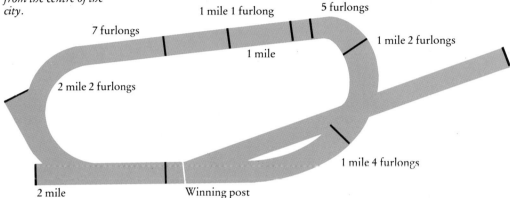

Another strength of Leopardstown lies in the width of the track which, by the simple process of constantly moving the guard rails can offer fresh ground day after day. This important attribute makes possible a varied diet of feature races, all capable of attracting foreign talent.

In February what was the Leopardstown Chase and is now called the Harold Clarke Memorial Leopardstown Chase (three miles) is a major test of form for the Cheltenham Gold Cup and the Aintree Grand National. It was won in three successive years from 1964 to 1966 by the great Arkle. On the same afternoon, a relatively new race but in a class of its own is the Erin Foods Champion Hurdle. Fred Rimell won this in 1979 with another great horse, Connaught Ranger. This is not the only big hurdle prize at Leopardstown won by Rimell, as Comedy of Errors won him successive runnings of the Irish Sweeps Hurdle (two miles), an event that tops the Christmas bill of fare.

The Larkspur Stakes (seven furlongs) for two-year-olds serves as a reminder that Vincent O'Brien's first Derby winner won on this course *en route* to his dramatic Epsom victory. However, in terms of value and prestige, the Joe McGrath Memorial Stakes (one mile two furlongs) is the main attraction. This is a weight-for-age race, which in its first four runnings, produced one French winner, Malacate, one English, North Stoke, and two Irish, Inkerman and Fordham.

Leopardstown. The course is modelled on Sandown Park in England and stages most of the major steeplechase and hurdle races in Ireland including the Irish Grand National, the Irish Sweeeps Hurdle and the Harold Clarke Memorial 'Chase.

Foxrock, Co Dublin

Turf, LH, flat and jumping. 1¾m circumference, 2f straight. 5f diagonal straight course. Inside jumping course 8 fences, run-in 240y.

Major races: Joe McGrath Memorial Stakes (Gp I), BMW Nijinsky Stakes (Gp II), Irish Sweeps H'cap Hurdle, Erin Foods Hurdle, Harold Clarke Leopardstown H'cap 'Chase.

Longchamp

Longchamp today is the product of a major building scheme undertaken by the Société d'Encouragement in the 1960s. The grandstand, which had been built in 1904, was replaced by the present one. The work was completed by the remodelling of the area behind the stands on two levels bordered by the re-designed paddock, the whole being capable of holding very large crowds.

Longchamp is a good galloping course, right-handed, rising in the back straight and falling as it turns into the straight. It is well watered, and there are often complaints of a false surface there. It is generally held that, to win the Prix de l'Arc de Triomphe, a horse must be within the first four as they turn into the straight, which is a little less than three furlongs. This theory was disproved somewhat, however, when Star Appeal, with Greville Starkey aboard, weaved through the field like a snipe to take the race in 1975.

Racing was established at Longchamp when the Emperor Napoleon III, encouraged his half-brother, the Duc de Morny, to establish a new racecourse in the Bois de Boulogne, which had been purchased by the city of Paris in 1852. Morny persuaded the Société d'Encouragement to lease the land for thirty years and to take charge of the new track. The chosen site was on the lands of the former Abbaye de Longchamp, which had been supressed by the revolutionary government in 1790. The first meeting, held on April 26, 1857, drew a crowd of 12,000 spectators. It was the first of seven that year.

Morny was also responsible for organizing the sponsorship of the Grand Prix de Paris, the race which first made Longchamp famous. As prefect of the city, he was well placed to persuade the municipal council to put up 50,000 francs as a prize and also to squeeze another 10,000 francs from each of the five great railway companies to add to it.

The initial Grand Prix was run on May 31, 1863, and attracted five challengers from England, all of whom had contested the Derby eleven days earlier. The favourite in a field of twelve was La Toucques, a French-trained filly who had won the Prix de Diane, although she, too, did much of her racing in England.

La Toucques was beaten by one length by The Ranger, owned by Henry Savile. The result was popular neither in France, where those who wished to bar foreign horses from French courses held the upper hand for most of the century, nor in England, where many were shocked by the news of their fellow countrymen racing – and gambling – on a Sunday. The vic-

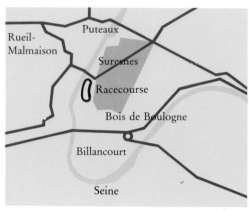

The course at Longchamp is in the Bois du Boulogne, a few miles from the centre of Paris.

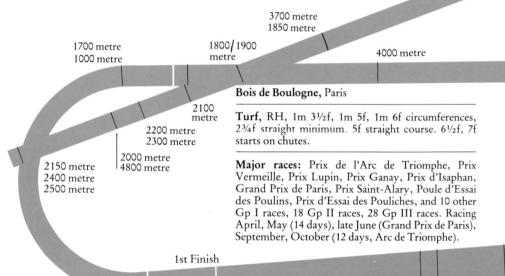

Bois de Boulogne, Paris

Turf, RH, 1m 3½f, 1m 5f, 1m 6f circumferences, 2¾f straight minimum. 5f straight course. 6½f, 7f starts on chutes.

Major races: Prix de l'Arc de Triomphe, Prix Vermeille, Prix Lupin, Prix Ganay, Prix d'Isaphan, Grand Prix de Paris, Prix Saint-Alary, Poule d'Essai des Poulins, Prix d'Essai des Pouliches, and 10 other Gp I races, 18 Gp II races, 28 Gp III races. Racing April, May (14 days), late June (Grand Prix de Paris), September, October (12 days, Arc de Triomphe).

Right A serious business anywhere in the world. French racegoers study form at Longchamp. **Top centre** The paddock at Longchamp, redesigned during the rebuilding of the stands in the early 1960s. **Bottom centre** The straight, with the massive stands behind. The comparatively short straight requires a horse to lie well up with the leaders to have a winning chance. **Far right** Setting out on a circuit. The course rises in the back straight and falls as it turns into the home straight.

The course at Longchamp is one mile, six furlongs round, although races of various distances can be run by the use of loops. The course is always well watered, with firm going rarely encountered. Horses with a marked low action sometimes fail to act on the course. The field for the Prix de L'Arc de Triomphe starts in front of the windmill, races behind a clump of trees and rises to the highest point of the course.

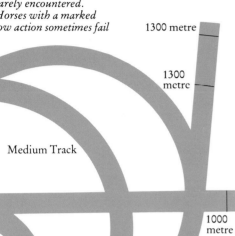

1300 metre

1300 metre

Medium Track

1000 metre

Track

New Track

torious owner did, however, enlist the sympathy of one section of the population, setting a handsome precedent by donating 10,000 francs from his prize to charity for the good of the poor of Paris.

English raiders also took third, fourth and fifth places, so the crowd was wound up for action when the Derby winner, Blair Athol, crossed the Channel to run in the race the following year. The horse was booed, but, perhaps fortunately for the future of international competition, he was beaten. French pride was fully restored when Gladiateur, 'The Avenger of Waterloo', who had already won the 2,000 Guineas and the Derby, made a sensational first appearance on his home soil in the 1865 Grand Prix. The favourite at 3-1, he was twenty lengths behind the leaders entering the straight but swept past to gain a two lengths' victory. His statue stands inside the gates at the main entrance to present-day Longchamp. His triumph so excited the crowd that they tore the rails down and burst on to the course. Worse destruction was to follow, however, during the Franco-Prussian War and the days of the Commune, when the stands were burnt down and the track badly damaged.

Nearco was the last foreign horse to win the Grand Prix. The British have run fewer runners in the last twenty years but the performances of Indiana (1964), Bustino (1974) and the Irish-trained Valinsky (1977), all of whom finished second, show that the race is still well within the range of their horses.

Longchamp's prestige race is now the Prix de l'Arc de Triomphe. This was established in 1920 in celebration of defeat of Germany (although the name had been carried by a selling race a few years earlier). It was won on its first running by the Grand Prix winner, Comrade. Nowadays, success in the Arc sets the seal on the career of a horse. Tesio, who put Italian racing on the map with the victories of Ortello (1929) and Crapom (1933), died too soon to see the greatest horse he ever bred, Ribot, destroying his rivals in 1955 and 1956.

The Arc has had many such memorable moments. One took place in 1965, when Sea Bird showed a brilliant turn of foot to leave Reliance and Diatome six lengths and five lengths in his wake. Anilin, the best horse ever to be bred in Russia was fifth, the Preakness Stakes and American Derby winner Tom Rolfe sixth and the Irish Sweeps Derby winner Meadow Court only ninth.

Ribot is one of only three dual Arc winners since the War, the others being Tanticme in 1950–51 and the Irish-trained Alleged in 1977–78. Other fine winners include Ballymoss in 1958, Vaguely Noble in 1968, Mill Reef in 1971 and Sea Bird's great daughter, Allez France, in 1974. But the Arc is equally capable of producing total surprises, such as the victories of the 81-1 outsider Topyo in 1967, the 52-1 Levmoss, who had apparently shown himself to be an out and out stayer by winning the Prix du Cadran and Ascot Gold Cup, two years later and of the 119-1 German-trained Star Appeal in 1975.

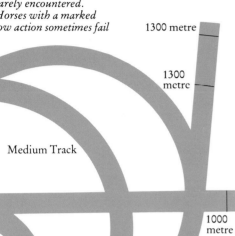

Chantilly

The reason for the comparative lack of popularity of racing in its early years in France was largely due to the unsatisfactory nature of the courses used – particularly the Champ de Mars in Paris itself – and of the only available training ground, the Bois de Boulogne. Thus it is not surprising that the news of an impromptu but wholly successful race at Chantilly, involving guests from the nearby château, soon spread throughout the world of French racing.

This contest took place in 1833, which was also the year of the foundation of the French Jockey Club, an organization which almost immediately proved unsuitable for its intended purpose – that of supervising racing in France. Its members were more interested in social matters and, within less than a year, its founder, Lord Henry Seymour, an Englishman living permanently in Paris, established a replacement, the *Société d'Encouragement pour l'Amelioration des Races de Chevaux en France.* The Société, which now owns Chantilly, Deauville and Longchamp as well as running the sport, organized its first meeting at the Champ de Mars on May 4, 1834 and its first on the new course at Chantilly, which had been laid out in immediate response to the chance discovery of its ideal turf in the previous year, on May 15 of the same year.

Chantilly was soon recognized as an ideal site for racing and many of the then-important fixtures were transferred from the Champ de Mars. Owners quickly realized the suitability of the area for training and most of the big stables were already established there by 1840.

The oldest French classic, the Prix du Jockey Club, was founded at the course in 1836 and was won in its first two years by horses belonging to Lord Henry Seymour – Franck and Lydia. Seven years later the initial Prix de Diane fell to Honesty, ridden by Z Caillotin, one of the first home-born riders. French jockeys soon became commonplace but English expatriates dominated training for most of the century and many of their descendents still live at Chantilly.

Other early innovations included the introduction of handicaps in 1837 and of the racing of two-year-olds in 1838. The course was popular with the rich, many of whom stayed in the neighbourhood for the eight days bounded by the two classics – *la Grande Semaine,* as it was known. The early facilities were primitive and the stands soon had to be replaced. The main feature of the course is the Grandes Ecuries, the palatial stables built for the Prince de Condé, which form an impres-

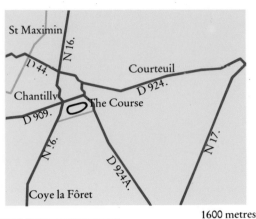

Chantilly, the main training area in France, is twenty-seven miles north of Paris and the home of the French Derby and Oaks.

Chantilly, Seine-et-Oise

Turf, RH, 1m 5f circumference, 3f straight. 9f straight course, round 7f start on chute.

Major races: Prix de Jockey-Club, Prix de Diane de Revlon (both Gp I), Prix Jean Prat (Gp II).

Right *Top hats are the order of the day for the Prix du Jockey Club and the Prix de Diane de Revlon, the French Derby and Oaks.* **Far right** *Part of the stands at Chantilly.*

0 metres

The Lawn

1100 metres
1400 metres

1000 metres
1300 metres
3000 metres

The Straight

Right *The paddock at Chantilly. Although the centre of training in France, with more than 3,000 horses in residence, there are only six days racing a year at the racecourse.*

Bottom left *The field sweeping past the former stables of the castle at Chantilly.*

sive backdrop as the runners begin the long right-handed turn for home.

The course itself has a complicated layout. There is a straight mile, allowing for the space needed for the horses to pull up, with the stands about halfway along it. Races from five to seven furlongs finish at two posts about one-and-a-half and three furlongs to the left of the stands respectively; patrons using them can only see races at those distances beginning to develop and learn about their conclusion second hand. The round course has a circuit of about eleven furlongs. Races from seven to nine furlongs, or at distances of two-and-a-quarter or two-and-a-half miles, begin in the back straight, while runners in one mile seven furlong events start at the end of the straight mile, come up to the stands and then complete a circuit.

The intermediate distance events, which include the ten-and-a-half furlongs of the Prix de Diane (sponsored by Revlon Cosmetics since 1977) and the mile-and-a-half of the Prix du Jockey Club, take place on a course which incorporates parts of both the other elements of the track.

The runners for the Prix de Jockey Club and others contested over the full length of this 'Piste du Jockey-Club' start to the left of the stands, close to the end of the straight mile, but soon cut away, bisecting the round course near where it bends out of the straight and then running across the centre until rejoining the main track, with about six furlongs to cover, shortly before passing the Grandes Ecuries. There is a run-in of almost three furlongs.

Foreign winners were not popular in the early years of French racing and both the Prix du Jockey Club and Prix de Diane remained closed to foreign horses until 1946. Foreigners did score notable successes in the few important events that were open to them; in 1857, for instance, Fisherman gained one of his 69 victories, at the expense of two other English-trained horses, Saunterer and Commotion, in the Prix de l'Empéreur at Chantilly.

Comte Frederic de Lagrange, who owned the first French winner of the Derby, Gladiateur, won the Prix du Jockey Club eight times, dominating it in the nineteenth century in much the same way that Marcel Boussac has in this. From Ramus in 1922 to Acamas in 1978, Boussac has gained twelve successes. The best of them was Pharis, who was baulked in the straight, yet came from well behind to win by five lengths in 1939.

About 2,700 horses were in training at Chantilly in the summer of 1979, some way below the highest figure of 3,346, which had been achieved four years earlier. In the same way that the Jockey Club slowly extended its control over Newmarket Heath, so the Société d'Encouragement, by purchase or lease or through bequests, has achieved the same object in Chantilly; nearby in the communes of Gouvieux, for instance, lie the Terrain des Aigles, the most famous and beautiful gallops in the world, Lamorlaye and Avilly-Saint-Leonard, where a complete training centre was built in response to the explosion in the thoroughbred population in the early 1970s.

Deauville

The story of Deauville goes back to the days of the Second Empire, when Charles, Duc de Morny, a half-brother to the Emperor Napoleon III, went touring in Normandy in 1860, in search of, among other things, a suitable place for a seaside resort.

Watering places were already popular in other countries but spa visiting was more usual than sea bathing in France. Morny's choice fell upon Deauville, close to the southern bank of the mouth of the Seine and, at 125 miles, about the nearest beach to Paris.

Horse racing was clearly high on the list of attractions considered necessary for the new resort because the racecourse there was opened as early as 1864. However, although the racegoers had to be persuaded to come from the cities for their holidays, the new track, which has always counted as part of the metropolitan circuit, had not been laid out in an area devoid of interest in the thoroughbred.

Several studs were already established in the district; the majority of the most important modern French breeding farms are within easy reach of the town. There are two Norman departments of Calvados, in which Deauville itself is situated, and Orne, which is immediately to the south.

One of the closest studs is the Rothschild family's Haras de Meautry, whose name is carried by a Group III sprint, one of the twelve pattern events run at the course during the sixteen days' racing which it presents each August.

The track, which is actually in the town, is a simple affair compared to most French courses. It has a straight mile, which crosses a branch of the River Touque, long since diverted, shortly before joining the round course. The main oval is right-handed, with a circumference of eleven-and-a-half furlongs. Races over a mile-and-a-quarter start in a chute to the left of the stands and the runners join the main track as it begins to turn into the back straight, passing another small chute from which events on the round mile are started.

Deauville is the only one of the principal French courses to retain the old-style

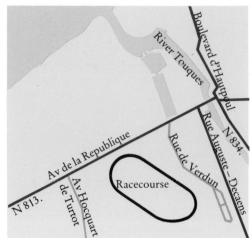

The holiday resort of Deauville is on the west coast of France, 125 miles south-west of Paris in the province of Calvados.

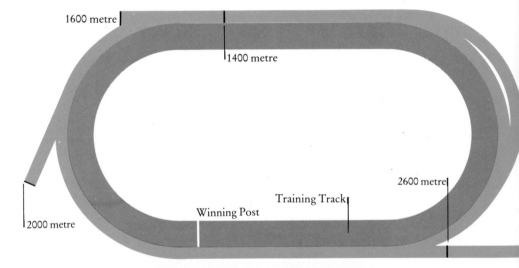

Deauville has a straight mile course, with chutes for one mile and ten furlong races on the round course. It is a flat, galloping track, and well watered.

Deauville, Calvados

Turf, RH, 1½m circumference, 2f straight. Straight 1m. 10f start on chute using outside bend.

Major races: Prix Jacques le Marois, Prix Morny (both Gp I), Grand Prix de Deauville, Prix Kergorlay (both Gp II), Prix Astarte, Prix Calvados, Prix de la Cote Normande, Prix Gontaut-Biron, Prix Maurice de Gheest, Prix Meautry, Prix Pomone, Prix Quincey (all Gp III). Racing in August.

Right Yves Saint Martin going out to the start at Deauville. It is the only principal French racecourse to retain an old style paddock, with racegoers able to inspect the horses from inside the enclosure.

paddock. It is still possible to walk through the gaps in the outside rails and the hedges, which bound the walking path, and join the throng inspecting the runners for the next race from inside, as it used to be at Longchamp and Auteuil until just a few years ago.

The two most important races at Deauville are the Prix Jacques le Marois, run on the straight mile, and the six-furlong Prix Morny. This big two-year-old race has not always commemorated Deauville's founder. For many years it was known as the Prix des Deux Ans, while Morny's contribution to racing in France was recognized in the title of the great spring prize at Longchamp, later known as the Grand Poule des Produits and now as the Prix Lupin. In its early days, the prize money for the Prix des Deux Ans was contributed by the nearby town of Trouville, while that for the Grand Prix de Deauville came partly from the town of Deauville and partly from its casino.

One exception to the rule was the Italian champion, Molvedo, who trounced the French champion Right Royal V by two lengths in the 1961 Arc. He had previously beaten Misti , the third-placed horse in the Arc, in the Grand Prix du Centenaire de Deauville, which celebrated the centenary of the town. However, Molvedo had missed the first half of the season through injury and the Grand Prix was only his second outing of the year. Another famous name on the list of Grand Prix victors is that of the great mare Kincsem, who came from Hungary in 1878 to gain her thirty-seventh success in an unbeaten career which stretched to fifty-four races.

There are other important events at Deauville, including the Group II Prix Kergorlay, over one mile and seven furlongs, but the races for two-year-olds usually attract as much interest as the more valuable ones for their seniors. This is because many future stars are given their first taste of the sport in August at the Normandy course.

Subsidies are paid to the owners of all runners and increase in generosity according to the number of times which the horses compete at either Deauville or neighbouring Clairefontaine. They are stabled at the Deauville course and do all the work on the training track which runs inside the main oval there. Those which race at Clairefontaine cover the brief journey by box. Since 'Parisian' racing takes place there throughout August, a large portion of the staff of the Société d'Encouragement also moves to the coast for the month to deal with its normal business of recording entries and forfeits.

For many years Deauville was merely part of the Normandy month, in which courses at the nearby towns of Caen and Dieppe also played a significant role. Even by the end of the nineteenth century, there were still only seven days racing a year at Deauville. The town's present popularity dates from the years between the two World Wars, when its success was re-inforced by the fashionable appeal of golf and polo as well as of the beach and racing.

Racing is not the only attraction for followers of the thoroughbred on the Normandy coast in August. Deauville is also the home of the only important yearling sales in France, while there are also sales of breeding stock in November.

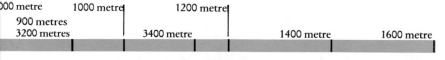

D00 metre 1000 metre 1200 metre
900 metres
3200 metres 3400 metre 1400 metre 1600 metre

Maisons-Laffitte/St-Cloud

While Chantilly was dominated by English trainers for most of the last century, the rival track at Maisons-Laffitte has always been the preserve of their French contemporaries. Four winners of the Prix du Jockey-Club since 1954 were trained there, including Herbager (1960) and Le Fabuleux (1964). However, the last winner of the premier classic from Maisons-Laffitte was Astec in 1968 and, since then, the trainers there have increasingly concentrated on jumping.

At its peak in 1975, the centre contained some 2,500 horses. It is equipped with the same elaborate facilities as Chantilly, both for the horses, with several excellent steeplechase and hurdle training courses, and the lads, particularly the young ones.

Maisons-Laffitte was 'discovered' by horsemen at about the same date and in much the same way as Chantilly, but, although trainers soon arrived there, it was not until 1891 that a racecourse was built. The track lies on the banks of the Seine, a perfect site for racing as long as the river is not too high.

It has several distinctive characteristics, among them a straight mile which can be extended to ten furlongs by the simple measure of having an extra finishing post two furlongs beyond the stands. It also has a finishing post at each end of the stand, sections at each end of the straight course which link it with the back straight and, also, the 'raquette' – a short stretch across the centre linking the two sides of the round course. Because of this, it is possible to run races left-handed from seven to twelve furlongs and right-handed from one to two miles.

In its early days, Maisons-Laffitte staged, at the beginning of August, the first two races of the season for two-year-olds permitted in France. It still runs the first pattern race for that age group, the Prix Robert Papin; this takes place on the last Sunday of July.

The Prix Robert Papin was first run in 1901. Run over five-and-a-half furlongs then, the distance was changed to six

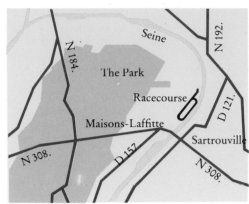

The racecourse at Maisons-Lafitte, the second largest training centre in France, lies on the banks of the Seine north of Paris.

furlongs from 1929 to 1942 and from 1946 to 1962. The Papin provides the first of the top four two-year-old races in France, followed by the six-furlong Prix Morny at Deauville, the seven-furlong Prix de la Salamandre and the one-mile Grand Criterium.

In 1970 it was won by the champion European two-year-old, My Swallow, who beat Mill Reef by a short head with the advantage of the draw. My Swallow went on to win the remaining top three races in France that year.

In 1971 the race was again won by a runner from England, Sir Michael Sobell's Sun Prince, and in 1976 by the top French two-year-old Blushing Groom, who was made favourite for the Derby the following year, but failed to stay the distance. It has been shown that a number of two-year-olds good enough to win the Papin in July fail to stay as three-year-olds.

Maisons-Laffitte, Seine-et-Oise.

Turf, straight course, races up to 10f. RH, 4f straight, 8f, 8½f, 10f, 10½f turf, 1½m circumference. Straight course, races up to 10f. RH, 4f straight, races up to 2¼m; 12½f, 13f starts on chute, 10½, 11½, 12, 12½f races on RH loop. LH, 2f straight, 10½f, 11f, 11½f, 12f starts on chute.

Major races: Prix Robert Papin (Gp I), Criterium de Maisons-Lafitte (Gp II), La Coupe de Maisons-Lafitte, Prix Messidor, Prix de Seine-et-Oise (all GP Gp III). Racing throughout season.

Below *The old stands at Maisons-Laffitte. A racecourse was established there in 1891, although horses had been trained in the area before* **that. Bottom** *The straight, showing how horses cut into the turf due to the proximity of the river and the poor drainage at the course.*

The course, flat throughout, has a straight mile which can be extended by moving the winning post. Races can be run either right-handed or left-handed.

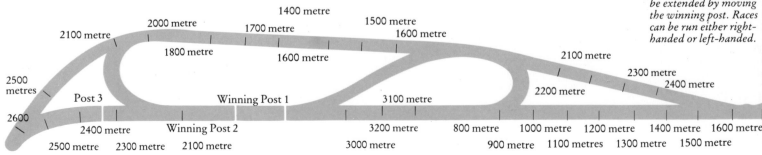

Saint-Cloud

Saint-Cloud in the suburbs of Paris on the western side of the Bois de Boulogne, provides most of the capital's racing fixtures in spring and autumn, when the weather is at its worst and fields at their largest. It is unique as the only left-handed course among the principal French tracks.

There are important races at Saint Cloud during both these periods. Among them is the first pattern event of the year in France, the Prix Edmond Blanc.

In July the racing includes the Grand Prix de Saint-Cloud, Prix Maurice de Nieuil and Prix Eugene Adam. All of these are run in the first half of the month, at a time when the course, with its modern stands built in 1954, and its paddock surrounded by tall hedges, looks at its best.

The Grand Prix used to be known as the Prix du Président de la Republique. Its title was changed to the Grand Prix during the German occupation from 1940 to 1944. It was run in its early years at Maisons-Laffitte – the other course belonging to the non-profit-making Société Sportive d'Encouragement. The same was the case as far as some of present-day Saint-Cloud's other important prizes were concerned; examples include the Prix de Flore and Prix Penelope.

One of the best horses ever to contest Saint-Cloud's greatest race was Ksar, winner of the Prix du Jockey-Club in 1921 and the Arc both that year and the next. Ksar, whose sire and dam both won the the Grand Prix de Paris, cost his owner a then record 151,000 francs as a yearling at Deauville.

A real champion, he was badly ridden in the Grand Prix de Paris and could finish only third behind the English-trained Lemonara, ridden by Joe Childs. The Chantilly-born Childs was booked for Ksar in the 1922 Prix du President but fared no better. Though the horse finished strongly, he failed by a short head to catch the 1921 Irish St Leger winner, Kircubbin, already a course winner three times that season. Some said that Ksar, who was trained nearby, did not like racing on his home course; others that he was given too much to do.

Saint-Cloud, Paris

Turf, LH, 1m 3½f circumference, 2¾f straight, 4½f straight course. 12f, 12½f races use diagonal across track.

Major races: Grand Prix de Saint-Cloud (Gp I), Criterium de Saint-Cloud, Prix Eugene Adam, Prix Jean de Chaudenay, Prix Maurice de Nieuil (all Gp II). Racing 45 days throughout season except August, September. Grand Prix 1st Sunday July.

The racecourse at Saint-Cloud is on the edge of the Bois du Boulogne, seven miles west of Paris and close to the Longchamp track.

Saint-Cloud is the only left-handed principal French track. The going is invariably good or good to firm, despite adverse weather conditions. The circuit is just under one-and-a-half miles, with a finishing straight of almost three furlongs.

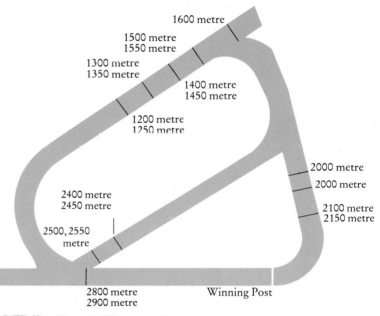

1600 metre
1500 metre
1550 metre
1300 metre
1350 metre
1400 metre
1450 metre
1200 metre
1250 metre
2000 metre
2000 metre
2100 metre
2150 metre
2400 metre
2450 metre
2500, 2550 metre
2800 metre
2900 metre
Winning Post

Left *The paddock at Saint-Cloud. The present stands were built in 1954 and comfortably accommodate crowds for the Gp I Grand Prix de Saint-Cloud, a title changed from the Prix du Président de la République during the German occupation in the Second World War. The Grand Prix is run on the first Sunday in July.* **Above** *Flat out inside the last furlong. The good going at Saint-Cloud provides high-class opportunities at both the beginning and the end of the French racing season. There is no racing there in August and September.*

Evry

In the middle of the 1960s, President de Gaulle decided that his vision of France required a new sports stadium in the suburbs of Paris. To the dismay of the racing community, he fixed on Le Tremblay, to the east of the city.

Le Tremblay belonged to the Société de Sport de France. This body was organized in 1882, at which time it conducted racing at Fontainebleau, where the sport had been first introduced to the country in 1776. For fifty years the Société prospered under the presidency of the Comte Henri Greffulhe, concentrating on the support of races for amateurs – over jumps as well as on the flat – and also for apprentices.

After a public enquiry, compensation for the expropriation of Le Tremblay, which closed on October 25, 1967, was agreed at 42,736,000 francs (then about £3,609,500), more than twice the sum originally proposed by the government. In the meantime the Société de Sport had found a potential new site and, after planning permission had been granted, became the owners of what was to be Evry racecourse in February, 1969.

Three round courses and a straight six-and-a-half furlongs were laid out and the necessary drainage work installed between January 1970 and August 1971. Then, while the turf settled, stands, with seats for 3,500 and including a completely new pari-mutuel system, were constructed. Racing began on March 15, 1973, the thirty-six fixtures from Le Tremblay, which had been distributed in the meantime among the other Parisian courses, were once again collected in one place.

Since its opening, Evry has met with mixed fortunes, even though its racing facilities are first class. The new pari-mutuel was a complete success. The system, which involves the issue of different types of bet on the same ticket and the automatic calculation of any dividends on the issuing machine, has since been introduced at Longchamp and Auteuil. It has also been imitated at many tracks in North America.

However, because of its newness – which means that it has a reputation to establish – and also because it is relatively difficult to reach whem compared to the other Parisian courses, Evry has had to try harder than most racecourses to attract both runners and racegoers, the latter with the aid of several special promotions.

The course itself is at Ris-Orangis, near the main road to the south. It is thus on the wrong side of the city from the point of view of the training centres, which, in turn, has led some trainers to be reluctant to make the journey.

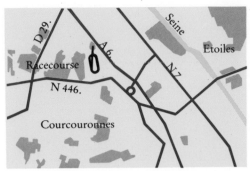

Evry racecourse is at Ris-Orange , twenty miles to the south of Paris, in the province of Yvelines.

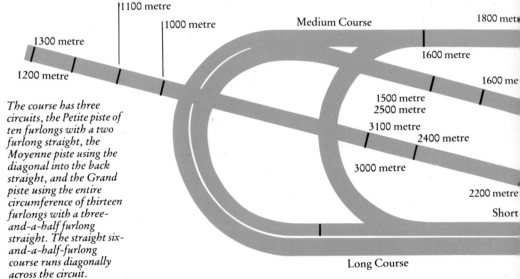

1100 metre
1000 metre
1300 metre
1200 metre
Medium Course
1800 metre
1600 metre
1600 me
1500 metre
2500 metre
3100 metre
2400 metre
3000 metre
2200 metre
Short
Long Course

The course has three circuits, the Petite piste of ten furlongs with a two furlong straight, the Moyenne piste using the diagonal into the back straight, and the Grand piste using the entire circumference of thirteen furlongs with a three-and-a-half furlong straight. The straight six-and-a-half-furlong course runs diagonally across the circuit.

Above *The dirt training tracks with the course and stands beyond. The course was laid out with drainage between 1970 and 1971. Two years later, with the turf settled and the stands completed, racing began in March 1973.* **Right** *The elaborate winners' enclosure. Despite being on the wrong side of Paris to easily attract runners trained at Chantilly and Maisons-Lafitte, the management at Evry* have done much towards offering inducements to provincial and foreign runners. One Group II and four Group III races are run there.

Ris-Orange, Yvelines. 20m from Paris.

Turf, LH, Petite Piste, 10f circumference, 2f straight. Moyenne Piste, horseshoe course for races between 7½f and 10½f, 3½f straight. Grande Piste, 13½f circumference, 3½f straight. Diagonal 6½f straight course.

Major races: Grand Prix d'Evry (Gp II), four Gp III races. Racing 36 days throughout season except August.

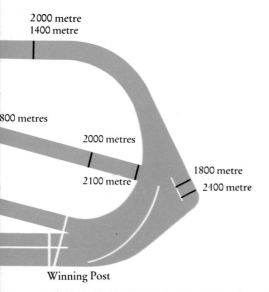

Right *Runners returning after a race. The start of the Moyenne piste can be seen, the course running diagonally across to join the Grand piste at the end of the back straight.* **Below** *The paddock at Evry, showing the considerable facilities afforded racegoers to view runners before the race.*

Baden-Baden/Köln/Hamburg

Baden-Baden's racecourse is the German equivalent of Deauville. It is situated at Iffezheim, a village about four miles away from the main spa. There, an ideal location for the track was found by the licensee of the town's casino in the mid-nineteenth century; he also had the wit to enlist the assistance of the Paris Jockey Club, under whose guidance racing began in 1858. The International Club, the administrators of Baden-Baden since 1873, took over the management of the track after the Franco-Prussian war.

The races were supported on a generous scale, attracted many of the wealthy and socially prominent; King Edward VII, for example, was very fond of the place. With surrounding scenery that includes the foothills of the Black Forest, Baden-Baden is the most attractive course in the Federal Republic and stages, with many recent improvements, one of the most enjoyable of Europe's race-meetings. National Hunt racing receives a fair share of about 100 races, whose prizes and trophies are among the most coveted in Germany. French and English stables, whose material was superior to the German-bred horse, then in the early stages of its development, won the course's main event, the Grosser Preis, year in and year out until 1873. This year saw the triumph of the German three-year-old Hochstapler. In 1908 Festa's good son, Faust, continued the revival by fighting off foreign attackers.

Nevertheless, both the Grosser Preis and the international test for two year-olds, the Zukunfts-Rennen, first run in 1859, continued to fall frequently to foreign owners. French trained runners for instance, had shorter journeys to cope with than their Berlin-prepared rivals. Though many good horses took the Grosser Preis trophy. It was, perhaps, La Camargo, heroine of the Prix de Diana, d'Essai de Pouliches, de Vermeille, du Cadran, Boiard, de la Forêt and Prix Ganay, who represented the best of all the outstanding contenders before 1914.

No winner of the Zukunfts-Rennen has done more for the improvement of the thoroughbred throughout the world than Tourbillon (1931 Prix du Jockey-Club), Marcel Boussac's first runner to acquire an international reputation. The race also saw the success of Frederico Tesio in his second venture abroad from Italy, when his five-year-old Scopas, a winner in France at four, beat with great ease the best that Germany could field against him in the 1924 Grosser Preis.

Two horses have so far won the great event three times, the incomparable Hungarian race mare, Kincsem (1877–79)

Baden-Baden racecourse is at Iffezheim, twelve miles west of the city and close to the Rhine and the French border.

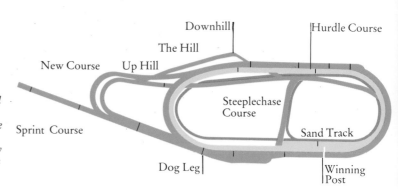

The main course has a circumference of ten furlongs with a three furlong straight. The old course has a one-and-a-half furlong straight. The six furlong course has a marked dog leg, and low numbers are favoured in the draw.

and the German Gestüt Schlenderhan's unforgettable Oleander (1927–29). Only two horses have been successful twice, the British-bred Espresso (1963–64) and German-bred Marduk (1974–75). Marduk's grand-sire, the nine-times leading stallion Ticino, triumphed in 1944, the year in which the event was run at Berlin-Hoppegarten. Arguably the best of all post-war winners was Sheshoon, champion stayer of 1960, who collected the Grand Prix de Saint-Cloud and Ascot's Gold Cup before he went to Baden-Baden.

The course's top mile event, the Oettingen-Rennen, run since 1927, fell to an unusually good horse in Oberwinter, a son of Landgraf, whilst Ace of Aces, by Vaguely Noble, who won in 1974, was the best foreign-bred winner of post-war years.

Baden-Baden's beautiful surroundings also provide, on two days during its end-of-August meeting, two independent sales of home-bred yearlings.

Iffezheim
12 miles west of Baden Baden City

Turf, LH, 10f circumference, 3f straight. Old course 1½f straight. 'Chase course RH (figure of 8).

Major races: Grosser Preis von Baden (1½m, Gp I), Grosser Preis von Badischen-Wirtschaft (9f, GpII), 6 of 18 German Gp III races. Racing mid-May, mid-June, last week August, first September.

Runners setting out on a circuit. Baden-Baden provides a season of racing for holidaymakers, and is similar to the August meeting at Deauville in France and the short Goodwood meeting in England in atmosphere. Crowds of 35,000 are common.

Köln

Notwithstanding Hamburg's great importance as Germany's Derby course, together with that of Baden-Baden, the most successful international meeting to be held in West Germany, the Kölner Rennverein (Cologne Racing Club) nevertheless plays a major role in the country's sport. Since its first day's racing, on September 3, 1889, the club and course have gone from strength to strength.

The crowning glory of Köln's many valuable events is now the Preis von Europa, a weight-for-age 2,400 metres Group I race for three-year-olds and older horses of all countries. The winner receives around 300,000 DM, a prize which compares favourably with those offered for classic races across Europe.

The club is the brain-child of businessmen, industrialists and bankers. Its racing calendar was planned to provide excellent racing from the moment of its inception. The course's early centre-piece was established, after some years, as the Grosser Preis, an event which drew most of Germany's best horses. Weissdorn (by Prunus, by Dark Ronald), the only horse to win the event twice, also won in England At stud he sired Play On, the winner of the 1934 Lincolnshire Handicap.

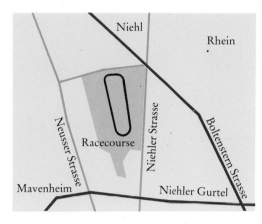

Köln racecourse is at Weidenpesch, three miles from the city centre and ten miles from Köln-Bonn airport.

Köln's Grosser Preis, however, has now yielded pride of place to the Preis von Europa. This has been won seven times by foreign-bred runners since its foundation in 1963. The Soviet Derby winner, Anilin, scored three times in 1965–67, while another Russian horse, Adan, took the prize in 1978. Wundwurf, a brilliant descendant of Waldrun,

Köln, where the 1947 Deutsches Derby was run before it moved to Hamburg-Horn, introduced Germany's most stringent test for two-year-olds, the 1,600 metres Preis des Winterfavoriten. Run since 1899, it is as valuable as Baden-Baden's international Zukunfts-Rennen and is the German equivalent of England's William Hill Futurity Stakes.

The track is right-handed, with a circumference almost one-and-a-quarter miles and a home straight of almost three furlongs. There is a five furlong straight course, and a diagonal steeplechase course.

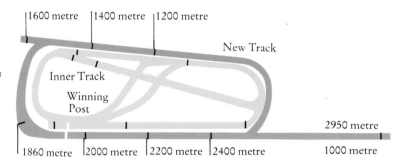

Hamburg-Horn

The Hamburger Renn-Club (Hamburg Racing Club) attained its real and lasting significance for the country's horse racing on the day the first German Derby was run in 1869. Then, two years before Bismarck created a united Germany, the 1,875 metres event for three-year-old colts, geldings and fillies was known as the Norddeutsches Derby. In common with other German turf clubs, Hamburg soon adopted the Epsom Derby distance; Hamburg, with the cosmopolitan outlook of its members and its windows always wide-open towards London, became the most English of all German racecourses. Although foreign horses are not allowed to enter the Deutsches Derby, trainers and jockeys of British origin were invariably preferred by owners. A listing of this century's successful Deutsches Derby riders produces names familiar to racing enthusiasts.

Two of Germany's five main races for two-year-olds are staged there, while the semi-classic Union-Rennen, the most serious test of form before the German Derby, found a home at Köln after the last war. National Hunt racing is well catered for. Planning permission has been granted for a new racecourse.

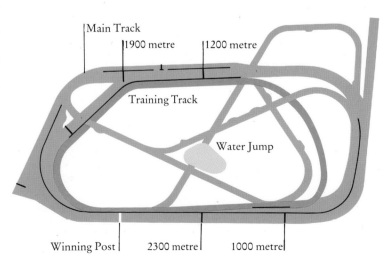

Round the home turn at Hamburg. The course is three miles from the centre of the city.

The course is dead flat, right-handed, with a circumference of ten furlongs. The straight is two-and-a-half furlongs long. There is a diagonal steeplechase course in the centre of the track with a lake used for one race each year.

San Siro/Rome

Milan was late in organizing racing, but when it finally did do so, it was fortunate enough to attract such men as Count Durini, Count Turati and Marquis Fossati. Together they created one of Europe's finest racecourses and a great training centre in the San Siro district.

The training facilities are excellent. They include an oval sand gallop, a steeplechase schooling ground and a well-watered oval turf track of 1800 metres as well as an 1800 metre turf straight on one side.

San Siro is known as 'the racecourse of truth' and it does indeed test every ability of the racehorse. To be successful there a horse has to be a true stayer, as it is a tough course. It is mainly flat, with wide, sweeping turns and a slightly uphill straight of about 700 metres. Italy's greatest horses have been tested here, including Ribot, who won twelve races over the course.

San Siro stages two of Italy's most important races for three-year-olds and upwards, the Gran Premio di Milano over 2400 metres in June and the Gran Premio del Jockey Club, also over 2400 metres, in October. Three of Italy's six classic races are also run here, the Oaks d'Italia over 2200 metres in late May, the Gran Premio d'Italia over 2400 metres in June and the St Leger Italiano over 2800 metres in late September.

San Siro, Milan

Turf, concentric figures-of-eight, 2m circumference, 4½f straight. Flat, RH, drained, watered.

Major races: Gran Premio di Milano (1½m, 3-y-o), Gran Premio del Jockey Club e Coppa d'Oro (1½m, all ages) (both Gp I).

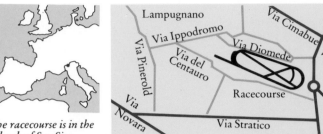

The racecourse is in the suburb of San Siro, 3 miles north of Milan.

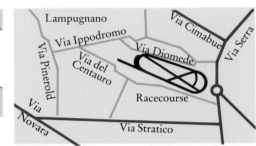

San Siro is a flat right-handed course of two miles, made up of figures-of-eight. There is a slight rise to the finishing post. The series of turns demand a well balanced horse.

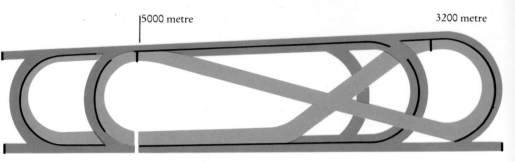

5000 metre | 3200 metre

Winning Post

Below *The stands at San Siro and* **right** *the turn out of the home straight. San Siro is also a training centre, and besides the racecourse there is an oval sand gallop, a steeplechase schooling ground and a watered oval turf gallop, with a straight nine furlong track.*

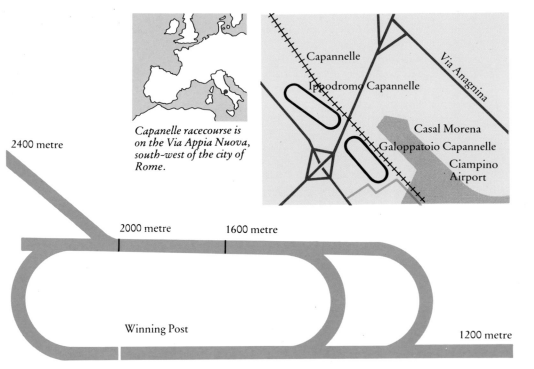

Capanelle racecourse is on the Via Appia Nuova, south-west of the city of Rome.

2400 metre

2000 metre 1600 metre

Winning Post

1200 metre

Capanelle

Capanelle, Rome's picturesque racecourse set against the background of the Castelli hills, is the home of the Italian Derby, as well as the first two Italian classics, the 2,000 Guineas and the 1,000 Guineas.

The course was founded in 1881, although occasional racecourses had been marked out in the Prati Fiscali and the Torre Spaccata since 1844. The first official Italian Derby (Derby Italiano) was run in April 1884.

The course is flat and right-handed, based on a chalk sub-surface which drains quickly. There is also an effective watering system. Five and six furlongs races are run over the straight course. The whole course has a circumference of one-and-a-half miles, with a four-and-a-half furlong straight. There are training facilities on both grass and sand, and with fifty trainers in residence at Capanelle there are more than 1000 horses in training there.

Via Appia Nuova, Rome

Turf, 1½m circumference, 6f straight. Flat, RH, drained on chalky soil, watered. **Sand** course used for lower class races in bad weather.

Major races: Premio Presidente della Repubblica (1m 2f, all ages), Premio Roma (1m 6f, 3-y-o), Derby Italiano (1½m, 3-y-o home bred only) (all Gp I).

Top left *Racing up the home straight at San Siro. Using the full circumference of the course, the straight can be four-and-a-half furlongs long and is one of the reasons why San Siro is known as the racecourse of truth. The unbeaten Ribot won twelve races at the course.*

Left *The paddock at San Siro. Racegoers in Italy are not known for their retiring nature, and are as likely to cheer as to castigate jockeys as thieves should they lose on a hot favourite.*

Aqueduct

Described as 'the wonder track of thoroughbred racing' when it opened in September 1959, the new Aqueduct racetrack replaced an older one, which survived from 1894 to 1955. The new stands are lavish, contemporary structures, standing 110 feet high, peering over the Belt Parkway in Queens, minutes from Kennedy Airport. The only track in America built with its own subway station, 'The Big A', as it is commonly known, is easily accessible from all parts of New York City and the surrounding suburbs. Built at a cost of $33,000,000, it can accommodate 80,000 people comfortably, with luxurious facilities for all classes of spectators.

Aqueduct is a mile-and-an-eighth in circumference with its stretch run of 1,174 feet being slightly longer than the two other New York tracks – Belmont and Saratoga. To accommodate year-round racing, a new winter inner track was constructed in 1975, replacing the main turf course. The inner track operates from December until March, when the main dirt track is re-opened.

The old Aqueduct provided US racing enthusiasts with two of the most memorable moments in the history of the sport. In 1944, the only triple dead-heat ever in a stakes race occurred in the seven-furlong Carter Handicap between Brownie, Bossuet and Wait a Bit. But the most unforgettable moment in the track's history was undoubtedly on July 10, 1920, when the immortal Man O' War turned certain defeat into his greatest triumph by coming again to defeat John P Grier in the Dwyer Handicap.

With no other challengers, the Dwyer turned into a match race between the two best three-year-olds in America. Man O' War, conceding 18lb, was headed by his rival at the furlong pole, as a stunned crowd watched in disbelief. Jockey Clarence Kummer lashed out twice with his whip, and 'Big Red', like a true champion, battled back to retake the lead. He went on to triumph by a length-and-a-half, setting a new American record for the mile-and-a-quarter distance. In commemoration of that great moment, the old furlong pole was preserved and embedded in the

Aqueduct racecourse is at Jamaica, New York, twelve miles from Manhattan, five miles from Kennedy airport and twelve miles from La Guardia airport.

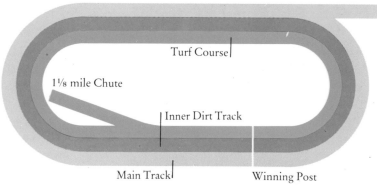

Turf Course
1⅛ mile Chute
1 mile Chute
Inner Dirt Track
Main Track
Winning Post

There are two dirt tracks, one of nine furlongs with a 385-yard straight and inner track of one mile with a 390-yard straight. There is a turf course of seven furlongs with a 390-yard straight.

Right *In the home straight. With tight turns and a short straight, horses tend to lie up with the leaders far more than in Europe.* **Below right** *Led out on to the track for a race. The huge stands behind are capable of seating 30,000, with a record crowd of more than 73,000 being recorded in 1965. Every available facility is provided for racegoers, with a subway station at the course.*

Jamaica, New York, NY.

Dirt, 9f circumference, 385y straight. 7f, 1m start on chutes. **Inner dirt,** 8f circumference, 390y straight (winter meetings). **Turf,** 7f 14y circumference, 390y straight. 9f start on chute. Seating 30,000. Record crowd 73,435 (1965). Racing October–May.

Major races: Ladies H'cap (10f), Top Flight H'cap (9f), Turf Classic (12f, turf), Wood Memorial (9f) (all Gr I).

ground just outside the entrance of the new track, a salute to the courage and determination of one of the greatest horses the world has ever seen.

It was not long before the new track was presenting classic moments of its own. Two weeks after it opened, Horse of the Year honours were decided when Brookmeade Stable's little chestnut Sword Dancer defeated the Californian sensation Hillsdale by a head in the Woodward Stakes, with the great Round Table a length-and-three-quarters behind in third place. The following year, Aqueduct saw its first real hero with the arrival of Mrs Allaire du Pont's mighty gelding Kelso. 'Kelly', as he was affectionately known, reigned supreme in New York for five years, winning twenty of his twenty-seven starts at Aqueduct. He captured the two-mile Jockey Club Gold Cup five times and the Woodward three times on his way to an unprecedented five Horse of the Year titles.

With the closing of Belmont Park for rebuilding in 1962, Aqueduct became the home of such championship races as the Belmont Stakes, the Woodward, the Jockey Club Gold Cup, the Man O' War Stakes and the Champagne Stakes. In 1967, the Woodward drew one of the most outstanding fields ever assembled when champions Buckpasser, Damascus and Dr Fager clashed for Horse of the Year honours. With the entire racing world predicting a tight finish, Damascus romped home by ten lengths to clinch his claim to the title. Aqueduct was also the scene of New York racing's emotional farewell to Secretariat in November 1973. A weekday crowd of almost 33,000 attended for a final look at the great colt, as he paraded before the spectators between races.

Everything about Aqueduct is designed for the convenience of great masses of people, including the many ramps and covered walks leading to and from the subway station. There are eighteen escalators and nine elevators to make it easy for the weary spectator to find his way around the massive grandstand, while numerous lounges allow him to take an occasional respite between races.

One facility no longer survives, however – at least, not on its original site. For many years, a barber's shop was open on the main floor for the public's convenience. However, it was moved when it was found that touts were observing which trainers went in for a shave, knowing they would soon be having their picture taken in the winner's circle.

Unlike Belmont and Saratoga, Aqueduct does not evoke visions of the past, or stimulate the hardened racegoer. Progress has in some ways passed it by and it is no longer the 'wonder track of American racing' it was two decades ago. However, it still remains 'America's Dream Track', because it is the prime refuge for America's number one dreamer, the horseplayer. At the 'Big A', he can fulfill his wildest dreams in the kind of comfort and luxury that no other race track can offer.

Below *Attacking round the home turn on the dirt track. Although the standard of racing is not as high as that at Belmont, racing takes place six days a week from October through to May. The inner dirt track is used in winter, while the most important race on the turf track is the one-and-a-half mile Turf Classic.*

Churchill Downs

For every horse lover in the world, the name of Churchill Downs is associated with one classic race – the world-famous Kentucky Derby. The magic associated with the race spills over on to the track itself; although it is located in a nondescript area of Louisville and its grandstand is antiquated when compared to the splendid modern structures of its rivals, Churchill Downs possesses an atmosphere all of its own. Seeing its famous twin spires for the first time is much like a first impression of the Eiffel Tower or the Statue of Liberty. This feeling was summed up by Irving S Cobb, the homespun philosopher of Peducah, Kentucky, who once said: 'Until you go to Kentucky, and with your own eyes behold the Derby, you ain't never been nowheres and you ain't never seen nothing.'

The Kentucky Derby is probably the most famous race in the USA. It is traditionally run on the first Saturday in May and attracts more than 100,000 spectators, most of whom set up camp in the infield to turn the Derby day into a carnival.

First run in 1875 – the year that Churchill Downs opened – the Kentucky Derby, strangely enough, took some little time to achieve its present prestige. It was nothing more than a local race, with little national significance, until 1902. Then, Colonel Matt Winn took over the financially-ailing track and began luring the big-name New York stables to compete there. But, although the race grew in stature throughout the years, it was not until 1915, when Harry Payne Whitney won with his magnificent filly, Regret. She led from start to finish, becoming the first filly ever to win the event. After the race, Whitney exclaimed: 'I don't care if she never wins another race, or if she never starts in another race. She has won the greatest race in America, and I am satisfied.'

The race itself starts at the head of the stretch, with a two-furlong run into the first turn. Although the track has one of the longest straights in America – aptly nicknamed 'Heartbreak Lane' – the race is, in fact, usually decided well before the finish. Of the last seventeen winners through 1979, sixteen had the lead a furlong out.

The surface is also a factor that trainers have to take into consideration. It is quick-drying, but tends to get on the 'cuppy', or

Churchill Downs is three miles from the centre of Louisville, Kentucky, and three miles from Standiford Field airport.

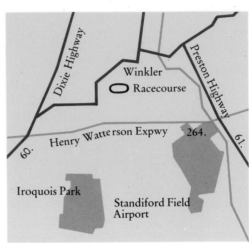

Churchill is a left-handed one mile circuit on sandy loam, with a chute for the one mile start. The straight is just under two furlongs long. There is no turf track.

Right *The start of the 1975 Kentucky Derby won by Foolish Pleasure. Handlers stand in the stalls to give a somewhat superfluous incentive to get going.*

Louisville, Kentucky

Dirt, 1m circumference, 412y straight. 1m start on chute. Seating 42,250. Record Crowd 163,628 (1974).
Racing May–June; November.

Major races: Kentucky Derby (10f), Kentucky Oaks (8½f) (both Gr I).

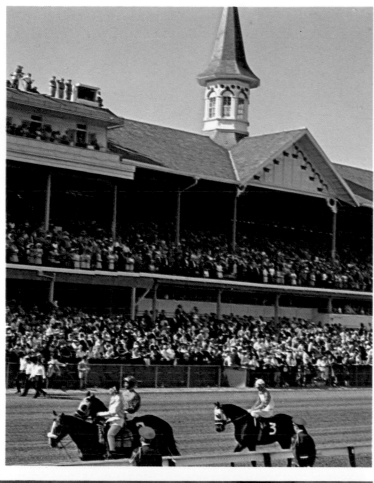

Left *Runners parading before the packed stands. More than 163,000 people watched Cannonade win the Derby in 1974.* **Below** *The back of the stands at Churchill, which seat almost 45,000. The infield is also opened for the Kentucky Derby, when racegoers turn it into a playground, campsite and fairground.* **Bottom** *What the average horse ever saw of Secretariat, streaking home in the 1973 Derby.*

loose, side. This can affect many horses, especially runners from California, who are used to the hard surfaces of Santa Anita and Hollywood Park. But, whatever complaints may be directed at the track or the race itself, the Derby can usually be relied upon to separate the good horses from the ordinary. Six of the last seven runnings have been won by the favourite, while seven of the past nine winners have gone on to become the champion three-year-old.

Because of the inconsistency of the surface, the Derby is not known for its fast times. The record of 1 minute 59 seconds set by the great Secretariat in 1973 has not been remotely threatened since that year. The previous record of 2 minutes flat was set in 1964 by Northern Dancer.

Belmont Park

Belmont Park is one of the most atmospheric and beautiful of all American racetracks. It is associated with some of the most celebrated moments in racing history and some of the greatest horses – names such as Man O' War, Sysonby, Zev, Count Fleet, Secretariat and Forego. All of these played their part in unforgettable match races, gruelling handicaps, and the classic Belmont Stakes.

Although it is not situated in scenic surroundings such as the Bois de Boulogne or the Sussex countryside, the beauty of Belmont Park lies within its own confines. Here, quietly nestled away from neighbouring avenues and highways, is a world truly apart. With its magnificent grandstand and tree-shaded paddock, Belmont ranks as one of the most picturesque racetracks in the world. Inside the walking ring, a 152-year-old White Pine tree and a striking sculpture of Secretariat link the past with the present. Racegoers are provided with a huge picnic area that includes a duck pond, many betting windows, television monitors and a variety of food stands to satisfy the racegoers' appetites.

The historic Belmont Stakes, the final leg of the Triple Crown, is the top attraction. This gruelling mile-and-a-half event has been the downfall of many a fine horse attempting to sweep the prestigious triad. Canonero II, Northern Dancer, Kauai King, Majestic Prince, Tim Tam, Forward Pass, and most recently Spectacular Bid, are just a few of the great names who came to Belmont with high hopes of achieving immortality only to fail.

After Calumet Farm's Citation swept the Triple Crown in 1948, there was a lapse of twenty-five years until Meadow Stable's Secretariat captured all three events in spectacular fashion, culminating with a thirty-one length victory in the Belmont. In 1977, Karen Taylor's Seattle Slew, a $17,500 yearling purchase, became the first undefeated horse in history to win the Triple Crown, scoring each time from the front. The following year, Harbor View Farm's Affirmed prevailed, defeating his arch-rival Alydar in all three events by a total margin of less that two lengths.

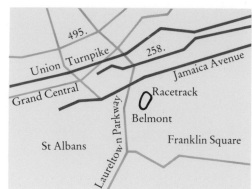

Belmont Park is at Hempstead, New York, twenty miles from New York and fifteen miles from Kennedy airport.

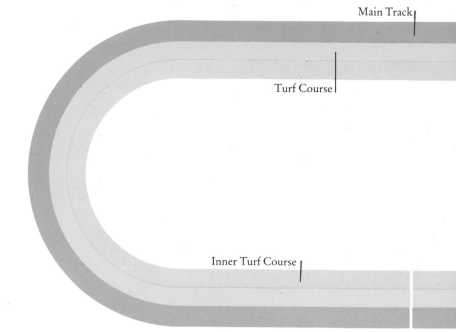

Main Track

Turf Course

Inner Turf Course

Winning Post

Hempstead, NY.

Dirt, 12f circumference, 10f start on chute. **Turf**, 10½f circumference, 336y straight. 8f, 10f starts on chute. **Inner turf**, 9½f circumference. Seating 30,000. Racing May–July, September–October.

Major races: Acorn Stakes (8f), Beldame Stakes (10f), Belmont Stakes (12f), Brooklyn H'cap (12f), Champagne Stakes (8f), Coaching Club of America Oaks (12f). Frizette Stakes (8f), Futurity Stakes (fillies), Jockey Club Gold Cup (12f), Man O'War (11f turf), Marlboro Cup H'cap (9f), Matron Stakes (7f), Metropolitan H'cap (8f), Mother Goose Stakes (9f), Ruffian H'cap (fillies), Suburban H'cap (10f), Woodward Stakes (10f) (all Gr I).

Belmont is one of the larger American courses, with a one-and-a-half mile circuit and a 336-yard straight. There is a ten-and-a-half furlong turf track, and an inner turf track of nine-and-a-half furlongs. There is a ten-furlong chute on the main track, and an adjacent training track.

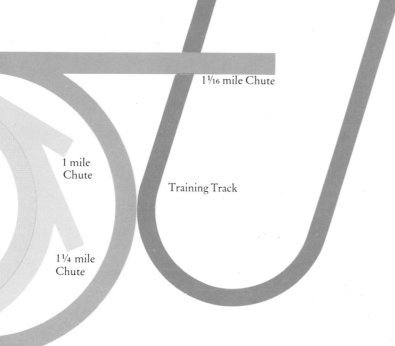

1 1/16 mile Chute

1 mile Chute

Training Track

1 1/4 mile Chute

In order to conquer the obstacles of the Belmont Stakes, a horse must be endowed with ehough stamina to endure a distance that is rarely run in the USA. He must be able to cope with the unusually long back stretch and sweeping turns, and, most of all, must possess the courage and fortitude to withstand the demanding final two furlongs. To the American breeder, therefore, the Belmont is truly the 'Test of the Champion'. Ten days after upsetting Spectacular Bid in last year's Belmont, William Haggin Perry's Coastal was syndicated for $5,400,000, which is perhaps four to five million dollars more than he was worth before the race.

Belmont Park is also the home of the 'Fall Championship Series', which is usually the final factor in determining Horse of the Year honours. It comprises the $300,000 Marlboro Cup at a mile-and-an-eighth, the $175,000 Woodward Stakes at a mile-and-a-quarter, and the $350,000 Jockey Club Gold Cup at a mile-and-a-half. The two main turf events are the $125,000 Man o' War Stakes at a mile and three-eighths and the $250,000 Turf Classic at a mile-and-a-half. Over the past few years, these races have attracted such top European runners as Trillion, Dahlia, Exceller, Crow and Arctic Tern.

The international tradition originated in 1923, when Joseph Widener came up with the idea of inviting the best three-year-old in America to meet the best three-year-old in England in an unforgettable match race. The honours went to Zev, winner of the Belmont Stakes, and Papyrus, winner of the English Derby. The Westchester Racing Association paid all expenses for shipping Papyrus to America. Advance sales were so high that a special ticket office was opened on Broadway to accommodate the demand. Unfortunately, three days of rain turned Belmont into a sea of mud and, despite being urged by American trainers to use mud caulks on his horse's hooves, Papyrus' trainer, Basil Jarvis, insisted on running his colt in the customary smooth plates. With Steve Donoghue aboard, Papyrus could never get hold of the track and Zev won by eight lengths.

The following year, Joseph Widener's innovative mind was at work again, this time in the construction of a seven-furlong chute that ran diagonally across the infield. Called the Widener Course, it provided racing fans with many years of first class sprint races until its removal in 1960. Two years later, Belmont closed for rebuilding until its grand opening in 1968. The old grandstand had become a hazard and a decision was made to tear it down for a new track.

Left *Heading for the line on the main dirt track. The great Forego holds three records at the track, as does Secretariat, one of those over the turf track.* **Right** *Part of the camera patrol system operating at the track.* **Below** *Horses being led out on to the track by lead horses, and* **below right** *the walkway leading up to the stands.*

Pimlico

On October 25, 1870, the Maryland Jockey Club staged its inaugural meeting at Pimlico Racecourse, just outside Baltimore. The first stakes race, the two-mile Dinner Party Stakes, was held two days later, with the surprise winner being a huge, coarse-looking colt named Preakness. Three years later, the Jockey Club honoured the colt by naming a race for him over the classic distance of a mile-and-a-half.

Preakness's future, however, was not as bright as the race for which he was named. He ran until the age of eight, when he was sent to England and later sold to the Duke of Hamilton for stud purposes. Unfortunately, the stallion developed a bad temper that was surpassed only by his owner's. One day, an inevitable clash took place in Preakness' stall, with the Duke coming out the loser. In a fit of anger, he seized his gun and, in a few moments, had one less stallion to feed.

The Preakness Stakes prospered over the years to become the second jewel in America's Triple Crown for three-year-olds. Its coveted trophy, the Woodlawn Vase, dates back to 1860, when it was created by Tiffany and Co for R Aitcheson Alexander. In 1917, it was presented to the Maryland Jockey Club, where it became the permanent trophy for the Preakness. The Woodlawn Vase was appraised in 1971 for $500,000, making it the richest trophy in American sport.

After experimenting with five different distances, it was decided in 1925 to keep the Preakness at a mile-and-three-sixteenths. It has proved a demanding race for horses that have run in the Kentucky Derby, as they are forced to drop back to a shorter distance while negotiating Pimlico's sharp turns.

While the Belmont Stakes, with its gruelling distance of a mile-and-a-half, has thwarted many pretenders to the Triple Crown, the Preakness has always found unpredictable and individual ways of accomplishing the same task.

In 1931, Greentree Stable's Twenty Grand won the Derby and Belmont, but in the Preakness was bumped badly, being knocked off stride on the first turn. After recovering, he was blocked by his own stablemate at the head of the stretch, losing all chance of victory. In 1939, Belair Stud's

Pimlico is in Baltimore, Maryland, twelve miles from the Baltimore-Washington International airport amd forty miles from Washington DC.

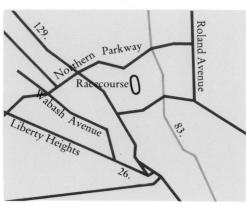

Main Course   6 furlong Chute

Turf Course

1¼ furlong Chute   Winning Post

Pimlico is a one mile oval track of soil and loam, with chutes for the six furlong and ten furlong starts. The straight is 384 yards. There is an inside turf course of seven furlongs.

Right *Lead horses taking runners down to the start at Pimlico. With a circumference of only eight furlongs, the nine-and-a-half furlongs of the Preakness Stakes, the second leg of the American Triple Crown, provides a stern test of a horse's ability to act round the turns.*

Baltimore, Maryland

Dirt, 1m circumference, 384y straight. 6f, 10f start on chutes. **Turf,** 7f circumference. Seating 23,672. Record crowd 77,346 (1977). Racing April–May.

Major races: Preakness Stakes (9½f, Gr I), Black-Eyed Susan Stakes (8½f, 3-y-o fillies), Dixie H'cap (1½m turf) (both Gr II).

Johnstown romped home by eight lengths in the Derby and easily captured the Belmont by five lengths. However, between the two races, he faltered badly in the Pimlico mud to finish fifth of six, beaten by twelve lengths. Greentree Stable's bad luck in the Preakness continued in 1942, when Shut Out was pinched back on the far turn, a factor which cost him the Triple Crown. In 1963, Darby Dan Farm's Chateaugay had defeated Candy Spots in the Derby, and would go on to defeat him handily in the Belmont. Unfortunately, a week before the Preakness, while working over a mile, his exercise rider lost control of him and he finished by breaking the track record for the distance. The workout took its toll as Chateaugay finished second to Candy Spots a week later.

In 1972, Meadow Stable's Riva Ridge suffered the same fate as Johnstown, when he romped home by four lengths in the Derby, and by seven lengths in the Belmont, only to flounder in the mud at Pimlico, finishing fourth to the lightly-regarded Bee Bee Bee. Four years later, Esteban Tizol's Bold Forbes was a wild free-running colt who won both the Derby and Belmont leading from start to finish with jockey Angel Cordero more or less along for the ride. However, on Preakness Day, the temperature soared to 95 degrees, causing Bold Forbes and the favourite Honest Pleasure to become extremely sweaty. The two ran each other dizzy in the sweltering heat, the fastest first six furlongs in the history of the race. Bold Forbes managed to stagger home third, returning with a bloody hoof.

Despite all these misfortunes, the Preakness has provided some of the most memorable moments in the annals of the Triple Crown. Because of its sharp turns, it encourages quick, unexpected moves. The most famous of these, without a doubt, was Secretariat's dynamic rush from last to first on the club house turn in 1973. None who witnessed it will ever forget the awesome power of the big chestnut as he devoured the entire field in a matter of seconds. There have been other extraordinary incidents, such as Damascus' dash from ninth to first on the far turn in 1967, and Little Current's dramatic charge in 1974, when he came from tenth at the head of the stretch to win by seven lengths. The unexpected also occurred in 1971, when Canonero II, after coming from seventeenth place to win the Derby, went right to the front in the Preakness. After battling neck and neck all the way with the swift Eastern Fleet, the $1,500 yearling purchase went on to win in a track record time of 1 minute 54 seconds, a time that has stood unbeaten by the three Triple Crown winners since that date.

Pimlico has had other great moments in its history, such as the memorable match race of 1938 in which Seabiscuit defeated Triple Crown winner War Admiral before a record crowd of more than 43,000.

Since the opening of the infield on a regular basis in 1967, the Preakness has become an event to rival the Kentucky Derby. Music varies from rock and roll to dixieland, and sports events from football to lacrosse. Pimlico and the Preakness have grown considerably over the years. Although the race may not have the publicity of the Derby or Belmont Stakes, it is the only one of the three always to have a horse in contention for the Triple Crown. History, in fact, has proven one thing about the race; no matter how the race shapes up, or how good a favourite looks, always expect the unexpected.

Below left *In the unsaddling enclosure.* **Bottom left** *A rousing finish, showing the American style of crouching into the horse. American jockeys hold their whips upright, through the front of the fist, throughout a race.* **Below** *The winners' enclosure before the start of the 104th Preakness Stakes in 1979. The race was won by Spectacular Bid. He also won the Kentucky Derby, but was beaten by Coastal in the Belmont Stakes.*

Santa Anita

Starting with its inaugural meeting on Christmas Day, 1934, in Arcadia, a suburb of sprawling Los Angeles, Santa Anita has been a racetrack apart from all others. Situated in the foothills of the hovering San Gabriel Mountains, it has one of the most spectacular backdrops of any racetrack in the world. It is also an elegant course, where tradition, warmth and dignity have not suffered during the increasingly brazen years since the Second World War.

At the back of the stands are park-like lawns, liberally dotted with antique statuary imported from England, shady trees and a statue of California's first modern-day equine hero, Seabiscuit. This is complemented by a bust of George Woolf, the finest rider of his time, who lost his life in a racing accident at the track in its early years. In front of the stands, facing the San Gabriels, is an attractive, but utilitarian, infield with gushing fountains, tall willowy palm trees, wine bar and picnic facilities for family and group outings.

Customer amenities have been Santa Anita's hallmark since its foundation. This was the work of Charles H Strub, a San Francisco dentist whose desire to build a racetrack in his own city became a reality when pari-mutuel wagering was legalized in 1933. He became the driving force behind the Lost Angeles Turf Club, operators of Santa Anita. Although conceived and opened during the great depression, Strub eschewed a 'free gate', surrounded his patrons with every possible sign of luxury and beauty, including original Munnings' and Stubbs' paintings, and announced a $100,000 purse, the richest to that date in the US, for the Santa Anita Handicap. After an impressive opening, however, Santa Anita struggled to survive, with some of Strub's friends using their own money to meet the payroll. Yet it was to become one of the most successful ventures in the history of American racing.

Santa Anita is part of the old Rancho Santa Anita, owned and developed by the Elias Jackson ('Lucky') Baldwin, one of the country's most prominent owners and

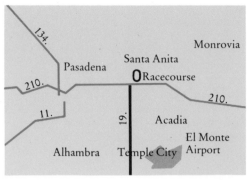

Santa Anita is in Arcadia, California, fourteen miles from the centre of Los Angeles and seventeen miles from Burbank airport.

Santa Anita is a one mile oval on sandy loam with a 330 yard straight. There are seven and ten furlong chutes. The turf course is a combination of the hillside track, crossing the main track at the entrance to the straight, and an inner circuit of just over seven furlongs.

Rounding the home turn on the dirt track. Besides the Santa Anita Derby, the Charles II Strub Stakes is an important Grade I race named after the founder of the course.
Far right *The San Gabriel Mountains provide a superb backdrop to the course with fountains in the centre of the course. A platform has been placed across the turf track to prevent it being damaged.*

Arcadia, California

Dirt, 1m circumference, 330y straight, 7f, 10f start on chutes. **Turf,** combination of 'Hillside' turf course (6f 88y) to junction with main track and inner turf course (7f 44y). Seating for 30,600. Record crowd 83,768 (1947). Racing end December–April, October–November (Oak Tree).

Major races: Charles H Strub Stakes (1¼m, 4-y-o), La Canada Stakes (9f, 4-y-o fillies), Oak Tree Invitational Stakes (1½m, turf), San Antonio Stakes (9f), San Juan Capistrano H'cap (1¾m, turf), San Luis Rey Stakes (1½m turf), Santa Anita Derby (9f), Santa Anita H'cap (1¼m), Santa Barbara H'cap (1¼m, turf, fillies and mares), Santa Margarita H'cap (9f, fillies and mares), Santa Susana Stakes (8½f, 3-y-o- fillies), Yellow Ribbon Stakes (1¼m turf, fillies and mares) (all Gr I).

breeders of the 1880s and 1890s. Breeder of such champions as Volante, Silver Cloud, Emperor of Norfolk and Rey El Santa Anita, 'Lucky' Baldwin also bred Rey Del Carreras. This horse, said to be one of the fastest horses seen up to that time, was a winner both in America and England. Sold to the notorious Richard ('Boss') Croker, the horse's name was changed to Americus. It was in England that he sired the immortal matriarch, Americus Girl, foundress of one of the most powerful and ramifying distaff families in the Stud Book. Baldwin built a track near the present course and racing was held there in 1907 and 1908, but its short-lived history closed with Baldwin's death early in 1909. Some of the relics of the Baldwin era are still evident at Santa Anita, especially on its colourful, dramatic, partially downhill turf course which early on passes by the old Baldwin winery.

The first Santa Anita Handicap attracted twenty of the most celebrated horses in the US, but it was the English-bred outsider, the gelding, Azucar, who startled the 34,269 crowd. His histrionics carried over to the winner's circle ceremony where he knocked down the guest of honour, Lucky Baldwin's daughter, Anita, snapped the cable on the live coast-to-coast radio broadcast and dragged his groom nearly a quarter of a mile down the track.

Santa Anita, whose main track is a mile dirt oval with chutes for races at seven and ten furlongs, has been a leader in American racing ever since its debut. It pioneered the photo finish, magnetic control starting gate and visual electric timing. Its turf course, inspired by those Dr Strub saw in Europe, has made Santa Anita's grass racing programme the finest and most exciting on the North American continent, highlighted by the $200,000-added San Juan Capistrano Handicap at about a mile-and-six furlongs.

For most of the past decade, Santa Anita and its crosstown equivalent, Hollywood Park, have been first and second respectively in average national daily attendance and average daily betting with Hollywood, due to its more central location and summertime weather, usually holding the number one spot. However, in 1978, Santa Anita led the nation in average daily attendance (26,437). Because of such patronage and because of its winter dates, the roster of winners of Santa Anita's most prestigious fixtures reads like a *Who's Who* of the most famous performers in American racing over the past forty-five years.

Keeneland/Hialeah Park

In its own way, Keeneland race track in Lexington, Kentucky, is, perhaps, the most visually stunning course in the USA. Located in the heart of the famed bluegrass country, it overlooks miles of white fencing set upon lush rolling hills. Lexington has always been the essence of American breeding; only at Keeneland can a horse be seen thundering down the finishing stretch to victory, just minutes from where he was born and raised.

Although it was built only forty-four years ago, and races a mere thirty days each year, Keeneland is a major contributor to racing in the USA. It was conceived by horsemen as a non-profit organization, dedicated to upholding the finest traditions of the sport. After considering numerous sites for the new track, a committee of Kentucky sportsmen selected a portion of John Keene's Keeneland Stud on Versailles Road in Lexington.

Keeneland is heir to a great tradition. Racing in Kentucky actually dates back to 1787, when races started on Main Street and continued up the hill to Ashland, the home of the American statesman Henry Clay. The first racetrack, known as Williams' Track, was constructed ten years later in Lee's Woods which is now part of the Lexington cemetery. In 1828, the newly-formed Kentucky Association built a track in the centre of the town, which operated until 1933. After it was closed, a group of central Kentuckians, headed by Hal Price Headley and Major Louie A Beard, joined forces to bring racing back to the bluegrass. Their efforts were rewarded three years later, when the Keeneland Association staged its inaugural nine-day meeting at the new track. The heroine of that meeting was Brownell Combs' filly Myrtlewood, who won three races, including stakes victories two days apart.

Divided into spring and autumn meetings, Keeneland is the ideal track for horses preparing for the Kentucky Derby. There is nothing more invigorating to the body and soul than April in Kentucky. Horses seem to thrive in the cool, crisp weather after coming from the warm climate of Florida or California.

Keeneland itself, with its ivy-covered walls, magnificent gardens, and tree-shaded saddling area, must rank as one of the most charming racetracks in the country. One unique factor is the absence of a public address system, thus making binoculars a necessity.

The big attraction of Keeneland's spring meeting is the mile-and-and-eighth Blue Grass Stakes, run nine days before the Derby. Since 1962, seven winners of the Blue Grass have gone on to capture the

Keeneland is in Kentucky, six miles west of Lexington and adjacent to the airport.

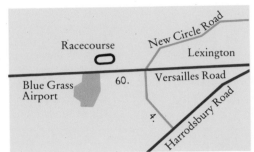

The track at Keeneland is an eight-and-a-half furlong oval on sand and loam, with a straight of 391 yards. There are chutes for the four-and-a-half furlongs and seven furlongs sixty-one yards starts. There is also a five-furlong training track.

7 furlong Chute

4½ furlong Chute

2nd Finishing Post
1st Finishing Post

Training Track

Lexington, Kentucky.

Dirt, 8½f circumference, 391y straight. 4½f, 7f 61y start on chutes. Seating for 7,000. Record crowd 22,303.
Racing April, October.

Major races: Blue Grass Stakes (9f), Spinster Stakes (9f) (both Gr I).

Above right The statue behind the stands at Keeneland. The winner of the Blue Grass Stakes, Keeneland's major race, has the right to paint the statue in the winning colours. **Below right** The

straight and infield at Keeneland, showing the totalisator board.

Churchill Downs classic, including the 1979 winner, Spectacular Bid. The highlight of the autumn meeting is the Spinster Stakes for fillies and mares, also run at a mile-and-an-eighth. Over the years it has been won by such outstanding champions as Primonetta, Bowl of Flowers, Lamb Chop, Straight Deal, Gallant Bloom, Numbered Account, Susan's Girl and Tempest Queen. The seven-furlong Breeders' Futurity for two-year-olds has served as a stepping stone for horses such as Whirlaway, Johnstown, Devil Diver and Round Table.

Hialeah

As winter blizzards immobilize major northern cities and shut down race tracks throughout the nation, thousands of horses, trainers, jockeys and racing enthusiasts bask in the warm Florida sun, enjoying first-class sport at Hialeah racetrack. Located near Miami Beach, Hialeah has lured holidaymakers from all over the USA since its foundation with its picturesque setting that includes 450 flamingos residing in the infield.

A crowd of 17,000 attended the track's opening meeting on January 15, 1925, which saw Mose Goldblatt's Corinth win the featured $1,500 Miami Handicap. Joseph E Widener, who patterned Hialeah after some of the finest racecourses in Europe, was named president in 1931 and the track immediately began to flourish. In the mid 1930s, it became recognized by the nation's top stables as the place to be during the winter. It began to attract some of the world's most noted celebrities and, through the years, has entertained such personalities as Winston Churchill, Harry Truman, Joseph Kennedy, Lord Derby and numerous others.

Like many tracks in America, Hialeah is a mile-and-an-eighth in circumference, with a three-furlong nursery chute for two-year-old races. The main attraction is the nine-furlong Flamingo Stakes for three-year-olds. Through the years it has served as a stepping stone for nine Kentucky Derby winners, including Citation, Carry Back, Northern Dancer, Tim Tam, Seattle Slew and Spectacular Bid. Citation, who won four races at the 1948 meeting, has been immortalized in a magnificent bronze statue gracing the paddock area. Perhaps the most memorable running of the Flamingo Stakes was in 1957, when Wheatley Stable's Bold Ruler held off a closing drive by Calumet Farm's Gen Duke to win by a neck in a track record time of 1 minute 47 seconds.

Another important fixture at Hialeah is the Widener Handicap for three-year-olds and upwards. This mile-and-a-quarter event has been won by such outstanding handicap stars as Forego, Armed, Nashua, War Admiral, Bull Lea and Coaltown.

In the 1970s, however, attendance and betting at Hialeah began to drop and the track's future was in jeopardy. In 1976 it was sold by John Galbreath to a New Jersey construction man John Brunetti for over $13,000,000. Hialeah now alternates each year with its neighbour Gulfstream Park for the choice middle dates from January to March and is a vacationers' paradise, providing high class racing in elegance and comfort.

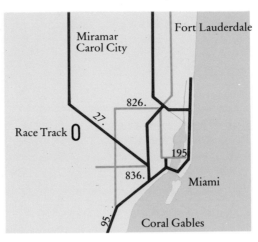

Hialeah is twelve miles from Miami, Florida, and two miles from Miami airport.

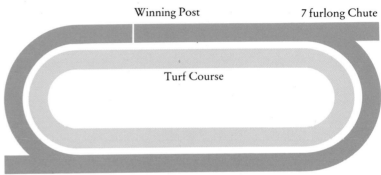

The track is a nine furlong oval on loam soil, with 358-yard straight. There are chutes for the seven furlong and nursery starts. The inner turf course of seven furlongs and 171 yards is banked on the turns with a 325-yard straight.

Hialeah, Florida

Dirt, 9f circumference, 358y, straight, 7f start on chute. **Turf,** 7f 171y circumference, 325y straight. Seating 20,000. Record crowd 42,366 (1956).
Racing (alternates annually with Gulfstream) January–March, March–May.

Major races: Flamingo Stakes (9f), Widener H'cap (10f), (both Gr I).

Below *Past the post with the infield lake in the background, the home of a flock of flamingoes. Hialeah races from January to March and from March to May, alternating annually with Gulfstream Park.*

Right *Runners being taken to the start by the lead horses.* **Below right** *The statue of Citation at Hialeah, one of the greatest horses to race in Florida.*

Saratoga

On August 15, 1863, less than a month after the Battle of Gettysburg, the first race meeting held at Saratoga Springs, New York was concluded. One of the sporting weeklies of the day, the *Spirit of the Times*, commented '. . . It must have laid the foundation for a great fashionable race meeting at the Springs, like that at Ascot in England, where the elegance and superb costumes of the ladies vie with the blood and beauty of the running horses . . .'

Saratoga had cast its first spell on the public. Over a century has passed, and although it has matured from its volatile infancy, the tiny town under the elms still possesses the power to lure people from all walks of life. Every August, buses, cars, trains, private jets, and most importantly, horse boxes converge on Saratoga in a mass influx of man and beast. A typical horse box leaving Belmont Park may contain the most diverse assortment of life since Noah's Ark. Humans, horses, dogs, cats, goats and an occasional rooster make up the average passenger list.

Once in Saratoga, visitors can see the remains of an era gone by. Small hotels stand wearily on last legs, a reminder of their majestic ancestors that sprawled over city blocks and catered to the opulent tastes of America's financial giants. From a visit to the museum in Canfield Casino one can visualize the celebrated gambler Diamond Jim Brady arriving at the Grand Union Hotel with his suite of twenty-seven Japanese houseboys, or the actress Lillian Russell riding about on a gold-plated bicycle with her name engraved on it in diamonds, a gift from Brady. There was also John 'Bet a Million' Gates, who once lost $400,000 at the track in a single day, then, to nurse his wounds, went to Canfield's gambling saloon, where he managed to lose another $150,000. By dawn, however, he had won back the $150,000, plus most of what he had lost at the track.

Saratoga's nefarious history can be traced to its founder John Morrisey. Nicknamed Old Smoke, Morrisey was a tough Irishman who had been a street gang leader in New York, a hired bully, a bouncer in brothels and saloons, an election-fixer and, eventually, US Congressman. He was also heavyweight boxing champion of America under London Prize Ring rules. At the age of thirty, Morrisey came to Saratoga, which had always been famous for its mineral waters, and opened the town's first big-time gambling hall. Witnin two years, he built a horse track. When it proved too small and primitive, he built a larger, more elaborate one on the site where Saratoga racetrack still stands.

Through the early 1900s, Saratoga's

Saratoga is at Saratoga Springs, thirty miles from Albany, New York.

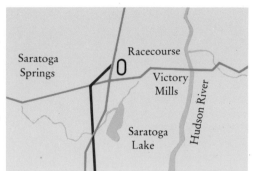

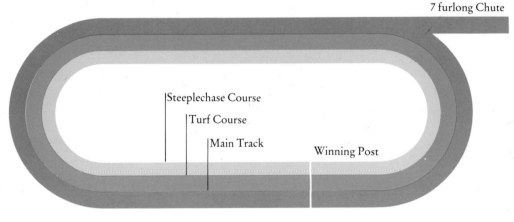

The track is a nine-furlong oval on sandy loam with a straight of 381 yards. There is a chute for the seven-furlong start. There is an inner turn course of seven furlongs and 171 yards, with banked turns. The inner steeplechase course has five obstacles.

7 furlong Chute

Steeplechase Course

Turf Course

Main Track

Winning Post

Saratoga Springs, NY.

Dirt, 9f circumference, 381y straight. 7f start on chute. **Turf**, 8f circumference. **Steeplechase** inside turf course. Seating 8,865. Record Crowd 35,530 (1977). Racing August.

Major races: Alabama Stakes (1¼m, 3-y-o fillies), Hopeful Stakes (6½f, 2-y-o-), Spinaway Stakes (6f, 2-y-o- fillies), Travers Stakes (1¼m, 3-y-o) (all Gr I).

decadence continued. All night gambling at Canfield's would be followed by a 6am breakfast of frogs legs and champagne served at the track. Screens would discreetly be put around anyone who collapsed from the food or, more probably, the drink. Harry Payne Whitney and his son William would play tennis for $10,000 a set and polo for even higher stakes. During poker games, when hard cash ran low, owners would often bet their horses.

In 1939 the first of these exciting elements vanished when the bookmakers were replaced by pari-mutuel machines. In 1950 the Kefauver hearings shut down the crap tables and roulette wheels. Finally in 1952, the last of the great hotels, the Grand Union was torn down thus ending one of the most flamboyant eras in American history. One tradition that is still observed, however, is the presentation of first-class racing. In 1979, nineteen stakes races were crammed into twenty-four days. These included four Grade I stakes – the Travers, Alabama, Hopeful and Spinaway Stakes.

Saratoga is also noted for one other factor. Even with all the great champions that have competed and won here, the track has always been known as 'The Graveyard of Favourites'. This tradition dates back to 1919, when the great Man O'War shocked the nation by suffering the only defeat of his career in the Sanford Stakes. His conqueror was the aptly-named Upset, who never came close to beating Man O'War again in their four subsequent meetings. Then in 1930, an obscure 100-1 outsider named Jim Dandy defeated the Triple Crown winner Gallant Fox by eight lengths in the Travers Stakes. It was Jim Dandy's only victory in twenty starts that year and Gallant Fox's only loss in ten races. In 1973, Saratoga opened the infield for the first time to accommodate the record crowd that poured in to see Secretariat in the Whitney Stakes. Unfortunately, 'Big Red' also fell prey to the Saratoga jinx, and was defeated by a lightly-regarded opponent named Onion, who was scoring the only stakes win of his career.

Far left *The side of the stands and the fountain at Keeneland.* **Left** *Early morning training on the track. Work riders do no more than ride the horses, handing them back to the grooms after their exercise.* **Below** *A finish on the turf track. Ogden Phipps, the Chairman of Saratoga, is a strong supporter of turf racing in Britain.* **Bottom** *Hosing down legs after exercise in the racecourse stables. Grooms tend to wash their horses clean.*

Hollywood Park/Arlington Park

Hollywood Park is at Inglewood, California, ten miles from Los Angeles, eight miles from Hollywood, and four miles from the International airport.

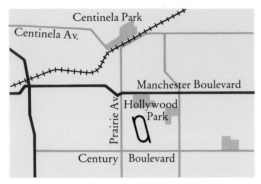

Hollywood Park, North America's leading race track during most of the 1970s in terms of average daily attendance, average daily wagering and purses paid, is not located, as might logically be assumed, in or near Hollywood, the capital of the world's entertainment industry. Its founders, who included many of Hollywood's most renowned film giants of the time, wanted it to be located there, but were unable to find a suitable parcel of land in the area. They therefore ventured a few miles south to the suburb of Inglewood. There, they acquired 315 acres of barren land on which to build the second major Los Angeles race track.

After various corporate problems, which found some of the original shareholders deserting the ship, Hollywood opened for thirty-four days of racing on June 10, 1938.

War and natural disaster, however, shut down Hollywood Park in turn. During the Second World War, its facilities were used by the military, the track re-opening in 1944. It was again closed five years later – this time by a disastrous fire, which led to its meetings being transferred to Santa Anita. Nevertheless, a 'new' Hollywood Park opened in 1951, the occasion being properly celebrated by Calumet Farm's mighty champion, Citation. He became the thoroughbred world's first millionaire by scoring easily in the Hollywood Gold Cup. In 1979 Harbor View Farm's champion, Affirmed, became racing's first two million dollar horse by winning the $500,000 Hollywood Gold Cup.

Between Citation and Affirmed, Hollywood Park patrons were treated to a steady stream of champions. These included horses such as Swaps, Round Table, Kelso, Native Diver, Fort Marcy, Dr Fager, Ack Ack, Riva Ridge, Seattle Slew and Cougar II, among many others.

The distaff stars who have graced the Hollywood Park stage are just as impressive as their male counterparts. They include Two Lea, Silver Spoon, Gamely, Princessnesian, Turkish Trousers, Convenience, Typecast, Susan's Girl, Cascapedia and Dahlia.

The season has now been extended to seventy-seven to seventy-eight days of summer sport. The centrepiece is a mile dirt track, with chutes for seven-furlong and ten-furlong races. The track also has a diagonal, inner grass course, which is used for a high percentage of its races.

The track is a one-mile oval on sandy loam with a 323 yards straight. The inner turf course is just over seven furlongs.

Training Track

Main Track

Turf Course

7 furlong Chute

1¼ mile Chute

Winning Post

Inglewood, Los Angeles, California.

Dirt, 1m circumference, 323y straight. 7f, 10f start on chutes. **Turf,** 7f 45y circumference. 9f start on chute (in centre of course). Seating 31,100. Record crowd 72,186 (1948).
Racing April–July.

Major races: Californian Stakes (8½f), Century H'cap (11f, turf), Hollywood Derby (9f), Hollywood Invitational H'cap (12f, turf), Hollywood Oaks (9f), Sunset H'cap (12f turf), Swaps Stakes (10f), Vanity H'cap (9f) (all Gr I).

Left *The back of the stands, with seating for 31,000. A record crowd of 72,186 attended in 1948. The course was opened in 1938.* **Right** *Runners approach the furlong pole, with the nine-furlong chute for the turf course in the background. The season at Hollywood is from mid-April to late July.*

Arlington Park

Arlington Park, which held its first meeting on October 13, 1927, has long been the keystone of mid-American racing. The track probably reached its height under Benjamin F Lindheimer, the executive director who died in June, 1960, at the age of sixty-nine. He was a revolutionary in turf circles, pioneering grass racing and increasing opportunities for fillies and mares. In the early 1950s he was responsible for the rich stakes programme that soon became *de rigueur* in the USA.

Lindheimer's attractive stakes schedules lured some of the outstanding performers to his mile-and-one-eighth track in Arlington Heights, Illinois. Citation, the 1948 Triple Crown winner and Horse of the Year, raced twice at the track, taking a five-eighths mile sprint in the third start of his career as a two-year-old and also capturing the Stars and Stripes Handicap at three. That race was one of fifteen stakes he won at three years, a figure that is still a record.

The roster of Arlington classic winners contains the names of some of the leading thoroughbred performers of all time. They include such horses as Blue Larkspur, Gallant Fox, Mate, Cavalcade, Omaha, Challedon, Attention (who beat that year's Triple Crown champion Whirlaway), Shut out, Slide Rule, Twilight Tear, Ponder, Mark-Ye-Well, Native Dancer, Nashua, Ridan, Tom Rolfe, Buckpasser (who covered the course in a world-record 1 minute 32³/₅ seconds for a mile), Dr Fager, Ack Ack and Alydar. Champions also abound in the Arlington Park Handicap and the Arlington Futurity and Lassie Stakes. In his great 1973 year, Secretariat scored an easy victory there.

On his death, Lindheimer was replaced as director by his daughter, Mrs Marjorie Everett. Under her aegis, the track tried night racing for the Arlington Futurity in 1969 and Silent Screen won the $206,075 for Sonny Werblin's Elberon Farm.

Arlington Park is at Arlington Heights, Palatine, twelve miles from O'Hare airport, in the western suburbs of Chicago, Illinois.

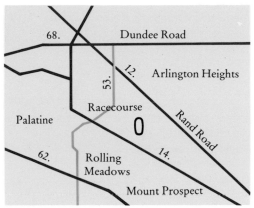

Arlington is a nine-furlong oval on sandy loam, with a chute for the seven and eight-furlong starts. The straight is 343 yards. The turf course is a one-mile circuit, with an inner turf course of seven furlongs. There is a six-furlong training track inside all three tracks.

1 mile 7 furlong Chute

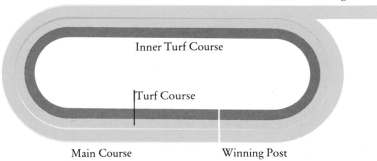

Inner Turf Course

Turf Course

Main Course   Winning Post

Above *The dirt and turf courses with the lake behind.*

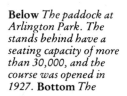

Below *The paddock at Arlington Park. The stands behind have a seating capacity of more than 30,000, and the course was opened in 1927.* **Bottom** *The enormous internal television screen in the betting hall. On September 2, 1974, the track handled more than $3 million in bets in one day.*

Arlington Heights, Chicago, Illinois

Dirt, 9f circumference, 343y straight. **Turf,** 8f circumference. **Inner turf,** 7f circumference. Seating 30,600. Record crowd 50,638 (1941). Racing June–September.

Major races: Arlington–Washington Futurity (7f, Gr I), American Derby (10f), Arlington Classic (10f), Secretariat Stakes (12f) (all Gr II).

Del Mar/Laurel/Meadowlands/Oaklawns

Among numerous highlights of racing at Del Mar, which has enjoyed immense attendance and growth of business in recent years, are the performances of C S Howard's immortal Seabiscuit and George Woolf's defeat of Crosby and Lin Howard's Ligaroti in a $25,000 winner-take-all match in 1938. Other memorable moments include John Longden surpassing England's Sir Gordon Richards as the world's most successful rider with his 4,871st winner, achieved on Arrogate in the 1956 Del Mar Handicap, and Bill Shoemaker overtaking Longden by scoring a record 6,033rd victory, on Dares J, fourteen years later on Labor Day, 1970.

Thoroughbred racing of a high quality is presented each summer from late July to mid-September. It is conducted under the aegis of the Del Mar Thoroughbred Club, a non-dividend paying corporation administered by a board of directors consisting of California thoroughbred breeders-owners. It operates the track on on twenty-year lease from the state of California.
Situated in the San Dieguito River valley, less than a half-mile from the shoreline of the Pacific Ocean and twenty-five miles north of the resort city of San Diego, Del Mar is one of the USA's most attractive and charming centres of thoroughbred racing. The track 'where the turf meets the surf', is visually distinguished. Its buildings are fashioned after the style of Spanish missions of the American west.

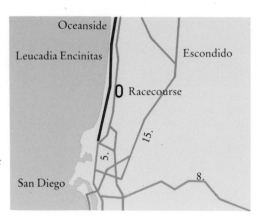

Del Mar racecourse is at Del Mar, twenty miles from San Diego and 100 miles south of Los Angeles. Palomar airport is sixteen miles away.

At the home turn on the seven-furlong turf course. Times are slower than on the one-mile dirt course, which has a straight of just over one furlong. There are six-furlong and ten-furlong chutes on the dirt course, made up of sand, loam and silt.

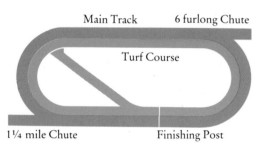

Del Mar, California.

Dirt, 1m circumference, 277y straight. 6f, 10f starts on chutes. **Turf,** 7f circumference, 9f start on chute (in centre of course). Seating 15,600. Record crowd 24,169 (1949).
Racing July–September

Major races: Del Mar Debutante Stakes (8f), Del Mar Futurity Stakes (8f), Del Mar H'cap (10f), Del Mar Oaks (9f), (all Gr II).

Laurel

Laurel Racecourse in Maryland is known throughout the world as the home of the Washington DC International. Since its inaugural running in 1952, horses from twenty-three countries have competed in the mile-and-a-half event, some coming from places as far apart as Singapore, New Zealand and the Soviet Union.

Laurel held its first meeting in 1911 The track changed ownership in 1947, when the Maryland Jockey Club bought a controlling interest, but three years later the club sold it to a Baltimore industrialist Morris Schapiro, who installed his youngest son, John, as president. Quickly the track began to prosper. The Schapiros built a new $3,000,000 clubhouse and turf club, refurbished the grandstand, built a new turf course and landscaped the surrounding area.

Two years after the Schapiros bought it, Laurel was ready to play host to the finest horses in the world. International racing had been tried in the past without success, largely due to various obstacles such as expenses, travel time and quarantine.

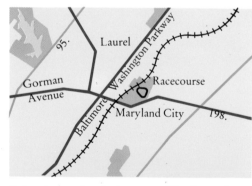

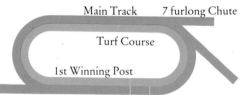

Schapiro solved these problems and on October 18, 1952, the Washington DC International became a reality.

The first running was won by the four-year-old English colt Wilwyn, who earned $32,500. In 1956, the high calibre of European racing was confirmed when the French colt Master Boing, after being soundly beaten by Ribot in Europe, galloped home by five lengths in the International. Two years later Vincent O'Brien brought John McShain's Ballymoss over from Ireland. The little son of Mossborough was the toast of Europe, winning the Arc de Triomphe, the King George VI

Laurel Park, is at Laurel, Maryland, twenty miles from Baltimore, twenty miles from Washington and twelve miles from the Baltimore-Washington International airport. The track is a nine-furlong oval on sand and

loam, with seven, eight and eleven-furlong chutes. The turf course is one mile round, with a one-and-a-half-furlong straight.

Laurel, Maryland.

Dirt, 9f circumference, 338y straight. 7f, 8f, 11f start on chutes. **Turf,** 8f circumference, 330y straight. Seating for 19,400. Record crowd 40,276 (1958). Racing October–December.

Major races: Laurel Futurity (8½f), Selima Stakes (8½f), Washington DC International (12f, turf) (all Gr I).

and Queen Elizabeth Stakes, the Eclipse Stakes, the Coronation Cup, the St Leger and the Irish Derby, while finishing second in the Epsom Derby. Unfortunately, he encountered difficulties during the International and finished third, as the 11-10 favourite.

In 1960, Cain Hoy Stable's Bald Eagle, under jockey Manuel Ycaza, became the first horse to win the race twice. Four years later, the great gelding Kelso, after suffering three tough losses, finally won the International in a record time of 2 minutes 23⅘ seconds. In 1967, Paul Mellon's Fort Marcy defeated the Horse of the Year Damascus in a thrilling stretch battle that saw the winner come again to prevail by a nose. The following year, it was a victory for Ireland as Raymond Guest's Epsom Derby winner Sir Ivor turned in a devastating run through the stretch to win by almost a length.

Paul Mellon became the first owner to win three Internationals when Fort Marcy and Run the Gauntlet scored in 1970 and 1971. That feat was duplicated by Nelson Bunker Hunt in 1973, 1974 and 1976, as Dahlia, Nobiliary and Youth all scored impressive wins representing France. The recent victories of Johnny D. and Mac Diarmida brought US horses back into the reckoning.

In its relatively short history, the International has been unique in its accomplishments. It became the first race in the world outside Great Britain in which a runner carried royal colours, when Queen Elizabeth's Landau competed in 1954. It has attracted such owners as Sir Winston Churchill, Prince Aly Khan and Karim Aga Khan, Baron Guy de Rothschild and the government of the USSR. What began as a dream almost thirty years ago has now evolved into one of the world's great international fixtures.

Meadowlands

Appointed as chairman of the New Jersey Sports and Exposition Authority in 1971, Sonny Werblin, then sixty-one, overcame a series of crises that might have broken the will of a less dedicated man in his determination to bring quality racing to New Jersey. In 1976, his hopes were realized when the Meadowlands racetrack, part of a larger New Jersey sports complex, rose on 588 acres of what used to be bog and marshland in East Rutherford. The leading night track in the land had been born.

By 1977, after a long spell of harness racing, thoroughbred racing made its debut at the one-mile track which is only four miles from the heart of New York City and has a three-state population of 18,000,000 on which to draw. That meeting ran for 100 nights, from the day after Labor Day until the end of December. It was established permanently by the prospectus that sold the $302,000,000 in bonds which kept the sports complex alive.

Werblin and the professional manager, Jack Krumpe, he hired to start the massive project moved on to New York not long after the thoroughbred track opened. But their successors have firmly established the course among the leaders of the sport in the east, topped only by New York Racing Association's Belmont, Aqueduct and Saratoga. The track has two chutes, a seven-furlong turf course and has already attracted horses of the class of Seattle Slew, Spectacular Bid, Valdez and Davona Dale. With further expansion still a possibility, it can hold, at capacity, 42,000 people.

East Rutherford, New Jersey.

Dirt, 8f circumference, 330y straight. 6f, 10f start on chutes. **Turf,** 7f circumference, 330y straight. Seating 10,000. Record crowd 42,000 (1979). Racing September–December.

Major races: Young America Stakes (Gr I), Meadowlands Cup H'cap (Gr II).

Oaklawn Park

Few racetracks in the USA can match the growth of Oaklawn Park over the past decade. Located in Hot Springs, Arkansas, Oaklawn's average daily attendance has risen from 9,932 in 1968 to 21,164 in 1978.

Although it first opened in 1904, Oaklawn is just beginning to establish itself as one of the top race tracks in America. Its purses are among the most lucrative in the country; as a consequence, the four big stake races – the Arkansas Derby, the Oaklawn Handicap, the Apple Blossom Handicap and the Fantasy Stakes – are now beginning to draw the nation's best horses.

Oaklawn is a one-mile oval, with a six-furlong chute, and a good run of 1,155 feet from the top of the stretch to the finish line. It is conducive to moves around the turn, and has favoured come-from-behind horses over recent years. For the third time in the past ten years, the managing authority is preparing a major improvement plan, which is expected to cost more than $2,500,000. It calls for the construction of seven to ten concrete and steel barns that will provide stalls for an estimated 450 horses. Also included is the building of tack rooms, living quarters, horse paths, service roads, utility lines, parking for track personnel and extensive landscaping. Over the last decade, Oaklawn has spent more than $12,000,000 on capital improvement.

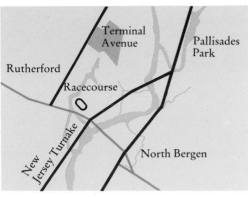

Meadowlands is at East Rutherford, New Jersey, four miles from the Lincoln Tunnel and eight miles from the George Washington Bridge. The course is a one-mile oval / *on sandy loam, with chutes for six and ten furlongs. The straight is one-and-a-half furlongs. The turf course is seven furlongs round*

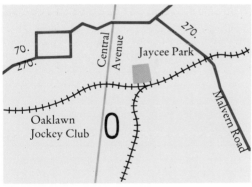

Oaklawn is at Hot Springs, Arkansas, two miles from the airport. The course is a one-mile / *oval on sand and clay, with a 383-yard straight. There is a six-furlong chute.*

Such ambitious planning is what makes Oaklawn Park one of the most profitable race tracks in America. It is constantly trying to improve itself, using its profits for the betterment of racing. If this philosophy is maintained, there is no telling how far it can develop in the future.

Woodbine

Since being built in June 1956, the new track at Woodbine, near Toronto, Canada, has grown not only into one of the great racecourses of North America, but also of the world. The old track, which had operated since 1881, was replaced by an elaborate $13,000,000 structure, conceived by and built largely through the efforts of the Ontario Jockey Club chairman Mr E P Taylor.

Perhaps the greatest boost to Woodbine over recent years has been the rapid emergence of the Canadian International Championship as one of the world's most important races. Once a local race, run as the Canadian Championship Stakes on a dirt track, the International was changed to a mile and five-eighths over the new two mile Marshall turf course in 1956. Each year the quality of the horses improved slightly, but it was not until 1973, when the Triple Crown winner, Secretariat, concluded his career with a six-and-a-half length victory, that the International first attracted a top class American star.

The race then began to take on an international flavour with the great French filly, Dahlia, winning in 1974. In 1975 the Epsom Derby winner Snow Knight defeated a star-studded field that included Dahlia, Admetus (the Washington International winner) and Comtesse de Loir, all from France. The French continued their strong influence over the next two years when Nelson Bunker Hunt's Youth and Exceller won. In 1978, however, Mac Diarmida turned the tables on the French, defeating Dom Alaric and Amazer.

The most important local event of the Canadian racing season is the historic Queen's Plate. First run in 1860, this is North America's oldest, continuously-run stake race. More than 4,000 spectators attended its first running at Carleton racetrack, outside Toronto, when the winner, Don Juan, received a prize of fifty guineas donated by Queen Victoria. In 1883, the Queen's Plate was moved to the old Woodbine, where it remained until 1956, when the Ontario Jockey Club transferred the race to the new track.

Over the years, E P Taylor has dominated the Plate, breeding eighteen winners and owning ten. These include Northern Dancer and Flaming Page, the sire and dam of the English Triple Crown winner Nijinsky.

Woodbine is one of the most unique tracks in North America. It has four separate chutes, and a one-mile dirt track that is encompassed by the seven-furlong and two-mile turf courses. It is not only the showcase of Canadian racing, but a major influence on international competition.

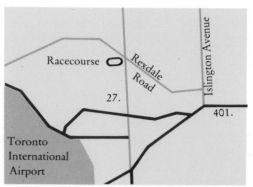

Top *The stands at Woodbine, with seating for 10,000. A further 3,000 can be seated in the clubhouse.* **Above** *The American Triple Crown winner Secretariat after winning the 1973 Canadian International Championship over one mile five furlongs on turf at Woodbine.* **Right** *The start in front of the stands on the dirt course.* **Far right** *Secretariat being led down to the start for the Canadian Championship. Later winners were Dahlia, the Epsom Derby winner Snow Knight, Youth and Exceller.*

Training Track

Woodbine dirt track is an eight-furlong oval on sandy loam, with a one-and-a-half-furlong straight. There are three-and seven-furlong chutes. The turf course is a combination of the outside Marshall course and the inner turf oval of six-and-a-half furlongs. Races of up to two miles can be run. There is a three-furlong chute, and an outside training track.

Etobicoke, Ontario

Dirt, 1m circumference, 325y straight. 3f, 7f start on chutes. **Turf**, combination of Marshall course (outside) and inner turf oval (6½f) (5f races inner oval, 6f Marshall, 7f, 1m, 8½f, 1½m either, 1¼m, 11f inner oval, 9f, 13f, 1¾m, 2m Marshall). Seating for 13,000. Record crowd 40,137 (1973). Racing May–July, September–October.

Major races: Canadian International Championship (13f turf) (US Gr I), Breeders' Stakes (1½m turf, 3-y-o), Canadian Oaks (9f, 3-y-o fillies), Coronation Futurity (9f, 2-y-o), Prince of Wales Stakes (11f turf, 3-y-o), Princess Elizabeth Stakes (8½f, 2-y-o fillies), Queen's Plate Stakes (1¼m, 3-y-o).

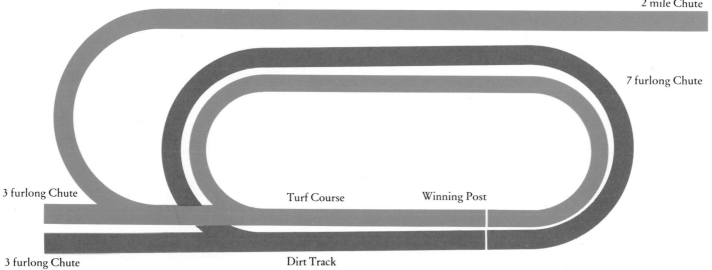

2 mile Chute

7 furlong Chute

3 furlong Chute

Turf Course   Winning Post

3 furlong Chute   Dirt Track

Caracas

Venezuela's main racecourse, La Rinconada, is set among the hills outside the
city of Caracas. Opened in 1939, the
course is a right-handed circuit of a mile
with a straight of just under two furlongs.
Despite the tightness of the turns, however, there is a chute of two-and-a-half
furlongs running into the home straight
which provides the start for one-and-a-
half-mile races, giving a run of five furlongs
before the first turn. Inside the dirt track is
a turf course of seven-and-a-half furlongs.
A training track of four furlongs lies
beyond the home turn.

The magnificent stands at La Rinconada
were designed by Arthur Froelich, responsible for the stands at Belmont,
Aqueduct and Hollywood Park. Air-
conditioned, they lack nothing in facilities
for racegoers and jockeys, with rest rooms,
a gymnasium, turkish baths and oxygen
rooms for those who feel the strain of
racing at 3,000ft. Costing some £24
million, a huge sum compared with the
£3.25 million spent on Goodwood and
Sandown's £1.75 million, they provide
seating for 12,500 and room for at least
60,000 in all.

The ability to pay for the stands, and the
substantial prize money that is offered at
La Rinconada compared with other South
American countries, comes from the
deduction of thirty-nine per cent from the
totalizator pool, a large amount by any
standards but insufficient to deter the
hardened Venezuelan punters. Their all-
abiding task is to win the five and six bet,
which requires punters to name six winners
with a consolation prize for those naming
five winners. In pursuit of this goal they are
prepared to invest doggedly, but the
rewards are enormous. A winner in 1978
received a prize of more than £400,000.

Although the standard of racing in
Venezuela is not high class, rare international successes have been achieved,
notably when the Venezuelan El Chama
and Prendase finished first and second in
the 1955 Washington International. The
record in the Clasico Internacional del
Caribe, a nine-furlong race for three-year-
olds confined to horses from countries in
or bordering on the Caribbean, is also unimpressive. Venezuelan horses have won
twice, compared with seven from Mexico.

While a large number of races have been
transferred from La Rinconada to
Valencia, the new coastal racecourse,
including the Venezuelan running of the
Internacional del Caribe so that it can be
run below 1,600ft, La Rinconada still
stages the major race in that country. This
is the Clasico Simon Bolivar, a weight-for-
age race run over one-and-a-half miles.

La Rinconada is at
Caracas, Venezuela, in
the hills outside the city.
The course is 3,000 ft
above sea level.

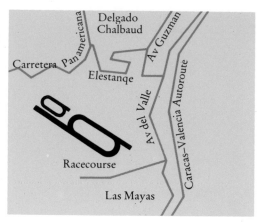

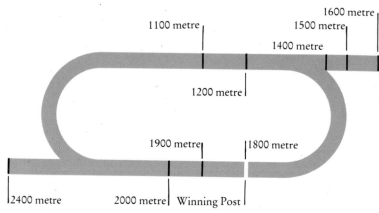

The one-mile dirt track
has chutes for the seven-
furlong and one-and-a-
half-mile starts. The
straight is 385 yards, and
there is an inside turf
track of seven furlongs.

Caracas, Venezuela.

Dirt, 1m circumference, 385y straight. 7f, 1½m start on chutes. Seating for 12,500, capacity 70,000. Racing all year round. Saturdays and Sundays (12 race cards).

Major race: Clasico Simon Bolivar.

Far right *The unsaddling enclosure at La Rinconada.* **Right** *The run to the line.* **Below** *La Rinconada cost £24 million to build, and is the home of the Classico Simon Bolivar, Venezuela's international classic event. The stands house a Hall of Fame, rest rooms, a gymnasium, Turkish baths and an oxygen room. They were designed by Arthur Froelich, responsible for the new stands at Belmont, Aqueduct and Hollywood Park, and were opened in 1959.*

São Paulo/Rio de Janeiro

Racing at São Paulo is the responsibility of the São Paulo Jockey Club, which was founded in 1875 and held its first meeting in October of the following year at Hipodromo da Moóca. Racing continued there until 1941, when a new course, Cidade Jardim, was built; this covers a total area of 600,000 square metres. There are two left-handed tracks – one sand and one grass – both of which are just over 2,000 metres in extent.

Though São Paulo's landscape has changed greatly over the years, the course retains much of its original character. The scene is still dominated by the track's imposing stands, which are packed to capacity for Cidade Jardim's two main races. These are the GP São Paulo and the GP Derby Paulista. Both of these are run over 2,400 metres, the former being an international event for three-year-olds and upwards. It was run for the first time in 1923. The Derby Paulista is slightly older than the São Paulo; run every November, it was introduced into the racing calendar in 1917.

Probably the best horse ever to race at the track was Adil, a bay imported *in utero* from England, whose breeding line included the great name of Nearco. Adil was successful in the 1954 Derby Paulista and, for three consecutive years from 1955, in the GP São Paulo – the only horse to date to perform this feat.

Cidade Jardim racecourse is at São Paulo, Brazil, five miles from the city centre.

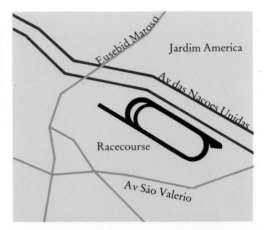

Above *Pomp and circumstances in the Presidential Box. Racing takes place at weekends on turf, and on Monday nights on dirt under lights.* **Right** *The course stages the São Paulo Triple Crown for colts and fillies on turf, and the Gran Premio São Paulo, a weight-for-age* race over one-and-a-half miles. The course in 2,500 ft above sea level, and is just south of the Equator.*

São Paulo, Brazil.

Turf, LH, 10f circumference, 3f straight. 5f straight course. 9f, 10f start on chutes. **Dirt**, 9¾f circumference, 2¾f straight. **Inside dirt**, 8¾f circumference, 2¼f straight.
Racing Saturday, Sunday on turf, Monday night under lights on dirt.

Major races: GP Criacao Nacional (1m), GP Diana (1¼m), GP Jose Guathemozin Nogueira (1½m) (fillies Triple Crown). GP Ipirange (1m), GP Derby Paulista (1½m), GP Consagracao (1m 7f) (Triple Crown).

Cidade Jardim is a left-handed ten-and-a-quarter-furlong turf track with a three-furlong straight. There is a straight five furlongs. Nine- and ten-furlong races start from a chute. There are two dirt tracks, of almost ten furlongs and nine furlongs, with one-and-a-half and one-furlong straights.

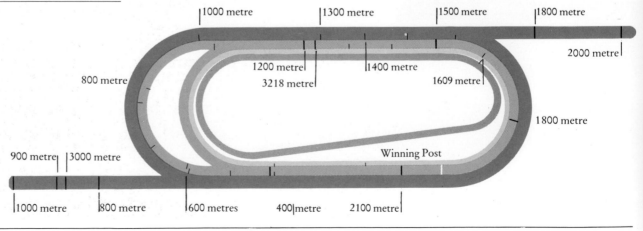

Rio de Janeiro

The Rio de Janeiro Jockey Club was founded in 1868. Their first racecourse there was called Prado Fluminense and the first meeting took place the following year. Fifty-seven years later, however, races were transferred to a new race course – the Hipódromo da Gavéa; this has been in operation since July 1926.

Gavéa has both a sand and a grass track. The tracks are left-handed and about 2,050 metres in extent. The course itself is located in a very suitable setting for the sport, one of the most attractive parts of Rio de Janeiro.

The best races at Gavéa are the GP Brasil and the GP Cruziero do Sol. The former is for four-year-olds and upwards; it is run in August over 2,400 metres. Introduced into the racing calendar in 1933, it is considered to be the most important race in Brazil. The GP Cruziero do Sul was first run in 1883; from 1933 onwards, it has been considered the Rio equivalent of the Derby.

The first GP Brasil winner was a grey colt called Mossoro. He was later sent to England, where he won at Bath in 1936 and was placed on several occasions. According to press reports, he was the first South American thoroughbred to race in England.

Gavéa racecourse is at Rid de Janeiro, Brazil, 300 miles from São Paulo. Left-handed, it has a ten-and-a-quarter furlong turf course and a nine-and-a-quarter furlong dirt course.

Rio de Janeiro, Brazil.

Turf, LH, 10¼f circumference, 3½f straight. 5f straight course. Dirt, 9¼f circumference, 3¼f straight.

Major races: Grande Premio Brasil (1½m, 4-y-o and up), GP Cruziero do Sul (Rio Derby, 1½m), GP Jockey Club Brasileiro (Rio St Leger, 1m 7f), GP General Couto de Magalhaes (2m, wfa), GP Major Suckow (5f, 3-y-o), GP Presidente da Republica (1m, 3-y-o and up).

Gavéa racecourse is hard by the sea. On the coastal side of the track can be seen the training track. The course stages similar races to those at São Paulo, although not at the same time, and a great rivalry exists between the two courses. Besides the Rio classic races, the course also stages the Grande Premio Brazil, a four-year-old and upward weight-for-age race over one-and-a-half miles and the GP Presidente da Republica for three-year-olds and up over a mile on turf.

Flemington

Melbourne's first race meeting was held on March 6 and 7, 1838, less than three years after the first settlers arrived. The first track was marked out on the present site of the North Melbourne Railway Station. With few horses there were only two races each day. Bullock trucks served as grandstands, and a clothes prop was stuck into the ground for a winning post. All bets were made and paid with bottles of rum.

Two years later saw the birth of Flemington, headquarters of the Victoria Racing Club, the controlling body of racing in that state, on a site on the banks of the Maribyrnong river. At first the site was known as 'The Racecourse', but it was later named Flemington after the local butcher, Bob Fleming. The inaugural fixture was a three-day event on March 3, 4 and 5, 1840, with a total of twelve races.

From its inception, Flemington was destined to be a great venue to attract the best horses for the richest prize-money. A succession of small clubs conducted the early race meetings at Flemington and it was the Victoria Turf Club which staged the first Melbourne Cup in 1861. This race, referred to in *Encyclopaedia Britannica* as the 'greatest all-age handicap in the world', has grown from strength to strength since the formation of the Victoria Racing Club; it is run on the first Tuesday in November each year.

In 1865 the Government declared Melbourne Cup day a half holiday, and since

Flemington is on the Epsom Road, Flemington, Victoria, four miles from Melbourne.

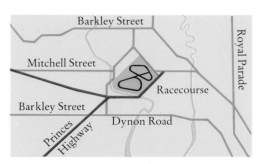

Right *Hyperno beats Salamander and Red Nose for the 1979 Melbourne Cup, Australia's greatest race.*
Below *First known as 'The Racecourse', the site on the banks of the Maribyrnong river later was called Flemington after the local butcher, Bob Fleming. Besides the*

huge stands, the densest gathering at Flemington is on The Hill. A ticket from Flinders Street station includes admittance to The Hill, an uncovered enclosure looking down on the winning post.

Flemington is a left-handed circuit of eleven-and-a-half furlongs, with a straight of just over two furlongs (253 metres). There is a straight six furlongs and a chute for the seven-furlong start. The Melbourne Cup field runs down the straight from the six-furlong course and completes a circuit. The hurdles and steeplechase course is inside the main course, looping outside on the left hand side.

Epsom Road, Flemington, Victoria. 4m from centre of Melbourne.

Turf, LH, 11½f circumference, 490¾y straight. 6f straight course. 7f start on chute. 'Chase/hurdle course inside. Record crowd 100,000.

Major races: Melbourne Cup H'cap, Craven 'A' H'cap, George Adams H'cap, Newmarket H'cap, Australian Cup, Blamey Stakes, Craiglee Stakes, LKS Mackinnon Stakes, Lightning Stakes, Linlithgow Stakes, Queen Elizabeth Stakes, Queen's Pte, Ascot Vale Stakes, Edward Manifold Stakes, Victoria Derby, VRC Oaks, Sires' Produce Stakes (all Gr I). Australian Grand National, Grand National Hurdle.

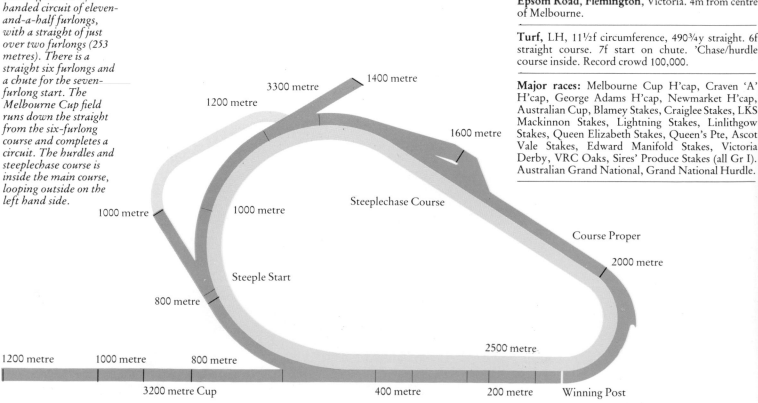

3300 metre
1400 metre
1200 metre
1600 metre
1000 metre
1000 metre
Steeplechase Course
Course Proper
2000 metre
Steeple Start
800 metre
2500 metre
1200 metre
1000 metre
800 metre
3200 metre Cup
400 metre
200 metre
Winning Post

1866 it has been a full holiday. An interesting runner in 1865 was Panic who had been foaled in England in 1858 and imported to Tasmania in 1860 by Mr S Blackwell. Panic, carrying 10st was beaten two lengths. He was an extraordinary horse, mixing racing with stud duty. He served his first mares as a three-year-old, and one of his sons, Nimblefoot, won the 1870 Melbourne Cup.

Imported horses who won the Mel-

bourne Cup were Comedy King (Persimmon–Tragedy Queen) in 1910 and Backwood (Bachelor's Double–Lady of Grace) in 1924, while The Grafter, winner of the 1898 Melbourne Cup, later won races in England, including the City and Suburban Handicap at Epsom.

Trenton, third in the 1885 Melbourne Cup and second the following year, provides an important reference point. Like Carbine, he was a son of the imported Musket. After racing, he was a successful sire in Australia before being sent to England, where he continued to prove himself. Trenton's daughter, Rosaline, was the dam of Rosedrop who won the English Oaks and produced Gainsborough.

Trenton's son, Torpoint sired Hamoaze, dam of Buchan, Saltash, and St Germans.

Flemington is a magnificent racecourse with the mile-and-a-half (2400 metres) start in front of the main grandstands, with a run from the home turn to the winning post of more than two furlongs. Another feature is the 'straight six' (now 1200 metres) which joins the main course at the home turn.

The birdcage area, sweeping lawns which extend the full length of the members' stands, a tree-lined lawn section for the public at the end of the straight, plus a new public grandstand complex, make Flemington a show-place. It is among the best racecourses in the world.

Flemington during Melbourne Cup Week is a mixture of the carnival atmosphere at Epsom on Derby Day, and the fashionable elegance of the Royal Ascot meeting, with the Victoria Derby on Saturday, the Cup on Tuesday and the Oaks on Thursday. The 1979 Melbourne Cup was worth $A310,000, which included a $A10,000 gold cup for the winner.

Left *Harry White and George Hanlon, the trainer. White has won the Melbourne Cup four times. The race was worth $A310,000 in 1979.*

Right *Fans jammed into the stands at Flemington. Melbourne Cup Day is a national holiday, when Australians start betting at the off-course tote offices soon after 9 am, and all other activities come to a standstill. At the course, fashion shows and beauty parades are held, with piped bands and various competitions for racegoers.*

Randwick

The course at Randwick, a few miles from the centre of Sydney and fringing Centennial Park, sits on a sandy base and is recognized as the finest wet weather track in Australia. It also provides one of the best turf racing surfaces in the world. Randwick has six training tracks inside the main grass track. They comprise two grass tracks, two sand tracks, one of sand and tan, and a dirt track (metal and ashes).

The Australian Jockey Club held its first meeting at Randwick on May 29, 1860, and on June 15, 1863, the crown finally granted Randwick racecourse to the trustees representing the Australian Jockey Club.

The AJC conducts its feature carnivals in the spring and autumn. The spring carnival in late September and early October features the Epsom Handicap over 1600 metres (one mile) and the Metropolitan Handicap over 2600 metres (thirteen furlongs). The AJC Derby has now been switched from the spring to the autumn, in the belief that three-year-olds are less strained by the 2,400 metres later in the season when they are more mature. The Doncaster Handicap (1600 metres) and Sydney Cup over 3,200 metres (two miles) are other major races at the Randwick Easter meeting.

Randwick operated its first automatic tote in December, 1917. In the first full year the Randwick tote investments were £705,456. Now with the on-course computer tote the Randwick 1977–78 racing year totalled some $A42.9 million.

There have been two revolutionary happenings in the history of the AJC which would cause some surprise in European racing countries. More than forty years ago the AJC banned all steeplechasing and hurdling on the grounds that jumping events were too difficult to control. Secondly the AJC dropped the St Leger from their turf calendar. Fields for the race were reduced to two or three runners, and the club decided that it was unprofitable to stage the classic when the stake money could be used to boost races with more public appeal.

Alison Road, Randwick, Sydney, NSW. 4m from city centre.

Turf, RH, 11f circumference, 2f straight. 5f, 6f, 7f and 8f starts from chutes.

Major races: Sydney Cup H'cap, Doncaster H'cap, Galaxy H'cap, Epsom H'cap, Metropolitan H'cap, Autumn Stakes, All-aged Stakes, Chelmsford Stakes, Craven Pte, George Main Stakes, Queen Elizabeth Stakes, AJC Derby, AJC Oaks, Spring Champion Stakes, Champagne Stakes, Sires' Produce Stakes (all Gr I).

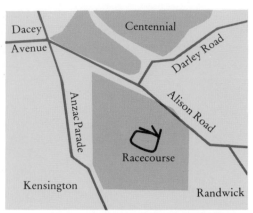

Randwick racecourse is on Allison Road, Randwick, New South Wales, four miles from the centre of Sydney.

A small field leaves the gate at Randwick. The turf at Randwick, which sits on a sandy base, provides one of the finest wet weather courses in Australia.

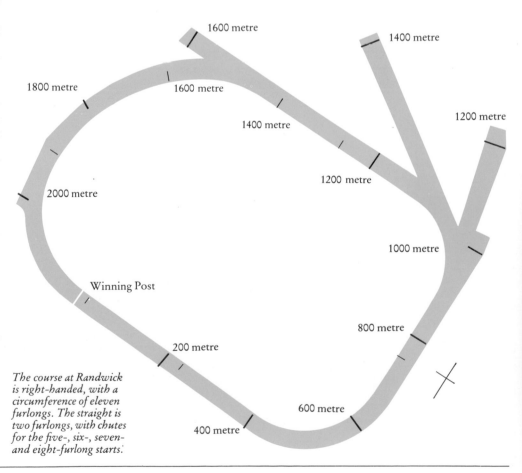

The course at Randwick is right-handed, with a circumference of eleven furlongs. The straight is two furlongs, with chutes for the five-, six-, seven- and eight-furlong starts.

Above *The stands and home straight at Randwick, showing some of the training tracks within the main course. Although surrounded by suburbs, Randwick serves as a* *training centre, with horses stables in nearby streets and on the racecourse.* **Below** *The 202 acres at Randwick were granted by Governor Darling in 1833. It has been the* *home of the Australian Jockey Club since 1860.* **Below right** *The parade ring in front of the ornate old stands, seen above on the right of the picture.*

Ascot

Since the Western Australian Turf Club introduced the first Australian Derby at Ascot (Perth) on December 26, 1972, that state's summer carnival has brought owners and trainers from all parts of the commonwealth and New Zealand. Runners for the Derby are invited to compete. If the top three-year-olds come through the AJC and VRC spring meetings, they clash again for the huge prize-money at Ascot. The classic, run over 2400 metres (1½m) is a $A250,000 race, with $A156,000 the winner's share.

The WATC summer racing carnival at Ascot has become an enormous money-spinner for the best horses from the Eastern States. The policy of the WATC has been to uplift stake money each year, so much so that the club has been accused of stirring up a stakes race with other major clubs. But off-course tote betting in the West is so big the WATC never misses an opportunity to plough back as much as possible to owners.

In 1829, when the first governor issued Official Notices, he included a regulation relating to Crown Lands and specifically declared expenditure 'for sites of towns, and racecourses . . .' Ascot had its first race meeting in 1840, but it was another twelve years before the WATC was founded in 1852. Today there is a new $A1.5 million grandstand at Ascot with world standard

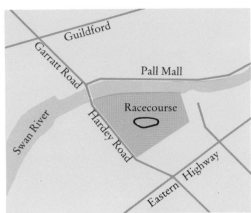

Ascot racecourse is at Perth, Western Australia. Five miles from the city centre, it is easily accessible by public transport and private cars.

facilities. The course, which has two grass tracks and two sand tracks, is ten furlongs round with a two furlong straight.

Racing in Western Australia was financially sound until the 1950s, when the Government legalized off-course betting shops in a move to stabilize the industry and to gain revenue from the large amount of illegal off-course betting. But book-

Below The course at Ascot is ten furlongs round, with a short straight of one-and-a-half furlongs. The home turn is a tight one, and local experience counts for much. There are chutes for the six-, seven-, seven-and-a-half-, eight- and twelve-furlong starts. **Right** Runners entering the short straight. The going at Ascot is invariably fast.

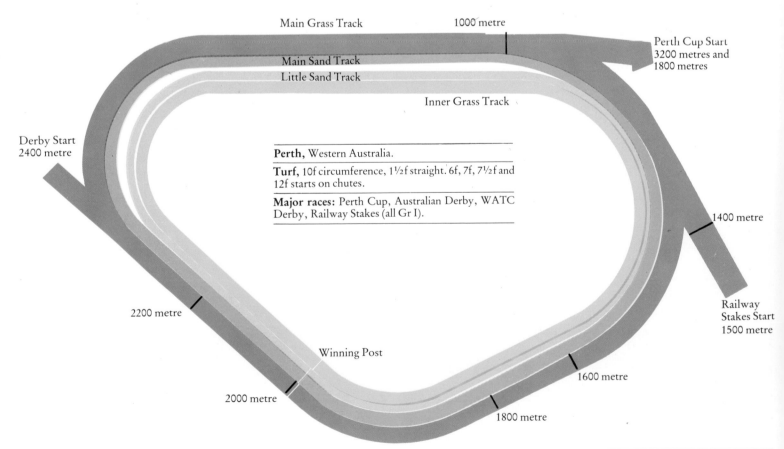

Main Grass Track

Main Sand Track

Little Sand Track

Inner Grass Track

1000 metre

Perth Cup Start
3200 metres and
1800 metres

Derby Start
2400 metre

1400 metre

2200 metre

Railway
Stakes Start
1500 metre

1600 metre

Winning Post

2000 metre

1800 metre

Perth, Western Australia.

Turf, 10f circumference, 1½f straight. 6f, 7f, 7½f and 12f starts on chutes.

Major races: Perth Cup, Australian Derby, WATC Derby, Railway Stakes (all Gr I).

makers channelled much of the public's money away from racing the industry suffered, and by 1959 racing in Western Australia was almost at a standstill.

A Royal Commission in 1960 introduced the off-course Totalisator Agency Board the following year. This new betting concept fed money back into the industry and asserted itself as a vital ingredient in the upgrading of racing. Since the inception of the off-course tote in Western Australia the Government has had a return of more than $A90 million in taxes from the racing industry, while the 1972 Perth Cup run on New Year's day was lifted to $A100,000 and now has increased to $A150,000. The history of the WATC is another story of how a full injection of revenue from off-course tote betting salvaged a club from bankruptcy.

Below *The parade ring in front of the stands. The Ascot festival meeting produces a huge betting turnover, which has enabled the club to raise prize money over the years.*

Caulfield/Rosehill

After the establishment of the Victoria Amateur Turf Club in 1876 the foundation committee decided to look for a suitable area around the wild country of Melbourne. A group of local sportsmen marked out a rough track through the heath at Caulfield, about seven miles south east of Melbourne. Today Caulfield is a great racecourse, eleven furlongs in circumference with a home run of two furlongs (400 metres).

The first meeting was held on August 5, 1876, and the first Caulfield Cup was run in the autumn of 1879 for a prize of £230. But in Melbourne spring was the important season for racing, when the Melbourne Cup occupied the attentions of the entire population. Realizing the appeal of that race, the VATC switched the 1881 Caulfield Cup to the spring.

The Caulfield Cup is usually run on the third Saturday in October and bookmakers' doubles' charts on the two Cups are published before the weights are declared at the end of July. The Caulfield Cup, like the Melbourne Cup, is a high-class handicap, attracting the best weight-for-age horses Australia and New Zealand can produce. Run over a mile and a half (2400 metres) the result and the overall form of the runners has a powerful influence on Melbourne Cup discussions.

During the First World War Caulfield received a boost from the English thoroughbred as a result of the general lapse in racing throughout the United Kingdom. Between 1915 and 1921 five imported horses won the Caulfield Cup, and in 1915 the first three horses, Lavendo (Chaucer–Lavella), William The Silent and Cyclon, were all imported from England. Other imported winners have been Shepherd King (Martagon–St Windeline), King Offa (Radium–Officious), Lucknow (Minoru–Amphora) and Violincello (Valens–Catgut). The 1931 Caulfield Cup winner, Denis Boy, was bred in Ireland, by Soldennis out of Blink Girl, while the imported 1968 winner, Bunratty Castle, was by Henry the Seventh out of Winter Solstice.

The VATC Spring Carnival is a three-day meeting on Saturday, Wednesday and Saturday, with the Cup run on the final day. The prelude to the meeting is the rich Marlboro Cup on Show Day in September. At the Club's autumn meeting at the end of February and early March the feature races are the Blue Diamond Stakes for two-year-olds, the Oakleigh Plate and the Futurity Stakes. The Blue Diamond, run over 1200 metres (six furlongs) is worth more than $A100,000, while the 1979 Caulfield Cup was worth $A156,000.

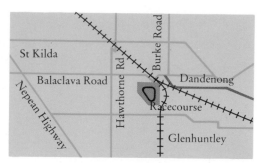

Caulfield racecourse is on Station Street, Caulfield, six miles from the centre of Melbourne.

Station St, Caulfield, Victoria. 6m from centre of Melbourne.

Turf, 10f circumference, 1½f straight. 6f, 7f start from chutes.

Major races: Caulfield Cup H'cap, Marlboro Cup H'cap, Oakleigh Pte H'cap, Toorak H'cap, Caulfield Stakes, Chirnside Stakes, Futurity Stakes, Memsie Stakes, St George Stakes, Underwood Stakes, Caulfield Guineas, 1,000 Guineas, Blue Diamond Stakes (all Gr I).

The stands at Caulfield with bookmakers' pitches in the foreground. The Caulfield Cup-Melbourne Cup double is a sporting institution in Melbourne, and was last completed by Gallilee in 1966. Even Stevens succeeded in the double in 1962.

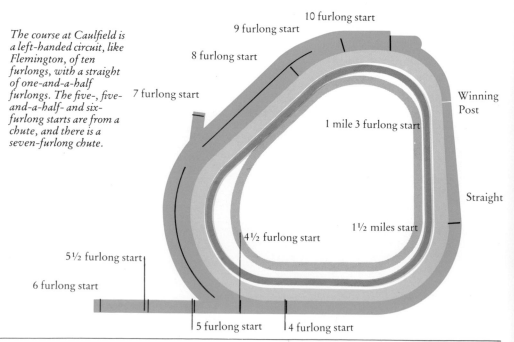

The course at Caulfield is a left-handed circuit, like Flemington, of ten furlongs, with a straight of one-and-a-half furlongs. The five-, five-and-a-half- and six-furlong starts are from a chute, and there is a seven-furlong chute.

10 furlong start
9 furlong start
8 furlong start
7 furlong start
Winning Post
1 mile 3 furlong start
Straight
1½ miles start
4½ furlong start
5½ furlong start
6 furlong start
5 furlong start
4 furlong start

Rosehill

Rosehill, one of Sydney's most attractive racecourses, is about twenty-two kilometres west of the city. Like all Australian racecourses it is a grass course with a circumference of ten furlongs and a two furlong straight. The course has an international distinction; it is the scene of the world's richest race for two-year-olds, the Golden Slipper Stakes. The 1200 metres (six furlong) weights race carries prize money of $250,000, with $150,000, plus trophies to the winner.

Racing at Rosehill is conducted by the Sydney Turf Club, which also controls racing at Canterbury. The club was set up by an Act of the New South Wales Parliament in August, 1943. It follows in a great tradition; since 1825 there have been three racing bodies in New South Wales with the name Sydney Turf Club, though the present club is not descended from any of them. A Sydney Turf Club raced in Hyde Park (Sydney) in 1825, before even the Australian Jockey Club was formed.

Rosehill racecourse was first opened in 1855 by the Rosehill Racing Club. The course itself was part of the notable settler John Macarthur's original land grant, where, interestingly enough, wheat was first successfully grown in Australia.

The club took over Rosehill on January 19, 1946. The club is one of the most progressive in Australia, with emphasis on public amenities being modernized each year and a racing policy which caters for all groups of horses from the top class to maidens. The Golden Slipper Stakes promotion, however, has been the club's chief glory, and a record 2,380 nominations were received for 1980.

Youngsters are nominated as foals and yearlings. Only the best survive final acceptance as two-year-olds, but if approaching the race there is a new-found champion youngster the club has a $A5,000 late entry clause.

Also on the card on Golden Slipper day is a $A150,000 weight-for-age race over 2,400 metres (1½m). The winner of this event takes away $A93,000; total prize money for the 1978 Golden Slipper festival was $A1,172,200.

In conjunction with the Australian Jockey Club the Sydney Turf Club has introduced one of the most modern computerized totalizator betting facilities in the world. It uses a multi-combination betting ticket which gives the punter a number of betting combinations on the one ticket issued. The off-course tote investments are transmitted to the course, and incorporated with on-course pools for dividend display and calculation.

Rosehill, Sydney, NSW. 14m from city centre.

Turf, RH, 10f circumference, 2f straight. 6f, 7½f start on chutes.

Major races: Marlboro Classic H'cap, HE Tancred Stakes, Hill Stakes, Rawson Stakes, Theo Marks Stakes, Gloaming Stakes, Peter Pan Stakes, Rosehill Guineas, Golden Slipper Stakes (all Gr I).

Rosehill racecourse is fourteen miles west of Sydney, at Rosehill, New South Wales.

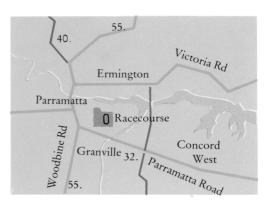

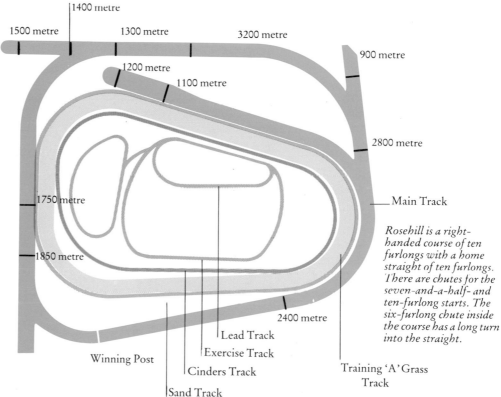

Rosehill is a right-handed course of ten furlongs with a home straight of ten furlongs. There are chutes for the seven-and-a-half- and ten-furlong starts. The six-furlong chute inside the course has a long turn into the straight.

Main Track

Winning Post — Sand Track — Cinders Track — Exercise Track — Lead Track — 2400 metre — Training 'A' Grass Track

Runners in the six-furlong Golden Slipper Stakes, the world's richest race for two-year-olds. The race carries a first prize of $A150,000, plus trophies. Rosehill is a fast course suited to sharp two-year-olds. It is also used as a large training centre, with several training tracks.

Morphettville/Trentham/Ellerslie

Morphettville racecourse, the home of the South Australian Jockey Club, was founded in 1874. The SAJC had been formed in January 1856, and the first Adelaide Cup was run on a track at Thebarton on April 20, 1861. Soon after the SAJC was forced into liquidation with a lack of funds, and the club was not re-formed until 1874, when it set up its new course at Morphettville.

The first meeting at Morphettville was in September 1875, and four years later totalizator betting was introduced. But in 1884 the Government repealed the Totalizator Act and betting was prohibited throughout the state. This brought racing in South Australia to a swift halt. The SAJC had already taken entries for its 1885 Adelaide Cup, but it was not possible to run the race without betting. The Victoria Racing Club offered the use of Flemington racecourse, and thus in 1885 the Adelaide Cup was run on the same track as the Melbourne Cup. But the venture was not a success and the SAJC had no alternative but to close down.

Four years later, in 1889, the totalizator ban was lifted, and racing has continued at Morphettville ever since. But it again suffered at the hands of the Government when off-course betting shops were licensed in 1933. In February 1942 the Government banned racing as a wartime measure, and it did not resume until October 30, 1943, with off-course betting shops never relicensed. The off-course tote was introduced in 1967 and has had a profound influence on the liquidity of clubs.

The biggest development in recent years in Adelaide has been the amalgamation of the three metropolitan clubs. In 1975 the SAJC absorbed both the Adelaide Racing Club and the Port Adelaide Racing Club, and as one club it now controls three courses, Morphettville (headquarters), Victoria Park and Cheltenham.

Morphettville, SA.

Turf, LH, 11½f circumference, 1¾f straight. 6f, 9f start from chutes.

Major races: Adelaide Cup H'cap, Marlboro Plate H'cap, SA Derby, SA Oaks (all Gr I).

Morphettville racecourse is near the ANZAC Highway, near Adelaide, South Australia.

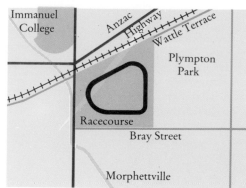

The left-handed course at Morphettville is a circuit of eleven-and-a-half furlongs, with a straight of just over one-and-a-half furlongs. There are chutes for the nine-and-a-quarter- and six-furlong starts.

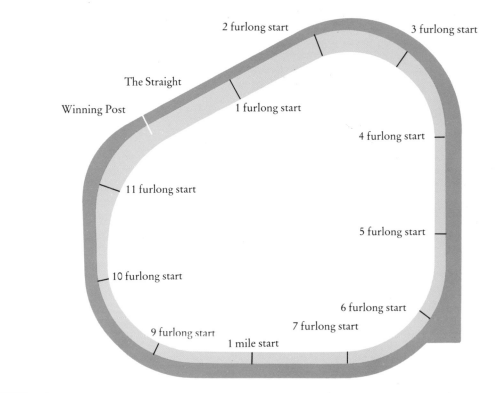

Morphettville is the home of the South Australian Jockey Club which stages four Group I races, the South Australian Derby and Oaks, the Adelaide Cup and the Marlboro Plate.

Ellerslie

Ellerslie racecourse, on the outskirts of Auckland, was opened in 1910 by the Auckland Racing Club. It stages the two miles Auckland Cup, worth more than 30,000 dollars, and two classic races, the Great Northern Derby and the Great Northern Guineas, besides the Grand Northern Steeplechase.

The course at Ellerslie is a fairly sharp right-handed circuit; the steeplechase course, over which the Grand Northern is run, includes a stiff hill on the far side of the course which has to be climbed three times during the race. The stands at Ellerslie were modernized in 1958 and opened in 1960, and now provide superb facilities which can match those of most racecourses anywhere in the world.

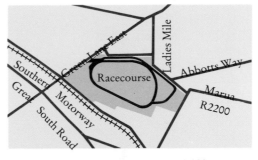

Ellerslie racecourse is on the outskirts of Aukland, on the North Island.

Ellerslie, Auckland, NZ.

Turf, 9½f circumference, 2½f straight. 4½f, 8f start on chutes.

Major races: Auckland Cup Handicap, Air New Zealand Stakes, Sires' Produce Stakes, Marlboro Easter Handicap, NZ Derby Railway Handicap (all Gr I).

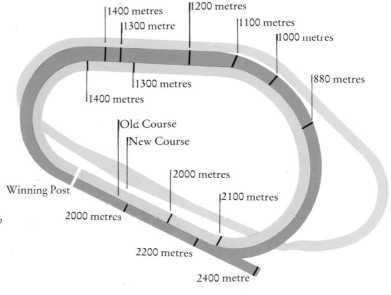

Ellerslie is a right-handed eight-and-a-half-furlong circuit, with a two-and-a-half-furlong straight. There are chutes for the four-and-a-half and eight-furlong starts. The track is a particularly fast one.

Trentham

Early records of racing in New Zealand show that a meeting was held on the beach at Wellington in 1840, when the town was little more than a village consisting of a few shacks. By the 1860s various racing clubs had been established, and the sport gradually spread. In 1924 the course at Trentham, the centre of racing at Wellington, was rebuilt. Trentham is now the home of the Wellington Gold Cup, worth more than 35,000 dollars and the richest prize in New Zealand racing, and the Wellington Derby over one-and-half miles.

The stands at Trentham are among the best in the world. Their cantilevered roofs give an uninterrupted view of the racing, which takes place against a backdrop of rolling hills. The races in New Zealand are not started until all betting has been completed, and horses can often be kept walking around the starting stall until betting operations have come to a halt.

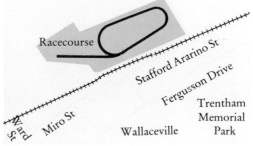

Above *Crowds at Trentham for the Wellington Cup, New Zealand's major handicap.*

Trentham, NZ.

Major races: George Adams H'cap, NZ Oaks, NZ St Leger, Wellington Cup H'cap (all Gr I).

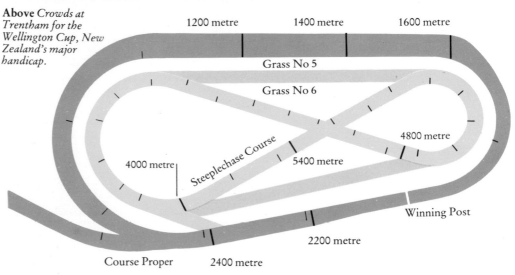

Bukit Timah/Happy Valley

The Singapore Turf Club, founded in 1842 as the Singapore Sporting Club, is the longest established club in the Malayan Racing Association. It initiated organized horse racing in south-east Asia and for almost 150 years, it has been progressive in development. The first recorded race in the region was The Singapore Cup, valued at $150, won by W H M Read – a great sporting figure for many years in Singapore – on the Colonel. The first course, which is now part of the Farrer Park sports centre, was a mile and a distance (eighty-three yards). Cleared of undergrowth – and shared for a time with the Singapore Volunteer Corps as a rifle range – it was to be the home of Singapore racing for some ninety years.

The Singapore racecourse is at Bukit Timah, seven miles from the centre of the city, in 350 acres of grounds.

The Sporting Club became the Turf Club in 1924 and moved in 1933 to Bukit Timah. Today the Club races on a course which, together with its associated facilities, matches the best in the world. Laid out in 350 acres of park-like grounds, Bukit Timah is a show place among world racecourses. It is situated about seven miles from the heart of Singapore and is part of a green complex of lush catchment areas for two great reservoirs, the last of the island's primary jungle and two superb golf courses. Its major races are the Gold Cup, the Singapore Derby, revived, after a lapse, in 1959, and the Queen Elizabeth II Cup. The course at Bukit Timah is nine furlongs and 110 yards in length. Races are run between distances of six furlongs and one-and-a-half miles. The second track is used for training and hurdle events at professional–amateur meetings. A third sand track is used for training. The Heath and Hill tracks at the northern end of the property are for training on. There is a two furlong sand track at the stables, where work can be done under floodlights, and a second track is being added. There is also a swimming pool where horses with leg or foot injuries can be exercised.

Because there are no legal betting facilities in Singapore, the track is used as a gigantic open-air betting shop with relayed betting information and commentaries from the other meetings. Up to 11,000 people attend Bukit Timah on a non-racing day compared to an average of 33,000 when the horses are present.

Prizes are excellent, with a minimum value of $8,000 (£1,785 at the official Jockey Club rate for 1979), of which the winner receives $5,600 (£1,250). On the other hand, there are no disproportionately large prizes. For instance, the winner of the Queen Elizabeth II Cup (1m 3f), run at Bukit Timah each July and one of the most important races of the year, received only $35,000 (£7,812) in 1979.

There are usually nine races each day, every one a handicap. All horses are graded into six classes, each sub-divided into divisions. Fields are large, with rarely fewer than ten runners and an upper limit of eighteen. Most of the competing horses are imported, either from Australasia or Britain, both parts of the world in which Malaysian owners have racing interests.

Each meeting lasts for four days, with racing taking place on consecutive Saturdays and Sundays. The weights are published on the Tuesday preceding the meeting. Six furlongs is the basic distance but mile events are common and longer races, up to at least the distance of the Singapore Gold Cup and Queen Elizabeth II Cup, are staged, particularly for the better horses.

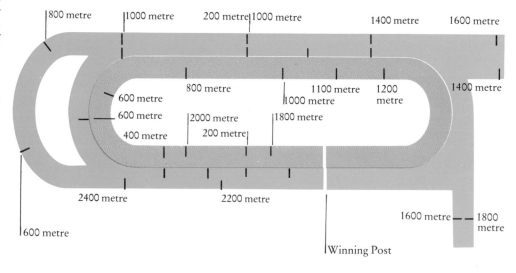

Right *The course at Bukit Timah, and* **above** *the nine-and-a-half-furlong left-handed circuit. Races are between six and twelve furlongs.*

Bukit Timah, Singapore. Bus service from city.

Turf, LH, 9½f circumference, 2½f straight. Inner turf and dirt training tracks. Racing 34 days, Saturday and Sundays.

Major races: Gold Cup (1m 3f), Singapore Derby (1½m), Stewards Cup (6f), Queen Elizabeth II Cup.

Happy Valley

Happy Valley is recognized as the home of racing in Hong Kong. Before the completion of Sha Tin, there was racing on fifty-eight days a year at Happy Valley, some of it at night. Because the course could not reasonably withstand that amount of racing, the figure has now been reduced to thirty-eight days per year.

Happy Valley is situated on Hong Kong Island. The course, slightly less than seven furlongs in circumference, is one of the tightest in the world, while the turns are exacerbated by not being cambered. The straight is fifty yards under two furlongs, and the last three furlongs of the track are particularly difficult to ride.

New grandstands are being constructed at Happy Valley and will be completed in the early summer of 1981, while the demolition of the stables there began in February 1980. Besides the new grandstands, other facilities at the course will be updated as part of a general scheme of improvement. However, the track itself cannot be enlarged, as there is not the space available to do so.

The finances for these improvements are to be raised by betting revenue, since there are an apparently unlimited amount of Chinese determined to gamble. With the course at Sha Tin completed, the vast sums that make up the revenue are to be directed towards putting Happy Valley on a par with it.

Happy Valley racecourse is on Hong Kong Island

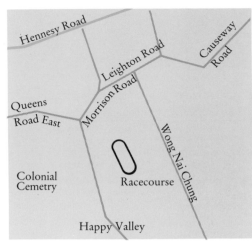

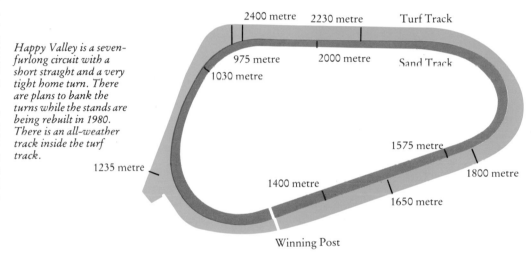

Happy Valley is a seven-furlong circuit with a short straight and a very tight home turn. There are plans to bank the turns while the stands are being rebuilt in 1980. There is an all-weather track inside the turf track.

Hong Kong Island.

Turf, RH, 7f circumference. Course being re-turfed during 1980, new stands to be completed 1980 providing room for 4,400 extra.

Left *An aerial view of Happy Valley showing the extent of building around the course. The new stands are designed to provide another 4,400 seats. The track is also being returfed during 1980, while racing is transferred to Sha Tin.* **Above** *Runners at the end of the home straight making the first turn.*

Sha Tin

The phenomenal growth of racing in Hong Kong after the Second World War inspired the establishment of the Hong Kong Jockey Club's fabulous new racing complex at Sha Tin in the New Territories, north of the Kowloon foothills and facing the borders of China. The club reclaimed 245 acres of water on the northern shore of Tide Cove and two entire hillsides were demolished by earth-moving equipment to provide earth filling. Heavy-duty trucks, working round the clock, dumped soil into

The Sha Tin racecourse is on the Chinese mainland, one hour by coach from Hong Kong Island.

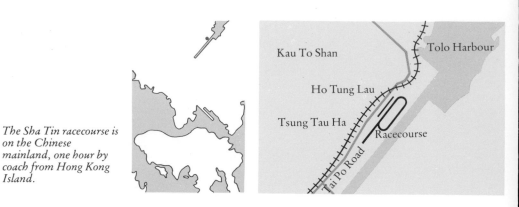

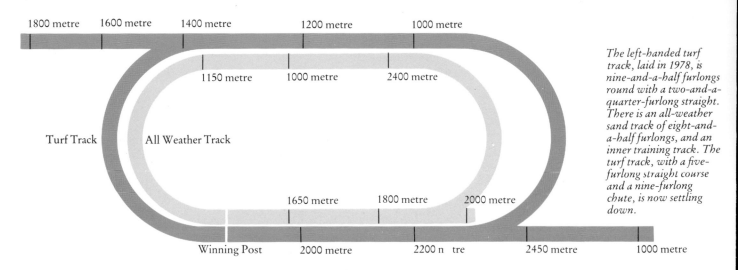

The left-handed turf track, laid in 1978, is nine-and-a-half furlongs round with a two-and-a-quarter-furlong straight. There is an all-weather sand track of eight-and-a-half furlongs, and an inner training track. The turf track, with a five-furlong straight course and a nine-furlong chute, is now settling down.

the bay at the rate of one truckload every thirteen seconds; altogether 16 million tons of soil were used.

Planning this amazing project started in the early 1970s. The Hong Kong government gave the go-ahead in 1972 and the first stage of filling in began in December 1973. By October 1978, the bay had been transformed into a modern racecourse, with a 1,900 metres grass track, a straight 1,000 metres grass track, a 75-foot wide all-weather circuit and a 35-foot wide training track inside the main 100-foot-wide course proper. The run-in from the home turn is 500 metres.

The straight five-furlong course has not yet fully settled down and there are undulations where the turf has sunk, due to subsidence. Horses training on the sand track become unbalanced when they meet the undulations, causing some upsets in form as a result. However, there are plans to level out the course in the near future.

The name Sha Tin means Sand Field. This is most appropriate for a combination of grass and all-weather tracks. Not only the tracks themselves, but the buildings and the associated facilities are equally imposing. The Sha Tin grandstand, for instance, covers sixteen-and-a-quarter

acres of floor area. It rises to eight storeys high and is 700 feet long. The course also has ten two-storey stable blocks, each accommodating fifty horses in twelve-foot-square boxes. To accommodate the moods of every horse, each box is equipped with piped music and air conditioning.

The Chinese mania for gambling is also fully accommodated. There are 500 ticket-selling machines at Sha Tin, serving a series of seventeen different computers. These are necessary to cope with the twelve different kinds of tote betting.

Without doubt, however, one of the most exciting features of Sha Tin is its video matrix screen, which pictures the running of a race from start to finish and is particularly effective during night racing under lights. The screen at Sha Tin is the first in Asia and the biggest in the world. It measures 66 feet 6 inches by 19 feet. The picture of the horses racing is formed by 32,256 separate lamp bulbs, more than all the street lamps in Hong Kong.

Hong Kong

Turf, 9½f circumference, 2¼f straight. 5f straight course, 9f chute. All-weather sand track 8½f circumference. Inner training track. Stands and seating for 30,000.

Left *The stands at Sha Tin stretch a furlong in front of the display board and beyond it the television screen. The all-weather track is inside the main turf course.* **Below** *Horses being led out for exercise on the sand. The horses are stabled in two-storey blocks at the course.* **Below right** *The computerized display board for tote prices in* front *of the stands. All betting relayed to the course is instantly shown on the board.* **Right** *The television screen, which shows races as they are being run, and shows replays after the race during enquiries.* **Above right** *Runners are taken out on to the course by lead horses.*

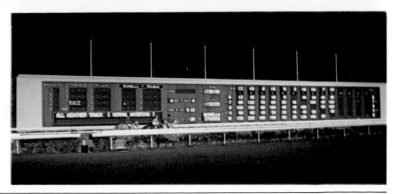

Tokyo/Kyoto/Nakayama

Although there was racing in Tokyo in the late nineteenth century it was not until November 1906, that a western-style racecourse was finally completed at Ikegami. As the racing there proved to be a great success, three other racecourses in and around Tokyo had opened by the following autumn; in 1910 the four courses were united under a single ruling authority. A process of rationalization followed with the result that the course at Meguro became the only racecourse in Tokyo. It was there that the first two runnings of the Tokyo Yuushun (the Japanese Derby), inaugurated in 1932, were held. Mainly because eighty-two per cent of the site was leased land, however, the course was moved in May 1933, to the town of Fuchu, twenty-seven kilometres from the centre of Tokyo, and this remains the Tokyo racecourse today.

The biggest crowd ever to assemble there was 169,174; this happened on May 6, 1973, when the attraction was Haiseikoh (by China Rock, an imported English stallion) winning the NHK Hai, the trial race for the Tokyo Yuushun. This boasts a record attendance of 167,263 in 1969. Haiseikoh's son Katsurano Haiseiko won the 2,400 metres Tokyo Yuushun in 1979 in the record time of 2 minutes 27.3 seconds, collecting a first prize of 55,000,000 yen (approximately £95,000).

Tokyo Yuushun winners include such truly outstanding horses as Kurifuji (by Tournesol) and Shinzan (by Hindostan). The winner in 1943, Kurifuji was never beaten in eleven starts, also winning the Japanese Oaks at Hanshin and the Japanese St Leger at Kyoto. She is probably the best race mare ever seen in Japan.

Besides the Tokyo Yuushun, Tokyo race course stages the Yuushun Hinba (the Japanese Oaks) and the Tennou Shou (the Emperor's Cup) for older horses over 3,200 metres.

Nakayama is in the city of Funabashi, Chiba Prefecture, eighteen miles from the centre of Tokyo. Tokyo racecourse is at Fuchu, sixteen miles from Tokyo. Kyoto racecourse is at Yodo railway station, twelve miles from Kyoto and twenty-five miles from Osaka.

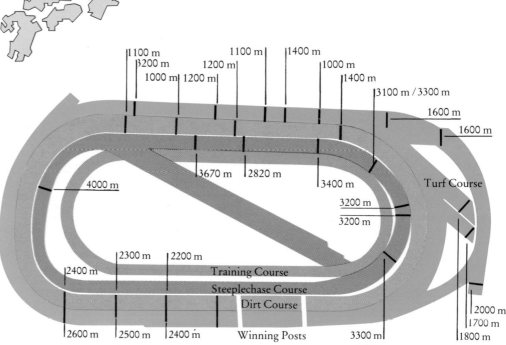

Fuchu, Tokyo Prefecture. Nearest station Fuchu Keibajo Semon-Mae.

Turf: 2,264y circumference, 540½y straight, undulation over course 2½y. **Dirt,** 2,046y circumference, 514¾y straight, undulation over course 2¼y. Racing 40 days.

Major races: Tokyo Yuushun (Japanese Derby) (1m 4f, 3-y-o), Tennou Shou (Emperor's Cup) (2m, 4-y-o+) (both Gr I).

Right *Katsurano Haiseiko wins the 1979 Tokyo Yuushun, the Japanese Derby, in record time.* **Below** *Tokyo racecourse is a ten-and-a-half-furlong circuit.*

Kyoto

Official horse racing in Kyoto, the old capital of Japan, began in May 1908, when a four-day meeting was held at Simabara. The course was moved first to Suchi in 1913 and then to the present site of Yodo in 1925, where the drainage of the marshy ground took eighteen months to complete. The water there remains in the form of a lake in the centre of the course.

The Kikuka Shou (the Japanese St Leger) was instituted at Kyoto in 1938; it us run over 3,000 metres in mid-November. The spring Tennou Shou is staged there on the Emperor's birthday, April 29, and was won in 1977 by Tenpointo (by Contrite), who won a Japanese record total of prize money of 328,415,400 yen. He also won that season's Arima Kinen. Tenpointo returned to Kyoto in January, 1978, for a handicap only to suffer a leg fracture which led to him being destroyed.

Kyoto is a left-handed circuit, with a straight of just over one-and-a-half furlongs. There is an eight-furlong inner dirt course, with a one-and-a-half-furlong straight and an inside steeplechase course of seven furlongs.

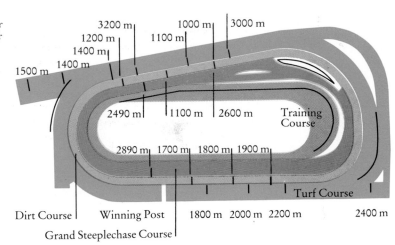

Kyoto stages the Japanese St Leger over one mile and seven furlongs, and one of the two races for the Emperor's Cup, the Tennou Shou, for four-year-olds and upwards over two miles.

Kyoto, Kyoto Prefecture. Nearest station Yodo.

Turf, RH, inner 1,944y circumference, 368y straight, undulation over course 3¼y. Outer 2,057y circumference, 439½y straight, undulation over course 4¾y. **Dirt,** RH, 1,751y circumference, 368y straight, undulation over course 2½y.
Racing 16 days.

Major races: Kikuka Shou (Japanese St Leger) (1m 7f, 3-y-o), Queen Elizabeth II Commemorative Cup (1½m, 3-y-o) (both Gr I).

Nakayama

Situated thirty kilometres east of the centre of Tokyo, Nakayama racecourse at Funabashi, Chiba Prefecture, held its first meeting in March 1920. Fourteen years later, the present Nakayama Daishougai, the most valuable steeplechase in Japan and run twice a year, was instituted there. The jumper Gurando Mahchisu (by Never Beat), winner of four successive Nakayama Dishougais in 1974 and 1975, has amassed 343,388,200 yen – more than £600,000.

In 1956 the grandstand at Nakayama was rebuilt in time for the first running of the Arima Kinen, set up at the suggestion of Yoriyasu Arima, the then president of the Japan Racing Association. An invitational races for three-year-olds only and limited to a field of twenty – ten of the runners being decided by popular vote and ten by a select committee consisting of owners trainers, pressmen and official handicappers – it is held in December.

Winner of the Arima Kinen, which is also open to foreign-bred horses, has always been given the title of Horse of the Year. The race set a betting turnover record in Japan of a staggering 20,507,061,500 yen – nearly £35 million – in 1978.

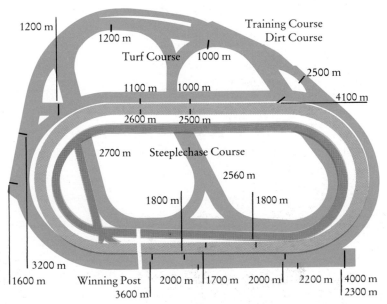

Nakayama is a wide, eight-furlong right-handed circuit with a one-and-a-half-furlong straight. There is an inner dirt course of seven-and-a-half furlongs and an inside steeplechase course with various tracks. The course stages the Satsuki Shou, the Japanese 2,000 Guineas, and the Arima Kinen, a weight-for-age race over twelve-and-a-half furlongs for horses invited by a panel of officials and journalists.

Funabashi, Chiba Prefecture, Tokyo. Nearest station Funabashi Hoten.

Turf, RH, inner 1,795y circumference, 333¾y straight. Outer 1,981½y circumference, 333¾y straight. Undulation over course 2¾y. **Dirt,** RH, 1,607¾y circumference, 331¾y straight, undulation over course 2½y.
Racing 40 days.

Major races: Satsuki Shou (2,000 Guineas) (1m 2f, 3-y-o), Arima Kinen (1m 4½f, all ages) (both Gr I).

The World's Great Horses

" Round-hoof'd, short jointed
fetlocks shag and long.
Broad breast,
full eye, small head
and nostril wide,
High crest, short ears,
straight legs
and passing strong.
Thin mane, thick tail,
broad buttock, tender hide:
look,
what a horse should have
he did not lack."
Venus and Adonis.

The World's Great Horses

Comparing the great horses of the past with those of today has always been a favourite pastime for racing enthusiasts. Unfortunately, it is impossible to state with any certainty how the great fore fathers of the modern racehorse would have contrasted with their modern equivalents, but it is possible, however, to scientifically contrast the horses of today with their immediate predecessors. In Britain, it is the policy of the Jockey Club to give an official rating for horses running on the flat. The rating, introduced with centralized handicapping and a grading system in 1973, is based on a norm of 100, taken to represent the average Derby winner.

David Swannell, an official Jockey Club handicapper since 1956 and the Jockey Club Handicapper (Flat Races) since 1973, has kept a record of personal assessments since 1959. These originated the system adopted by the Jockey Club and his ratings are those now published officially in the Racing Calendar. Major Swannell has agreed to extend his ratings back to 1955 to take in the last quarter century, and writes as follows.

'The early 1970s were a vintage period of racing; Nijinsky made 1970 a year to remember but, just one season later, the deeds of Mill Reef and Brigadier Gerard will not be forgotten as long as racing survives. In four seasons these three brilliant colts won a staggering total of eighteen Group 1 races between them; in all their forty-five runs they were beaten on only five occasions. They raised racing in this country to an unrepeated level.

'How, though, do they and those of the sixties compare with the three great racehorses of the mid-fifties? Since my original records date only from 1959, I have, by some rather laborious but absorbing back tracking, included in the ratings published here Ribot, Crepello and Ballymoss for the first time. In doing so, I made the fullest use of the relevant Free Handicaps compiled by that master of handicapping, Geoffrey Freer. It would, of course, have been highly presumptious not to do so and at least, through having done this, much possible controversy is removed.

'Sea Bird II and Ribot were the two outstanding individuals to have run in this country during the last twenty-five years. It is possibly not yet forgotten that the race for the Prix de l'Arc de Triomphe of 1965 contained, amongst other top-class winners, five Derby winners and Diatome, who a few weeks later was to beat a truly international field in the Washington DC International. In quality that Arc field is never likely to be equalled, yet Sea Bird ran away from it. Even if the field for the

	Foaled	At 3 years	At 4 years and over
Sea Bird II (FR)	1962	110	—
Ribot (ITY)	1952	—	108
Crepello	1954	106	—
Exbury	1959	—	106
Vaguely Noble	1965	106	—
Brigadier Gerard	1968	106	106
Mill Reef (USA)	1968	106	106
Busted	1963	—	104
Levmoss	1965	—	104
Nijinsky (CAN)	1967	104	—
Sassafras	1967	104	—
Ballymoss	1954	103	103
Right Royal V	1958	103	—
Floribunda	1958	103	—
Relko	1960	103	—
Petite Etoile (filly)	1956	102	101
Charlottesville	1957	102	—
Match III	1958	(97)	102
Ragusa	1959	102	102
Karabas	1965	—	102
Arctic Storm	1958	101	—
Royal Palace	1964	101	101
Park Top (filly)	1964	—	101
Sir Ivor (USA)	1965	101	—
Jimmy Reppin (1965)	1965	—	101
Habitat (USA)	1966	101	—
Dahlia (USA) (filly)	1970	101	101
Thatch (USA)	1970	101	—
Grundy	1972	101	—
St Paddy	1967	100	(99)
Santa Claus	1961	100	—
Hethersett	1959	100	(92)
Provoke	1962	100	—
Alleged (USA)	1974	(98)	100

Epsom Derby was less inspiring, he disposed of it without coming off the bit.

'Without detracting from the truly great Ribot, it is notable that in his two principal victories as a four-year-old, in the King George VI and Queen Elizabeth Stakes and the Arc de Triomphe (for the second year), the opposition on both occasions was, compared to the field for Sea Bird's Arc, undistinguished to say the least. He could do no more than trounce it and he was the second best racehorse I am ever likely to see. Of the others, I believe Crepello to have been outstanding; a view much strengthened by the subsequent career of Ballymoss, his runner-up at Epsom.

'Looking back over a quarter of a century, the supreme champion Sea Bird and Ribot, the runner-up, must stand comparison with any of the great racehorses that have run in this country. The 1960s were enriched by the deeds of Exbury, Relko and Vaguely Noble. The early 1970s promised much, but so strange are the ways of breeding that the Derby winners of 1976, 1977, and 1978 were unable to improve on an average of 92, while Troy, in 1979, winner of the English and Irish Derbies and the King George VI and Queen Elizabeth Diamond Stakes but beaten by Three Troikas in the Arc de Triomphe, received a rating of 98.'

Sea Bird II coasts home in the 1965 Derby from Meadow Court and I Say. At stud Sea Bird II sired the great filly Allez France and other classic winners.

How the Swannell system works

The Swannell rating system is based on what David Swannell terms the 'X' factor. In 1959, Swannell started to keep each year an assessment of the comparative merit of the Derby winner against a 'mean' figure, which he represented as 'X'. Thus, if he considered a horse to be superior to the average Derby winner by 2lb, that horse would have a merit rating of X+2; whereas in another year a horse, which was lucky enough to be just the best of a moderate crop and in his assessment 4lb below the quality normally required of a winner of the Derby, would be rated at X−4. It was a simple and logical extension of his system to extend his ratings not only to the classic winners but to all the best horses of the respective three-year-old crops and then to rate those horses which had stayed in training at four years and later.

The information he had to draw on was and is contained in various handicaps published in France and Britain. Some of the handicaps and races available to him for the top ten horses in his ratings are shown here.

Sea Bird II, rated by David Swannell the best horse to have raced in Europe in the last twenty-five years, raced only once in Britain, when he won the Derby. At the end of his three-year-old season in 1965 Sea Bird II was rated 10 lb better than the next horse, Provoke, in the official British three-year-old handicap.

Sea Bird II	10 st 2 lb
Provoke	9 st 7 lb
Meadow Court	9st 2 lb
Aunt Edith	9 st 1 lb

Provoke won the St Leger for Lord Astor in 1965, while Meadow Court ran second to Sea Bird II in the Derby and went on to win the Irish Derby and the King George VI and Queen Elizabeth Stakes that year.

Ribot twice won the Prix de l'Arc de Triomphe, and the King George VI and Queen Elizabeth Stakes. In the 1956 Free Handicap, the year in which Ribot won the Ascot race and the Arc for the first time, Talgo was rated the best horse in Britain.

Talgo	9 st 7 lb
Donald	9 st 6 lb
Hornbeam	9 st 5 lb
Le Pretendant	9 st 4 lb
High Veldt	9 st 3 lb

In the Arc Ribot beat Talgo by six lengths, giving him 10 lb, while in the 'King George' Ribot gave High Veldt 14 lb and beat him five lengths.

In the 1957 official handicap of three-year-olds, Crepello was rated at 9 st 7 lb.

Crepello	9 st 7 lb
Ballymoss	9 st 2 lb
Rose Royale	9 st 0 lb
Almeria	9 st 0 lb

Crepello beat Ballymoss in the Derby, and that horse went on to win the Irish Derby, the King George, and the following year's Arc de Triomphe.

A clue to the comparative greatness of Exbury can be found in the weights for the Prix de la Pelluse in 1963, before he won the Prix de l'Arc de Triomphe but after he had won the Coronation Cup at Epsom.

Exbury	4	10 st 10 lb
Val de Loir	4	10 st 8 lb
Misti	5	10 st 6 lb
Cirio	4	10 st 6 lb

In the 1968 French Handicap Optional Vaguely Noble was rated the best horse in France after he had won the Arc.

Vaguely Noble	3	10 st 9 lb
Carmarthen	4	10 st 7 lb
Hopeful Venture	4	10st 6 lb
Pardallo	5	10 st 6 lb
Sir Ivor	3	10 st 5 lb

The Queen's Hopeful Venture had won the Grand Prix de Saint Cloud in France, while Pardallo won the Ascot Gold Cup and Sir Ivor the Derby and the Washington International.

The two great rivals, Mill Reef and Brigadier Gerard, met only once, when Brigadier Gerard beat Mill Reef in the 2,000 Guineas. But the weights for the official three-year-old handicap at the end of the 1971 season put Mill Reef above Brigadier Gerard, as they assumed the distance of the theoretical race to be one-and-a-half miles.

Mill Reef	9 st 7 lb
Brigadier Gerard	9 st 3 lb
Linden Tree	8 st 12 lb
Altesse Royale	8 st 11 lb

Linden Tree ran second to Mill Reef in the Derby, while Altesse Royale won the 1,000 Guineas and the Oaks.

Busted is a difficult horse to rate as he did not really develop until he was a four-year-old. However, when he won the King George VI and Queen Elizabeth Stakes, Busted beat Salvo and Ribocco three lengths and a neck. Ribocco, who had been second to Royal Palace in the Derby and went on to win the St Leger, was rated only one pound below Royal Palace.

Levmoss is another difficult horse to assess, as he also developed as a four-year-old. But after he won the Prix de l'Arc de Triomphe, beating Park Top three-quarters of a length, Levmoss was rated the best horse in the French Handicap.

Levmoss	4	68 kg
Park Top	5	66½ kg
Carmarthen	5	66½ kg
Karabas	4	66 kg

Taking into account an allowance for her sex, the handicap rates Park Top almost the equal of Levmoss. The year before, in 1968, Carmarthen had been rated two pounds below Vaguely Noble, while Karabas won the Washington International.

The next two horses in Swannell's ratings are Nijinsky and Sassafras. In 1970, after his three-year-old career, Nijinsky was rated the best horse in Britain.

Nijinsky	9 st 7 lb
Humble Duty	9 st 0 lb
Highest Hopes	8 st 13 lb
Meadowville	8 st 10 lb

Sassafras just beat Nijinsky in the Arc, but there are doubts as to whether Nijinsky was absolutely at his best at the time.

Finally of the top ten horses in the ratings, Right Royal V was rated below Molvedo in the French Handicap Optional.

Sea Bird II

Trained at Chantilly by Etienne Pollet for the textile manufacturer Jean Ternyck, Sea Bird II, a tall chestnut with a blaze and two white socks behind, followed an orthodox training programme for a high-class European middle-distance horse. Having been allowed to mature in the first half of his first season, he gave the first demonstration of his remarkable turn of foot by beating a pair of dead-heaters by a short neck in the seven furlongs Prix Blaison at Chantilly in September, 1964. A fortnight later he won by the same margin, over the same distance and in the same way at Maisons-Laffitte, but in the last of his three races as a juvenile he was to sustain the only defeat of his career. As a result of his being held in check a long way out of his ground, the devastating late run that was already becoming his hall-mark could gain him no more than second place in the Grand Criterium behind his better-fancied stable mate Grey Dawn, who beat him by two lengths.

Returning to action in the £11,000 Prix de Greffuhle over a mile and 2½ furlongs at Longchamp in early April in his three-year-old season, Sea Bird II won by three lengths and then ran out a still more convincing winner by beating Diatome by six lengths in the £25,000 Prix Lupin over the same course and distance. On the strength of those performances he started as the 7/4 favourite for the 1965 Epsom Derby, but even those who had complete confidence that he would win the race could never have envisaged how triumphantly he would win it. Though the chestnut colt was still hard held on the bit when his Australian jockey Pat Glennon asked him to improve his position 300 yards out, onlookers still tensed in the expectation of the race beginning in earnest – only to experience a sense of anti-climax mixed with stupefaction. Having produced a burst of acceleration that was as phenomenal as it was instantaneous, Sea Bird II did not meet the vestige of a challenge – nor did he come under the faintest pressure – to beat Meadow Court by two lengths (that distance would have been very much longer had Glennon let out any rein instead of easing up in the last fifty yards). Derbies have been won by much wider margins but never with such overwhelming authority from such good horses.

Ribot

David Swannell regards Ribot as the outstanding horse of the St Simon line to race in Europe in the middle of the twentieth century. Although so puny as a yearling that the stable lads dubbed him 'Il Piccolo' – the little one – Ribot grew into a fine bay colt of great range and strength, though retaining a gentle and amenable temperament throughout his days in training. His sire, Tenerani, had won the Goodwood Cup, the Italian Derby and eight other races, while his dam, Romanella, had revealed ability of a high order by winning five of her seven races as a two-year-old in 1945. His breeding was the last and supreme triumph of Federico Tesio and the Marchese Incisa della Rochetta, who were partners in the Razzo Dormello-Olgiata Stud, founded near Arona on the western shore of Italy's Lake Maggiore in 1898.

Unlike Nearco, Donatello II and Appelle, the three other great horses bred by the partnership, Ribot had parents who had both been bred at Dormello, as were both his grand-sires, Bellini and El Greco. Trained by Ugo Penco and always ridden by Enrico Camici, he had his first outing on July 4, 1954, when he made all the running over five furlongs at Milan. He led all the way again over a furlong further there in September, but on his final appearance as a two-year-old, the Gran Criterium over 7½ furlongs at Milan, he faced defeat for the only time in his career. Camici was told to hold him up early on, but the free-running Ribot resented these tactics so bitterly that he finished up having to fight to beat Gail by a head.

As no classic engagements had been made for the once disregarded 'Il Piccolo', Ribot had no opportunities to meet rivals remotely worthy of him in Italy as a three-year-old. After little more than an exercise canter at Pisa he met stiffer opposition in the Premio Emanuele Filiberto at Milan, where he beat his old rival Gail by ten lengths, though pulling up so lame that it was five minutes before he could reach the winner's enclosure. More than possibly a leg was feeling the strain of the traditional Tesio training schedule, which took the form of frequent gallops on firm ground. Real fears that Ribot might never run again proved groundless, however, and, although he also succumbed to a cough in the early summer of 1955, he was able to stage a successful return to Milan in the middle of July.

After winning at Milan yet again in September Ribot at last made his debut on the international scene in the Prix de l'Arc de Triomphe in October when he humbled the pride of Europe as effortlessly as he had the most insignificant of his compatriots. Forging ahead from the turn into the straight he beat Beau Prince by a ridiculously easy three lengths. Among those trailing in unplaced were Rapace (winner of the French Derby), Zarathustra (Irish Derby), Douve (French Oaks), Macip (French St Leger) and Hugh Lupus (Irish 2,000 Guineas). The effort took so little out of Ribot that, instead of retiring for the season, he reappeared at Milan a fortnight later to win the Premio de Jockey Club by fifteen lengths from Norman, who had been successful in the race in each of the two previous years.

Ribot won four more races with effortless ease at Milan in the first half of his four-year-old season in 1956 before coming to England for the King George VI and Queen Elizabeth Stakes in July. English racegoers expecting a spectacular exhibition from him were to be disappointed, though the opposition was far from strong. Hating the soft ground at Ascot, Ribot was under pressure to go the pace early on. Turning into the short straight he was still being hard ridden, but, on reaching the better ground two furlongs out, he found his action and strode away to beat the Queen's High Veldt by five lengths.

On his return to Italy, Ribot won by ten lengths at Milan and then came to the crescendo of his career by taking the Prix de l'Arc de Triomphe a second time. Settling the issue on the final turn again, he loped away from the rest of the field, as though they were equine statues, to beat the Irish Derby winner Talgo by six lengths. After that breathtaking performance Ribot retired as the unbeaten winner of sixteen races.

Ribot spent his first season at stud at Lord Derby's Woodland Stud at Newmarket and then returned to Italy. In 1961 he was sent to the United States for five years but the once equable temperament and deteriorated so badly that it was considered dangerous for him to make the return journey to Europe.

He died in 1972, after proving himself a major sire of classic winners throughout the world. It can be argued that, by the nature of its racing, his full potential was not realised in the United States. But, mainly through the late Charles W Engelhard and his manager, David McCall, many of his yearlings were purchased for racing in the United Kingdon with brilliantly successful results.

Vaguely Noble

A rare individual who combined size, strength and quality, Vaguely Noble was a bay colt by Vienna out of the Nearco mare Noble Lassie. He was the last and by far away the best of the many good horses bred by the late Major L B Holliday, perhaps the greatest British studmaster of the second half of the twentieth century. Yet the major never saw him run – nor was the breeding of Vaguely Noble destined to be the major's final and finest service to the British thoroughbred.

When Holliday died at the age of eighty-five in December 1965, his horses were being trained by Walter Wharton at Lagrange, his private stable at Newmarket. Arrangements for the winding up of the estate necessarily took a long time, so it was not until the December sales of 1967 that the final consignment of his blood-stock, which included Vaguely Noble, was due to be sold. In the meantime Walter Wharton carried on the stable as usual, with Vaguely Noble as a yearling in the autumn of 1966.

Coming events hardly cast their shadow on Vaguely Noble's first two racecourse appearances. Making his debut at Newcastle towards the end of August he was beaten by a neck by Sweet Thanks. The following month he lost by three-parts of a length to Saraceno, after leading until passed by the winner inside the last of the seven furlongs of the Feversham Stakes at Doncaster, where the going was firm. Not until he came to race on soft ground at Ascot in the middle of October did he give the first glimpse of his real potential by beating Moorings by twelve lengths in the seven furlongs Sandwich Stakes. A fortnight later, he was still more impressive – although seriously hampered two furlongs out – when beating Doon by an easy seven lengths in the Observer Gold Cup at Doncaster (now the William Hill Futurity).

Despite the immense promise of his late autumn performances, there was no change in the plan to sell Vaguely Noble. While speculation about how much he would make was rife, allowance had to be made for his having no classic entries. The sale itself was a singularly cursory affair. After the then enormous opening bid of 80,000 guineas, it was less than three minutes before he had been knocked down for 136,000 guineas – then a world record price for a racehorse – to an agent acting for Dr Robert Franklyn, a Hollywood plastic surgeon. Vaguely Noble was then sent to Ireland to be trained by Paddy Prendergast, but he was speedily transferred to Étienne Pollet in France when the Texas oil magnate Nelson Bunker Hunt purchased a half share in him.

Having acquired Vaguely Noble, the partners had to protect their investment, which, despite the talent of the property, was not necessarily easy. With the classics closed to him, Vaguely Noble could have been hard put to it to earn a high enough reputation to command the stud fee that would show them a satisfactory return on their huge outlay. It followed, therefore, that he had to win either the King George VI and Queen Elizabeth Stakes or the Prix de l'Arc de Triomphe. The latter was chosen as his target.

On his first two appearances in France Vaguely Noble won the Prix de Guiche over ten furlongs at Longchamp in April and the Prix de Lys over two furlongs further at Chantilly in June, but was then beaten into third place behind the Queen's Hopeful Venture in the Grand Prix de Saint-Cloud. Vaguely Noble looked a most unlucky loser of that event, as Jean Deforge had laid a long way out of his ground on him in a truly-run race. Whatever the rights and wrongs of the matter, when Vaguely Noble turned out for the Prix de Chantilly in September, Deforge was replaced by the Australian Bill Williamson, who had ridden the colt to win both his races in England and was promptly successful on him for a third time. Partnered by Williamson yet again in the Prix de l'Arc de Triomphe, Vaguely Noble showed what he was really made of by settling the issue as soon as he went to the front two furlongs out. He drew away to beat the Epsom Derby winner Sir Ivor by three lengths with the winners of two other Derbies, two Oaks, four St Legers and a Grand Prix de Paris trailing behind.

Since being retired to stud in the USA, Vaguely Noble has transmitted his excellence in abundance. Bunker Hunt has reason to be most especially grateful for this, as it was in his colours that Vaguely Noble's daughter Dahlia won two King George VI and Queen Elizabeth Stakes and his son Empery the Derby. Vaguely Noble stands at Gainesway Farm in Lexington.

Alleged

The greatest achievement of Alleged was to win the Prix de l'Arc de Triomphe for a second time. The manner in which he accomplished this arguably represented the ultimate in the training achievements of Vincent O'Brien. In the summer of 1978, Alleged, then a four-year-old, was among the several inmates of O'Brien's Ballydoyle stable in Ireland's Co Tipperary to be stricken by a virus. Plans to run him in the King George VI and Queen Elizabeth Stakes had to be scrapped and soon the time available to prepare him for his second Arc began to look perilously short.

Alleged had begun the season by winning the Royal Whip for the second time at The Curragh on May 12. Shortly afterwards, he succumbed to the virus and, when at last he was back in full work, O'Brien was desperately racing against the clock. Not until September 17, just a fortnight before the Arc, was Alleged ready to resume his career in the Prix du Prince d'Orange at Longchamp. Having spent four months on the sidelines, he showed that his troubles were far behind him by winning in record time for the course and distance.

Fourteen days later Alleged reached the summit and the end of his career simultaneously by carrying Robert Sangster's emerald green and royal blue colours to that second success in the Prix de l'Arc de Triomphe. In the same split second that Lester Piggott asked Alleged to go away to win his race two furlongs out, Freddie Head put the same question to Dancing Maid, the best three-year-old filly in France.

The answers both jockeys received were different. Whereas Alleged sprinted to the front without further encouragement, Dancing Maid was soon under heavy pressure through trying to go with him, with the result that she was run out of second place by Trillion. Alleged beat the latter by a nonchalant couple of lengths to the Gallic cheers of a crowd that loves to see Europe's richest race won with the authority of a true champion.

A level bay colt of length and strength, Alleged is by Ribot's grandson Hoist the Flag out of Princess Pout, by Prince John.

Events in his early life made it unlikely that he would leave his native America, as he was purchased for $34,000 at Keeneland Yearling Sales and put into training. In March 1976, however, he was back on the market again at the Hollywood Park Sale, where he was bought by a syndicate of which Robert Sangster was to become the principal shareholder.

Sent across the Atlantic to be trained by O'Brien, Alleged took his time to come to hand after the manner of the Ribot line. Therefore it was not until the backend of his two-year-old days that he made his racecourse debut by running out an eight-lengths winner over seven furlongs at The Curragh on November 1, 1976. Reappearing at Leopardstown the following April, Alleged duly won again. Though still unbeaten in that late spring of 1977 he was as yet unrecognized. When, with Paedar Matthews up, he accompanied his stablemates Valinsky, ridden by Lester Piggott, and Meneval, partnered by T Murphy, to the post for The Royal Whip at The Curragh, Alleged started the 33-1 outsider of seven, with Valinsky the 5-4 favourite.

Giving the complete lie to the market, Alleged beat Valinsky by a length and thereafter Piggott never missed the mount on him. In August he stepped out into the European limelight by making all the running to win York's 1½ miles Great Voltigeur Stakes by seven lengths from Classic Example and Lucky Sovereign, the placed horses in the Irish Sweeps Derby, with, in fourth place, Hot Grove, beaten by a neck in the Epsom Derby. Starting a hot favourite for the St Leger, Alleged sustained his only defeat in ten starts through finding the 1¾ miles just too far for him, so that he was beaten by 1½ lengths. Reverting to 1½ miles in the Prix de l'Arc de Triomphe three weeks later, he took his revenge by going to the front after just three furlongs and keeping that initiative to beat the New Zealand ace Balmerino by a length and a half, with Dunfermline – the horse that had beaten him in the St Leger – fourth.

The view that the other jockeys played into Piggott's hand by letting him dictate the pace was dispelled twelve months later when it was clearly demonstrated that there was nothing they could have done to prevent him placing Alleged anywhere he chose at any stage of the race. Alleged was, indeed, a truly brilliant racehorse who will almost certainly prove a mainstay of the Ribot line now that he has retired to stud. He stood his first season in 1979 at Walmac-Warnerton Association Farm, Lexington.

Brigadier Gerard and Mill Reef

Rarely has British racing been dominated by two horses of the sheer excellence of Brigadier Gerard and Mill Reef, who were foaled against very different backgrounds in 1968. Whereas Brigadier Gerard, a fine, powerful bay by Queen's Hussar out of La Paiva, was bred by his owners, Mr and Mrs John Hislop on their East Woodhay Stud in Berkshire, Mill Reef, a neater, darker bay by Never Bend, was reared on the 1,000 rolling acres of Paul Mellon's Rokeby Stud in the magnificent Virginian countryside. Brigadier Gerard was to go into training with Dick Hern at West Ilsley, Berkshire, while Mellon sent Mill Reef to join Ian Balding's Kingsclere stable just a few miles away across the Hampshire border.

Mill Reef was the first of the two to run, when winning at Salisbury on May 13, 1970. He went on to triumphs in Royal Ascot's Coventry Stakes, the Gimcrack Stakes, Kempton's Imperial Stakes and the Dewhurst Stakes, his only two-year-old defeat being by a mere short-head by Mr Swallow in the Prix Robert Papin at Maisons-Laffitte. Starting on a quieter note, Brigadier Gerard won a minor event at Newbury in June, another at Salisbury and then Newbury's Washington Singer Stakes before stepping into the limelight with a comfortable success in the Middle Park Stakes at Newmarket in the autumn.

The epic clash between Brigadier Gerard and Mill Reef came in the 2,000 Guineas on May 1, 1971, when they were ridden by their regular jockeys, Joe Mercer and Geoff Lewis respectively. Unlike Mill Reef, who had been an impressive winner of the Greenham Stakes, Brigadier Gerard was without a previous race of the season. Nevertheless he showed that he was as fit as human hands could make him by taking the lead well over a furlong out and bounding away to beat the hard-ridden Mill Reef by three lengths.

Thereafter their paths diverged. Whereas Brigadier Gerard consolidated his reputation as the supreme miler, Mill Reef proved himself the outstanding middle-distance horse in Europe. Having justified being made favourite for the Derby, he reverted to ten furlongs successfully in the Eclipse Stakes, beat off a strong international challenge by six lengths in the King George VI and Queen Elizabeth Stakes and then showed a clean pair of heels to the best that Europe could pit against him in the Prix de l'Arc de Triomphe at Longchamp. There, he beat the high class French filly Pistol Packer by a convincing three lengths.

Meanwhile Brigadier Gerard maintained his triumphal progress over a mile by winning the St James's Palace Stakes at Royal Ascot, Goodwood's Sussex Stakes, the Goodwood Mile and then the Queen Elizabeth II Stakes at Ascot. In October he tackled 1¼ miles in the Champion Stakes at Newmarket, where it was not the extra distance but the soft ground he hated that obliged him to draw on his courage for the first time in his life in order to beat Rarity by a short-head.

A renewal of rivalry between Brigadier Gerard and Mill Reef as four-year-olds in either the Eclipse Stakes or York's Benson & Hedges Gold Cup was eagerly anticipated, but this never materialized. After winning the Prix Ganay at Longchamp and the Coronation Cup, Mill Reef caught a virus before shattering four bones in his near fore while working at Kingsclere on August 30. Superb veterinary skill saved his life and since retiring to the National Stud he has made his mark by siring both the English and French Derby winners of

1978 – Shirley Heights and Acamas.

Following four more successes in the first half of 1972, Brigadier Gerard put his unbeaten record into jeopardy by venturing as far as 1½ miles in the King George VI and Queen Elizabeth Stakes at Ascot, where his class, rather than his innate stamina, enabled him to beat Parnell by a length and a half. Next time out he met with a shock defeat by that year's Derby winner Roberto, who made all the running in the hands of American jockey Braulio Baeza to beat him by three lengths in the Benson & Hedges Gold Cup. The only certain thing about that controversial contest is that Brigadier Gerard did not run below his form, as he also broke the record for the course and distance.

Though beaten at last, Brigadier Gerard was far from the end of his career, as he showed by winning both the Queen Elizabeth II Stakes and the Champion Stakes for a second time with characteristic authority. He then retired to the Egerton Stud, just across the road from the new quarters of Mill Reef on the western outskirts of Newmarket.

Crepello

Crepello was an extremely handsome though distinctly top-heavy, chestnut colt by Donatello II out of Crepuscule, by Mieuxce – breeding that represents some of the best English, French and Italian blood. He was bred and owned by the late Sir Victor Sassoon and trained by Sir Noel Murless at Warren Place, Newmarket; having been foaled in 1954, he was a year younger than his half-sister Honeylight, who won the 1,000 Guineas.

The tragedy of Crepello was that he had to be taken out of training long before he could realise his full potential, but a measure of his greatness can be inferred from the fact that all three of his triumphs were achieved when circumstances were against him. Although bred for stamina and late maturity, he made his mark in the top flight as a two-year-old. After being second in the Windsor Castle Stakes at Royal Ascot first time out, he was fourth to Pipe of Peace in the Middle Park Stakes, before beating the more forward Doutelle by three-quarters of a length in the Dewhurst Stakes.

Crepello ran just twice as a three-year-old. In the 2,000 Guineas he beat Quorum by half a length, with Pipe of Peace a head away third. In the Derby he beat the Irish horse Ballymoss by a length and a half, with his old rival Pipe of Peace third again. The Guineas had been run over a distance that was already too short for him on

Top Left *Brigadier Gerard (Queen's Hussar – La Paiva), yet to produce a horse as good as himself.* **Top right** *Levmoss (Le Levanstell – Feemoss) had the speed to win the Arc de Triomphe and the* stamina to win the Prix du Cadran and the Ascot Gold Cup. **Centre right** *Mill Reef (Never Bend – Milan Mill), a brilliant career shattered on the downs.* **Above left** *Crepello (Donatello II – Crepescule) has had a* lasting influence at stud. **Above right** *The unbeaten Ribot (Tenerani – Romanella) was a champion in three countries and had a profound influence at stud.*

ground that was too firm, while the Derby was also run on firm ground round a switchback course that was hardly calculated to suit a long-striding colt.

After the Derby, Crepello was to have run in the King George VI and Queen Elizabeth Stakes at Ascot but, despite the unpopularity he necessarily incurred with ante-post backers, his trainer withdrew him on the morning of the race because of the unsuitability of the dead going on Ascot Heath. Three weeks later the strain that carrying his massive top imposed on his legs told when he broke down on his near fore. The following month Ballymoss paid him the most handsome of compliments by winning the St Leger.

Crepello, who had a perfect temperament for a stallion, retired to the Beech House Stud at Cheveley, near Newmarket. Among the many high-class horses he sired was Busted, winner of the King George VI and Queen Elizabeth Stakes and the Eclipse Stakes, and the classic winning fillies Caergwrle and Mysterious. Like many of his male line, he lived to a ripe old age, being destroyed in 1974 at the age of twenty. Though circumstances conspired to prevent racegoers seeing much of Crepello himself, his descendants are going to be much in evidence as he is becoming a powerful influence in maintaining the Donatello II branch of the Blandford male line. His daughters are also most highly prized as brood-mares.

Levmoss

Bred by the McGrath Trust Company, Levmoss – ranked equal eighth with Busted by David Swannell in his ratings – carried the colours of Seamus McGrath, who trained him at Sandyford, Co Dublin. A rangy bay, he was by the sprint-bred Le Levanstell, who showed top-class form over a mile, out of Feemoss, by Ballymoss out of the Yorkshire Oaks winner, Feevagh. Thus, it was from the dam's side of his pedigree that his stamina came. The same breeding produced Le Moss, winner of the Ascot Gold Cup in 1979.

In common with all stayers, Levmoss improved with age, but, unlike most others, he also had the speed and precocity to make his mark as a two-year-old, as he showed by winning at Gowran Park on the second of this two appearances at that age. In the light of hindsight, this early success was extremely significant. Levmoss was a progressive type of horse, but it was not only his ability to hold his own in increasingly better staying races that was to develop. His speed developed as well – hence his eventual success in the Prix de l'Arc de Triomphe.

On his first outing as a three-year-old, Levmoss won over a mile-and-a-quarter at Pheonix Park, but his next appearance made it plain that he was still a good way behind the best. The first public indication that Levmoss might be in the top class came when he beat Canterbury by a neck in the Oxfordshire Stakes at Newbury. The value of that form was underlined by Canterbury running Ribero to a short head in the Doncaster St Leger the following month.

Levmoss himself was placed third in the French St Leger, being beaten four lengths and three lengths by Dhaudevia and Torpid. He finished the season by using his stamina to beat older horses over the two miles of the Leopardstown November Handicap.

Having been unplaced over a mile at the Curragh first time out in 1969 and coming third to Zamazaan in the Prix Jean Prat at Longchamp, Levmoss gave notice that he was coming to the height of his powers by beating Zamazaan by a neck in the Prix du Cadran, the French equivalent of the Ascot Gold Cup. Just over three weeks later, he completed the great stayers' double by reversing earlier form by beating Torpid, who had won the French St Leger, by four lengths in the Ascot Gold Cup.

Next time out Levmoss took the transitional step to reverting to middle distance by carrying the huge weight of 10st 10lb to win a handicap over a mile and six furlongs at The Curragh in mid-September. Then came his bid for the Arc on his final appearance in public.

As the runners turned into the straight at Longchamp, the Italian horse Bonconte di Montefeltro made the running, with Levmoss and three others lying close up. When Levmoss made his break for the line shortly afterwards, none of the other leaders could find the pace to go with him. Though Park Top, ridden by Lester Piggot, put in a late challenge from the rear of the field, Levmoss won by three-quarters of a length.

Given that Levmoss had his fair share of luck – Park Top had been hopelessly boxed in on the rails – the quality of the rest of the field showed his supremacy. It included no fewer than four of that year's Derby winners – Blakeney (English), Prince Regent (Irish), Goodly (French) and Bonconte di Montefeltro (Italian).

Levmoss thus became the only horse to date to win the Arc, the Prix du Cadran and the Ascot Gold Cup. He retired to the Brownstone stud, from which he was moved to France in 1976. He died the following year. Nevertheless, he was at stud long enough to sire M. Lolshan, winner of the Irish St Leger in 1978.

Exbury

The French horse Exbury, whom David Swannell rates on a par with Crepello, was a complete contrast to the 1957 Derby winner. An exquisitely-made little chestnut colt, he radiated quality and never stopped improving throughout the three seasons that he was in training. As a two-year-old he proved useful by winning once and being placed in his other three races. At three he established himself in the top class by winning twice and obtaining a place in three of his other five races. As a four-year-old, he showed absolute brilliance by winning each of his five races and emerged as the outstanding middle-distance horse in Europe.

Owned and bred by Baron Guy de Rothschild and trained by Geoffrey Watson at Chantilly, Exbury, like Crepello, came from the Blandford male line, being by Le Haar out of the English-bred Greensward, a daughter of the Nearco horse Mossborough. Having obtained his solitary success as a two-year-old over the seven furlongs of the Prix Reine Mathilde at Deauville in August, 1961, Exbury won both the Prix Daru over a mile and 2½ furlongs and the Prix Henri Foy over half a furlong further at Longchamp as a three-year-old. At the same age he was beaten by a length into second place behind Match III in the Grand Prix de Saint-Cloud and was third in the Prix de Jockey Club, beaten a length and a neck by Val de Loir.

As a four-year-old, Exbury left that form a long way behind. Having won the Prix Poiard at Saint-Cloud in late March he had his revenge on Val de Loir by beating him four lengths at level weights in the 1¼ miles Prix Ganay. Next time out he gave English racegoers a taste of his excellence by winning the Coronation Cup at Epsom. Taking the lead 300 yards from home, he stormed away to beat the previous season's St Leger winner, Hethersett, by an impressive six lengths, with another of the 1962 classic winners, Monade, who had been successful in the Oaks, down the field.

In July, Exbury avenged his defeat of twelve months previously in the Grand Prix de Saint-Cloud be reasserting his superiority over Val de Loir. Finally he won the Prix de l'Arc de Triomphe. Making his extraordinary finishing speed tell irresistably, he took the lead a furlong out and went away to beat Le Mesnil by two lengths, with the Derby winner, Relko, who had started at a shade odds-on, unplaced.

Top left *Relko (Tanerko – Relance III), the six-length winner of the Derby and unbeaten as a four-year-old.*
Top right *The Aga Khan leads in his Oaks winner Petite Étoile, with the young Lester Piggott aboard. By Petition – Star of Iran, her fourth dam was the* great Mumtaz Mahal. **Centre left** *Nijinsky (Northern Dancer – Flaming Page) lasts out the St Leger to win the Triple Crown. He was bred in Canada by E P Taylor.* **Above left** *Busted (Crepello – Sans le Sou), a powerful bay who developed into a champion as a* four-year-old. **Above right** *Sassafras (Sheshoon – Ruta), the winner of the Prix de l'Arc de Triomphe and the first horse to beat Nijinsky. At stud he has already sired the classic winners Henri de Balafre and Marmolada.*

Busted

A fine, big bay colt foaled in 1963, Busted was bred by the Snailwell Stud – Crepello – Sans le Sou, by Vimy out of Martial Loan, by the 2,000 Guineas winner, Court Martial – and was owned by the late Stanhope Joel. In common with Levmoss, he shared eighth place in David Swannell's championship ratings; both horses, too, were trained originally in Ireland, but, whereas Levmoss was based in Ireland throughout his career, Busted was sent to England, where he reached his peak as a four-year-old.

As a two-year-old and in the following season, however, Busted was trained by 'Brud' Fetherstonhaugh at the Curragh. Because of his backwardness, he was unplaced in both his two-year-old races, while in 1966 he proved too headstrong for his own good in the Irish Derby. He led two furlongs from home, but soon ran out of steam and dropped back to finish only twelfth to Sodium. Inability to settle did not prevent the horse from winning the next year, however, as he won by a head from Pieces of Eight in the 1¼-mile Gallinule Stakes at the Curragh.

On being sent to Newmarket to be trained by Sir Noel Murless, Busted learned the priceless lesson of how to relax and drop himself out in his work. This proved the key to unlocking the huge reserves of talent that enabled him to show an almost unrecognizable improvement on his form of his first two seasons. Making his first appearance in England at Sandown Park in late April, he did not take the lead until inside the last of the ten furlongs. Having done so, he drew away to beat Haymarket by three lengths.

For the second of his four appearances as a four-year-old, Busted returned to Sandown Park for the Eclipse Stakes in early July. Sir Noel Murless's jockey, George Moore, chose to ride the stable's other runner, Fleet, and, judged by form, this was a sensible decision. But Busted held up was a very different horse from Busted given his head, as Bill Rickaby was to demonstrate. Starting to make ground three furlongs from home, Rickaby sent him to the front at the distance. The colt sprinted away to beat Great Nephew by two-and-a-half lengths, with Fleet fourth and Sodium, the horse that had beaten Busted so decisively in the Irish Derby, only fifth.

A week later, Busted consolidated his new-found reputation as a top-class international performer by winning the King George VI and Queen Elizabeth Stakes at Ascot. Now ridden by George Moore, he trailed the field until making rapid headway six furlongs out. Taking the lead again at the distance, he beat Salvo by three lengths.

Busted's next target was the Prix de l'Arc de Triomphe and, in preparation for this, he was sent to France in early September. There, he beat Fiasco by a comfortable four lengths in the Prix Henri Foy at Longchamp. But this was to be his last race, as he damaged a tendon while working a few days before the Arc and was then retired to the Snailwell Stud, at which he had been reared. His progeny there have included the St Leger winner Bustino, the Irish Sweeps Derby winner Weavers' Hall and the leading two-year-old of 1978, Tromos.

Right Royal V

Right Royal V, a strapping brown horse by Owen Tudor out of Bastia, was trained at Chantilly by Etienne Pollet for Mme J Couturie, his breeder. Having won three of his four races as a two-year-old in 1960, Right Royal scored five times and was placed in his other two races in 1961. On his only visit to England he put up the performance of a very high-class horse indeed by beating the previous year's Derby winner, St Paddy, by three lengths in the King George VI and Queen Elizabeth Stakes.

The finest achievements of Right Royal V in his own country were to beat Match III by two lengths in the Prix Lupin and by three lengths in the Prix du Jockey-Club. The following season Match III was to pay him tribute by winning the King George VI and Queen Elizabeth Stakes. Right Royal V also won the Poule d'Essai des Poulains but was probably past his best for the season by the time he was beaten by two lengths into second place behind the Italian horse Molvedo in the Prix de l'Arc de Triomphe. Right Royal stood in France, where he sired the Irish Derby winner Prince Regent, and died in 1973.

Nijinsky

Another of the outstanding horses to have been trained in Ireland in recent years was Nijinsky, who became the fifteenth winner of the Triple Crown in 1970 – the first horse to do so since Bahram in 1935. Unlike Levmoss, he was not Irish-bred but a product of E P Taylor's famous Canadian Windfield's Stud. Sent to Toronto's Woodbine Sale, he was bought by the Charles W Engelhard for $84,000 on the advice of Vincent O'Brien, who was to train him at Ballydoyle.

A fine big bay colt, with a great barrel of a body set on strong limbs, Nijinsky was by Nearco's grandson Northern Dancer out of Flaming Page, by Bull Page. Unbeaten as a two-year-old he already looked a good year older when he came to Newmarket to win the Dewhurst Stakes with absurd ease on his final appearance at that age.

Carrying on his triumphal progress by treating his contemporaries with utter contempt in 1970, Nijinsky won the Gladness Stakes and the 2,000 Guineas before disposing of the highly regarded French colt, Gyr, in The Derby and then completing the double in the Irish Derby.

Nijinsky met older horses for the first time in the King George VI and Queen Elizabeth Stakes at Ascot in July, but this did not worry him either – even though the previous year's Derby winner Blakeney was one of the runners. Riding with supreme confidence, Lester Piggott sent him to the front just below the distance and had restrained him to a mere canter by the time they passed the post two lengths clear of Blakeney. Seven weeks later Nijinsky completed the Triple Crown in the St Leger at Doncaster, where he accelerated on the bit just below the distance to beat Meadowville by a length.

Nijinsky's success in the St Leger was his eleventh in as many outings but thereafter began the autumn of discontent that was to be the anticlimax of a great racecourse career. Arguably he was left with too much to do in the Prix de l'Arc de Triomphe, as he was still in the last four with half a mile to go, but if he had been his old self he must have won. As it was, he hit the front a hundred yards out, only to start hanging away to his left. The result was that Sassafras was able to get up to beat him by a head. The obvious cause for any loss of form on the part of Nijinsky was that he had insufficient time to recover after the St Leger, for which he had a necessarily hurried preparation as a result of a severe attack of ringworm in early August.

Be that as it may, it was decided that Nijinsky had to be allowed to wind up his career on a winning note, so he was sent to the post for the Champion Stakes at Newmarket on October 17. He was submitted to almost impossible pressure from the television and press photographers and, instead of being the proud, commanding individual that he used to be, he was in a lather of sweat by the time he reached the start. Lorenzaccio set off to make all the running and, when Nijinsky was asked to go after him in earnest a furlong out, there was no response to the pressure. Lorenzaccio was able to maintain the initiative to beat him by a length and a half into second place for his sad farewell. Returning across the Atlantic, he took up stud duties in 1971 at Claiborne Stud with immediate success, his winners including the King George VI and Queen Elizabeth Stakes winner, Ile de Bourbon.

Ballymoss

Ballymoss, the outstanding horse to be trained in Ireland during the 1950s, is ranked close to Crepello in the list of all-time greats. After being second to the latter in the Derby, he developed into a high-class middle-distance horse. A chesnut colt by Mossborough out of the Singapore mare, Indian Call, he carried John McShain's colours to win the Irish Derby next time out after the Derby and later returned to England to beat Court Harwell by a length in the St Leger.

As a four-year-old, Ballymoss proved to be the best horse in Europe in 1958. At Epsom he beat the French horse Fric by two lengths in the Coronation Cup without being extended and at Sandown Park put up a still more impressive performance in the Eclipse Stakes by storming home six lengths clear of Restoration, with Arctic Explorer, winner of the race a year previously, third. A fortnight later Ballymoss completed a great hat-trick by slamming the Queen's high-class filly Almeria by three lengths in the King George VI and Queen Elizabeth Stakes. Having been rested in the late summer, he put the finishing touch to his career by beating Fric again in the Prix de l'Arc de Triomphe. Like Alleged, Nijinsky and so many other good horses who have been based in Ireland during the last 20 years Ballymoss was trained by Vincent O'Brien. His lengthy stud career was spent at Whitsbury Manor Stud in Hampshire and he died there of a heart attack in July 1979. While there he sired the good horse Royal Palace, winner of the Derby and Eclipse Stakes.

Sassafras

By reason of his success in the Prix de l'Arc de Triomphe, Sassafras figures on the same mark as Nijinsky. A bay colt by the Ascot Gold Cup winner Sheshoon out of Ruta, by Ratification, Sassafras was bred by the wife of his owner, the late Arpad Plesch, at the Dollarstown Stud in Ireland and was trained by Francois Mathet in France. He never ran outside that country.

Sassafras won at Vichy on his first time out and had three other races as a two-year-old. The following season he won five times and was placed in his other two races. In the Prix du Jockey-Club, he beat Roll of Honour by three-quarters of a length and gained a second classic success in the Prix Royal Oak although only on the disqualification of Hallez, who had outstayed him by three lengths. Then on his 11th and final appearance in public he obtained a dramatic success over Nijinsky in the Prix de l'Arc de Triomphe.

Relko

Relko was a bay colt by Tanerko out of Relance III. He was trained by Francois Mathet at Chantilly for the late Francois Dupré and was, in effect, a Triple Crown winner in 1963, as he was successful in the Poule d'Essai des Poulains, beat Merchant Venturer by a most convincing six lengths in the Derby at Epsom and won the Prix Royal Oak by three lengths from Deboule. He was an odds-on favourite to win the Irish Derby but had to be withdrawn on being found to be lame at the start.

Unbeaten as a four-year-old, Relko returned to Epsom to win the Coronation Cup by a neck from Khalkis. He was also successful in the Prix Ganay and the Grand Prix de Saint-Cloud. At the age of nineteen he was still covering successfully at Burley Lodge Stud near Reading in Berkshire.

Floribunda

Floribunda, the first sprinter to appear in David Swannell's list of great European horses, was a strong well-balanced bay colt of medium size trained in Ireland by Paddy Prendergast for Mrs J R Mullion. Both his sire, Princely Gift, and his maternal grandsire, Denturius, had been sprinters of outstanding ability.

Having won in Ireland on his first two appearances as a juvenile in 1960, Floribunda came to England to put up an extraordinarily impressive performance by beating Praise by no less than eight lengths at the end of the five furlongs of the New Stakes (now the Norfolk Stakes) at Royal Ascot. On his only subsequent appearance during his first season, however, he disappointed by finishing only third to Test Case in the Gimcrack Stakes.

Returning to York a year later, Floribunda avenged that defeat in no uncertain manner by beating the fast filly Cynara by the easiest of three lengths in the Nunthorpe Stakes (now the William Hill Sprint Championship). He had also beaten Cynara in the King George Stakes at Goodwood on his previous appearance. After standing for nine seasons in England, he was exported to Japan in 1970.

Petite Etoile

The grey Petite Etoile, the first filly to appear in David Swannell's assessments, used to be freely compared with Pretty Polly and Sceptre, the now legendary heroines of the early years of the century. Trained by Sir Noel Murless for the late Prince Aly Khan and subsequently his son, the present Aga Khan, she continued racing until she was a five-year-old. Unusually burly for one of her sex, she had immense power in her quarters. She was by Petition out of Star of Iran, whose third dam was the late Aga Khan's great foundation mare Mumtaz Mahal.

Having made a satisfactory. though hardly auspicious, start by winning two of her four races as a two-year-old in 1958, Petite Etoile took the Free Handicap first time out in 1959. The stable jockey, Lester Piggott, passed over the ride on her in favour of Collyria in the 1,000 Guineas, and it was Doug Smith who brought her home a length clear of Rosalba. Continuing through her second season unbeaten and improving all the time, Petite Etoile proceeded to win the Oaks, The Sussex Stakes at Goodwood, the Yorkshire Oaks and the Champion Stakes.

After winning the Victor Wild Stakes on the now defunct Hurst Park course first time out in 1960, Petite Etoile beat the previous year's Derby winner Parthia with ruthless brilliance in the Coronation Cup, but lost by half a length to Agressor in the King George VI and Queen Elizabeth Stakes at Ascot. There Piggott's tactics came in for widespread criticism, while the going was probably rather softer than she liked it. A bout of coughing prevented her from running again that season.

The decision to keep her in training for a fourth season in 1961 was justified though it was unfortunate that she should have been beaten on the two occasions on which public emotion was most behind her – in the Aly Khan Memorial Gold Cup at Kempton Park, where she could not catch the pillar-to-post winner, Sir Winston Churchill's High Hat, and on her farewell appearance in the Queen Elizabeth II Stakes at Ascot, which she was beaten half a length by Le Levanstell. On the credit side though, Petite Etoile won a second Coronation Cup, Sandown Park's Coronation Stakes and the Scarborough Stakes at Doncaster as a five-year-old. In as much as she went on racing for longer than any of the colts that Swannell rates above her, Petite Etoile earned her high rating amongst the great horses of her time the hard way.

Just as the Senior British Jockey Club Handicapper, David Swannell, has provided his rating of European racehorses of the past twenty-five years, so it proved possible to provide authoritative ratings for the great horses of the USA. Frank E (Jimmy) Kilroe, perhaps America's best known handicapper, has provided these assessments. For six years, Kilroe was racing secretary and handicapper at the New York Racing Association tracks, Aqueduct, Belmont Park and Saratoga. At the same time he carried out the same job at Santa Anita, continuing there until 1960, also serving periods as director of racing at Del Mar, Hollywood Park and Oak Tree. He is currently Vice President-Racing of the Los Angeles Turf Club Inc, at Santa Anita.

'If it seems rash to attempt a grading of the best horses of the past twenty-five years in American racing, how much more so is it to relate that rating to a similar effort in England? Where perhaps six races determine the best in England, there may be twenty-four that have a bearing on such judgements in this country and at least ten of those are handicaps as against none in England. To complete the disparities, all the definitive races in England are run on grass while most US races remain on dirt.

'David Swannell and I have agreed to use a common scale starting at 100 for the average Kentucky Derby winner. Assuming that to be equivalent to 126lb in our weights, the upward span of 12lb in these ratings may gain in significance. The exclusion of fillies and mares is not an evidence of male chauvinism, but rather of an absence of form for the distaff group racing against the other sex. It should be stated that those weights are based on a hypothetical distance of 1¼ miles.

'Despite the advent of computers, the assignment of weights is still pretty much a matter of opinion. The superiority of one horse to his contemporaries involves an evaluation of his competition; geldings such as Forego, Kelso and Bardstown, while they benefit from a longer racing career, lose a certain glamour that comes to dominant sires like Bold Ruler.

'The American quarter-century to 1979 just excludes Native Dancer's abbreviated four-year-old season which was still long enough to gain him Horse-of-the-Year honours. Like Nijinsky, he might have been retired undefeated with a little bit of luck. The following years were dominated by Nashua, Swaps, Bold Ruler and Round Table in that chronological order. Nashua was as good as he cared to be and swamped Swaps in a celebrated match race in

Chicago. Bold Ruler was brilliant, despite his infirmities, while Round Table, who seemed to have no weaknesses, held his form as long as any horse.

'Then came the Kelso years – five in all. He sprung to fame in the autumn of his three-year-old year, having missed all the Triple Crown races, but once he found the path to the winner's circle, he seldom lost his way. As a gelding, his dreams were limited to the racecourse, and he had the further advantage as he grew older of the undying support of half a decade of New York horseplayers. After Kelso came Buckpasser, who liked to draw his finishes fine, but timed thirteen in a row perfectly while sitting out the Triple Crown. People are still debating the relative merits of Damascus and Dr Fager. Dr Fager, perhaps the most brilliant miler of all, did run that distance at Arlington Park in 1 minute 32 seconds, but ten furlongs was his absolute limit, while Damascus could run around again.

'Of our other high weights, one can hardly overlook Forego, whose reign, despite a number of physical handicaps, was just as unchallenged as Kelso's. An enormous gelding, he was as genuine as he was big, and withstood all but a few of the handicapper's best efforts to bring him back to the field. Seattle Slew went through the Triple Crown series undefeated and scarcely extended, a singular achievement.

'Affirmed and Alydar are perhaps the two best horses to race in the same season in memory. The gap between them, never wide, narrowed to a few inches at the finish of twelve furlongs in the Belmont.

'Spectacular Bid was definitely the best two-year-old of 1978, and he made short work of his contemporaries through two-thirds of our Triple Crown, only to fail in the Belmont whan Coastal sailed past him in the last quarter mile. At the time of writing he is on the inactive list while Coastal has gone from strength to strength.'

Secretariat	112	Coastal	105
Forego	111	Ack Ack	105
Affirmed	111	Cougar II	105
Kelso	110	Bardstown	104
Bold Ruler	108	Majestic Prince	104
Buckpasser	108	Arts and Letters	103
Nashua	108	Needles	103
Seattle Slew	108	Tom Rolfe	103
Spectacular Bid	108	Sword Dancer	102
Alydar	107	High Gun	101
Dr Fager	107	Carry Back	100
Gallant Man	107	Foolish Pleasure	100
Northern Dancer	107	Key to the Mint	100
Swaps	107		
Coastal	106		
Damascus	106		
Riva Ridge	106		
Round Table	106		
Tim Tam	106		

Secretariat

Secretariat, a huge chestnut colt by Bold Ruler out of Somethingroyal, was so precocious and successful as a two-year-old that he was syndicated for $6,080,000 at the end of his first season, having been nominated the US Horse of the Year. Even before the start of that season (1972) Secretariat, when worked over five furlongs, had returned a time of 57⅗ seconds. His three-year-old campaign was marked with such brilliance that it still remains unparalleled in racing history. After dazzling performances in the seven furlongs Bay Shore Stakes and the one mile Gotham Stakes at Aqueduct, Secretariat shocked the nation by finishing third to his own stable mate Angle Light in the Wood Memorial. It was later discovered that a boil had infected Secretariat's mouth just prior to the race.

Luckily, he was fully recovered by Derby Day, and on that first Saturday in May, 1973, Secretariat took the first step to racing immortality by coming from last place easily to defeat the Santa Anita Derby winner Sham, while also shattering the track record. His time of 1 minute 59⅖ seconds was three-fifths of a second faster than the previous record, set nine years earlier by Northern Dancer.

Two weeks later Secretariat added the Preakness to his laurels, after making a move on the first turn that became part of racing folklore. Running last, some six lengths off the lead, he was given his head by his jockey and he literally leaped at the rest of the field, like a tiger attacking some unfortunate victim. Before anyone could comprehend this unorthodox move, 'Big Red', as he was now known, was two lengths in front, and there he stayed, with the unlucky Sham trying gallantly to close the gap. But he was unable to make up an inch on Secretariat, who was under no pressure whatsoever to maintain a 2½ length advantage to the post.

Secretariat's Derby and Preakness wins were indeed the mark of an extraordinary animal. However, there is not a superlative in the English language that could do justice to his performance in the Belmont Stakes. Secretariat won the Belmont by an unbelievable thirty-one lengths, shattering the race record by over two full seconds. His jockey unable to pull him up, he also beat the record for thirteen furlongs at Belmont, Secretariat being the first horse to complete the triple crown in twenty-five years.

Secretariat ran six more races, winning four, including the Arlington Invitational, a world-record performance in the Marlboro Cup, and spectacular wins over the turf in the Man O' War Stakes and Canadian International Turf Championship. After his defeat to Onion in the Whitney Stakes, it was discovered that Secretariat was suffering from a virus and fever, forcing him to miss the Travers. He was defeated by Prove Out in the Woodward Stakes, as a last-minute stand-in for his stablemate Riva Ridge.

Secretariat was retired to Claiborne Farm in Kentucky with sixteen wins in twenty-one starts (including one disqualification) for earnings of $1,316,808.

Forego

In fifty-seven starts, Forego won thirty-four races and earned $1,938,957. On only three occasions did he finish worse than fourth, two of those being on slippery types of track he disliked. To illustrate his remarkable consistency, after finishing fifth in the 1973 Blue Grass Stakes at Keeneland, he ran in forty-six consecutive races without finishing lower down the field than fourth. Thirty-one of those races were handicaps and Forego was the top weight in all of them. He was voted Horse of the Year in 1974, 1975 and 1976, finishing second to the Triple Crown winner Seattle Slew in 1977.

Forego was not an ideal two-year-old. He was an enormous individual, with a malicious temperament, and an acute case of sexual precocity. Already looking, and acting, like a five-year-old stud horse, he would go into a frenzy at the mere sight of a filly, and his habit of attempting to remove any anatomical parts he could reach had left a trail of gnarled grooms and exercise riders.

After eight unsuccessful months of trying to tame this raging brute, his trainer, Sherrill Ward, and his owner, Martha Gerry, decided that the only course of action was to geld him and hope for the best. Sent to Florida later that year, Forego was already an imposing figure standing seventeen hands tall and weighing approximately 1,200 lb. Although he gave away seasoning to the other two-year-olds, Forego would often outwork them in the morning, suggesting to Ward that he was a colt of enormous ability.

When he turned three, Forego was working well for his debut, but Ward was already concerned about the colt's left foreleg. Inflamed branches of the suspensory ligaments attached to the outside of both round sesamoid bones had deposited a disquieting amount of calcium there and, as a result, one sesamoid was

enlarged by about one-third. This meant that Ward would have to keep him away from any kind of track with a slippery or loose surface. The condition, sesamoiditis, plagued the gelding throughout his career.

At three, Forego equalled two track records and set another, all in New York. In his final two starts, he captured the Discovery and Roamer Handicaps at Aqueduct. He improved considerably at four. He won the nine furlongs Donn Handicap, 10 furlongs Gulfstream Park Handicap, and 10 furlongs Widener Handicap, all in Florida. Then, after almost two month's rest, he returned to New York for the seven furlongs Carter Handicap against the fastest colt in the east, Mr Prospector. Carrrying top weight of 129 lb, in what was supposed to be only a preparatory race for the mile Metropolitan Handicap nine days later, Forego went from last to first on the turn, and coasted by Mr Prospector, while under a pull, to score easily by 2¼ lengths. His jockey, Heliodoro Gustines, never moved his hands, as Forego appeared to be galloping along as if in a morning workout.

The big gelding won only one of his next five starts, but emerged in the autumn better than ever. His final three victories that year will certainly go down as one of the most unique feats in the annals of American racing. In a five-week span, this extraordinary animal captured the Woodward Stakes at a mile and a half, followed by the Vosburgh Handicap, defeating the nation's top sprinters at seven furlongs, and culminated with an impressive win over the leading stayers in the two-mile Jockey Club Gold Cup. Never before had a horse demonstrated such an unparalleled display of versatility. He was voted Horse of the Year, and became the first horse to be voted Champion Sprinter while winning the two miles Gold Cup.

The following year, Forego continued his dominance, by winning the Seminole and Widener Handicaps in Florida, plus another win in the Carter Handicap, carrying 134 lb. After finishing third, under 136 lb, in the Metropolitan, he won the Brooklyn Handicap, setting a new track record, under 132 lb, and the mile and a half Suburban Handicap, carrying 134 lb. He returned in the fall to defeat the champion three-year-old Wajima in the Woodward Stakes, winning his second Horse of the Year title.

In 1976, Forego's trainer, Sherrill Ward, was not in the best of health and Mrs Gerry decided to turn Forego over to the veteran trainer Frank Whiteley. Under Whiteley's patient and meticulous handling, Forego finally won the elusive Metropolitan from

the Preakness Stakes winner Master Derby, was beaten by a nose by Kentucky Derby winner Foolish Pleasure in the Suburban under 134 lb and then took his revenge by winning the Brooklyn by two lengths, again carrying 134 lb.

Later that year, under a new jockey, Bill Shoemaker, Forego won the Woodward, carrying 135 lb, running the nine furlongs in 1 minute 45⅘ seconds – just two-fifths of a second off the world record. Then came the Marlboro Cup, and Forego's greatest moment. Carrying a staggering 137 lb, he beat Honest Pleasure by a head, stamping himself as one of the premier weight carriers of all time. The time on a sloppy track was 2 minutes flat, just a fifth of a second off his own track record.

The following year, Forego won four of seven races, including victories in the Metropolitan, Nassau County, and the Woodward for the fourth time.

In 1978, at the age of eight, Forego won his first start, beating the subsequent champion sprinter Dr Patches at seven furlongs. In his next start, the Suburban, he couldn't handle the slippery track, and finished fifth. One week later the news came that he had been retired. Heat was discovered in his leg, and x-rays revealed the presence of calcium chips.

Throughout his career, Forego required special treatment, although not once in fifty-seven starts did he ever back off under fire. He was always the aggressor, an imposing figure ready and willing to do battle at all times. For this, he was respected and appreciated by racegoers throughout the USA.

Affirmed and Alydar

Although they had met twice early in 1977, it was not until the Hopeful Stakes at Saratoga in August that Affirmed and Alydar developed their intense rivalry. Alydar had scored four brilliant victories after his debut, when he finished fifth to Affirmed in the Youthful Stakes, but turned the tables on the Harbor View Farm colt in the Great American Stakes. By Raise A Native out of Sweet Tooth, Alydar was considered to be the top two-year-old.

Affirmed, who had journeyed to California to win the Hollywood Juvenile after his loss to Alydar, then returned to Saratoga, where he captured the Sanford Stakes in impressive fashion. The son of Exclusive Native by Won't Tell You, he could not match Alydar in looks, being tall and lanky but with enormous scope for improvement.

As they turned for home in the Hopeful Stakes, Affirmed and Alydar formally met for the first time. Alydar, the even-money favourite, stormed up alongside Affirmed and seemed like a sure thing to add the Hopeful to his laurels. But, though Alydar maintained his momentum, he could not pass the Harbor View colt and was beaten by half a length.

In the historic Futurity Stakes at Belmont Park two weeks later Affirmed on the inside and Alydar on the outside came down the Belmont straight locked together. Alydar got his nose in front, with his jockey, Eddie Maple, working furiously to stay there. However, Affirmed, under the urging of Steve Cauthen, came again to snatch victory by a nose in a time of 1 minute 21⅗ seconds. The brilliance of this performance was substantiated by the eleven length margin over the third horse Nasty and Bold.

The mile Champagne Stakes was their next meeting with Alydar under a new jockey in Jorge Velasquez. Tucked in along the rail for most of the race, Velasquez saw Affirmed was busy on the inside with Darby Creek Road and quickly took his mount to the middle of the track. Down the stretch, Alydar came on the outside and swept past Affirmed to win by a length and a quarter.

Instead of putting his colt away for the year, trainer John Veitch decided to show the world that Alydar was the better horse, and sent him to Laurel for a final showdown with Affirmed in the eight and a half furlong Futurity. This time Alydar had the rail and a good head lead turning into the stretch, but he was worn down by Affirmed in the straight and lost by a head. The Futurity secured the two-year-old championship for Affirmed, but many felt Alydar was more the classic horse, and would turn the tables when the distances were extended.

Trainer Laz Barrera sent Affirmed to Santa Anita for his three-year-old campaign, while John Veitch employed the more conventional Florida-Kentucky route for Alydar. Events could not have worked out better, as Affirmed won an allowance race by five lengths, captured the San Felipe Handicap under the Derby weight of 126 lb, ran away with the Santa Anita Derby by eight lengths, and culminated his California stay with a two length win in the Hollywood Derby.

Alydar, meanwhile, was brilliant in Florida, winning an allowance race easily, then defeating the top Derby contender Believe It in the Flamingo Stakes and Florida Derby, winning both races in near track record time. Sent to Keeneland for the Blue Grass Stakes, Alydar came from eleven lengths behind to win by thirteen.

The stage was now set for the Kentucky Derby. Alydar was installed as the 6/5 favourite, with Affirmed second choice at 9/5. Others in the star-studded field included Believe It, impressive winner of the Wood Memorial at Aqueduct, and Sensitive Prince, unbeaten in six races, and already the holder of two track records.

With Sensitive Prince setting a scorching pace, Cauthen was able to settle Affirmed into third place, five lengths off the leader. Alydar, however, was trailing the field by as much as seventeen lengths down the back-stretch. Around the final turn, Affirmed and Believe It disposed of Sensitive Prince, and turned for home head and head, with Alydar beginning his run. Down the stretch, Believe It proved no match for Affirmed who easily opened a clear lead at the furlong pole. Alydar closed gamely in the middle of the track but fell short by a length and a half, confirming Affirmed as the best three-year-old in America.

In the Preakness two weeks later, Affirmed went for an early lead with Cauthen able to set an easy pace. Jorge Velasquez moved Alydar to within five lengths of Affirmed and at the three-furlong pole went to within a half-length of the leader. Although Alydar opened up six lengths on the third horse Believe It, he was unable to gain an inch on Affirmed. Three times the Calumet colt came again, and three times Affirmed resisted him. The final margin was a neck, and the time of 1 minute 54⅖ seconds was the second fastest Preakness ever to be run.

Of all the great moments provided by these two remarkable horses, nothing could remotely compare to the monumental struggle that took place three weeks later in the Belmont Stakes. For the final mile of this gruelling mile and a half event, Affirmed and Alydar were flat out and neck and neck. At the three-sixteenths pole Alydar seemed to get his nose in front, but Affirmed fought back as usual, with Cauthen and Velasquez both flailing away with left and right-handed whips. They came to the post together with Affirmed the winner by a head and Alydar thirteen lengths ahead of the third horse Darby Creek Road. Affirmed had become racing's eleventh triple crown winner.

Following the Belmont, Alydar devastated his opponents by thirteen lengths in the Arlington Classic and ten lengths in the Whitney Stakes, while Affirmed defeated Sensitive Prince by a half-length in the Jim Dandy Stakes. The tenth meeting took place thirteen days later in the mile-and-a-quarter Travers Stakes at Saratoga. With Steve Cauthen ill, Laffit Pincay

was summoned from California to ride Affirmed. Two others, Nasty and Bold and Shake Shake Shake, completed the field. Going into the far turn, Affirmed was leading as Alydar moved through along the rail to challenge. As he did so Pincay brought Affirmed in on Alydar, causing the Calumet colt to stumble badly, almost unseating Velasquez. Falling some six lengths back, Alydar remarkably came on again and was actually alongside Affirmed as they turned for home. However, the incident had taken its toll and Affirmed was able gamely to resist the challenge to win by almost two lengths. That victory was short lived as the stewards, after reviewing the films, disqualified Affirmed and placed Alydar first.

These two great competitors were never to meet again.

While training for the Marlboro Cup, Alydar broke a bone in his ankle and, although he recovered enough to run six times the following year, he was never the same horse. He broke down again preparing for the Brooklyn Handicap, and was retired to stud in Kentucky.

Affirmed, after going through some lean months with jockey Steve Cauthen, finally came good in 1979 to score some of his most brilliant victories under Laffit Pincay, and became the first horse ever to earn $2,000,000.

After winning the prestigious Santa Anita Handicap in track record time, he won the Californian Stakes, Hollywood Gold Cup under 132 lb, Woodward Stakes, and then defeated Spectacular Bid for Horse of the Year honours in the Jockey Club Gold Cup.

Kelso

When retired at nine, Kelso was an institution. He was Horse of the Year in America for an unprecedented five consecutive years from 1960 to 1964, even though usually he did not find his best form until the autumn. Then he was virtually unbeatable. He captured the two-mile Jockey Club Gold Cup five times, the Woodward Stakes three times, and the Aqueduct Stakes and Stymie Handicap twice, all these races being run in September and October. However, it would be a mistake to assume that Kelso was a seasonal horse. In 1961, he became only the third horse in history to sweep the Handicap Triple Crown, consisting of the mile Metropolitan in May, and the 10-furlong Suburban and Brooklyn Handicaps in July. He retired with record earnings of $1,977,896 from thirty-nine wins in sixty-three starts.

As a weanling at Woodstock Farm in

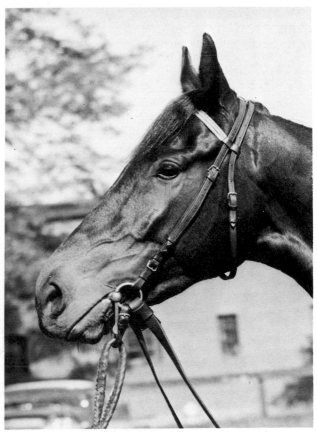

Top left *Bold Ruler (Nasrullah – Miss Disco), seven times champion sire in America and the sire of Secretariat.* **Top right** *Damascus (Sword Dancer – Kerala) is congratulated by his jockey, Willie Shoemaker, after winner the 1967 Belmont Stakes.*

Centre left *Affirmed (Exclusive Native – Won't Tell You) stretches out in the home straight. Affirmed narrowly established superiority over Alydar in 1978, but was a true champion in 1979.* **Above left** *Secretariat (Bold Ruler – Somethingroyal), storming*

home in the Belmont Stakes by thirty-one lengths. **Above right** *The head of the immortal Kelso (Your Host – Maid of Flight).*

Maryland, Kelso's action showed a slight fault in stride, and the farm veterinarian, Dr John Lee, thought this might be caused by a strangulated condition. Hoping to correct this fault – and possible increase in his size – it was decided that Kelso, the son of Your Host and Maid of Flight, should be gelded.

Kelso's stride did improve, but because of backwardness, he did not start his two-year-old campaign until September 4 at Atlantic City. With Dr Lee training, Kelso came from seventh to win by a length and a quarter at odds of 6-1. He raced twice more that year, finishing second on each occasion. The following year, his owner Mrs du Pont decided to expand her racing operation and hired ex-jockey Carl Hanford as trainer. Kelso, meanwhile, had grown into a healthy individual, standing 15.3hh. Although still unimpressive to look at, he displayed a smooth flowing stride that carried him to eight wins in nine starts at three, earning him his first Horse of the Year title.

The next year, with Eddie Arcaro now his regular rider, Kelso made racing history by sweeping the arduous Handicap Triple Crown, carrying 130, 133 and 136 lb respectively. He returned in the fall to capture the Woodward and Jockey Club Gold Cup to seal his second title. After the retirement of Arcaro, Bill Shoemaker became Kelso's regular rider, but after winning only one of his first four starts, he admitted that he wasn't the right rider for the horse, and was replaced by Ishmael 'Milo' Valenzuela. Later that year, Kelso won his second Woodward, defeating the Belmont and Travers winner Jaipur, followed by his third Gold Cup, a 10-length win in track record time.

Although this was far from his best year, Kelso had done enough to merit another Horse of the Year title. In 1963, at the age of six, the mighty gelding, now standing a shade under 16hh, won nine of his twelve starts, including still another Woodward and Gold Cup. He was unanimously voted best horse in America for the fourth consecutive years.

In 1964, after an unsuccessful trip to California, where he was unplaced in two stakes at Hollywood Park, Kelso returned home and won an overnight handicap under 136 lb, then lost a stirring battle to the swift Iron Peg in the Suburban Handicap, giving away 15 lb.

On September 4, Kelso met Gun Bow at equal weights in the nine furlong Aqueduct Stakes and defeated him by three-quarters of a length. In the Woodward, a race that Kelso had dominated over the past three seasons, he met Gun Bow again, and turn-

ing for home, the two were level and raced for the line locked together. After a long delay Gun Bow was announced the winner by the shortest of margins. The next stop for Kelso was the Gold Cup. Gun Bow wisely took the day off, conceding the overwhelming superiority of his rival over two miles. As he had four times before, Kelso romped home by 5½ lengths, breaking his own track record.

Kelso met Gun Bow for the third time in the Washington International at Laurel. Gun Bow, as was his custom, went for the early lead, with Kelso four lengths back in second. Down the backstretch, Valenzuela decided to test the leader early, and sent Kelso up to challenge. For a while it looked like a repeat of the Woodward with both horses coming away from the rest of the field. As they turned into the stretch, however Kelso pulled away from Gun Bow and coasted home by 4½ lengths in a course record time of 2 minutes 23⅘ seconds, a time that has not been remotely threatened since. He was subsequently awarded his fifth consecutive Horse of the Year title. Kelso's thirst for competition was so strong that he became too difficult to handle at Woodstock Farm and Mrs du Pont and Hanford decided to race him the following year. He managed three wins in six starts, including a dramatic win by a nose over the three-year-old Malicious in the Whitney Stakes. During the running of the Stymie Handicap, which he won by eight lengths, Kelso was hit in the eye with a clod of dirt, suffering an eye injury that worsened each time he worked. Put away for the rest of the year, he became so nervous and restless that Mrs du Pont was forced to bring him back at the age of nine. He finished fourth in a six-furlong allowance race at Hialeah, then, while preparing for the Donn Handicap, he took a false step. X-rays revealed a hairline fracture of the right inside sesamoid and he was retired.

Dr Fager and Damascus

Dr Fager and Damascus dominated racing in the United States in 1967 and 1968, eclipsing even the exploits of the 1966 champion Buckpasser in their first season of rivalry. Dr Fager was essentially no more than a miler, although he could win over a mile-and-a-quarter, taking the lead from the start in his races and challenging all to beat him. Those who did take him on from the start were run off their feet. Damascus, however, was more of a stayer, and would come with a late run to win his races.

In 1967, Damascus was overwhelming,

winning twelve of sixteen starts for earnings of $817,941. After an early season loss to Dr Fager – the start of their rivalry – in the Gotham Stakes at Aqueduct, the son of Sword Dancer out of Kerala captured eight of his next ten starts. These included wins in the Wood Memorial, Preakness, Belmont Stakes, Dwyer Handicap, American Derby (setting a new track record), Aqueduct Stakes, and a twenty-two-length success in the Travers. Dr Fager, meanwhile, was also in brilliant form winning the Withers mile by six lengths in 1 minute 33⅘ seconds, but disqualified after easily winning the Jersey Derby. Sent to Rockingham Park, the son of Rough n' Tumble and Aspidistra set two track records in the Rockingham Special and New Hampshire Sweepstakes.

In the mile-and-a-quarter Woodward Stakes, the two three-year-olds met the defending champion Buckpasser. Hailed as the 'Race of the Century', it turned into an easy victory for Damascus, as he stormed past Dr Fager to win by ten lengths, with Buckpasser just getting up for second. Damascus later added the two-mile Jockey Club Gold Cup to his laurels and was unanimously voted Horse of the Year, as well as leading three-year-old and top handicap horse. Dr Fager salvaged the title of best sprinter.

The following year, however, it was a different story. Even though they defeated each other once, Dr Fager showed such brilliance and versatility that he ended up as Horse of the Year, top handicap horse, top grass horse and top sprinter – the only horse ever to win the four titles in a single season. After capturing the Roseben Handicap and Californian Stakes, he carried 132 lb to defeat Damascus (133 lb) in the Suburban Handicap in track record time. Two weeks later, in the Brooklyn, Dr Fager gave his rival 5lb, but, as in the previous year's Woodward Stakes, was used up fighting a pacesetter, finishing second, as Damascus broke his short-lived record.

Dr Fager made four more starts that year, each race being more spectacular than the other. After easily winning the Whitney Stakes, he set a new world record for the mile in the Washington Park Handicap, winning by ten lengths in 1 minute 32⅕ seconds carrying 134lb. He then made his first appearance on grass in the United Nations Handicap and, conceding 22 lb, he defeated Advocator by a neck after losing the lead no less than four times. Dr Fager finished his career in brilliant fashion by setting a track record in the seven-furlong Vosburgh Handicap, winning by six lengths under a staggering 139lb.

Damascus, after defeating Dr Fager in the Brooklyn, captured the William du Pont Handicap and Aqueduct Stakes under 134 lb. Then, after two tough losses, he suffered a bowed tendon in the Jockey Club Gold Cup and was retired. In four meetings, Dr Fager and Damascus each won two races. They shared eight titles and eight track records between them, while totally dominating their opposition.

Bold Ruler and Gallant Man

On July 11, 1971, after conferring with owner Ogden Phipps, A B 'Bull' Hancock, master of Claiborne Farm, made the most difficult decision of his life. The grand old champion Bold Ruler would be put to sleep at the age of seventeen, the victim of cancer. He had sired eighty-two stakes winners and ten champions.

For seven consecutive years, from 1963 to 1969, Bold Ruler was the leading sire in America. He regained the title four years later, when the great Secretariat became the first horse in a quarter of a century to sweep the Triple Crown. Bold Ruler had left his greatest legacy two years after his death.

The son of Nasrullah – Miss Disco was also a sensational racehorse. He won twenty-three races in thirty-three starts, competing against one of the finest crops of thoroughbreds ever produced in the USA – such as Round Table, General Duke, Iron Leige and his number one rival Gallant Man. Bred in England, the last-named won fourteen of twenty-six races, including the Metropolitan Handicap, Travers, Jockey Club Gold Cup, Hollywood Gold Cup, and a brilliant performance in the Belmont Stakes. He won this by eight lengths in 2 minutes 26⅗ seconds, a record that would stand for sixteen years.

Bold Ruler, meanwhile, was brilliant at two, winning seven of his first eight starts, before falling off form late in the year. At three he captured the Bahamas and Flamingo Stakes at Hialeah and then went to New York, where he beat Gallant Man by a nose in the Wood Memorial. Starting as the 6/5 favourite in the Kentucky Derby, he finished fourth, having wasted all his energy fighting his jockey, Eddie Arcaro, who was determined to hold back the free-running colt. The race was won by Calumet Farm's Iron Leige, as Gallant Man, too, fell short by a nose, after Bill Shoemaker had misjudged the finish line. In the Preakness, Arcaro gave in to Bold Ruler's temperament, and he responded by leading all the way for a two-length victory (Gallant Man missed the race to prepare for the Belmont). In the final leg, Bold Ruler

fell victim to Gallant Man's pacesetter and finished third, as the English-bred colt achieved his record setting win.

Following the Triple Crown, Bold Ruler won six of his final seven starts, including a clear-cut win in the Trenton Handicap, defeating Gallant Man and Round Table. Gallant Man was equally brilliant the rest of the year, winning the Travers and Gold Cup, but the Horse of the Year honours went to Bold Ruler.

The following year Bold Ruler removed all doubts about his greatness, capturing the six furlong Toboggan Handicap under 133 lb, the seven furlong Carter Handicap under 135 lb – there defeating Gallant Man – the nine furlong Stymie Handicap carrying 133 lb, and the 10 furlong Suburban and Monmouth Handicaps, each under 134 lb. His string of victories was interrupted by a loss to none other than Gallant Man in the Metropolitan, when he conceded 5 lb to his rival. In his final start, the Brooklyn Handicap, he had a rough race, finishing seventh of eight. Gallant Man, after winning the Met, journeyed to California, and captured the Hollywood Gold Cup and Sunset Handicap, before returning east to finish fifth in the Sysonby Mile.

Gallant Man was retired to Spendthrift Farm in Lexington, Kentucky, where he sired many outstanding stakes winners, such as the champion filly Gallant Bloom. Bold Ruler was sent to Claiborne Farm in Paris, Kentucky, where he changed the course of US breeding. Believed by many to be the greatest sire ever to stand in the USA, Bold Ruler was an institution for over a decade. To illustrate his total dominance of the sport even now, every Kentucky Derby winner since 1973 (with the exception of Affirmed) has been sired by a son or grandson of Bold Ruler.

Nashua and Swaps

The two great rivals Swaps and Nashua were foaled a month and a half apart on opposite ends of the country. Swaps was born on March 1 at Ontario Ranch, just east of Los Angeles, California, while Nashua was foaled on April 14 at Claiborne Farm in Paris, Kentucky. Swaps' owner Rex Ellsworth had once been a cowhand in Arizona, working for $50 a month. He saved up enough money to purchase six mares and two weanlings in Kentucky for $600 and from that initial venture, built up a multi-million dollar empire. Nashua's owner, William Woodward Jr, was born into racing's élite. Although he had no interest in the sport, he inherited the powerful Belair Stud.

By 1954 Nashua had grown into a

marvellous-looking individual with everything in his favour. He had the breeding, being by the great Nasrullah out of Segula, the trainer in Sunny Jim Fitzsimmons, and the jockey in Eddie Arcaro. It was no surprise that he was voted champion two-year-old, winning six of his eight starts, including the Hopeful and Futurity, in which he defeated the swift Summer Tan by a head and neck. Meanwhile, in California, little attention was paid to Swaps, who won three of his six starts, including a small stake at Hollywood Park.

The following year, Nashua continued his winning ways in the Flamingo Stakes, Florida Derby and Wood Memorial. In the latter event, he was determined to defeat Summer Tan by a neck, setting up a confrontation in the Kentucky Derby. Swaps, who had won the the San Vicente Stakes and Santa Anita Derby, was also aimed for the Kentucky Derby, and after being moved to Churchill Downs for the race won the six-furlong Jefferson Purse by 8½ lengths, covering the distance a full second faster than the featured Churchill Downs Handicap the same afternoon.

In the Derby Nashua was sent off as the 13/10 favourite, with Swaps 5/2 and Summer Tan 9/2. Swaps, under Bill Shoemaker, set off in front with Nashua behind in second, followed by Summer Tan. As the field rounded the far turn and headed for home, Nashua went after Swaps. But driving for all he was worth, Arcaro could not get Nashua past Swaps, who pulled away to win by a length and a half.

With Swaps gone, Nashua was unbeatable, winning the Preakness, Belmont, Dwyer and Arlington Classic. Returning to California, Swaps won his next four races, including three track records. On August 31, 1955, a $100,000, winner take all match was set for Washington Park, Illinois.

Unfortunately, a black cloud hovered over the race, as Swaps injured his right foreleg a few days before the event. However, because of the importance of the race, Ellsworth and trainer Mesh Tenney decided to take the risk. Coming out of the gate Swaps swerved badly, falling lengths behind Nashua. He tried gallantly to make up the ground, but the Belair colt drew away to win by 6½ lengths. Following the race, the soft spot between the frog and Swaps' right foot was cut away, and he was retired for the year. Nashua, after losing the Sysonby Handicap, easily won the Jockey Club Gold Cup and was voted Horse of the Year.

The two colts never met again. The following year Nashua won six of ten races, including the Widener, Grey Lag, Suburban and Monmouth Handicaps, and another success in the Gold Cup. He was syndicated by Leslie Combs II after the death of Woodward, and was retired to Spendthrift Farm in Lexington, Kentucky, where he still resides at the age of twenty-seven.

Swaps' four-year-old campaign justly earned him Horse of the Year honours. With the exception of a poor showing on the turf, he won eight of nine races, while equalling or breaking seven track records and four world records. His only loss was when Shoemaker mistakenly eased him in the Californian Stakes and he was beaten a head by Porterhouse. While preparing at Garden State for the Washington DC International, he suffered two fractures of the cannon bone, but miraculously recovered and was retired to John Galbreath's Darby Dan Farm in Lexington. He was later moved to Spendthrift, where he died in November 1972.

Buckpasser

Buckpasser won twenty-five of his thirty-one races, earned over $1,400,000, won four titles, including Horse of the Year, and turned his fans into nervous wrecks every time he ran. As a three-year-old, for instance, he won thirteen consecutive races, but nine of them by less than a length. Whether he was overly competitive, or overly lazy, no one knows for sure. What is certain is that he could defeat a horse by a head with the same authority as if it had been five lengths.

Owned by the Jockey Club chairman, Ogden Phipps, Buckpasser, under jockey Braulio Baeza, won nine of eleven starts at two, including the Sapling, Hopeful, Arlington Futurity and Champagne Stakes. His only loss, after finishing fourth in his career debut, was in the Futurity Stakes at Aqueduct when at the sixteenth pole his coltish precocity prevented him passing the filly Priceless Gem and he was beaten a half-length.

The following year, despite missing the Triple Crown because of an injury, Buckpasser was overwhelming, winning thirteen of fourteen starts. The Hialeah management thought he was a certainty for their most prestigious event, the Flamingo Stakes, and ran it as an exhibition race, despite a field of nine horses. With no wagering, the press billed it as the 'Chicken Flamingo'. But the officials almost fell out of their boxes as Buckpasser was passed by Abe's Hope at the sixteenth-pole and appeared totally beaten. However, with fifty yards to go, he came again at Abe's

Hope to snatch victory by a nose.

After missing three months of action, Buckpasser returned to set a new world record for a mile, winning the Arlington Classic in 1 minute 32⅗ seconds. He added victories in the Brooklyn Handicap, American Derby, Travers, Woodward and Jockey Club Gold Cup to be unanimously voted Horse of the Year.

At four, Buckpasser won the Metropolitan Handicap under 130 lb and the Suburban under 133 lb. After being beaten by ten lengths by Damascus in the Woodward, he was retired to stud at Claiborne Farm in Kentucky.

Seattle Slew

Seattle Slew, the only undefeated winner of America's Triple Crown was purchased by Karen and Mickey Taylor for a mere $17,500 at the 1975 Fasig-Tipton Kentucky Sale, and won fourteen of his seventeen races for earnings of $1,208,726. His style was to take the lead and stay there, defying all others to try and outrun him. Those who did were nowhere to be found at the finish. Major stakes winners such as Cormorant, For The Moment, Jatski, Spirit Level and even the Triple Crown winner Affirmed attempted to run with him early on, only to finish well down the field.

When the trainer William Turner took over the training of Seattle Slew as a two-year-old, he was greeted, not by the high-spirited, competitive animal 'Slew' was to become, but a big, floppy colt – so lazy he was nicknamed 'Baby Huey' after the cartoon character. However, this completely changed the first time he worked with another horse. 'Slew' progressed so quickly that Turner was forced to put him away for two months.

Seattle Slew made his first start on September 20, and won by five lengths as the 5/2 favourite. After winning an allowance race easily, he galloped home by ten lengths in the Champagne Stakes, setting a new stakes record. His performance was so brilliant he was voted two-year-old champion on that one stakes.

At three Seattle Slew continued his dominance by winning an allowance race at Hialeah in track record time and by coasting home in the Flamingo Stakes and Wood Memorial before tackling the Triple Crown. In the Derby, he was left at the gate. Jockey Jean Cruguet was to force his way through the entire field to take the lead. Once in front, Seattle Slew had to fight it out with the Blue Grass Stakes winner For The Moment, before winning a clear lead at the quarter-pole. Opening up

in the straight, he won in hand by almost two lengths.

In the Preakness, Seattle Slew ran head and head with the speedy Cormorant before disposing of him at the head of the stretch. He drew clear to win by a length and a half in a near record time. In the Belmont, he toyed with his opponents to win handily by four lengths, becoming the only undefeated horse in history to sweep the Triple Crown. He made his final start of the year only three weeks later, when the Taylors sent him to California for the $300,000 Swaps Stakes. Knocked out by his efforts in the Triple Crown, he struggled home fourth, sixteen lengths behind J O Tobin.

The following year, after a virus that kept him out for the early part of the year, Seattle Slew easily won an allowance race at Aqueduct in May, but, preparing for the Metropolitan Handicap, he developed a filling in his leg that kept him out of action. Returning with another allowance score at Saratoga, he was upset by Dr Patches in the Paterson Handicap at Meadowlands. In the Marlboro Cup, eleven days later, he defeated Affirmed by three lengths under a new jockey Angel Cordero and then beat Exceller in the Woodward Stakes, before suffering a tough loss in the Jockey Club Gold Cup. In his final start, he carried 134 lb to victory in the Stuyvesant Handicap at Aqueduct. He was then retired to Spendthrift Farm in Kentucky and syndicated for $12,000,000.

Riva Ridge

Even as a two-year-old, when he won seven of his nine starts, and was voted leading juvenile of 1971, Riva Ridge was an unlucky horse. In his only two losses of the year, he was bumped badly, losing all chance of winning in his first start, while he lost a shoe as he was being steadied in the Great American Stakes. Even after winning the Futurity, the Champagne Stakes by seven lengths and the Laurel Futurity by eleven lengths, he still had to prove himself against Ogden Phipps' brilliant filly Numbered Account in the Garden State Stakes. Not until he scored convincingly by 2½ lengths was Riva Ridge accepted as the best two-year-old in America.

The son of First Landing–Iberia, Riva Ridge won the Hibiscus Stakes at three, defeating the speedy New Prospect, but in the heavy going of the nine furlong Everglades Stakes finished a disappointing fourth behind Head of the River. Sent to Kentucky, he easily won the Blue Grass Stakes by four lengths and then scored a

Top left *The elegant Buckpasser (Tom Fool – Busanda), who won thirteen consecutive races at three, nine of them by less than a length.* **Top right** *Seattle Slew (Bold Reasoning – My Charmer), the* only horse to be undefeated up to his Triple Crown successes. **Centre left** *Gallant Man (Migoli – Majideh) was bred in England and won the Belmont Stakes by eight lengths.* **Above left** *Swaps (Khaled – Iron Reward) won eight of his nine races at four, breaking seven track records and four world records.* **Above right** *Nashua (Nasrullah – Segula), Swaps' great rival and beaten by him in the Kentucky Derby.*

brilliant all the way win in the Kentucky Derby. Unfortunately, the Preakness two weeks later was run in heavy going and he once again finished fourth to the lightly regarded Bee Bee Bee. Riva Ridge rebounded to walk home by seven lengths in the Belmont Stakes, again leading throughout the race.

Three weeks later he was shipped to California for the Hollywood Derby, where he carried 129 lb and gamely resisted challenges from four different horses to win by a neck. It was a magnificent performance, but it took its toll as Riva Ridge did not win another race for the rest of the year. In the Monmouth Invitational Handicap, in which he finished a sluggish fourth, urine samples showed the presence of a tranquilizer, but the case was not taken any further. In the Stymie Handicap, he caught the previous year's Derby winner Canonero II on one of his greatest days and succumbed by five lengths as the winner equalled the American record for a mile and an eighth.

In the Woodward Stakes, Riva Ridge met Rokeby Stable's Key to the Mint in a showdown for three-year-old championship honours. Key to the Mint had scored late season victories in the Brooklyn Handicap, Whitney Stakes and Travers to challenge the Meadow Stable colt for division leadership. Unfortunately, the track was again sloppy and he could finish only fourth to the Rokeby colt. This loss cost him the title.

The following year, however, Riva Ridge was brilliant, winning the Brooklyn Handicap in world record time, the Massachusetts Handicap, equalling the track record, and the Stuyvesant Handicap, carrying 130 lb, setting a new track record. However, he still had to take a back seat to his illustrious stablemate Secretariat, and virtually went unnoticed. On September 15, Meadow Stable staged a coup as Secretariat and Riva Ridge ran first and second in the nine-furlong Marlboro Cup in world record time. They were both then retired to Claiborne Farm in Kentucky.

Northern Dancer

The theory that a ' good big horse will beat a good little horse every time' was shattered in the 1964 Kentucky Derby, when the diminutive Northern Dancer defeated the big Californian colt Hill Rise in record time. Standing less than 15.2hh and weighing a mere 950 lb, the son of Nearctic–Natalma became the first Derby winner in a quarter of a century to win the classic before reaching his third birthday.

Born on May 27 at his owner E P Taylor's Windfields' Farm in Canada, Northern Dancer was put up for sale as a yearling, but did not make his reserve price of $25,000. After being broken by Peter Richards, son of Sir Gordon Richards, he was sent to the trainer Horatio Luro to begin serious training. Luro was immediately impressed with the little colt and had him ready for his first start on August 2 at Fort Erie. There he won by almost seven lengths. After losing the Vandal Stakes to the more seasoned Ramblin' Road, Northern Dancer scored impressive wins in the Summer Stakes on turf, the Coronation Futurity and the Carleton Stakes. Shipped to Aqueduct, he romped home by eight lengths in an allowance race and set a stakes record by winning the mile Ramsen Stakes by two lengths.

Put away until February, Northern Dancer made his first start of the new year in an allowance race, in which he finished third after being bumped at the start. Luro, displeased with jockey Bob Ussery's abusive treatment of the colt, replaced him with Bill Shoemaker for the Flamingo Stakes and Northern Dancer responded with a two-length win, covering the nine furlongs in a swift 1 minute 47⅘ seconds. After winning the Florida Derby by a length in the ordinary time of 1 minute 50⅘ seconds, Shoemaker decided to switch horses for the Derby, choosing the Santa Anita Derby winner Hill Rise, a colt he had never ridden.

Luro named Bill Hartack as Northern Dancer's new rider and the two combined to capture the Blue Grass Stakes at Keeneland by a half-length. Hill Rise, meanwhile, with his new jockey aboard, won the seven-furlong Forerunner Purse at Keeneland and the mile Derby Trial at Churchill Downs to become the new Derby favourite. Northern Dancer's neck win over the favourite in two minutes flat was a track record.

In the Preakness two weeks later, however, Hill Rise was again favourite at 4/5 with Northern Dancer 2/1. Shoemaker kept Hill Rise close by Northern Dancer and, when Hartack sent his colt to the lead on the far turn, Hill Rise was already alongside him. Straightening into the stretch, Northern Dancer, to the surprise of almost everyone, began pulling away from the favourite to win convincingly by 2¼ lengths, as Hill Rise lost second place to the Scoundrel in the final jump.

The Windfields colt looked certain to sweep the Triple Crown, but failed to stay the mile-and-a-half Belmont Stakes, fading to third behind Quandrangle and Roman Brother. Two weeks later, he returned to his homeland to breeze home by 7½ lengths in the historic Queen's Plate, receiving a hero's welcome.

In August, while preparing for his return, it was discovered that Northern Dancer had suffered a bowed tendon, however, and he was retired to Taylor's National Stud in Canada. He became one of the most influential stallions in the world siring over sixty stakes winners, including the classic winners Nijinsky and The Minstrel. He was the leading sire in North America in 1971, and twice led the sire list in England.

Round Table

An entire horse and the son of Princequillo–Knight's Daughter. Round Table raced sixty-six times in four years of competition, winning forty-three races for record earnings of $1,749,869. He equalled or established fifteen track records, on grass and dirt, carried 130 lb or more to victory sixteen times, and won stakes at thirteen different race tracks. During one season alone, from May 30, 1957 to May 11, 1958, he won twenty of twenty-one starts.

Bred by A B 'Bull' Hancock and foaled at Claiborne Farm in Kentucky, Round Table won five of his ten starts as a two-year-old, including the Breeders' Futurity at Keeneland. The following year, after two poor showings at Hialeah, he was sold to the Oklahoma oilman Travis Kerr for $135,000, with Hancock retaining an interest for future breeding purposes. Turned over to a new trainer Bill Molter, Round Table showed immediate improvement by winning an allowance race by six lengths. He went on to capture the Blue Grass Stakes, setting a new track record, finished third in the Kentucky Derby and then scored victories in the Hollywood Gold Cup, United Nations Handicap, American Derby and Hawthorne Gold Cup. By the end of the year, he had won fifteen races in twenty-two starts, for earnings of over $600,000, and was voted champion grass horse.

The next year, Round Table won his first seven races, while setting five consecutive track records. He captured the Santa Anita Maturity, Santa Anita Handicap, Gulf-stream Park Handicap, Hawthorne Gold Cup, Arlington Handicap and journeyed to Mexico where he easily won the Caliente Handicap. With fourteen victories in twenty starts, Round Table was voted Horse of the Year and champion grass horse for the second time.

Kerr decided to keep Round Table in training as a five-year-old and, instead of losing his thirst for competition as do most

Top *Spectacular Bid (Bold Bidder – Spectacular) bursts from the stalls. He was defeated by Coastal in his attempt at the third leg of the Triple Crown, the Belmont Stakes.* **Above left** *Northern Dancer* *(Nearctic – Natalma), sire of Nijinsky, The Minstrel and Lyphard and one of the most influential stallions in the world today.* **Centre right** *Riva Ridge (First Landing – Iberia), winner of the Kentucky Derby and* *the Belmont Stakes.* **Above right** *Round Table (Princequillo – Knight's Daughter), the winner of forty-three of his sixty-six races and a champion sire during nineteen seasons at stud.*

horses of his age, the little colt was still as brilliant as ever. He won eight of eleven starts, including the Arlington, Washington Park and Manhattan Handicaps. In his greatest performance, he captured the United Nations Handicap, under a staggering 136 lb. For the third consecutive year, he was voted champion grass horse in America.

Round Table was retired to Claiborne Farm as sound as the day he began racing. Facing top stars such as Bold Ruler, Gallant Man, Iron Leige, Clem and Porterhouse, Round Table outlasted them all, while setting a new record for career earnings. He continued his toughness and durability at stud. He was the leading sire in 1972 and sired seventy-seven stakes winners to 1978. In that year, he retired from stud duty at the age of twenty-five after serving for nineteen years.

As both racehorse and sire, Round Table was truely a unique individual. His courage, honesty and consistency, which spanned two decades, will never be forgotten.

Spectacular Bid and Coastal

Purchased for $37,000 at the Keeneland Fall Sales by Harry Meyerhoff, a Baltimore construction magnate, Spectacular Bid exploded on the racing scene in 1978 to chalk up a remarkable string of victories that continued through to the following year's Preakness Stakes. In the span of eight months, he captured twelve consecutive stake races by an average margin of almost seven lengths.

Conditioned by the outspoken Grover 'Buddy' Delp, Spectacular Bid lived up to his trainer's accolades by capturing the World's Playground, Champagne Stakes, Young America Stakes and the Laurel Futurity in track record time, as well as the Heritage Stakes, *en route* to the two-year-old Championship.

Sent to Florida for his three-year-old campaign, the son of Bold Bidder – Spectacular went from strength to strength, scoring easy victories in the Hutcheson Stakes by 4½ lengths, the Fountain of Youth by just under double the distance, the Florida Derby by 4½ lengths, the Flamingo Stakes by twelve lengths and Blue Grass Stakes by seven. Meanwhile, in California, Benjamin Ridder's Flying Paster was winning the Santa Anita and Hollywood Derbies by a combined margin of sixteen lengths, thus setting up an east–west confrontation between the two horses in the Kentucky Derby. Starting as the 3/5 favourite, Spectacular Bid showed his superiority by coming from ten lengths

behind to beat General Assembly by almost three lengths, with Flying Paster a well-beaten fifth. Two weeks later, Spectacular Bid returned home to Maryland with trainer Delp and jockey Ronnie Franklin to score a brilliant victory in the Preakness Stakes, winning by five lengths in near record time. It looked as if there was nothing that could stop the 'Grey Tornado' from sweeping the pretigious Triple Crown.

Two weeks before the Belmont Stakes, however, a relatively unknown but vastly improved colt named Coastal romped home by thirteen lengths in the nine furlong Peter Pan Stakes to establish himself as a possible Belmont threat. Owned by William Haggin Perry and trained by David Whiteley, Coastal had won the Tyro Stakes at Monmouth Park as a two-year-old, but then turned in two poor efforts in the World's Playground and Marlboro Nursery. In the latter, the son of Majestic Prince – Alluvial was hit in the eye by a clod of dirt, suffering an injury that later required surgery. Turned over to Whiteley during the winter, Coastal thrived in the warm Californian sun, then returned east to win two allowance races impressively before capturing the Peter Pan.

In the Belmont Stakes, Ronnie Franklin sent the 3/10 Spectacular Bid to the lead on the back stretch and appeared on his way to completing the Triple. However, as the runners turned for home, Coastal, under Ruben Hernandez, came storming along the rail to challenge him for the lead. At the furlong pole Coastal drew away to win by 3¼ lengths, with Spectacular Bid losing second place to Golden Act.

Following the race, it was revealed that Spectacular Bid had stepped on a safety pin that morning, leaving a deep hole in the bottom of his foot. The next day, infection and fever set in, causing the colt to miss over two months of action.

Coastal, meanwhile, was in brilliant form, winning the Dwyer Stakes at Belmont, and the Monmouth Invitational Handicap, giving away large weight concessions on both occasions. On August 26, Spectacular Bid returned to competition, under a new jockey, Bill Shoemaker, and scored a seventeen-length victory in allowance company, thus setting up a further confrontation in the nine furlong Marlboro Cup.

With Spectacular Bid the favourite at 1/2, Shoemaker took the lead early on and steadily drew away to win by five lengths, with Coastal finishing a dull third. The two met again in the mile-and-a-half Jockey Club Gold Cup, but there they both fell victim to the great four-year-old Affirmed,

who defeated Spectacular Bid by three-quarters of a length, with Coastal another three lengths further back.

Tim Tam

As the runners rounded the long, sweeping turn in the 1958 Belmont Stakes, jockey Milo Valenzuela moved Calumet Farm's Derby and Preakness winner Tim Tam within striking range of the Irish-bred Cavan. With two furlongs standing between them and Triple Crown immortality, Tim Tam suddenly swerved repeatedly as Cavan drew clear to score a six-length win. The Calumet colt, who struggled on gamely to finish second, had suffered a cracked sesamoid bone and was retired to stud.

A son of Tom Fool – Two Lea, Tim Tam had compiled a brilliant record as a three-year-old, winning the Everglades Stakes, Flamingo, Fountain of Youth, Florida Derby, Derby Trial. He then scored courageous wins over the speedy Lincoln Road in the Kentucky Derby and Preakness Stakes. The 15/100 favourite in the Belmont Stakes, Tim Tam seemed on his way to sweeping the Triple Crown when he suffered his fateful injury, but it is the sight of him wobbling down the Belmont stretch, refusing to give up, that will always be remembered as his greatest moment.

Ack Ack

When E E 'Buddy' Fogelson purchased the five-year-old Ack Ack for $500,000 in January 1971, he was buying a fast, consistent stakes winner who had won twelve of his nineteen starts for Harry Guggenheim's Cain Hoy Stable. However, the son of Battle Joined – Fast Turn was basically a sprinter, never having won a stake race over a mile.

Under the care of the trainer Charlie Whittingham, however, Ack Ack suddenly changed complexion at the age of five to win seven of eight starts at distances ranging from seven furlongs to a mile and a quarter, and was voted Horse of the Year. After finishing second in his first start, Ack Ack won the seven-furlong San Carlos Handicap in a blazing 1 minute 21 seconds on good going. He then took the mile and a sixteenth San Pasqual Handicap under 129lb and the nine furlong San Antonio Stakes. Facing his illustrious stablemate Cougar II in the Santa Anita Handicap, Ack Ack won by a length and a half under 130lb, giving 5lb to his rival.

Dropping down to five-and-a-half furlongs, he again carried 130lb to victory in the Hollywood Express, missing the track record by a fifth of a second. He then continued to demonstrate his remarkable versatility by capturing the nine furlong American Handicap on grass, setting a new course record. In his final appearance, he put the finishing touch on a brilliant career by carrying 134lb to a four-length win in the mile-and-a-quarter Hollywood Gold Cup.

Ack Ack was retired to Claiborne Farm in Kentucky, where he sired the international champion Youth, winner of the French Derby, Canadian International Championship and Washington DC International.

Cougar II

Bred and raced in Chile, Cougar II came to America as a four-year-old after winning the Grade II Premio Municipal de Vina del Mar and being placed in the Chilean Derby. Turned over to trainer Charlie Whittingham by his new owner Mary Jones, Cougar II won two small stakes races at Del Mar and was placed in the Manhattan Handicap and Oak Tree Stakes. The following year, at the age of five he finally came into his own, winning the San Marcos Handicap, San Juan Capistrano, and Hollywood Invitational, on grass, and the mile and sixteenth California Stakes on the main track.

Sent to New York in quest of Horse of the Year honours, Cougar II galloped home by five lengths in the Woodward Stakes, only to be disqualified for ducking in during the final stretch run. But, by demonstrating his total superiority over the best horses in the east, Cougar II opened the way for his stablemate Ack Ack to be voted Horse of the Year, as Ack Ack had defeated him earlier in the Santa Anita Handicap.

In 1972, after being beaten by a head in the Santa Anita Handicap, Cougar II scored in the Century Handicap, Californian Stakes, Carleton F Burke Handicap and Oak Tree Stakes, earning him champion grass horse honours. The following year, at the age of seven, he finally captured the Santa Anita Handicap in his first start of the year. Then he added the Century and Sunset Handicaps to his score before finishing third to Secretariat in the Marlboro Cup, and to Prove Out in the Woodward Stakes. The son of Tale of Two Cities – Cindy Lou II was then retired to Spendthrift Farm with twenty wins in fifty starts for earnings of $1,162,725. He was later moved to Arthur Hancock's Stone Farm in Paris, Kentucky, where he still stands.

Ruffian

Bred and owned by Mr and Mrs Stuart Janney, Ruffian was foaled at Claiborne Farm in Kentucky, and turned over to the veteran trainer Frank Whiteley as a two-year-old. Almost jet black in colour, the daughter of Reviewer – Shenanigans was overwhelming in appearance, standing over 16.1hh and girthing an incredible 75½in.

Ruffian made her first start on May 22 at Belmont in one of the most awesome debuts ever seen in the USA. She cantered home by fifteen lengths and equalling the track record. In the 5½ furlong Fashion Stakes on June 12, she won by almost seven lengths over the promising filly Copernica, who finished thirteen lengths ahead of the third horse. In Aqueduct's Astoria Stakes a month later, Ruffian toyed with the opposition, scoring by nine lengths over the speedy Laughing Bridge and missing the track record by a fifth of a second. Sent to Monmouth Park for the $100,000 Sorority Stakes, she faced her biggest challenge in the form of Dan Lasater's undefeated Hot N Nasty, who had won her only three starts by a total of twenty-nine lengths. After a neck and neck battle, Ruffian finally asserted herself in the stretch and drew away to a two-and-a-quarter-length win, with Hot N Nasty twenty-two lengths ahead of the third horse.

Put away for a month, Ruffian returned to action in Saratoga's six furlong Spinaway Stakes against Laughing Bridge. Although she had beaten her easily in the Astoria, Neil Hellman's filly had improved drastically at Saratoga, winning two stakes with ease. However, in the Spinaway, Ruffian never raised a sweat, galloping home by thirteen lengths in stakes record time of 1 minute 08⅗ seconds. Unfortunately, while preparing for the mile Frizette Stakes at Belmont Park, Ruffian suffered a hairline fracture and was retired for the year.

In 1975 she returned to the track in as brilliant form as ever, winning an allowance race by five lengths and the Comely Stakes by seven in a blazing 1 minute 21⅕ seconds for the seven furlongs. In the first two legs of the fillies Triple Crown, Ruffian set new stakes records, taking the mile Acorn Stakes by eight-and-a-quarter lengths, and the nine furlong Mother Goose Stakes by fourteen. In the gruelling mile-and-a-half Coaching Club American Oaks, she led all the way easily to defeat King Ranch's fine filly Equal Change by almost three lengths.

With no other filly in America remotely able to compete with her on equal terms, a match race was proposed by the New York Racing Association against Kentucky Derby winner Foolish Pleasure. Both parties agreed, and on Sunday, July 6, with over 50,000 fans in attendance, Ruffian stepped on to the track for her date with destiny. With less than four furlongs of the race run, the big filly suddenly pulled up, as a stunned crowd watched in horror. Jockey Jacinto Vasquez quickly dismounted, as Ruffian stood helplessly, her leg dangling in mid air. She was loaded into the horse ambulance and brought back to her stall, still in shock.

X-rays revealed both sesamoids had been shattered. Sent across the street to Dr William Reed's hospital, a delicate operation was performed in an attempt to save her. However, after emerging from anesthesia, Ruffian lashed out violently, breaking the cast that held her leg together. She was in terrible pain, and at 2.20 am, eight hours after her fatal mishap, Janney gave the authority to put her out of her misery. Two days later Ruffian was buried in the infield at Belmont Park, the first horse ever bestowed that honour in New York.

Majestic Prince

Majestic Prince, a son of Raise A Native out of Gay Hostess, was the record priced yearling in America in 1967, selling for $250,000 at the Keeneland Summer Sales. A small but beautifully proportioned chestnut colt, his progress was watched with great interest. In his first season he won his only two races in California, although neither of them with the class he was to show as a three-year-old. At three he was taken to Churchill Downs for the seven furlong Stepping Stone Purse a week before the Kentucky Derby, and gave the first real indication of his talent by winning easily and breaking the track record. He confirmed this promise by beating Arts And Letters in the Derby, and followed up by winning the Preakness Stakes. In doing so he established himself as the best three-year-old colt in the United States.

His trainer, John Longden, decided after the second leg of the Triple Crown to give the horse a rest, but his owner, Frank McMahon, felt duty bound to run his colt in the Belmont Stakes, giving his horse the opportunity to become the first Triple Crown winner since Citation in 1948. But Majestic Prince, who was beginning to develop trouble with his legs, could not pass Arts And Letters in the home straight, and was beaten five lengths.

With an even greater diversity of racing in Australasia than in the USA it has not proved possible to provide an accurate rating for great horses running in the Southern Hemisphere. But James Ahern, the Victoria Racing Club's former Chairman of Stewards, has listed ten of the best over the past twenty-five years in order of preference. A former amateur rider and a steward of the VRC since 1953, James Ahern was appointed chairman of the stipendary stewards panel in 1961.

Tulloch	1	Tobin Bronze	6
Rising Fast	2	Redcraze	7
Gallilee	3	Leilani	8
Light Fingers	4	Gunsynd	9
Rain Lover	5	Family of Man	10

Tulloch

Only 15.2hh but a giant as a racehorse with a tremendous stride, Tulloch (Khorassan – Florida) was bred in New Zealand. The best horse to race in Australia in post-war years – and one of the best Australian horses ever – his trainer, Tommy Smith, was able to buy him for only 750 guineas at the 1956 New Zealand yearling sales due to Tulloch's hollow back.

As a spring two-year-old Tulloch won three races and was second twice from five starts, winning the Canonbury Stakes, the VATC Gwyn Nursery and the VRC Byron Moore Stakes. In the autumn of 1957 he won the VRC Sires' Produce Stakes, the AJC Fairfield Handicap, the AJC Sires' Produce Stakes and the QTC Sires' Produce Stakes.

He began his three-year-old career by winning the AJC Warwick Stakes and followed with the STC Rosehill Guineas, the AJC Derby and VATC Caulfield Guineas. He then contested the Caulfield Cup carrying 7st 8lb, a pound more than weight-for-age, but nevertheless started at 6/4 on, the first horse ever to be quoted at odds-on for the race. Not only did he win easily but he also set an Australasian record of 2 minutes 26.9 seconds for twelve furlongs. Before the season was over he completed the eastern States Derbys treble – the Victoria and Queensland Turf Club (Brisbane) Derbys as well as the AJC and VRC St Legers. He then became seriously ill with a virus infection and was unable to race for two years.

Although never quite the same horse, Tulloch won his last race, the Brisbane Cup of 1961, with 9st 12lb. He failed as a stallion, however, though this was perhaps due to the heavy and prolonged antibiotic treatment he endured fighting off the severe virus infection which almost cost him his life. Although he fell away to skin and bone, his recovery was remarkable and his ability to win further races was indicative of his great heart and character. In fifty-three starts he won thirty-six, was second twelve times, third four times and was once unplaced for $A220,247.

Rising Fast

Not surprisingly when his breeding is considered, Rising Fast was sold as a yearling for only 325 guineas. His sire Alonzo, bred in 1943 in England, was an ordinary racehorse (by Mid-day Sun – Sardana, by Sardanafale) who won only two races, one of them a humble hurdle event, while Rising Fast's dam, Faster, started only twice and was unplaced. He did, however, have three crosses of Musket, sire of the great Carbine, in his pedigree.

Rising Fast gave no indication of his coming greatness as a two-year-old when he raced five times, his only placing being third. He did far better as a three-year-old, winning four and being second four times.

Over the next two years Rising Fast proved to be an outstanding racehorse, as much at home with heavy weights in handicaps as in the best weight-for-age company. He won the Caulfield Cup with 8st 10lb and the Melbourne Cup with 9st 5lb. In between, he won the richest weight-for-age race in Australia, the W S Cox Plate at Moonee Valley.

A year later Rising Fast won the Caulfield Cup again, this time with 9st 10lb, then the highest weight any horse had carried to victory in the race. He then attempted an unprecedented double-double, the Caulfield–Melbourne Cups in successive years. He failed, but only just. Carrying a crushing weight of 10st, he ran second in a controversial finish to Toparoa, carrying 7st 8lb.

In all Rising Fast ran sixty-eight times, winning on twenty-four occasions. He was second seventeen times and third twice.

Light Fingers

Light Fingers (NZ), by Le Filou out of Cuddlesome, was a delicate mare and, according to Bart Cummings, one of the best horses he ever trained. As a two-year-old, she won three races and was second once from four starts; the following season, she showed considerable improvement on this form to win the Triple Crown for fillies at the VRC Spring Carnival – the Manifold, Wakeful and Oaks Stakes – and the AJC Oaks and the Sandown Guineas.

At four Light Fingers won her first start over five furlongs and then won the one mile weight-for-age VRC Craiglee Stakes. Troubled by a virus for three weeks during her Cups preparation, she almost fell in the Caulfield Stakes and ricked a shoulder muscle. As a consequence, she went into the Melbourne Cup on a very light preparation and, carrying 8 st 4 lb, she showed great courage in defeating her stable-mate Ziema. The previous weight-carrying record for a mare in the cup was 8 st.

The following year Light Fingers was beaten by Ziema in the Melbourne Cup, but then won the Sandown Cup on a waterlogged track with 9st 0lb. Injury and illness limited her opportunities, but she nevertheless won fifteen races from thirty-three starts, with eight seconds and five thirds for winnings of $A109,470.

Gallilee

Gallilee (NZ), by Alcimedes out of Salsoon, did his early racing in South Australia, where he won the Birthday Cup as a three-year-old with 8st 3lb. This was one of his seven wins in eleven starts that season. The following year, he impressed Melbourne racegoers when he won the Patrohus Welter at Caulfield in September, carrying 9st 11lb, and then ran second in the Epsom Handicap at Sydney.

Returning to Melbourne, Galillee won the mile VATC Toorak Handicap. On the following Saturday, he continued this winning streak when he comfortably won the Caulfield Cup with 8st 7lb. He completed the Cups double by winning the Melbourne Cup with 8st 13lb, and then easily won the C B Fisher Plate.

The following autumn Galillee won the VRC 10 furlongs Queen's Plate, the twelve furlongs Queen Elizabeth Stakes (by ten lengths) the AJC Autumn Stakes and the Sydney Cup with 9st 7lb by six lengths at 6/4 on – the shortest price favourite in the history of the race.

Galillee then developed a splint which kept him off the racecourse for seventeen months. Although he won two more weight-for-age races he was never again the same champion of 1966/7. He was regarded by Bart Cummings, his trainer, as the best horse he has ever had, and from thirty six starts won eighteen, was second six times and third four times for winnings of $A169,970.

Rain Lover

Rain Lover, by Latin Lover out of Rain Spot, first drew attention to his great class as a stayer when he won the Adelaide Cup

Top left Gallilee (Alcimedes – Salsoon), one of only two horses to have completed the Caulfield Cup–Melbourne Cup double in the last twenty-five years. **Top right** Rising Fast (Alonzo – Faster), who completed the Cup double in 1954, won the Caulfield Cup in 1955 and was just beaten in the Melbourne Cup under 10st. **Centre left** Leilani (Oncidium – Lei) winning the 1974 Caulfield Cup in a canter. **Above left** The great Tulloch (Khorassan – Florida), bred in New Zealand and the best horse to race in Australia since the war. **Above right** Tobin Bronze (Arctic Explorer – Amarco) won twenty-two races in Australia and two in America.

of 1967 as a three-year-old carrying 8 st 3 lb. He won three more races that season. In eight days as a four-year-old he scored three great victories at the Melbourne Cup Carnival – the LKS MacKinnon Stakes, the Melbourne Cup and the C B Fisher Plate. His Cup win was remarkable on two counts; he won by a record eight lengths in a record time of 3 minutes 19.1 seconds.

In the autumn of 1969 Rain Lover won the VATC St George Stakes, the VRC Queen's Plate and the Queen Elizabeth Stakes, and carried 9 st 6 lb to second place in the Sydney Cup. As a five-year-old he won the Craiglee Stakes and the Underwood Stakes before scoring a remarkable second victory in the Melbourne Cup. Carrying 9 st 7 lb he won in a photo finish from Alsop, to whom he was conceding two stone. The only previous horse to win successive Melbourne Cups was Archer, successful in 1861/62. Rain Lover's record was forty-six starts, seventeen wins, ten seconds, eight thirds, and a total in prize money of $A195,000.

Tobin Bronze

Tobin Bronze, by Arctic Explorer out of Amarco, was in the top class of Australian horses, both in weight-for-age events and handicaps. He won three races as a two-year-old, the SAJC Breeders' Stakes, the VATC Trenton Stakes and the VRC Gibson Carmichael Stakes. The following year he won the 1965 Victoria Derby and in the autumn took the VRC Blamey Stakes.

As a four-year-old, Tobin Bronze was almost invincible at weight-for-age, winning ten such events. He also won the top mile handicap, the AJC Doncaster Handicap, under 9 st 5 lb. He began his five-year-old season suffering from the virus, which affected his spring preparation, but won his two starts before the Caulfield Cup. In the Cup itself he showed great courage to win under the huge weight of 9 st 10 lb. In his last race in Australia Tobin Bronze won the W. S. Cox Plate for the second time.

Tobin Bronze was then sent to America, where he won two of his three races before being retired to stud. In his forty-four starts he won twenty-four races, was second seven times and four times third for winnings of $A233,551 and $56,380 in the United States.

Redcraze

Redcraze (NZ), by Red Mass out of Myarion, showed good form in New Zealand before his owner-breeders, Mr and Mrs J. B. Bradley, brought him to Australia in 1955. In the former country

his wins had included the Awapuni Gold Cup and the Wanganui Cup.

In Australia, Redcraze demonstrated his class by defeating Rising Fast in the twelve furlong Turnbull Stakes of 1955 at Flemington. Soon after this Mr Bradley died, but the horse continued to race in his wife's name. On June 2, 1956, Redcraze began a sequence of seven wins in the highest class by winning the P J O'Shea Stakes in Brisbane and then the Brisbane Cup. In September of that year, he won the AJC Hill Stakes and followed up by winning the Colin Stephens Stakes and the premier handicap at the Sydney Spring Carnival – the thirteen furlongs Metropolitan Handicap – under 9 st 8 lb. Taken to Melbourne, he defeated Rising Fast again in the weight-for-age VATC Caulfield Stakes; in his next start, he set a new weight-carrying record when he won the world-famous Caulfield Cup in heavy going with 9 st 13 lb.

Attempting the double in the Melbourne Cup under 10 st 3 lb, he failed by half a neck, being beaten by the quality mare Evening Peal, to whom he was giving 27 lb. From eighty-four starts Redcraze recorded thirty-two wins, ten seconds, and ten thirds, winning $A142,962.

Leilani

A mare of great brilliance and stamina whose career was cut short by a tragic accident, Leilani (NZ), by Oncidium out of Lei, did not race at two and was lightly raced in the spring of her three-year-old career. In the autumn she won the VATC St Clair Handicap and the AJC Oaks, but suffered a hairline fracture in a hock bone.

She recovered by the start of her four-year-old season and won the VRC Turnbull Stakes at Melbourne in very heavy going. In her next two starts she won the Toorak Handicap easily and the Caulfield Cup in a canter, followed by the LKS Mackinnon Stakes. Carrying 8 st 10 lb in the Melbourne Cup, she ran a brave second to Think Big, but she won five more races that season – the Queen's Cup, the C F Orr Stakes, the St George Stakes, the Queen's Plate and the Australian Cup.

Leilani looked set for an even greater season in 1975/76, when she met with her tragic accident. While being loaded for a flight to Melbourne, she slipped on the concrete tarmac at Sydney airport, but, despite suffering severe muscle damage, she made a comeback to win one race. Then she retired with thirteen wins from twenty-three starts, six seconds and three thirds for $A254,305 in prize money. Trained by Bart Cummings and ridden by

the champion jockey Roy Higgins, she was considered almost the equal of Light Fingers.

Gunsynd

Gunsynd (Sunset Hue – Woodie Wonder), a great stayer, was something of a genetic freak as both his sire and his dam were pure sprinters, while Woodie Wonder was a twin who achieved nothing on the race track. An appealing grey, Gunsynd was bred for speed only, but he excelled as a stayer and a weight-for-age performer.

A precocious two-year-old, Gunsynd won five of his six starts then and went on to win five of his fifteen starts as a three-year-old. These included the weight-for-age Chelmsford and STC Rawson Stakes. At four, he began the season by winning the Epsom and Toorak Handicaps and, after twice running fourth in the Caulfield Cup and the W S Cox Plate, took the George Adams Handicap.

Gunsynd then belied his breeding by winning the twelve furlong Sandown Cup and, in the autumn of that season, the VATC Futurity with 9 st 13 lb, the VRC Queen's Plate and the Queen Elizabeth Stakes. Following these middle-distance events, he recorded a great win in the one mile AJC Doncaster Handicap with 9 st 7 lb.

In his final year, at five, Gunsynd ran third in the Caulfield Cup, third in the two-mile Melbourne Cup, and won the W S Cox Plate, to become the then highest stakes winner in Australian racing history with $A280,455 from twenty-nine wins, five and a half seconds and eight thirds in fifty-four starts.

Family of Man

Family of Man (Lots of Man – Colleen) consistently won important races over four seasons in four states and the Australian capital territory (Canberra), where he won the National Stakes. With 19½ wins to his credit, including the Western Australian Derby and the W S Cox Plate, he amassed the record sum of $A590,840 in stakes. He also ran nine and a half seconds and twelve thirds. Although the horse won handicaps, including a rich mile event at Flemington, his real strength was at weight-for-age. A genuine classic racehorse, he won his conditions races with style and assurance.

Now retired to stud in Western Australia, Family of Man has gained tenth rating at the expense of the brilliant milers Vain and Todman, and two horses with international reputations, Balmerino and Darly's Joy.

Statistical Glossary

The Pattern System

The term 'Pattern Race' originated in the title of the Duke of Norfolk's committee on the Pattern of Racing. The committee was asked by the Jockey Club in Britain to make recommendations on the general programme of all prestige races and stakes, with emphasis on top-class horses of all ages and the general improvement of the thoroughbred. As a result of their report and subsequent developments, Pattern Races are now run throughout Europe, and the system has now been adopted in every major racing country.

The first step in this process was the appointment by the Jockey Club of a Race Planning Committee to ensure that a series of races over the right distances at the right time of year are available to test the best horses of all ages. The aim was to plan races and prize money to make it worthwhile for horses to remain in training long enough to be tested properly for constitution and soundness. Pattern Racing was introduced from the 1968 season onwards. There are currently 100 such races in Britain each year, thirty-two in Ireland and 102 in France. Italy and Germany have forty-seven and thirty-one respectively.

As well as providing a programme for two-year-olds with championship races over five, six, seven and eight furlongs, Pattern racing provides sufficient valuable races over all distances for four-year-olds and over to counteract the tendency to retire good horses to stud before they have been properly tested.

Prize money

The International Pattern Committee keep the races under constant review. This has led to a smoother programme. At the 1979 meeting in Ireland, for instance, the French agreed to move the date of their mile-long Prix du Moulin de Longchamp for three-year-olds, as it clashed with Britain's longer established Queen Elizabeth II Stakes at Ascot. The committee is also responsible for the allocation of prize money awarded to Pattern Races. In Britain, for example, the Flat Race Pattern Committee, chaired since its inception by Lord Porchester, the Queen's Racing Manager, includes the Controller of Programmes of the Jockey Club, leading bloodstock breeders, representatives of the various administrative bodies in racing, and a member of the Horserace Betting Levy Board. Over £2½ million a year is channelled into British Pattern Races, slightly less than half of it from the Levy Board and the remainder from sponsors and the courses themselves. In the 1979 season, £1,034,000 of the £2,270,000 Pattern Race prize money came from the Levy Board. In 1980 the figure was £2,572,000, £1,104,000 from the Board.

The Group System

Prize money, or the lack of it, led to the introduction of the Group System in the late 1960s. Then the comparatively low levels of prize money in Britain and Ireland meant that the winners of important races in the British Isles were able to run in big French races with small penalties or no penalties at all. This was because the penalty system in France depends on the amount of money already accrued to any one horse.

The Société d'Encouragement were also being pressed by French owners and breeders to close races to horses trained abroad, except where horses competed on a weight-for-age basis. This restrictive policy would have spoiled international competition, but with the enormous amount of money pumped into French racing each year by the State-owned pari-mutuel, the complaints were justified.

Following discussion between the English, Irish and French turf authorities, a solution was found in the introduction of the group system for the 1971 season. In this, Pattern Races are divided into Groups I, II and III, according to their importance as tests of the horse rather than their monetary value. Penalties are graded on the basis of victories within the various groups.

Broadly, the groups are defined as follows: **Group I**, Championship races including classic races, in which horses meet on weight-for-age terms with no penalties or allowances. **Group II**, Races just below championship standard, in which there may be some penalties and allowances. **Group III**, Races of mainly domestic interest, including classic trials, which are required to complete the series of tests for the best horses.

International ratings

The Pattern Race Group system thus provides the most reliable formula yet devised for indicating the quality of performance of racehorses. It is a method that transcends national frontiers, having great potential value to breeders and an obvious application in methods of cataloguing for bloodstock sales. The catalogues of leading sales in Great Britain, Ireland, France and the United States indicate the winners of Pattern Races, with Group suffixes in the pedigrees of horses for sale and these form the basis of a horse's International Classification.

Although there is no central racing authority in the United States and consequently no official Pattern of Racing, American owners and breeders have adopted the Group System. The Thoroughbred Owners and Breeders Association and The Blood-Horse magazine jointly compiled a list of the most important American races and divided them into three grades according to the quality of the fields that contested them over a period of years and not according to their monetary value. There are now roughly 270 Graded Races in the thirty racing states of the USA and these are considered as Pattern Races for qualifications, penalties and allowances.

Most other racing countries of the world use the Group System but at the present time these act as a guide only and are not internationally recognized. Australia has 262 races based on a list approved by a Conference of Principal Clubs in 1971: the ninety or so races in Grade I are considered to be the most prestigious events on the Australian turf. The Jockey Club of Canada lists forty-seven graded races, including seven Grade I; New Zealand has seventy-two, sixteen of which are Grade I; Spain holds twenty-four graded races each year, Argentina 127. The Japan Racing Authority hold eighty-four graded races each year, including two Grade I races for two-year-olds, six Grade I for three-year-olds and four for three-year-olds and over.

Statistical Glossary

The Hungarian mare Kincsem, *foaled in 1874, was unbeaten in fifty-four races, including the 1878 Goodwood Cup. The Puerto Rican horse* Camarero *was unbeaten in fifty-six consecutive races from April 1953 to August* 1955, *and died of colic the following year having won seventy-three of the seventy-six races of his career. The world record for the fastest long-distance horse is held by* Champion Crabbet *who in 1920 covered 300 miles*

Great Britain

Leading races

1,000 Guineas Stakes		Oaks Stakes		King George VI and Queen Elizabeth Diamond Stakes		2,000 Guineas Stakes		St Leger Stakes		Derby Stakes	
Newmarket 1m		*Epsom 1m 4f*		*Ascot 1m 4f*		*Newmarket 1m*		*Doncaster 1m 6f 132 yds*		*Epsom 1m 4f*	
1960	Never Too Late	1960	Never Too Late	1960	Agressor	1960	Martial	1960	St Paddy	1960	St Paddy
1961	Sweet Solera	1961	Sweet Solera	1961	Right Royal V	1961	Rockavon	1961	Aurelius	1961	Psidium
1962	Abermaid	1962	Monade	1962	Match III	1962	Privy Councillor	1962	Hethersett	1962	Larkspur
1963	Hula Dancer	1963	Noblesse	1963	Ragusa	1963	Only For Life	1963	Ragusa	1963	Relko
1964	Pourparler	1964	Homeward Bound	1964	Nasram II	1964	Baldric II	1964	Indiana	1964	Santa Claus
1965	Night Off	1965	Long Look	1965	Meadow Court	1965	Niksar	1965	Provoke	1965	Sea Bird II
1966	Glad Rags	1966	Valoris	1966	Aunt Edith	1966	Kashmir II	1966	Sodium	1966	Charlottown
1967	Fleet	1967	Pia	1967	Busted	1967	Royal Palace	1967	Ribocco	1967	Royal Palace
1968	Caergwrle	1968	La Lagune	1968	Royal Palace	1968	Sir Ivor	1968	Ribero	1968	Sir Ivor
1969	Full Dress II	1969	Sleeping Partner	1969	Park Top	1969	Right Tack	1969	Intermezzo	1969	Blakeney
1970	Humble Duty	1970	Lupe	1970	Nijinsky	1970	Nijinsky	1970	Nijinsky	1970	Nijinsky
1971	Altesse Royale	1971	Altesse Royale	1971	Mill Reef	1971	Brigadier Gerard	1971	Athens Wood	1971	Mill Reef
1972	Waterloo	1972	Ginevra	1972	Brigadier Gerard	1972	High Top	1972	Boucher	1972	Roberto
1973	Mysterious	1973	Mysterious	1973	Dahlia	1973	Mon Fils	1973	Peleid	1973	Morston
1974	Highclere	1974	Polygamy	1974	Dahlia	1974	Nonoalco	1974	Bustino	1974	Snow Knight
1975	Nocturnal Spree	1975	Juliette Marny	1975	Grundy	1975	Bolkonski	1975	Bruni	1975	Grundy
1976	Flying Water	1976	Pawneese	1976	Pawneese	1976	Wollow	1976	Crow	1976	Empery
1977	Mrs McArdy	1977	Dunfermline	1977	The Minstrel	1977	Nebbiolo	1977	Dunfermline	1977	The Minstrel
1978	Enstone Spark	1978	Fair Salinia	1978	Île de Bourbon	1978	Roland Gardens	1978	Julio Mariner	1978	Shirley Heights
1979	One In A Million	1979	Scintillate	1979	Troy	1979	Tap On Wood	1979	Son Of Love	1979	Troy

Group I Pattern races	Age		Distance	Racecourse		Leading Owners	Winning horses	Races won	£
Benson and Hedges Gold Cup	3+	CF	10 f	York	1960	Sir Victor Saesoon	15	29	90,069
Coral Eclipse Stakes	3+	CF	10 f	Sandown Park	1961	Maj L. B. Holliday	25	37	39,227
Champion Stakes	3+	CF	10 f	Newmarket	1962	Maj L. B. Holliday	24	39	70,206
Coronation Cup	3+	CF	12 f	Epsom	1963	Mr J. R. Mullon	5	9	68,882
Derby Stakes	3	CF	12 f	Epsom	1964	Mrs H. E. Jackson	2	3	98,270
Gold Cup	3+	CF	20 f	Royal Ascot	1965	M. J. Ternynck	1	1	65,301
King George VI and Queen					1966	Lady Zia Wernher	1	2	78,075
Elizabeth Diamond Stakes	3+	CF	12 f	Ascot	1967	Mr H. J. Joel	22	34	120,925
King's Stand Stakes	3+	CF	5 f	Royal Ascot	1968	Mr Raymond R. Guest	1	4	97,075
Oaks Stakes	3	F	12 f	Epsom	1969	Mr D. Robinson	42	96	92,553
1,000 Guineas Stakes	3	F	8 f	Newmarket	1970	Mr S. Engelhard	20	30	182,059
St Leger Stakes	3	CF	14 f	Doncaster	1971	Mr P. Mellou	11	22	138,786
Sussex Stakes	3+	CF	8 f	Goodwood	1972	Mr J. Hislop	3	10	155,190
2,000 Guineas Stakes	3	CF	8 f	Newmarket	1973	Mr N. B. Hunt	8	11	124,771
William Hill Cheveley Park					1974	Mr N. B. Hunt	7	8	147,217
Stakes	2	F	6 f	Newmarket	1975	Dr C. Vittadini	6	12	209,492
William Hill Dewhurst Stakes	2	CF	7 f	Newmarket	1976	Mr D. Wildenstein	5	10	244,500
William Hill Futurity Stakes	2	CF	8 f	Doncaster	1977	Mr R. Sangster	16	21	348,023
William Hill July Cup	3+	CF	6 f	Newmarket	1978	Mr R. Sangster	51	27	160,405
William Hill Middle Park					1979	Sir M. Sobell	5	13	339,751
Stakes	2	CF	6 f	Newmarket					
Yorkshire Oaks	3	F	12 f	York					

carrying seventeen and a half stones in 522 hours. The tallest horse to race in recorded history is the English-owned Fort d'Or standing 18.2 hands (187 cm) though his Irish dam, Golden Sunset, was a mere 15.1 hands.

The horse that has won the most money ever is the American horse Affirmed who collected $2,044,218 between 1977 and June 1979. In one year, 1978, Affirmed won $901,541. After winning the 1978 American Triple Crown,

Trainers		Winning horses	Races won	£	Breeders		Winning horses	Races won	£			Races won
1960	C. F. Murless	24	42	118,327	1960	Eve Stud Ltd	17	37	96,689	1960	L. Piggott	170
1961	C. F. N. Murless	21	36	95,972	1961	Eve Stud Ltd	10	19	39,653	1961	A. Breasley	171
1962	W. Hern	24	39	70,206	1962	Maj L. B. Holliday	28	47	72,617	1962	A. Breasley	179
1963	P. Prendergast (in Ireland)	14	19	125,294	1963	Mr H. F. Guggenheim	1	3	66,011	1963	A. Breasley	176
1964	P. Prendergast (in Ireland)	14	17	128,102	1964	Bull Run Stud	2	3	98,270	1964	L. Piggott	140
1965	P. Prendergast (in Ireland)	10	11	75,323	1965	Mr J. Ternynck	1	1	65,301	1965	L. Piggott	160
1966	M. V. O'Brien (in Ireland)	7	8	123,848	1966	Someries Stud	2	3	80,153	1966	L. Piggott	191
1967	C. F. N. Murless	34	60	256,899	1967	Mr H. J. Joel	14	22	109,882	1967	L. Piggott	117
1968	C. F. N. Murless	30	47	141,508	1968	Mill Ridge Farm	1	4	97,075	1968	L. Piggott	139
1969	A. M. Budgett	22	35	105,349	1969	Lord Rosebery	17	28	65,591	1969	L. Piggott	163
1970	C. F. N. Murless	35	53	199,524	1970	Mr E. P. Taylor	3	7	161,302	1970	L. Piggott	162
1971	I. Balding	25	45	157,488	1971	Mr P. Mellon	8	16	133,902	1971	L. Piggott	162
1972	W. Hern	24	42	206,767	1972	Mr J. Hislop	4	11	155,571	1972	W. Carson	132
1973	C. F. N. Murless	21	34	132,984	1973	Chalborne Farm	3	5	88,250	1973	W. Carson	164
1974	P. Walwyn	54	96	206,781	1974	Mr N. B. Hunt	3	5	123,702	1974	P. Eddery	148
1975	P. Walwyn	69	121	382,527	1975	Overbury Stud	7	11	194,480	1975	P. Eddery	164
1976	H. Cecil	24	52	261,301	1976	Dayton Ltd	5	10	232,599	1976	P. Eddery	162
1977	M. V. O'Brien (in Ireland)	13	18	439,124	1977	Mr E. P. Taylor	2	4	241,120	1977	P. Eddery	176
1978	H. Cecil	60	109	382,301	1978	Cragwood Estates Inc	1	3	136,012	1978	W. Carson	182
1979	H. Cecil	56	128	683,971	1979	Ballymacoll Stud	6	14	346,981	1979	J. Mercer	164

Ireland

Group I races	Added Money in 1979 (£)	Age		Distance	Racecourse	Race	Added Money in 1979 (£)	Age		Distance	Racecourse
Gallaghouse Phoenix	15,000	2		5 f	Curragh	Irish 1,000 Guineas	20,000	3	F	8 f	Curragh
(formerly Patrick S.						Irish St Leger	15,000	3	CF	8 f	Curragh
Gallagher Phoenix)						Irish 2,000 Guineas	30,000	3	CF	8 f	Curragh
Irish Sweeps Derby	50,000	3	CF	12 f	Curragh	Joe McGrath Memorial					
Irish Guiness Oaks	25,000	3	F	12 f	Curragh	Stakes	20,000	3+		10 f	Leopardstown.

Irish Guinness Oaks
The Curragh   1m 4f

1960	Lynchris
1961	Ambergris
1962	French Cream
1963	Hibernia III
1964	Ancasta
1965	Aurabella
1966	Merry Mate
1967	Pampalina
1968	Celina
1969	Gaia
1970	Santa Tina
1971	Altesse Royale
1972	Regal Exception
1973	Dahlia
1974	Dibidale
1975	Juliette Marny
1976	Lagunette
1977	Olwyn
1978	Fair Salinia
1979	Godetia

Irish 1,000 Guineas
The Curragh   1m

1960	Zenobia
1961	Lady Senator
1962	Shandon Belle
1963	Gazpacho
1964	Royal Danseuse
1965	Ardent Dancer
1966	Valoris
1967	Lacquer
1968	Front Row
1969	Wenduyne
1970	Black Satin
1971	Favoletta
1972	Pidget
1973	Cloonagh
1974	Gaily
1975	Miralla
1976	Sarah Siddons
1977	Lady Capulet
1978	More So
1979	Godetia

Irish St Leger
The Curragh   1m 6f

1960	Lynchris
1961	Vimadee
1962	Arctic Vale
1963	Christmas Island
1964	Biscayne
1965	Craighouse
1966	White Gloves
1967	Dan Kano
1968	Giolla Mear
1969	Reindeer
1970	Allangrange
1971	Parnell
1972	Pidget
1973	Conor Pass
1974	Mistigri
1975	Caucasus
1976	Meneval
1977	Transworld
1978	M-Lolshan
1979	Niniski

Irish Sweeps Derby
The Curragh   1m 4f

1960	Chamour
1961	Your Highness
1962	Tambourine II
1963	Ragusa
1964	Santa Claus
1965	Meadow Court
1966	Sodium
1967	Ribocco
1968	Ribero
1969	Prince Regent
1970	Nijinsky
1971	Irish Ball
1972	Steel Pulse
1973	Weaver's Hall
1974	English Prince
1975	Grundy
1976	Malacate
1977	The Minstrel
1978	Shirley Heights
1979	Troy

Irish 2,000 Guineas
The Curragh   1m

1960	Kythnos
1961	Light year
1962	Arctic Storm
1963	Linacre
1964	Santa Claus
1965	Green Banner
1966	Paveh
1967	Atherstone
1968	Mistigo
1969	Right Tack
1970	Decies
1971	King's Company
1972	Ballymore
1973	Sharp Edge
1974	Furry Glen
1975	Grundy
1976	Northern Treasure
1977	Pampapaul
1978	Jaazeiro
1979	Dickens Hill

Affirmed was sold to a syndicate in November of the same year for $14.4m in 36 shares of $400,000 each. The shortest odds ever quoted on a horse were 10,000 to 1 on when Dragon Blond *was ridden by the English champion* jockey Lester Piggott *in the Premio Naviglio in Milan, June 1967. The American horse* Man o' War *was three times quoted at odds of 100 to 1 on in one year – 1920. Joint record holders amongst jockeys for winning most races on one*

France

Group I races	Added Money in 1979 (fr)	Age		Distance	Racecourse	Race	Added Money in 1979 (fr)	Age		Distance	Racecourse
Abbaye de Longchamp	250,000	2+	CF	1,000 m	Longchamp	Jockey Club	900,000	3	CF	2,400 m	Chantilly
Arc de Triomphe	1,200,000	3+	CF	2,400 m	Longchamp	Lupin	500,000	3	CF	2,100 m	Longchamp
Cadran	300,000	4+	CF	4,000 m	Longchamp	Morny	250,000	2	CF	1,200 m	Deauville
Critérium des Pouliches	250,000	2	F	1,600 m	Longchamp	Moulin de Longchamp	300,000	3+	CF	1,600 m	Longchamp
Diane	700,000	3	F	2,100 m	Chantilly	Poule d'Essai des Poulains	350,000	3	C	1,600 m	Longchamp
Forêt	300,000	2+	CF	1,400 m	Longchamp	Poule d'Essai des Pouliches	350,000	3	F	1,600 m	Longchamp
Ganay	400,000	4+	CF	2,200 m	Longchamp	Robert Papin	200,000	2	CF	1,100 m	Maisons-Laffitte
Grand Critérium	500,000	2	CF	1,600 m	Longchamp	Royal-Oak	300,000	3+	CF	3,100 m	Longchamp
Grand Prix de Paris	400,000	3	CF	3,100 m	Longchamp	Saint-Alary	350,000	3	F	2,000 m	Longchamp
Grand Prix de Saint-Cloud	600,000	3+	CF	2,500 m	Saint-Cloud	Salamandre	250,000	2	CF	1,400 m	Longchamp
Ispahan	400,000	3+	CF	1,850 m	Longchamp	Vermeille	600,000	3	F	2,400 m	Longchamp
Jacques Le Marois	300,000	3+	CF	1,600 m	Deauville						

Poule d'Essai des Pouliches	Prix de Diane	Prix de l'Arc de Triomphe	Poule d'Essai des Poulains	Prix Royal-Oak	Prix de Jockey-Club
Longchamp 1m	*Chantilly 1m 2f 110yds*	*Longchamp 1m 4f*	*Longchamp 1m*	*Longchamp 1m 7f*	*Chantilly 1m 4f*
1960 Timandra	1960 Timandra	1960 Puissant Chef	1960 Mincio	1960 Puissant Chef	1960 Charlottesville
1961 Solitude	1961 Hermieres	1961 Molvedo	1961 Right Royal V	1961 Match III	1961 Right Royal V
1962 Le Sega	1962 Le Sega	1962 Soltikoff	1962 Adamastor	1962 Sicilian Prince	1962 Val de Loir
1963 Altissima	1963 Belle Ferroniere	1963 Exbury	1963 Relko	1963 Relko	1963 Sanctus
1964 Rajput Princess	1964 Belle Sicambre	1964 Prince Royal II	1964 Neptunus	1964 Barbieri	1964 Le Fabuleux
1965 La Sarre	1965 Blabal	1965 Sea Bird II	1965 Cambremont	1965 Reliance	1965 Reliance II
1966 Right Away	1966 Fine Pearl	1966 Bon Mot	1966 Soleil	1966 Vasco da Gama	1966 Nelcius
1967 Gazala	1967 Gazala	1967 Topyo	1967 Blue Tom	1967 Samos III	1967 Astec
1968 Pola Bella	1968 Roseliere	1968 Vaguely Noble	1968 Zeddaan	1968 Dhaudevi	1968 Tapalque
1969 Koblenza	1969 Crepellana	1969 Levmoss	1969 Don II	1969 Le Chouin	1969 Goodly
1970 Pampered Miss	1970 Sweet Mimosa	1970 Sassafras	1970 Caro	1970 Sassafras	1970 Sassafras
1971 Bold Fascinator	1971 Pistol Packer	1971 Mill Reef	1971 Zug	1971 Bourbon	1971 Rheffic
1972 Mata Hari	1972 Rescousse	1972 San San	1972 Riverman	1972 Pleben	1972 Hard to Beat
1973 Allez France	1973 Allez France	1973 Rheingold	1973 Kalamoun	1973 Lady Berry	1973 Roi Lear
1974 Dumka	1974 Highclere	1974 Allez France	1974 Moulines	1974 Busiris	1974 Caracolero
1975 Ivanjica	1975 No race	1975 Star Appeal	1975 Green Dancer	1975 Henri Le Balafre	1975 Val de L'Orne
1976 Riverqueen	1976 Pawneese	1976 Ivanjica	1976 Red Lord	1976 Exceller	1976 Youth
1977 Madelia	**Prix de Diane de Revlon**	1977 Alleged	1977 Blushing Groom	1977 Rex Magna	1977 Crystal Palace
1978 Dancing Maid	1977 Madelia	1978 Alleged	1978 Nishapour	1978 Brave Johnny	1978 Acamas
1979 Three Troikas	1978 Reine de Saba	1979 Three Troikas	1979 Irish River	1979 Niniski	1979 Top Ville
	1979 Dunette				

	Leading Owners	Races won	New Francs		Leading owners	Races Won	New Francs
1963	F. Dupré	73	3,404,330	1972	Mme. P. Wertheimer	44	4,956,259
1964	Baron G. de Rothschild	34	2,945,336	1973	D. Wildenstein	87	8,044,810
1965	Baron G. de Rothschild	43	3,455,751	1974	D. Wildenstein	74	9,313,215
1966	Late F. Dupré (and Mme)	54	3,033,942	1975	J. Wertheimer	60	7,295,343
1967	Mme F. Dupré	41	2,813,775	1976	D. Wildenstein	42	6,107,500
1968	Mme F. Dupré	42	2,494,234	1977	D. Wildenstein	47	5,731,000
1969	D. Wildenstein	42	3,458,548	1978	J. Wertheimer	62	7,072,300
1970	A. Plesch	24	3,916,963	1979	Aga Khan	97	6,106,000
1971	Mme F. Dupré	39	4,112,956				

card are Hubert S. Jones, aged seventeen, at Caliente in California, and the Argentinian Oscar Barattuci at Rosario City. Both won eight out of thirteen races on the card – Jones in June 1944, and Barattuci in December 1957.

The longest winning streak was by the English jockey Sir Gordon Richards who rode twelve consecutive winners – in the last race at Nottingham on October 3, 1933, in six out of six races at Chepstow the following day, and

	Leading Sires	Races won	First prize money won (new francs)		Leading Trainers	Races won	New Francs	Leading Jockeys	Races won	Leading Breeders	New Francs
1960	Prince Chevalier	11	1,061,215								
1961	Wild Risk	59	989,914								
1962	Tantieme	22	1,464,454								
1963	Le Haar	19	2,687,559	1963	E. Pollet	39	4,392,105	Y. Saint-Martin	172	Baron G. de Rothschild	293,500
1964	Wild Risk	35	2,483,735	1964	F. Mathet	125	4,347,975	Y. Saint-Martin	184	Baron G. de Rothschild	288,065
1965	Tantieme	14	2,530,224	1965	F. Mathet	135	4,935,930	Y. Saint-Martin	142	Baron G. de Rothschild	342,822
1966	Sicambre	31	2,677,718	1966	F. Mathet	146	6,682,430	Y. Saint-Martin	170	Executors of F. Dupré	295,560
1967	Prince Taj	40	4,010,742	1967	F. Mathet	127	5,691,457	Y. Saint-Martin	155	Executors of F. Dupré	272,970
1968	Prince Taj	41	2,076,208	1968	F. Mathet	116	6,848,038	Y. Saint-Martin	138½	Executors of F. Dupré	217,110
1969	Snob	23	2,829,544	1969	F. Mathet	118½	6,203,649	Y. Saint-Martin	120	Executors of G. Wildenstein	225,290
1970	Sheshoon	17	4,475,680	1970	F. Mathet	105	6,758,239	Y. Saint-Martin	116	Baron G. de Rothschild	156,320
1971	Traffic	26	3,266,391	1971	F. Mathet	141	7,470,519	F. Head	132	Mme F. Dupré	456,820
1972	Sanctus	38	2,671,961	1972	G. Watson	44	6,817,624	F. Head	103	Baron G. de Rothschild	313,390
1973	Val de Loir	30	3,065,611	1973	F. Mathet	140	8,656,288	Y. Saint-Martin	117	Baron G. de Rothschild	398,100
1974	Val de Loir	29	3,433,397	1974	A. Penna	59	8,380,186	Y. Saint-Martin	121	M. Boussac	525,840
1975	Val de Loir	33	3,856,576	1975	A. Head	60	7,295,343	Y. Saint-Martin	125	W. Stora	370,080
1976	Luthier	33	5,241,100	1976	F. Boutin	95	8,486,900	Y. Saint-Martin	109	Dayton Limited	668,200
1977	Caro	27	4,596,500	1977	F. Mathet	144	10,828,150	P. Paquet	108	Dayton Limited	1,061,120
1978	Lyphard	61	6,636,850	1978	F. Boutin	108	9,135,150	A. Gilbert	116	Mme P. & J. Wertheimer	865,155
1979	Lyphard	51	7,218,000	1979	F Boutin	116	14,800,000	P Paquet	116	M Pfaff	857,000

Italy

Group I races	Added Money in 1979 (lire)	Age			Distance	Racecourse
Derby Italiano	55,000,000	3	CF		2,400 m	Rome
Emilio Turati	35,000,000	3+			1,600 m	Milan
Gran Critérium	32,500,000	2	CF		1,600 m	Milan
Gran Premio d'Italia	37,500,000	3	CF		2,400 m	Milan
Gran Premio del Jockey Club	60,000,000	3+	CF		2,400 m	Milan
Gran Premio di Milano	60,000,000	3+	CF		2,400 m	Milan
Lydia Tesio	32,500,000	3,4	F		2,000 m	Rome
Oaks d'Italia	36,000,000	3	F		2,200 m	Milan
Presidente della Republica	32,500,000	3+	CF		2,000 m	Rome
Roma	40,000,000	3+	CF		2,800 m	Rome

Germany

Group I races	Added Money in 1979 (DM)	Age				Distance	Racecourse
Aral-Pokal	100,000	3+	CF			2,400 m	Gelsenkirchen
Deutsches Derby	150,000	3	CF			2,400 m	Hamburg
Grosser Preis Von Baden	175,000	3+	CF;	3,4	F	2,400 m	Baden-Baden
Grosser Preis Von Berlin (formerly Von Nordrhein Westfalen)	120,000	3+	CF			2,400 m	Dusseldorf
Preis Von Europa	300,000	3+	CF			2,400 m	Cologne

the first five races on the same course the day after that. The youngest jockey ever to ride was Frank Wootton who was only nine years and ten months old when he rode his first winner in South Africa at the turn of the century and went

on to become English champion jockey from 1909 to 1912. In 1932, Levi Barlingame rode his last race in Kansas, aged eighty. The oldest 'first winner' was ridden by amateur jockey Mr Victor Morley Lawson on Ocean King *at*

Canada

Grade I races	Foaled in Canada	Fillies and Mares	Age	Track	Distance (Furlongs)	Turf
Breeder's Stakes	※		3	Woodbine	12	T
Canadian International Championship			3+	Woodbine	13	T
Canadian Oaks Stakes	※	F	3	Woodbine	9	
Coronation Futurity	※		2	Woodbine	9	
Prince of Wales Stakes	※		3	Woodbine	11	T
Princess Elizabeth Stakes	※	F	2	Woodbine	8½	
Queen's Plate Stakes	※		3	Woodbine	10	

United States

Grade I races	Age		Track	Furlongs		Grade I races	Age		Track	Furlongs	
Acorn S	3 yo	f	Bel	8		Metropolitan H	3 & up		Bel	8	
Alabama S	3 yo	f	Sar	10		Monmouth Invitational H	3 yo		Mth	9	
Amory L. Haskell H	3 & up		Mth	9		Monmouth Oaks	3 yo	f	Mth	9	
Arlington-Washington Futurity	2 yo		AP	7		Mother Goose S	3 yo	f	Bel	9	
Beldame S	3 & up	f/m	Bel	10		Oak Tree Invitational S	3 & up		SA	12	T
Belmont S	3 yo		Bel	12		Preakness S	3 yo		Pim	9.5	
Blue Grass S	3 yo		Kee	9		Ruffian H	3 & up	f/m	Bel	9	
Brooklyn H	3 & up		Bel	12		San Antonio S	4 & up		SA	9	
Californian S	3 & up		Hol	8.5		San Juan Capistrano Invitational H	4 & up		SA	14	T(abt)
Century H	3 & up		Hol	11	T	San Luis Rey S	4 & up		SA	12	T
Champagne S	2 yo		Bel	8		Santa Anita Derby	3 yo		SA	9	
Charles H. Strub S	4 yo		SA	10		Santa Anita H	4 & up		SA	10	
Coaching Club American Oaks	3 yo	f	Bel	12		Santa Barbara H	4 & up	f/m	SA	10	T
Delaware H	3 & up	f/m	Del	10		Santa Margarita Invitational H	4 & up	f/m	SA	9	
Delaware Oaks	3 yo	f	Del	9		Santa Susana S	3 yo	f	SA	8.5	
Fantasy S	3 yo	f	OP	8.5		Sapling S	2 yo		Mth	6	
Flamingo S	3 yo		Hia	9		Selima S	2 yo	f	Lrl	8.5	
Florida Derby	3 yo		GP	9		Sorority S	2 yo	f	Mth	6	
Frizette S	2 yo	f	Bel	8		Spinaway S	2 yo	f	Sar	6	
Futurity S	2 yo		Bel	7		Spinster S	3 & up	f/m	Kee	9	
Gulfstream Park H	3 & up		GP	10		Suburban H	3 & up		Ble	10	
Hollywood Derby	3 yo		Hol	9		Sunset H	3 & up		Hol	12	T
Hollywood Invitational H	3 & up		Hol	12	T	Swaps S	3 yo		Hol	10	
Hollywood Oaks	3 yo	f	Hol	9		Top Flight H	3 & up	f/m	Aqu	9	
Hopeful S	2 yo		Sar	6.5		Travers S	3 yo		Sar	10	
Jockey Club Gold Cup S	3 & up		Bel	12		Turf Classic	3 & up		Aqu	12	T
Kentucky Derby	3 yo		CD	10		United Nations H	3 & up		Atl	9.5	T
Kentucky Oaks	3 yo	f	CD	8.5		Vanity H	3 & up	f/m	Hol	9	
La Canada S	4 yo	f	SA	9		Washington D.C. International S	3 & up		Lrl	12	T
Ladies H	3 & up	f/m	Aqu	10		Widener H	3 & up		Hia	10	
Laurel Futurity	2 yo		Lrl	8.5		Wood Memorial S	3 yo		Aqu	9	
Man o' War	3 & up		Bel	11	T	Woodward S	3 & up		Bel	10	
Marlboro Cup H	3 & up		Bel	9		Yellow Ribbon S	3 & up	f/m	SA	10	T
Matchmaker S	3 & up	f/m	Atl	9.5		Young America S	2 yo		Med	8.5	
Matron S	2 yo	f	Bel	7							

Warwick, England, in October 1973, then aged sixty-seven. The most successful money-winning jockey of all time is the American Willie Shoemaker. He has earned over $70,000,000 from 7,598 winners on 32,184 rides, between March 1949 and the end of the 1978 season. He was born in 1931 weighing two and a half pounds and now at 4 ft 11½ in he weighs less than one hundred pounds. The lightest jockey on record was Kitchener who

Belmont Stakes		**Kentucky Derby**		**Preakness Stakes**		**Washington International**	
Belmont Park 1m 4f		*Churchill Downs 1m 2f*		*Pimlico 1m 1f 110yds*		*Laurel Park 1m 4f*	
1960	Celtic Ash	1960	Venetian Way	1960	Bally Ache	1960	Bald Eagle (USA)
1961	Sherluck	1961	Carry Back	1961	Carry Back	1961	T.V. Lark (USA)
1962	Jaipur	1962	Decidedly	1962	Greek Money	1962	Match III (France)
1963	Chateaugay	1963	Chateaugay	1963	Candy Spots	1963	Mongo (USA)
1964	Quadrangle	1964	Northern Dancer	1964	Northern Dancer	1964	Kelso (USA)
1965	Hail to All	1965	Lucky Debonair	1965	Tom Rolfe	1965	Diatome (France)
1966	Amberoid	1966	Kauai King	1966	Kauai King	1966	Behistoun (France)
1967	Damascus	1967	Proud Clarion	1967	Damascus	1967	Fort Marcy (USA)
1968	Stage Door Johnny	1968	Forward Pass	1968	Forward Pass	1968	Sir Ivor (Ireland)
1969	Arts and Letters	1969	Majestic Prince	1969	Majestic Prince	1969	Karabas (England)
1970	High Echelon	1970	Dust Commander	1970	Personality	1970	Fort Marcy (USA)
1971	Pass Catcher	1971	Canonero II	1971	Canonero II	1971	Run The Gantlet (USA)
1972	Riva Ridge	1972	Riva Ridge	1972	Bee Bee Bee	1972	Droll Role (USA)
1973	Secretariat	1973	Secretariat	1973	Secretariat	1973	Dahlia (France)
1974	Little Current	1974	Cannonade	1974	Little Current	1974	Admetus (France)
1975	Avatar	1975	Foolish Pleasure	1975	Master Derby	1975	Nobiliary (France)
1976	Bold Forbes	1976	Bold Forbes	1976	Elocutionist	1976	Youth (France)
1977	Seattle Slew	1977	Seattle Slew	1977	Seattle Slew	1977	Johnny D (USA)
1978	Affirmed	1978	Affirmed	1978	Affirmed	1978	Mac Diarmida (USA)
1979	Coastal	1979	Spectacular Bid	1979	Spectacular Bid	1979	Bowl Game (USA)

	Leading Owners	**Wins**	**Total Earnings $**		**Leading Trainers**	**Wins**	**Total Earnings $**
1960	C. V. Whitney	66	1,039,091	1960	Hirsch Jacobs	97	748,349
1961	Calumet Farm	62	759,856	1961	Horace A. Jones	62	759,856
1962	R. C. Ellsworth	80	1,154,454	1962	M. A. Tenney	59	1,099,474
1963	R. C. Ellsworth	75	1,096,863	1963	M. A. Tenney	40	860,703
1964	Wheatley Stable	38	1,073,572	1964	W. C. Winfrey	61	1,350,534
1965	M. H. Van Berg	270	895,246	1965	Hirsch Jacobs	91	1,331,628
1966	Wheatley Stable	44	1,225,861	1966	E. A. Neloy	93	2,456,250
1967	Hobeau Farm	87	1,120,143	1967	E. A. Neloy	72	1,776,089
1968	M. H. Van Berg Stable Inc	339	1,105,388	1968	E. A. Neloy	52	1,233,101
1969	M. H. Van Berg Stable Inc	383	1,453,679	1969	Elliott Burch	26	1,067,936
1970	M. H. Van Berg Stable Inc	391	1,347,289	1970	Charles Whittingham	82	1,302,354
1971				1971	Charles Whittingham		
1972	Sigmund Sommer	96	1,605,896	1972	Charles Whittingham	79	1,734,020
1973	Dan Lasater	234	1,498,785	1973	Charles Whittingham	85	1,865,385
1974	Dan Lasater	494	3,022,960	1974	F. Martin	166	2,408,419
1975	Dan Lasater	459	2,894,726	1975	Charles Whittingham	93	2,437,244
1976	Dan Lasater	403	2,891,854	1976	J. C. Van Berg	494	2,972,218
1977	Elmendorf Farm	114	2,309,200	1977	Lazaro S. Barrera	127	2,715,848
1978	Harbor View Farm	64	2,097,443	1978	Lazaro S. Barrera	100	3,314,564
1979	Harbor View Farm	78	2,701,741	1979	Lazaro S. Barrera	97	3,563,147

died in 1872. He was an English jockey who won the Chester Cup on Red Deer in 1844 weighing only forty-nine pounds. Four years earlier he weighed in for races at thirty-five pounds but there is no accurate record of his *height. The most money won in one season, $6,188,353, was by the American jockey Darrell McHargue in 1978. Fellow American Chris McCarron, four years earlier, rode 546 winners in one year from 2,199 starts – both*

	Leading Sires	Wins	$		Leading Jockeys	Wins	Leading Breeders	$
1960	Nasrullah	122	1,019,547	1960	W. Shoemaker	274		
1961	Ambiorix	148	679,427	1961	W. Shoemaker	304		
1962	Nasrullah	107	1,092,440	1962	W. Shoemaker	311		
1963	Bold Ruler	56	917,531	1963	W. Shoemaker	271	R. C. Ellsworth	1,465,069
1964	Bold Ruler	88	1,457,156	1964	W. Shoemaker	246	Bieber-Jacobs Stable	1,301,643
1965	Bold Ruler	90	1,091,124	1965	B. Baeza	270	Bieber-Jacobs Stable	1,994,649
1966	Bold Ruler	107	2,309,523	1966	B. Baeza	298	Wheatley Stable and O. Phipps	3,096,416
1967	Bold Ruler	136	2,252,847	1967	B. Baeza	256	Wheatley Stable and O. Phipps	1,975,539
1968	Bold Ruler	99	1,988,427	1968	B. Baeza	201	Claiborne Farm and partners	1,506,908
1969	Bold Ruler	90	1,357,111	1969	J. Velasquez	258	Leslie Combs II and partners	1,467,664
1970	Hail to Reason	82	1,402,829	1970	Laffit Pincay Jr	265	Leslie Combs II and partners	1,730,242
1971	Northern Dancer	93	1,288,580	1971	Laffit Pincay Jr	380	Leslie Combs II and partners	0,000,000
1972	Round Table	98	1,199,933	1972	Laffit Pincay Jr	289	Leslie Combs II and partners	1,916,337
1973	Bold Ruler	74	1,488,619	1973	Laffit Pincay Jr	350	Elmendorf Farm	2,128,080
1974	T. V. Lark	120	1,242,003	1974	Laffit Pincay Jr	341	Leslie Combs II and partners	1,998,419
1975	What a Pleasure	101	2,011,878	1975	C. J. McCarron	468	E. P. Taylor	2,366,571
1976	What a Pleasure	108	1,622,159	1976	S. Hawley	413	E. P. Taylor	3,022,181
1977	Dr Fager	124	1,593,079	1977	S. Cauthen	487	E. P. Taylor	3,413,984
1978	Exclusive Native	106	1,969,867	1978	D. G. McHargue	375	E. P. Taylor	3,387,945
1979	Exclusive Native	110	2,903,995	1979	Laffit Pincay Jr	400	E. P. Taylor	3,001,108

Argentina

Grade I races	Age	Metres	Hippodrome
Gran Premio Ciudad de Buenos Aires (Internacional)	3+	1000	Argentino
Maipú	3+	1000	Argentino
Saturnino J. Unzué	2 f	1100	Argentino
Santiago Luro	2 m	1100	Argentino
Eliseo Ramirez	2 f	1400	Argentino
Raúl u Raúl E. Chevalier	2 m	1400	Argentino
Jorge Atucha	2 f	1500	Argentino
Montevideo	2 m	1500	Argentino
Organización Sudamericana de Fomento del Pura Sangre de Carrera (Internacional)	3 f	1600	Argentino
Polla de Potrancas	3 f	1600	Argentino
Polla de Potrillos	2 m	1600	Argentino
Palermo	3+	1600	Argentino
General San Martin	4+	1800	Argentino
Gran Premio Selección	3 f	2000	Argentino
Gran Premio Jockey Club	3	2000	Argentino
Criadores	3+ f	2500	Argentino
Gran Premio 25 de Mayo	3+	2500	Argentino
Ignacio é Ignacio F. Correas	4+ f	2500	Argentino
Enrique Acebal	3 f	2500	Argentino
Gran Premio Nacional	3	2500	Argentino
Gran Premio San Isidro	3	2500	Argentino
Gran Premio Dirección Provincial de Hipódromos	3	2500	La Plata
Gran Premio República Argentina –Carlos Pellegrini (Internacional)	3+	3000	Argentino
Gran Premio Dardo Rocha (Internacional)	3+	3000	La Plata
Gran Premio de Honor	4+	3500	Argentino

world records. In 1974, owner Dan R. Lasater (U.S.A.) had 494 winners, a world record for an owner earning him a record $3,022,960 in prize money. Also in America, trainer Jack Van Berg had the same record number of winners in 1976, although the record for prize money to a trainer is held by Lazaro S. Barrera who, in 1979, won $3,563,147 with only 97 winners America hold the world's richest horserace – the All-American Futurity, a two-furlong sprint for

Australia

Grade I races

HANDICAPS	Club	Age	Distance Metres	Track
Adelaide Cup	S.A.J.C.	3 up	3,200	Morphettville
Brisbane Cup	Q.T.C.	3 up	3,200	Eagle Farm
Caulfield Cup	V.A.T.C.	3 up	2,400	Caulfield
Craven 'A' S	V.R.C.	3 up	1,200	Flemington
Doncaster H	A.J.C.	3 up	1,600	Randwick
Doomben Cup	B.A.T.C.	3 up	2,200	Doomben
Epsom H	A.J.C.	3 up	1,600	Randwick
The Galaxy	A.J.C.	2 up	1,100	Randwick
George Adams H	V.R.C.	3 up	1,600	Flemington
Marlboro Classic	S.T.C.	3 up f and m	1,500	Rosehill
Marlboro Cup	V.A.T.C.	3 up	1,400	Caulfield
Marlboro Plate*	S.A.J.C.	3 up	1,200	Morphettville
Melbourne Cup	V.R.C.	3 up	3,200	Flemington
Metropolitan, The	A.J.C.	3 up	2,600	Randwick
Newmarket H	V.R.C.	3 up	1,200	Flemington
Oakleigh Plate	V.A.T.C.	2 up	1,100	Caulfield
Perth Cup	W.A.T.C.	3 up	3,200	Ascot
Railway S	W.A.T.C.	3 up	1,500	Ascot
Rothmans 'Hundred Thousand'**	B.A.T.C.	2 up	1,350	Doomben
Stradbroke H	Q.T.C.	2 up	1,400	Eagle Farm
Sydney Cup	A.J.C.	3 up	3,200	Randwick
Toorak H	V.A.T.C.	3 up	1,600	Caulfield

Prior to 1975 was known as Goodwood Handicap.
**Prior to 1978 was known as Doomben Ten Thousand.*

WEIGHT FOR AGE Race	Club	Age	Distance Metres	Track
A. J. Moir S	M.V.R.C.	3 up	1,000	Moonee Valley
Alister Clark S	M.V.R.C.	3 up	1,600	Moonee Valley
All-Aged S	A.J.C.	2 up	1,600	Randwick
Australian Cup*	V.R.C.	3 up	2,000	Flemington
Autumn S	A.J.C.	3 up	2,000	Randwick
Blamey S	V.R.C.	3 up	1,600	Flemington
C. B. Cox S	W.A.T.C.	3 up	2,400	Ascot
C. F. Orr S	V.A.T.C.	3 up	1,400	Sandown
Caulfield S	V.A.T.C.	3 up	2,000	Caulfield
Chelmsford S	Tatt's (N.S.W.)	3 up	1,800	Randwick
Chipping Norton S	A.J.C.	3 up	2,100	Warwick Farm
Chirnside S	V.A.T.C.	3 up	1,200	Caulfield
Craiglee S	V.R.C.	3 up	1,600	Flemington
Craven Plate	A.J.C.	3 up	2,000	Randwick
Freeway S	M.V.R.C.	3 up	1,200	Moonee Valley
Futurity S	V.A.T.C.	2 up	1,400	Caulfield
George Main S	A.J.C.	3 up	1,600	Randwick
H.E. Tancred S**	S.T.C.	3 up	2,400	Rosehill
Hill S	S.T.C.	3 up	1,700	Rosehill
J. F. Freehan S	M.V.R.C.	3 up	1,600	Moonee Valley
J. J. Liston S	V.A.T.C.	3 up	1,400	Sandown
L. K. S. Mackinnon S	V.R.C.	3 up	2,000	Flemington
Lightning S	V.R.C.	2 up	1,000	Flemington
Linlithgow S	V.R.C.	3 up	1,400	Flemington
Marlboro '50,000'	W.A.T.C.	3 up	1,800	Ascot
Memsie S	V.A.T.C.	3 up	1,600	Caulfield
Queen Elizabeth S	V.R.C.	3 up	2,500	Flemington

2-YEAR-OLDS	Club	Distance Metres	Track
Blue Diamond S	V.A.T.C.	1,200	Caulfield
Champagne S	A.J.C.	1,600	Randwick
Golden Slipper S	S.T.C.	1,200	Rosehill
Karrakatta Plate	W.A.T.C.	1,000	Ascot
Marlboro S	Q.T.C.	1,600	Eagle Farm
Queensland Sires' Produce S	Q.T.C.	1,400	Eagle Farm
Sires' Produce S	A.J.C.	1,400	Randwick
Sires' Produce S	V.R.C.	1,400	Flemington

3-YEAR-OLDS	Club	Distance Metres	Track
A.J.C. Derby	A.J.C.	2,400	Randwick
A.J.C. Oaks (F)	A.J.C.	2,400	Randwick
Ascot Vale St	V.R.C.	1,200	Flemington
Australian Derby	W.A.T.C.	2,400	Ascot
Canterbury Guineas	S.T.C.	1,900	Canterbury
Caulfield Guineas	V.A.T.C.	1,600	Caulfield
Edward Manifold St (F)	V.R.C.	1,600	Flemington
Gloaming St	S.T.C.	1,850	Rosehill
Grand Prix St	Q.T.C.	2,200	Eagle Farm
Moonee Valley	M.V.R.C.	1,600	Moonee Valley
One Thousand Guineas (F)	V.A.T.C.	1,600	Caulfield
Peter Pan St	S.T.C.	1,500	Rosehill
Queensland Derby	Q.T.C.	2,400	Eagle Farm
Queensland Oaks (F)	Q.T.C.	2,400	Eagle Farm
Rosehill Guineas	S.T.C.	2,000	Rosehill
Sandown Guineas	V.A.T.C.	1,600	Sandown
South Australian Derby	S.A.J.C.	2,500	Morphettville
South Australian Oaks (F)	S.A.J.C.	2,000	Morphettville
Spring Champion Stakes	A.J.C.	2,000	Randwick
Victoria Derby	V.R.C.	2,500	Flemington
V.R.C. Oaks (F)	V.R.C.	2,500	Flemington
Western Australian Derby	W.A.T.C.	2,400	Ascot
Western Australian Oaks (F)	W.A.T.C.	2,400	Ascot

quarter horses held at Ruidoso Downs in New Mexico. In 1978, the total prize money was $1,280,000, the world record for first prize for any horse being Moon Lark's 1978 win of $437,500. The introduction of the electronic camera and the photo-finish have eliminated some of the multiple dead-heats of the past. Although there is no record in turf history of a quintuple dead-heat, in the 1880 Astley Stakes at Lewes, Sussex, England, there was a triple

Grade I races	Club	Age	Distance	Track	Grade I races	Club	Age	Distance	Track
Queen Elizabeth Randwick S	A.J.C.	3 up	2,400	Randwick	Underwood S	V.A.T.C.	3 up	2,000	Caulfield
Queen's Plate	V.R.C.	3 up	2,000	Flemington	W. S. Cox Plate	M.V.R.C.	3 up	2,050	Moonee Valley
Rawson S	S.T.C.	3 up	1,500	Rosehill	Warwick S	A.J.C.	3 up	1,400	Warwick Farm
St George S	V.A.T.C.	3 up	1,800	Caulfield	William Reid S	M.V.R.C.	3 up	1,200	Moonee Valley
Theo Marks S	S.T.C.	3 up	1,400	Rosehill					

Year	Melbourne Cup	Caulfield Cup	Year	Leading Sires	Wins	Races	£
1960	Hi Jinx	Ilumquh	1960/1	Star Kingdom	34	78	81,862
1961	Lord Fury	Summer Fair	1961/2	Star Kingdom	38	85	74,521
1962	Even Stevens	Even Stevens	1962/3	Wilkes	48	109½	94,529
1963	Gatum Gatum	Sometime					£A
1964	Polo Prince	Yangtze	1963/4	Wilkes	44	96½	110,244
1965	Light Fingers	Borehead	1964/5	Star Kingdom	33	82½	105,138
1966	Galilee	Galilee					$A
1967	Red Handed	Tobin Bronze	1965/6	Better Boy	37	85	176,220
1968	Rain Lover	Bunratty Castle	1966/7	Alcimedes	18	40	216,977
1969	Rain Lover	Big Philou	1967/8	Agricola	17	49	212,776
1970	Baghdad Note	Beer Street	1968/9	Wilkes	53	124	312,148
1971	Silver Knight	Gay Icarus	1969/70	Alcimedes	33	71	254,520
1972	Piping Lane	Sobar	1970/1	Better Boy	65	123	285,236
1973	Gala Supreme	Swell Time	1971/2	Better Boy	56	129	283,605
1974	Think Big	Leilani	1972/3	Oncidium	25	64	363,775
1975	Think Big	Analight	1973/4	Matrice	48	107	365,011
1976	Van Der Hum	How Now	1974/5	Oncidium	31	75	756,981
1977	Gold and Black	Ming Dynasty	1975/6	Showdown	54	115½	472,266
1978	Arwon	Taksan	1976/7	Better Boy	39	73½	563,195
1979	Hyperus	Mighty Kingdom	1977/8	Showdown	51	105	584,269
			1978/9	Century	27	58	621,093

New Zealand

Grade I races	Club	Age	Distance Metres	Track
Air New Zealand S	A.R.C.	3+	2000	Ellerslie
Auckland Cup Hcp	A.R.C.	3+	3200	Ellerslie
Avondale Cup Hcp	Av.J.C.	3+	2200	Avondale
Ellerslie Sires Produce S	A.R.C.	2	1400	Ellerslie
George Adams Hcp	W.R.C.	3+	1600	Trentham
Lion Brown Sprint	Wkto.R.C.	3+	1400	Te Rapa
Manawatu Sires Produce S	Mtu.R.C.	2	1400	Awapuni
Marlboro Easter Hcp	A.R.C.	3+	1600	Ellerslie
New Zealand Cup Hcp	C.J.C.	3+	3200	Riccarton
New Zealand Derby	A.R.C.	3	2400	Ellerslie
New Zealand Oaks	W.R.C.	3f	2400	Trentham
New Zealand One Thousand Guineas	C.J.C.	3f	1600	Riccarton
New Zealand Two Thousand Guineas	C.J.C.	3	1600	Riccarton
New Zealand St Leger	W.R.C.	3	2800	Trentham
Railway Hcp	A.R.C.	3+	1200	Ellerslie
Wellington Cup Hcp	W.R.C.(16)	3+	3200	Trentham

dead heat for first place, a head in front of a dead-heat for fourth place. Every one of the five jockeys thought he had won. There are, however, three recorded instances of quadruple dead-heats: in the Omnibus Stakes at The Hoo, *Hertfordshire, England, in April 1851; at the Houghton Meeting at Newmarket in October 1955, and in Ireland at Bogside, June 1808. There have been several triple dead-heats recorded by photo-finish in recent years. The*

	New Zealand Derby	New Zealand Oaks	Wellington Cup	Auckland Cup
1960	Blue Lodge	Challen	Jalna	Marie Brizard
1961	Burgos	Fair Symbol	Great Sensation	Ruato
1962	Algalon	Blyton	Great Sensation	Floutulla
1963	Royal Duty	Cicada	Great Sensation	Stipulate
1964	Trial Offer	Trial Offer	Gay Fillou	Senor
1965	Roman Consul	Natter	Eiffel Tower	Lucky Son
1966	Fair Account	Star Belle	Red Crest	Apa
1967	Jazz	Aquarelle	Michael Molloy	Royal Sheen
1968	Pep	Brazil	Loofah	Bright Chief
1969	Piko		City Court	Il Tempo
1970	Fairview Lad		Il Tempo	Il Tempo
1971	Master John	Young Ida	Ansin	Sailing Home
1972	Classic View	Brown Satin	Simon de Montfort	Sailing Home
1973	Fury's Order		Rustler	Apollo Eleven
1974	Mansingh	Sweet Offer	Battle Heights	Rose Mellay
1975	Balmerino	Princess Patrice	Timon	Kia Maia
1976	Silver Lad	Eastern Time	Guest Star	Perhaps
1977	Uncle Remus	La Mer	Good Lord	Royal Cadenza
1978	Kaiser	Athenaia	Good Lord	Stylemaster
1979	Ruling Lord	Supreme Glory	Cubacade	Blue Denim

	Owners	Stakes		Trainers	Winners		Jockeys	Wins
1959/60	J. G. Alexander	£12,565	1959/60	E. Ropiha	43	1959/60	R. J. Skelton	69
1960/1	Hon W. S. Goosman	£12,575	1960/1	H. A. Anderton	56	1960/1	W. D. Skelton	80
1961/2	Hon W. S. Goosman	£11,527	1961/2	E. Temperton	35	1961/2	R. J. Skelton	91
1962/3	A. E. Davis	£18,625	1962/3	E. A. Winsloe	45	1962/3	R. J. Skelton	79
1963/4	I. Robinson	£13,155	1963/4	E. A. Winsloe	41	1963/4	J. R. Dowling	70
1964/5	W. E. Hazlett	£22,013		H. A. Anderton		1964/5	R. J. Skelton	78
1965/6	W. E. Hazlett	£25,615	1964/5	E. A. Winsloe	61	1965/6	R. J. Skelton	76
1966/7	W. E. Hazlett	£27,473	1965/6	W. J. Hillis	52	1966/7	R. J. Skelton	96
1967/8	W. E. Hazlett	$41,880	1966/7	W. J. Hillis	53	1967/8	W. D. Skelton	124
1968/9	W. E. Hazlett	$36,985	1967/8	S. A. Brown	46	1968/9	R. J. Skelton	94
1969/70	B. Priscott	$59,950	1968/9	S. A. Brown	49	1969/70	E. J. Didham	99
1970/1	Mrs M. Greene	$38,635	1969/70	R. Cochrane	55	1970/1	B. Andrews	102
1971/2	Miss J. Edgar Jones	$62,700	1970/1	R. Cochrane	54	1971/2	D. A. Peake	84
1972/3	J. D. Foote	$60,640	1971/2	R. Cochrane	53	1972/3	D. A. Peake	91
1973/4	Mr and Mrs T. Douglas	$81,545	1972/3	G. K. and W. Sanders	63		N. Harris	
1974/5			1973/4	G. K. and W. Sanders	67	1973/4	R. J. Skelton	81
1975/6	R. K. Stuart	$87,452	1974/5	G. K. and W. Sanders	76	1974/5	D. A. Peake	92
			1975/6	G. K. and W. Sanders	83	1975/6	R. J. Skelton	98
			1976/7	G. Ivil	64	1976/7	D. A. Peake	86
				G. K. and W. Sanders		1977/8	D. A. Peake	107
			1977/8	R. Verner	54			

longest ever horserace, in Portugal, was for 1,200 miles won by an Egyptian-bred Blunt Arab horse called Emir. The oldest race in the world still being run is the Lanark Silver Bell in Scotland, instituted by William the Lion in the 12th century. Britain also has the world's largest racecourse at Newmarket, England, where the Beacon Course, one of nineteen raced there, is four miles 397 yards long (6.8km).

	Leading Sires	Winners	Wins	Stakes		Leading Sires	Winners	Wins	Stakes
1959/60	Summertime	35	65	£42,289	1969/70	Copenhagen	29	56	$104,305
1960/1	Summertime	36	63	£40,549½	1970/1	Pakistan	36	90	$138,360
1961/2	Le Filou	18	45	£40,086	1971/2	Better Honey	36	71	$146,180
1962/3	Count Rendered	34	62	£57,157	1972/3	Mellay	47	103	$188,569
1963/4	Le Filou	26	42	£43,139	1973/4	Pakistan		76	$222,767
1964/5	Summertime	28	58	£47,251	1974/5	Copenhagen		88	$180,787½
1965/6	Le Filou	30	67	£68,207	1975/6	Copenhagen		77	$187,599½
1966/7	Le Filou	26	59	£59,447	1976/7	Mellay		133	$266,198
1967/8	Copenhagen	36	93	$101,537	1977/8	Bandmaster	10	32	$241,225
1968/9	Pakistan	33	78	$103,388	1978/9	Gate Keeper	26	53	$185,230½

Japan

2-YEAR-OLDS

Race	Grade	Furlongs	Track
Asahi Hai Sansai S	I	8	Nakayama
Hanshin Sansai S	I	8	Hanshin

3-YEAR-OLDS

Race		Grade	Furlongs	Track
Kikuka Shou	F C	I	15	Hanshin
Ouka Shou	F	I	8	Hanshin
Tokyo Yuushun	F C	I	12	Tokyo
The Queen Elizabeth II Commemorative Cup	F	I	12	Hanshin
Yuunshun Hinba	F	I	12	Tokyo

3-YEAR-OLDS AND UP

Race	Age	Grade	Furlongs	Track
Arima Kinen	3+	I	12.5	Nakayama
Takarazuka Kinen	4+	I	11	Hanshin
Tennou Shou (Spring)	4+C F	I	16	Kyoto
Tennou Shou (Autumn)	4+C F	I	16	Tokyo

Index

Page numbers in italic refer to illustrations.

Acknowledgements

2. Zefa. **5.** George Selwyn. **10.** Cooper Bridgeman Library. **12.** *Penny Magazine*, The Mansell Collection. *Charles II*, National Picture gallery. **13.** The Mansell Collection. **14.** Cooper Bridgeman Library. **15.** Cooper Bridgeman Library. **16/17.** The Mansell Collection. **18.** The Mansell Collection. **19.** *Arkle*, Keystone Press Agency. *V O'Brien*, Horseman Photography. **20/21.** The Mansell Collection. **22.** The Mansell Collection. **23.** Keystone Press Agency. **24/25.** New York Public Library Picture Collection. **26/27.** New York Public Library Picture Collection. **28.** *Tod Sloan*, W W Rouch & Co Ltd. *Kentucky Derby*, The Mansell Collection. **29.** Barnabys Picture Library. **30.** *Milan Grand Prix*, Popperphoto. *Sienna*, The Mansell Collection. **31.** Keystone Press Agency. **32.** Popperphoto. **33.** Keystone Press Agency. **35.** Keystone Press Agency. **36.** High Commissioner for New Zealand. **38/39.** *Fields of Sekiya*, Cooper Bridgeman Library. *Kikuka*, Kyoto Race Course. *Derby*, Tokyo Race Course. **40/41.** *Greyville*, South African Tourist Corporation. **42.** Bernard Gourier. **44.** *Winners Circle*, Keystone Press Agency. *The Queen*, Press Association. **45.** John Wyatt. **46/47.** *Both Tattersalls*, David Hastings. *Ballsbridge*, Ed Byrne. *Deauville*, Bernard Gourier. **51.** George Selwyn. **52.** Press Association. **55.** *The Queen, Cecil*, Ed Byrne. *Hunt, Sangster*, Bernard Gourier. *Galbraith, Whitney*, Jerry Cooke. **57.** *Aga Khan*, Ed Byrne. *R Guest*, Bobby Hopkins. *Vittadini*, Central Press. *Ken Cox*, Victoria Racing Club. *Lanzarote*, Sporting Pictures. **59.** *Mellon, Taylor*, Jerry Cooke. *Wildenstein, Rothschild*, Gourier. *The Queen*, George Selwyn. **60.** George Selwyn. **62/63.** Mrs Vincent O'Brien. **65.** George Selwyn. **66.** *Belmont*, William Stravitz. *Covered Ride*, Ed Byrne. *Deauville*, Bernard Gourier. **67.** *Main Picture*, George Selwyn. *Training Run*, Laurie Morton. **68.** Laurie Morton. **69.** George Selwyn. **70/71.** Laurie Morton. **72.** Laurie Morton. **75.** *Penna*, Bernard Gourier. *Dick Hern*, Ed Byrne. *Whitingham*, Jerry Cooke. **77.** *Rimmel, Boutin, Wragg*, Press Association. *Price, Hills*, Sporting Pictures. **79.** *Zilber, Head*, Bernard Gourier. *Whitely, Luro*, Jerry Cooke. *Walwyn*, Ed Byrne. **81.** *Prendegast, Walwyn*, Press Association. *Cecil*, Ed Byrne. **82.** Zefa. **84.** Press Association. **85.** *F Head*, Bernard Gourier. *Gold Cup*, Sport and General. **86/87.** *Winner, Belmont, Laytown, Changing Rooms*, Ed Byrne. *Sha Tin*, David Hsiung. **88/89.** *Fence, Fallers, O'Neill*, George Selwyn. *Birds Nest*, Sporting Pictures. *Pendil*, Ed Byrne. **90.** *Leopardstown*, Ed Byrne. *Newton Abbott*, George Selwyn. **91.** *Greville Starkey*, Laurie Morton. *Colours*, George Selwyn. **92.** *Valet*, George Selwyn. *Cauthen*, Sporting Pictures. **93.** George Selwyn. **94.** Ed Byrne. **97.** *Mercer*, George Selwyn. *Shoemaker*, Press Association. *Roche*, Peter Mooney. *Valasquez*, Jerry Cooke. *Higgins*, T Kennedy. **99.** *Carson, Piggott*, David Hastings. *Francome, Starkey*, George Selwyn. **101.** *Swinburn*, Ruth Rogers. *Yves St Martin*, Gourier. *Cordero*, Bob Coglianese. *Cauthen*, Provincial Press Association. **103.** Zefa. **104.** Keystone Press Agency. **106/107.** *National Stud Newmarket*, Laurie Morton. *Irish National Stud*, Ed Byrne. **110/111.** Colin Meyer. **112/113.** Keystone Press Agency. **117.** Laurie Morton. **114.** *Foal*, Laurie Morton. *Jumping*, George Selwyn. **120/121.** *Jockey Club (both)*, John Slater. *Ken Alday*, George Selwyn. **122/123.** *Aqueduct*, John Wyand. *Belmont*, Ed Byrne. *Santa Anita Racecourse, from Course*. **124.** *Melbourne Cup*, Australian Information Service. *Longchamp*, George Selwyn. **127.** Japanese Tourist Board. **129.** *Computor*, Australian News. *Punter*, Nigel Osborne. **130.** Bernard Gourier. **131.** Hong Kong Tourist Board. **132/133.** *Newmarket*, Zefa. *Punters*, George Selwyn. *William Hills*, David Weeks. **136/137.** *Epsom 1976, 1977*, George Selwyn. *Derby, Princess Gate*, David Hastings. **138/139.** George Selwyn. **140/141.** George Selwyn. **142/143.** *Parade Ring, Winners Enclosure*, George Selwyn. *Rolls Royce*, David Hastings. *Stand*, Popperphoto. **144/145.** George Selwyn. **146/147.** George Selwyn. **150.** George Selwyn. **153.** *Racing*, Ed Byrne. *Walking Out*, Zefa. **154.** Ed Byrne. **156/157.** Bernard Gourier. **158/159.** Bernard Gourier. **160/161.** Bernard Gourier. **162/163.** Bernard Gourier. **164/165.** Bernard Gourier. **166.** Liefershein. **167.** Zefa. **168/169.** Photo Perrucci. **170/171.** Jerry Cooke. **172/173.** *Starting Gate, Walking Out, A Long Straight*, Jerry Cooke. *Gardens*, Steve Haskin. **174/175.** *Parade Ring, Winning Post*, Jerry Cooke. *Paddock, Camera Patrol*, Ed Byrne. **176/177.** Ed Byrne. **178.** Barnabys Picture Library. **179.** Popperphoto. **180.** *Statue*, Steve Haskin. *Finish*, Jerry Cooke. **181.** *Parade Ring, Cantering*, Jerry Cooke. *Citation*, William Stravitz. **183.** *Flowers, Backstretch*, William Stravitz. *Training, Cantering*, Jerry Cooke. **184.** Jerry Cooke. **185.** Jerry Cooke. **186.** Barnabys Picture Library. **187.** Jerry Cooke. **188/189.** *Secretariat's Last Race, Walking Out*, Jerry Cooke. *Stand*, William Stravitz. *Start*, Michael Burns. **191.** Macquitty International Collection. **192.** Brazilian Tourist Board. **193.** Brazilian Tourist Board. **194/195.** *Red Nose, Harry White*, Keystone Press Agency. *Stands*, Jerry Cooke. **196.** John Fairfax and Sons Ltd. **197.** *Aerial Views*, Australian News. *Parade Ring*, Jerry Cooke. **198.** R Voldendorp. **200.** Tony Simon. **201.** Australian News. **202.** Department of Immigration. **203.** National Publicity Studios. **204.** R Carter. **205.** Ray Cranbourne. **206/207.** *Stands, Readout Board, Placing Board*, David Hsiung. *Paddock*, CJLA. **208.** Japanese National Tourist Organization. **209.** Japanese National Tourist Organization. **210.** George Selwyn. **211.** George Selwyn. **212/213.** Sport and General. **217.** *Levmoss, Mill Reef*, Fiona Forbes. *Brigadier Gerard*, Press Association. *Crepello*, Steve Haskin. *Ribot*, UNIC. **219.** *Relko, Sassafras*, APRH. *Petite Etoile*, Sport and General. *Nijinsky*, Alec Russell. *Ballymoss*, R Anscombe. **225.** Thoroughbred Record. **228.** Thoroughbred Record. **281.** *Northern Dancer*, Thoroughbred Record. *All Other Pictures*, Jerry Cooke. **235.** *Tobin Bronze*, Australian News. *All Other Pictures*, Sun Herald. **237.** George Selwyn.